Six Sigma
DeMYSTiFieD®

DeMYSTiFieD® Series

Accounting Demystified
Advanced Statistics Demystified
Algebra Demystified
Alternative Energy Demystified
Anatomy Demystified
ASP.NET 2.0 Demystified
Astronomy Demystified
Audio Demystified
Biology Demystified
Biotechnology Demystified
Business Calculus Demystified
Business Math Demystified
Business Statistics Demystified
C++ Demystified
Calculus Demystified
Chemistry Demystified
College Algebra Demystified
Corporate Finance Demystified
Data Structures Demystified
Databases Demystified
Differential Equations Demystified
Digital Electronics Demystified
Earth Science Demystified
Electricity Demystified
Electronics Demystified
Environmental Science Demystified
Everyday Math Demystified
Forensics Demystified
Genetics Demystified
Geometry Demystified
Home Networking Demystified
Investing Demystified
Java Demystified
JavaScript Demystified
Linear Algebra Demystified
Macroeconomics Demystified
Management Accounting Demystified

Math Proofs Demystified
Math Word Problems Demystified
Medical Billing and Coding Demystified
Medical Terminology Demystified
Meteorology Demystified
Microbiology Demystified
Microeconomics Demystified
Nanotechnology Demystified
Nurse Management Demystified
OOP Demystified
Options Demystified
Organic Chemistry Demystified
Personal Computing Demystified
Pharmacology Demystified
Physics Demystified
Physiology Demystified
Pre-Algebra Demystified
Precalculus Demystified
Probability Demystified
Project Management Demystified
Psychology Demystified
Quality Management Demystified
Quantum Mechanics Demystified
Relativity Demystified
Robotics Demystified
Signals and Systems Demystified
Six Sigma Demystified
SQL Demystified
Statics and Dynamics Demystified
Statistics Demystified
Technical Math Demystified
Trigonometry Demystified
UML Demystified
Visual Basic 2005 Demystified
Visual C# 2005 Demystified
XML Demystified

Six Sigma
DeMYSTiFieD®

2ND EDITION

Paul Keller

New York   Chicago   San Francisco   Lisbon   London   Madrid   Mexico City
New Delhi   San Juan   Seoul   Singapore   Sydney   Toronto

The McGraw·Hill Companies

1 2 3 4 5 6 7 8 9 10 QFR/QFR 1 9 8 7 6 5 4 3 2 1 0

ISBN 978-0-07-174679-3

MHID   0-07-174679-X

This publication is designed to provide accurate and authoritative information in regard to the subject matter covered. It is sold with the understanding that neither the author nor the publisher is engaged in rendering legal, accounting, securities trading, or other professional services. If legal advice or other expert assistance is required, the services of a competent professional person should be sought.

—From a Declaration of Principles Jointly Adopted by a Committee of the American Bar Association and a Committee of Publishers and Associations

Library of Congress Cataloging-in-Publication Data

Keller, Paul A.
Six sigma demystified / by Paul Keller.—2nd ed.
p.   cm.
Includes bibliographical references and index.
ISBN 978-0-07-174679-3 (alk. paper)
1. Six sigma (Quality control standard)   I. Title.
TX156.K41 2011
658.4'013—dc22   2010029966

McGraw-Hill books are available at special quantity discounts to use as premiums and sales promotions or for use in corporate training programs. To contact a representative, please e-mail us at bulksales@mcgraw-hill.com

This book is printed on acid-free paper.

To my wife Roxy, my girls Jessica, Melanie, and Ashley, and my boys Harry, Macklin, and Finian.
Thanks for the inspiration and the free time to work on this project.
I mention you often in my courses to demonstrate the relevance of these
problem-solving methods in meeting life's many challenges.
Did I mention Black Belts get a higher allowance?
Love Dad.

About the Author

Paul Keller is president and chief operating officer at Quality America, Inc. (www.qualityamerica.com), a provider of quality improvement software, training, and training materials since 1983. As a senior consultant, Paul has developed and implemented successful Six Sigma and quality improvement programs in service and manufacturing environments. Before launching Quality America's training and consulting business in 1992, Paul specialized in quality engineering in the masters program at the University of Arizona. He applied these techniques as a quality manager for a consumer goods manufacturer (1990–1992), and an SPC director at an industrial products manufacturer (1987–1990). In these roles, he developed company-wide quality systems to meet the demands of a diverse customer base, including the automotive and aerospace industries.

Contents

Introduction

There are now many excellent books on Six Sigma. Many of these emphasize the deployment issues of Six Sigma, providing valuable insight into the big-picture issues required for successful implementation of Six Sigma at an organizational level. These issues, including management responsibility, resource allocation, and customer focus, are summarized in Chapter 1.

Successful Six Sigma deployment involves continual success of projects, each incrementally moving the organization closer to its strategic goals of shareholder return, employee growth, and customer satisfaction. Each project, in turn, progresses from its initial definition through the *d*efine, *m*easure, *a*nalyze, *i*mprove, and *c*ontrol (DMAIC) cycle to the maturity of financial reward. This project evolution requires much attention to detail by the project team, including its black belt, green belts, and sponsor. Unfortunately, many Six Sigma books fail to develop the detail of the tools necessary for practical use, or they cover only a small handful of the tools required for an organization's projects. Readers are not provided clear benefits for the tools or may wonder if the tools may be applied to their specific processes and projects.

I am often asked by clients, "How does Six Sigma apply to us?" Each industry tends to approach problems as if no other market segment has experienced the same problems, now or ever. Even if the problems were the same, the solutions certainly can't apply across industries.

Some books provide far too much statistical back-ground for the tools. Readers are forced to endure aca-demic derivations of formulas or statistical tests that have limited use in today's computerized world. This tends to force the focus away from the practical use and limitations of the tools.

Six Sigma Demystified is written to address these needs. This Second Edition has taken the input of the many thousands of readers of the First Edition to further refine specific topics, as well as to provide further detail on using Minitab and Excel to solve common problems found in both service and industrial settings, as well as certification exams.

How to Use This Book

The book's presentation is based on the implementation strategy for Six Sigma. Part 1 addresses the management responsibilities for developing a coherent infrastructure to support successful Six Sigma projects. Part 2 addresses the details of deploying Six Sigma projects using the Six Sigma *define, measure, analyze, improve,* and *control* (DMAIC) problem-solving methodology. Each chapter in Parts 1 and 2 concludes with exercises to test the subject matter expertise of the reader. Section exams are also provided for Parts 1 and 2, in addition to a final exam addressing the entire scope of the text. Solutions to the questions are provided at the end of the book.

Part 3 of the book serves as a reference guide to detail the statistical, lean, and problem-solving tools used most often in the DMAIC project deployment. It includes a variety of tools useful to Six Sigma teams, each presented within the context of an objective for a particular stage of DMAIC. Since many tools have applications within multiple stages of DMAIC, each tool description includes a "When to Use" section relating to the DMAIC methodology and its objectives. Detailed interpretation of each tool is also provided, with reference to other tools that should be used in conjunction with that tool for full effectiveness. Calculations and assumptions are provided as needed, as are detailed examples of their use in popular software such as *MS Excel, Minitab,* and *Green Belt XL*. To attract interest from the widest audience, many examples are provided for service processes.

This book may be used for training groups of black belts and green belts or for self-study to master the tools and methodology of Six Sigma. Students may download example files and free (limited-time use) copies of the *Green Belt XL* software at www.qualityamerica.com\downloads.

I hope that you will find this book useful in your Six Sigma journey.

PART I

Preparing for Deployment

chapter 1

Deployment Strategy

What Is Six Sigma?

Sigma (σ) is the Greek letter used by statisticians to denote the standard deviation for a set of data. The standard deviation provides an estimate of the variation in a set of measured data. A stated sigma level, such as Six Sigma, is used to describe how well the process variation meets the customer's requirements.

Figure 1.1 illustrates the Six Sigma level of performance for a stable process. The process data are represented by the bell-shaped distribution shown. Using the calculated value of the standard deviation (σ), the distance from the process centerline to any value can be expressed in sigma units. For example, consider the teller station at a bank whose average customer wait time (or time in queue) is 7.5 minutes with a standard deviation of the wait time calculated as 1 minute. Six standard deviations, or 6σ, from the average is 1.5 minutes (in the negative direction) and 13.5 minutes (in the positive direction).

Separately, through the use of customer surveys, focus groups, or simple feedback, customer requirements may have been established for the process. In this case, the process is likely to have only an upper specification limit defined by the customers; there is no minimum limit to desirable wait times.

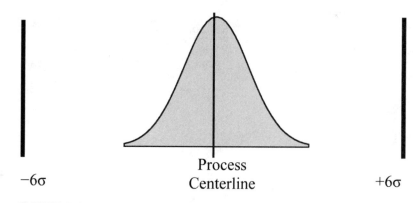

-6σ Process
           Centerline $+6\sigma$

FIGURE 1.1 Six Sigma level of performance for a stable process.

If this upper specification coincides exactly with the plus 6σ level (i.e., 13.5 minutes), then the process is at the Six Sigma level of performance. The implication is that the customer wait time will exceed the customer requirements only a very small percentage of the time. Similarly, if the maximum allowable customer wait time is 10 minutes, then the process would be operating at only a 2.5σ level of performance, indicating an increased risk of customers exceeding this maximum wait time.

Although the normal distribution tables discussed later in this text indicate that the probability of exceeding 6 standard deviations (i.e., $z = 6$) is two times in a billion opportunities, the accepted error rate for Six Sigma processes is 3.4 defects per million opportunities (DPMO). Why the difference? When Motorola was developing the quality system that would become Six Sigma, an engineer named Bill Smith, considered the father of Six Sigma, noticed that external failure rates were not well predicted by internal estimates. Instead, external defect rates seemed to be consistently higher than expected. Smith reasoned that a long-term shift of 1.5σ in the process mean would explain the difference. In this way, Motorola defined the Six Sigma process as one that will achieve a long-term error rate of 3.4 DPMO, which equates to 4.5 standard deviations from the average. While this may seem arbitrary, it has become the industry standard for both product and service industries.

These concepts have been applied successfully across a broad range of processes, organizations, and business sectors with low and high volumes and millions or billions in revenue and even in nonprofit organizations. Any process can experience an error, or defect, from a customer's point of view. The error may be related to the quality, timeliness, or cost of the product or service. Once

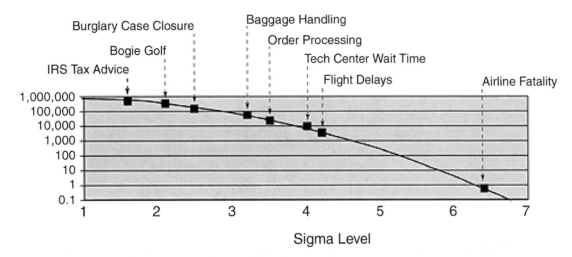

FIGURE 1.2 Sigma ranges for the activities shown, based on published defect rates. (*Keller, 2001.*)

defined, the Six Sigma techniques can be applied to methodically reduce the error rate to improve customer satisfaction.

Using the curve shown in Figure 1.2 (Keller, 2001), any known process error rate can be converted directly to a σ level. Most companies, including those with typical total quality management (TQM)-type programs, operate in the 3σ to 4σ range based on their published defect rates. In Figure 1.2, airline baggage handling, order processing, tech center wait time, and flight on-time performance fall in the general area from 3σ to 4σ.

Moving from left to right along the curve in Figure 1.2, the quality levels improve. Companies operating at between 2σ and 3σ levels cannot be profitable for very long, so, not surprisingly, only monopolies, government agencies, or others with captive customers can afford to operate at these levels.

Notice that the *y* axis, representing DPMO, is logarithmically scaled. As sigma level is increased, the defects per million opportunities decreases exponentially. For example, in moving from 3σ to 4σ, the DPMO drops from 67,000 to 6,500 and then to just over 200 at 5σ.

It's clear that significant improvement in customer satisfaction is realized in moving from 3σ to 4σ. Moving beyond 4σ or 5σ involves squeezing out every last drop of potential improvement. Six Sigma is truly a significant achievement, requiring what Joseph Juran termed *breakthrough thinking* (Juran and Gryna, 1988).

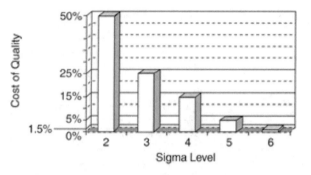

FIGURE 1.3 Cost of quality as a percent of sales for organizations at a specified sigma level. (*Keller, 2001.*)

There is some criticism of the DPMO focus, specifically with the definition of an *opportunity*. In counting opportunities for error in a deposit transaction at a bank, how many opportunities are there for error? Is each contact with a customer a single opportunity for error? Or should all the possible opportunities for error be counted, such as the recording of an incorrect deposit sum, providing the wrong change to the customer, depositing to the wrong account, and so on? This is an important distinction because increasing the number of potential opportunities in the denominator of the DPMO calculation decreases the resulting DPMO, increasing the sigma level.

Obviously, an artificially inflated sigma level does not lead to higher levels of customer satisfaction or profitability. Unfortunately, there will always be some who try to "game" the system in this manner, which detracts from the Six Sigma programs that estimate customer satisfaction levels honestly.

Since DPMO calculations can be misleading, many successful Six Sigma programs shun the focus on DPMO. In these programs, progress is measured in other terms, including profitability, customer satisfaction, and employee retention. Characteristics of appropriate metrics are discussed in more detail later in this section.

The financial contributions made by Six Sigma processes are perhaps the most interesting to focus on. The cost of quality can be measured for any organization using established criteria and categories of cost. In Figure 1.3, the y axis represents the cost of quality as a percentage of sales. For a 2σ organization, roughly 50 percent of sales is spent on non-value-added activities. It's easy to see now why for-profit organizations can't exist at the 2σ level.

At 3σ to 4σ, where most organizations operate, an organization spends about 15 to 25 percent of its sales on "quality-related" activities. If this sounds high, consider all the non-value-added costs associated with poor quality: quality assurance departments, customer complaint departments, returns, and warranty repairs. These associated activities and costs are sometimes referred to as the "hidden factory," illustrating the resource drain they place on the organization.

For many organizations, quality costs are hidden costs. Unless specific quality cost identification efforts have been undertaken, few accounting systems include provision for identifying quality costs. Because of this, unmeasured quality costs tend to increase. Poor quality affects companies in two ways: higher cost and lower customer satisfaction. The lower satisfaction creates price pressure and lost sales, which results in lower revenues. The combination of higher cost and lower revenues eventually brings on a crisis that may threaten the very existence of the company. Rigorous cost of quality measurement is one technique for preventing such a crisis from occurring.

It's not uncommon for detailed quality audits to reveal that 50 percent of the quality costs go unreported to management, buried in general operating costs. Often these costs are considered "the cost of doing business" to ensure a high-quality product or service to the customer. Reworking, fine-tuning, touch-ups, management approvals, next-day deliveries to compensate for delayed or failed processes, and fixing invoice errors are all non-value-added costs that may go unreported.

As an organization moves to a 5σ level of performance, its cost of quality drops to around 5 percent of sales. The Six Sigma organization can expect to spend between 1 and 2 percent of sales on quality-related issues.

How are these cost savings achieved? As a company moves from 3σ to 4σ and then to 5σ, its quality costs move from "failure costs" (such as warranty repairs, customer complaints, and so on) to "prevention costs" (such as reliability analysis in design or customer surveys to reveal requirements). Consider the increased costs incurred when customers detect problems. A common rule of thumb is that an error costing $1 to prevent will cost $10 to detect and correct in-house and $100 to remedy if the customer detects it. These orders of magnitude provide an incentive to move toward error prevention.

The cost of quality also drops quickly as dollars that go to waste in a 3σ organization (owing to failure costs) go directly to the bottom line in a Six Sigma organization to be reinvested in value-added activities that boost revenue. Thus, while the 3σ organization is forever in "catch-up" or "firefighting" mode, the Six Sigma organization is able to fully use its resources for revenue generation. This infusion of capital helps the sales side of the equation, so the cost of quality as a percentage of sales (shown in Figure 1.3) drops more quickly.

Differences Between Six Sigma and Total Quality Management (TQM)

There are four key differences between a Six Sigma deployment and TQM-style implementations (Keller, 2001):

- *Project focus and duration.* Six Sigma deployment revolves around Six Sigma projects. Projects are defined that will concentrate on one or more key areas: cost, schedule, and quality. (Note that other possible considerations, such as safety or product development, could be restated in terms of cost, schedule, and/or quality, as will be described later in this book.) Projects may be developed by senior leaders for deployment at the business level or developed with process owners at an operational level. In all cases, projects are linked directly to the strategic goals of the organization and approved for deployment by high-ranking sponsors.

  The project sponsor, as a leader in the organization, works with the project leader (usually a black belt) to define the scope, objective(s), and deliverables of the project. The sponsor ensures that resources are available for the project members and that person builds support for the project at upper levels of management as needed. All this is documented in a project charter, which serves as a contract between the sponsor and the project team.

  The scope of a project is typically set for completion in a three- to four-month time frame. Management sets criteria for minimal annualized return on projects, such as $100,000. The structure of the project and its charter keep the project focused. The project has a planned conclusion date with known deliverables. And it has buy-in from top management. These requirements, together with the Six Sigma tools and techniques, build project success.

- *Organizational support and infrastructure.* As shown in the next section, a proper Six Sigma deployment provides an infrastructure for success. The deployment is led by the executive staff, who use Six Sigma projects to further their strategic goals and objectives. The program is actively championed by middle- and upper-level leaders, who sponsor specific projects in their functional areas to meet the challenges laid down by their divisional leaders (in terms of the strategic goals). Black belts are trained as full-time project leaders in the area of statistical analysis, whereas process personnel are trained as green belts to assist in projects as process experts. Master black belts serve as mentors to the black belts and deployment experts to the managerial staff.

- *Clear and consistent methodology.* A somewhat standard methodology has been developed for Six Sigma projects, abbreviated as DMAIC (pronounced "dah-may-ick"), an acronym for the *define, measure, analyze, improve,* and *control* stages of the project. This discipline ensures that Six Sigma projects are clearly defined and implemented and prevents the recurrence of issues.

- *Top-down training.* A properly structured deployment starts at the top, with training of key management. Six Sigma champions, consisting of executive-level decision makers and functional managers, are necessary to align the Six Sigma program with the organization's business objectives through project sponsorship and to allocate resources to project teams. Without committed champions supporting them, black belts lack the authority, resources, and business integration necessary for project success.

The result of a properly implemented Six Sigma deployment is data-driven decision making at all levels of the organization that is geared toward satisfying critical needs of key stakeholders.

Six Sigma deployment doesn't cost, it pays. With minimum savings of $100,000 per project, the Six Sigma training projects will provide financial returns that far exceed the cost of the training. This "reward as you go" deployment strategy has proven beneficial to organizations of all sizes.

If you're still unsure whether a Six Sigma program is the right path for your organization, consider the impact on market share if your closest competitor implemented a Six Sigma program and you didn't.

Six Sigma and Lean

A proper Six Sigma deployment includes use of the lean tools and methods. In this regard, there is no difference between a properly developed Six Sigma program and a lean Six Sigma program. Six Sigma (aka lean Six Sigma) is a deployment strategy for implementing value-added improvement projects aligned with an organization's business needs. These focused projects target critical-to-quality (CTQ), critical-to-schedule (CTS), and/or critical-to-cost (CTC) opportunities within an organization. Six Sigma uses a variety of tools and methods, including statistical (i.e., enumerative stats, statistical process control, and designed experiments), problem-solving, consensus-building, and lean tools. A given project may not use all the tools, yet most organizations find that they need most of the tools at any given time. Lean provides essential methods to define value and waste to improve an organization's responsiveness to customer needs. As such, the lean methods provide a critical means of accomplishing the Six Sigma goals. Similarly, the lean methods require the use of data, and statistics provide the necessary methods for data analysis. It's unfortunate that some lean advocates and some lean Six Sigma programs do not stress the critical importance of the statistical tools in their analysis because this lack of rigor will prevent lean-focused projects from realizing their full potential.

Elements of a Successful Deployment

Jack Welch, former CEO of General Electric, said: "This is not the program of the month. This is a discipline. This will be forever" (Slater, 1999).

Six Sigma is primarily a management program. For many organizations, it will fundamentally change the way they operate. It must, if it is to achieve the levels of improvement shown earlier. Consider that moving from 3σ to 4σ means a 91 percent reduction in defects; from 4σ to 5σ, an additional 96 percent; and from 5σ to Six Sigma, a 99 percent further reduction. Without strong management and leadership, the time, effort, and expertise of the Six Sigma project team will be wasted, and results will not be achieved.

Program success is based on the following four factors, presented in order of importance:

- Support and participation of top management
- Sufficient resource allocation to improvement teams
- Data-driven decision making using DMAIC
- Measurement and feedback of key process characteristics

Management Support and Participation

A successful Six Sigma program must be integrated into the organization's business strategy. Active participation by leaders in the organization will ensure program survival.

As with most initiatives he launched as CEO of General Electric, Jack Welch was nearly fanatical about the Six Sigma program. In a January 1997 meeting, only a year after officially announcing the inception of the program to his managers, he challenged them:

> You've got to be passionate lunatics about the quality issue. . . . This has to be central to everything you do every day. Your meetings. Your speeches. Your reviews. Your hiring. Every one of you here is a quality champion or you shouldn't be here. . . . If you're not driving quality, you should take your skills elsewhere. Because quality is what this company is all about. Six Sigma must become the common language of this company. . . . This is all about better business and better operating results. In 1997, I want you to promote your best people. Show the world that people who make the big quality leadership contributions are the leaders we want across the business [Slater, 1999].

To get the most from the endeavor, management must actively support the Six Sigma initiative. Welch urged management to find opportunities to motivate employees to use Six Sigma in meetings, speeches, reviews, and hiring.

Jack Welch further challenged his executive vice presidents by tying 40 percent of their bonuses to specific bottom-line improvements from their Six Sigma initiatives (Slater, 1999). He realized that it was critical to move beyond mere words and to demonstrate commitment with leadership and results. This participation from senior management, through integration with the company's business strategy and practices, marked a key departure from run-of-the-mill TQM initiatives, where leadership was delegated to departments with little authority or few resources.

The key priorities for management leadership include

- *Define objectives and goals of the program.* How is program success measured?
- *Develop the business strategy based on key customer requirements and market conditions.* Are there market opportunities that build on the core competencies of the business? Are there competitor weaknesses that can be challenged? By reviewing market, operational, and customer-feedback data, areas of opportunity are identified. Which improvements will have the greatest impact on the financial status of the organization? Where are its key losses, the "low-hanging fruit," for the first wave of projects? Some of these data are probably already compiled. A review may reveal gaps in

the information that require changes to data-acquisition methods. Business-level Six Sigma projects provide a sound approach to understanding these issues.

- *Define business-level metrics for customer, employee, and shareholder requirements.* Establish baselines and dashboards (measurement standards) for easy synthesis of data needed to gauge the success of the program and highlight hot opportunities. (Metrics are discussed further in the "Measurement and Feedback" section later in this chapter.)

- *Establish project selection, assignment, and approval criteria.* Project selection criteria should be aligned with the business strategy. (This is discussed further in the "Project Selection" section of Chapter 3.) Define key players for assigning and approving projects.

- *Market the program to the organization.* Construct, conduct, and analyze organizational assessment to identify obstacles to deployment within organizational levels. These perceptions are important to understand so that strengths can be built on and weaknesses addressed. Larger organizations always need this internal buy-in. Many times, smaller organizations do as well. Use an employee-focused dashboard to track progress.

- *Select and train the deployment team.* Personnel moves send strong signals. By selecting the best and brightest (the A team) for key black belt, champion, and green belt positions in the first wave of deployment, management sends a clear signal: This effort is not just important—it is the most important thing we're doing. Training people to do it right sends the message that failure is not an option.

- *Develop a human resource strategy to retain black belts and motivate middle management to support and contribute to the program.* By giving employees incentives and ensuring that leadership maintains its priority, management says that there is no going back.

Resource Allocation

Organizations need to plan effectively for the human resource needs of their Six Sigma projects. Access to other resources, such as operational processes, also will require difficult prioritization decisions.

Resource allocation is a critical challenge for any organization. You often hear, "Our people already feel overworked." In many smaller organizations, resource allocation is further complicated because employees "wear several hats," usually because each function can't be cost-justified as a full-time position. Furthermore, many of these functions include tasks that are critical to the daily operations, not just the longer-term survival of the firm. Managers may question how they can afford to "lose" key people to the black belt role.

The key to resource allocation is the realization that the Six Sigma program will very quickly pay for itself. When the huge amount of waste in a 3σ organization (25 percent of revenue) is considered, it's clear that there are tremendous opportunities for these organizations. Many of these opportunities exist simply because of resource constraints: People know the problem exists, have a good understanding of potential solutions, yet lack the time to investigate and deploy the best solution. Only by diverting or adding resources to the system can waste be reduced and profitability improved. The deployment plan should balance expenditures for training and project deployment with the achievable savings predicted in the coming one to three years.

A mature Six Sigma program usually has about 1 percent of its workforce committed as black belts. Once trained properly, these individuals work only on black belt projects. In this regard, they are strictly overhead and contribute nothing directly to the everyday operations.

Full-time black belts will lead four to seven project teams per year. Each team consists of green belts, line personnel, and subject-matter experts involved in the process targeted for improvement. These team members maintain their operational roles in the organization and participate only when serving on a project team. Team facilitators are also sometimes needed to help manage group dynamics and build consensus.

In some organizations, green belts are also designated as project leaders, responsible for completing one to five projects per year. Since this can present conflicts with their daily operational duties, a preferred strategy is for full-time black belts to lead projects. In Chapter 2 we will also discuss the limitations of the green belt's expertise as an issue with project leadership.

Master black belts provide coaching and other expertise to black belts. They typically have expertise in advanced statistical analysis methods and change management. One master black belt for every 10 black belts is the recommended staffing. In addition, it is useful to appoint a master black belt to assist the executive staff with Six Sigma deployment, technical training development, and technical support for business-level Six Sigma projects.

Smaller companies may have floating black belts who provide expertise to a number of Six Sigma teams throughout the organization. Companies with less than a few hundred employees may use key support personnel in part-time black belt roles, utilizing consultants as master black belts, particularly for the first year or two of deployment. When part-time black belts are used, management assumes a risk in losing project focus to daily operational issues. These resources must be managed effectively by the Six Sigma champions.

Sponsors are middle- to upper-level managers, trained as champions, who authorize, fund, and support the projects through allocation of resources.

Six Sigma project team members will be excused periodically from daily operational duties to work on project-related activities. Other resources (such as equipment and materials) will be diverted from daily operations to gather data. Line managers will need clear signals that upper management not only authorizes this reallocation of resources but also requires it.

Each Six Sigma project should include an estimate of the costs related to deploying the project. These costs are calculated by the accounting department and include labor, materials, and lost production time. Costs are debited against the financial benefits of the project, which also are calculated by the accounting department.

Data-Driven Decision Making

Management needs to lead by example. Managers need to *walk the talk*. Decisions regarding project selection, incentives to sales or production units, resource allocation, and so on all must be based on sound data analysis. Consider, for example, project selection. If line supervisors have sole authority to allocate resources for projects, then projects might not be aligned with the strategic direction of the business unit or the needs of the external customer simply because line supervisors lack access to that information.

Instead, project selection is a management activity that needs to consider a variety of factors: benefit to customers, probability of success, cost to implement, and time to implement, to name just a few. (See also "Project Selection" in Chapter 3.) By quantifying these factors, management is able to choose projects objectively that use the company's limited resources effectively.

The DMAIC problem-solving methodology introduced earlier typically is used to acquire data and glean information from the data in the context of a Six Sigma project. The DMAIC methodology is designed to

- *Define* the problem
- *Measure* the extent of the problem
- *Analyze* the sources of variation

- *Improve* the process
- *Control* the process for sustained improvement

Readers familiar with quality improvement methods will be reminded of Shewhart's plan-do-check-act (PDCA) and Deming's plan-do-study-act (PDSA). These methods are quite similar in their approach, employing cycles of improvement. Once the final step is completed, a new cycle may begin for an additional level of improvement. The key differences between DMAIC and PDSA/PDCA include the prescribed use of specific tools and techniques, particularly in the measure, analyze, and improve stages, as well as the project sponsorship (define stage) and detailed control plans (control stage). DMAIC seeks to address the shortcomings in PDSA/PDCA effectively, at least as PDSA/PDCA were often practiced, if not defined.

Motorola used the MAIC (measure, analyze, improve, control) acronym. General Electric and Allied Signal used DMAIC, which has become more of the standard. General Electric also has varied the methodology for use in product design areas, calling it DMADV, where the second *D* stands for design and the *V* for verify. This acronym is used in conjunction with the DFSS (design for Six Sigma) nomenclature. The objectives and approach of the design stage are remarkably similar to those of the improve stage, as is verify to control, making the differences between DMADV and DMAIC subtle. Some companies choose to call it DMAIC in either case for ease of implementation.

Some consultants brand the methodology by adding even more steps. Harry and Schroeder added recognize to the front and standardize and integrate to the end, referring to the product as their "breakthrough strategy," which takes its name from Juran's concept of breakthrough developed years earlier to describe methods for achieving orders-of-magnitude improvements in quality. A review of Harry and Schroeder's definitions of these additional terms shows similarity to the objectives described for each stage of DMAIC in Part 2 of this book. A casual review of Six Sigma practitioners found the DMAIC methodology to be the one used most commonly. Apparently everyone agrees on what essentially will be done; they just don't agree on what to call it!

Putting these semantics aside, the importance of DMAIC is in its structured approach. This discipline ensures that Six Sigma projects are clearly defined and implemented and that results are standardized in the daily operations.

The DMAIC methodology should be applied from the leadership levels of the organization all the way down to the process level. Whether a project begins at the business level or the process level, the methodology is the same. DMAIC is covered in more detail in Chapters 4 through 8. Part 3 of this book addresses the specific tools referenced in each stage of DMAIC.

Project sponsorship ensures that projects will not be authorized or funded if they fail to provide bottom-line benefits or are too broadly scoped to be achievable in an agreed-on timetable. The sponsor provides the functional authority to break organizational roadblocks and works with other sponsors within the managerial ranks to coordinate projects with overall business needs.

Business projects are championed at the top level of the organization. They concentrate on vital aspects of business success, such as market share, viability, profitability, employee retention, and so on. They may involve purchasing or selling business units or ways to attract or maintain customer base. Because of the scope of business-level projects, the time scale is measured in years rather than months. Some business-level projects may take three to five years to cycle through the Six Sigma process (Harry and Schroeder, 2000), whereas others are completed in less than a year.

As projects are deployed, decisions need to reflect the data. Where data do not exist, sponsors need to motivate the project team to acquire sufficient data to justify decisions made at each stage of DMAIC by asking the right questions. For example: Is the project defined for the correct problems? Does the project attack the root cause or just the symptom? Are the best metrics used to gauge project success? Have the data been analyzed properly? Is the improvement plan sustainable?

Business success will be more closely aligned with project success when management consistently integrates this way of thinking into its daily decisions. Rather than reacting to the crisis of the day, management should understand the differences between common and special causes of variation and react accordingly. Financial incentives to sales or production should be based on metrics encouraging long-term customer satisfaction, business growth, and viability. For example, yield estimates that ignore the hidden costs of rework or customer returns provide poor incentive for production to satisfy external customer needs or longer-term viability.

There is a wealth of information available to management on which to base decision making. Six Sigma projects deployed at the organizational level can be used to define, collect, and synthesize the data necessary for proper decision making.

- *Reliable customer data provide the distinction between internal perceptions and actual customer needs.* There may be a disconnect between internal perceptions and customer perceptions. To ensure thoroughness, conduct a complete value-stream analysis. While site visits are a popular means of collecting these data, they can be costly and may not be necessary. Indeed, their usefulness certainly will be improved if surveys are conducted beforehand. Critical-incident surveys, described in the *Six Sigma Handbook* (Pyzdek and Keller, 2009), also can be a great source of customer insight.

- *Data mining sometimes is used for discovering opportunities but often is insufficient for conclusive decision making.* Data mining involves the statistical analysis of databases, either to understand the nature of a particular variable (a *directed* analysis) or to search for patterns (an *undirected* analysis). For example, customer data may be mined to look for buying patterns by price and time of year. Because of the nature of this statistical analysis, it is often wise to conduct designed experiments to verify the suspected patterns before committing resources.

- *Benchmarking, like data mining, can provide a wealth of ideas for defining direction but often does not provide sufficient information for direct commitment of resources.* Benchmarking can be used to understand best practices and discover new methods. Often the information is readily available from suppliers, books, magazines, and the Internet. Benchmarking helps to define the potential for processes, especially those that may represent a new direction, where no internal experience exists in the organization. This information can be used to conduct pilot trials or experiments that serve as valid data-collection strategies for decision making.

- *Process data is perhaps the most prolific and reliable source of data for decision making, given its relative ease of acquisition and low cost.* Unfortunately, process data often are analyzed incorrectly, which can lead to more process degradation than improvement.

It's not uncommon for management reports to use bar graphs or pie charts to represent changes over time. Although bar graphs certainly are easy to interpret, they may not really provide the necessary context for a decision.

In the bar graph shown in Figure 1.4, it would appear that the process error rate has decreased in March. Apparently, the process change initiated in February was effective in preventing further increases in the failure rate, as observed from January to February.

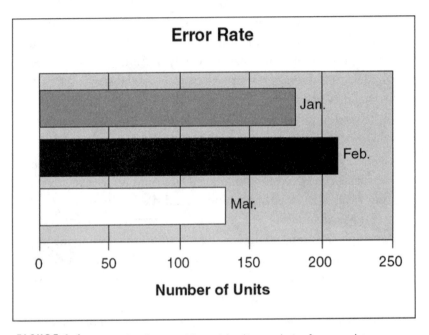

FIGURE 1.4 Bar graphs often provide a misleading analysis of process data.

A proper analysis of the data in Figure 1.5 shows that the process did not change significantly over time. The bar graph in Figure 1.4 is missing context. It does not show how much month-to-month variation is usual or should be expected.

Confidence intervals and hypothesis tests are also incorrect tools to use for this analysis because (as enumerative statistical tools) they cannot properly detect changes to a process over time. Instead, the analytical control chart shown in Figure 1.5 is the correct tool to estimate process variation over time. Through use of the control chart, the variation expected from the process (sometimes called the *common-cause variation*) can be differentiated from the variation owing to process changes (referred to as *special-cause variation*).

When all changes to the process are assumed to be due to special causes (as is done using a bar-graph analysis), the process variation can be increased by responding to the natural fluctuation with intentional process changes. This concept of process tampering is discussed in more detail in Chapters 5 and 6.

Obviously, correct analysis of process data is necessary for true improvements to customer service and the bottom line.

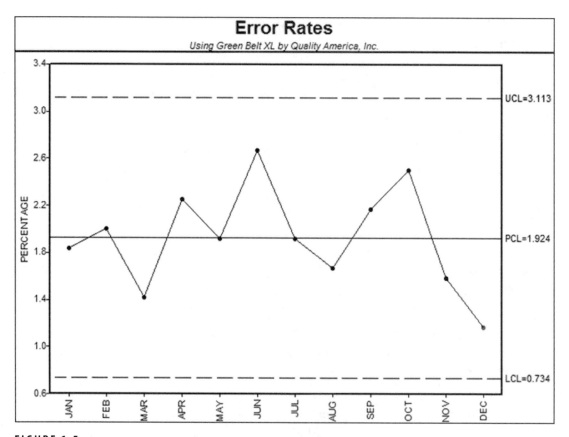

FIGURE 1.5 The process control chart shows process variation over time.

Measurement and Feedback

Employees need to understand the impact of their processes on customers. It is management's responsibility to establish a continuous flow of information from customers to the process employees. This constant feedback of data enables employees to respond quickly to problems to limit the negative impact on customers.

Metrics provide a quantitative means to assess what is critical to quality, cost, or scheduling. At the business level, these metrics provide feedback from the stakeholders in terms consistent over time and relevant to the business strategy. Six Sigma projects can be used to understand how these CTQ, CTC, and CTS metrics correlate with key process variables and controls to achieve system-wide improvements. Project deliverables will be defined in terms of these metrics and will provide an indication of project completion and success.

Appropriate metrics for tracking performance have the following characteristics:

- *A good metric is primarily customer-centered.* If a parameter is important to the customer, it should be important to your operations. Processes that have a direct impact on customer-centered parameters must be measured and controlled. Conversely, if issues that add no value to the customer experience are the focus, then resources are wasted, and the focus should be redirected. Chapter 3 provides techniques for focusing on the needs of customers. Chapter 5 provides flow-down functions (big Y, little y) for defining process-level metrics that meet business-level customer requirements.

- *A good metric is linked to your organization's strategy so that it can be clearly identified by all as critical.* The dashboard metrics discussed in this section are linked to each of the main stakeholder groups (customers, shareholders, and employees), providing high visibility throughout the organization.

- *A good metric is developed collaboratively, ensuring buy-in from all parties.* The collaborative development of the metric is realized by the Six Sigma project team in the measure stage, improving buy-in by stakeholders.

- *A good metric measures performance over time.* Use of the metric to evaluate the process over time is discussed below and further explained in the "Metric Definition" section of Chapter 5.

- *A good metric provides direct information so that it can be applied nearly immediately without further processing.* Immediate feedback allows for quick responses to changing conditions.

An effective means of presenting business-level metrics is through the use of dashboards. *Dashboards*, as the name implies, are like the gauges in a car: They provide immediate feedback of system status.

To understand how a car's engine is performing, the most direct method is to open the hood and look. At highway speeds, this can be messy, and even at idle, the results are often less than conclusive. Unless there is catastrophic damage, such as oil or steam shooting from the engine, most problems would be undetected.

So it is with customer feedback. Waiting for feedback from the customer, even requesting direct feedback of unfavorable conditions, may provide incomplete, inconclusive, or untimely information.

In most automobiles, gauges, connected to sensors, are provided to constantly measure and report on critical precursors to unfavorable conditions. For example, the temperature gauge, oil pressure gauge, and fuel gauge each provide immediate feedback of impending problems. Better still, today's cars include electronic displays to indicate a drop in coolant level or tire pressure, providing even more advanced notice of a potential problem.

Clearly, similar metrics are available to business processes for measuring real-time precursors to meet or exceed key stakeholder expectations. These metrics will provide input for data-driven decision making and communicate the performance of the business or process relative to key goals and objectives.

Effective dashboards should provide more than just single numbers or a table of historical values. Instead, dashboards should provide clean and clear graphic displays, where historical context is readily apparent. If the dashboard metric changes, it should be clear whether the change is statistically significant. As discussed in the preceding section, a statistical control chart provides the necessary context for this analysis.

From these business-level metrics, drill-down capability to subsets of the data or to the operations or process levels of the organization provides further understanding of the key drivers influencing trends.

In a Six Sigma deployment, dashboard metrics should be defined for each of the three main stakeholder groups: customers, employees, and shareholders. Each of the indices is measured using representative data for a current time period. As in an automobile, too many dashboard indicators will cause confusion and lack of focus in the short term and accidents or fatalities in the longer term. At the business level, no more than three or four metrics for each stakeholder type should suffice.

Once these metrics are defined, their performance should be tracked over time and shared within the organization. The operational drivers for these business-level metrics should be defined and monitored at the lower levels of the organization and linked effectively to the higher-level management metrics. These drivers are discovered as a result of DMAIC projects aligned with the higher-level metrics. For example, if revenue from existing customers is closely linked with on-time delivery, customer-service response time, and initial defect rate, then these metrics should be monitored closely at the operational level, with regular feedback provided to operating units. Six Sigma projects should be sponsored to improve performance relative to these metrics.

In practice, it is useful to think of metrics as big Y's and little y's. The little y's are the drivers of the big Y's. Mathematically,

$$Y_1 = \text{function of } \{y_1, y_2, \ldots, y_n\}$$

$$Y_2 = \text{function of } \{y_1, y_2, \ldots, y_n\}$$

$$\ldots$$

$$Y_m = \text{function of } \{y_1, y_2, \ldots, y_n\} \quad \text{for } m \text{ big } Y\text{'s}$$

Big Y's and their corresponding little y's are defined at each level of the organization—the business level, the operations level, and the process level. The *transfer functions* (or flow-down functions) provide a means of understanding the relationships between the process-level metrics and the bigger-picture organizational metrics that guide the business operations and the Six Sigma program.

Starting at the business level, then down to the operations level, and finally the process level, the little y's at each stage become the big Y's at the next stage down. While the big Y's are useful for tracking, the little y's provide the detail necessary for controlling processes and improving the organization.

This flow-down of the metrics from one level to the next provides direct linkage of the operational and process metrics to the key stakeholder big Y metrics used in the dashboards at the business level.

For example, the big Y's related to the customer stakeholders' group may be as follows:

$$Y_1 = \text{satisfaction score}$$

$$Y_2 = \text{retention rate}$$

$$Y_3 = \text{order turnaround time}$$

$$Y_4 = \text{sales revenue}$$

The metrics at this level provide a good high-level stakeholder view but do not yet provide the details necessary to optimize operations. It would be helpful to drill down on each of these big Y's to understand their little y drivers. Conversely, those at the operations or process levels in the organization can drill up to understand how their metrics relate to stakeholder value.

For example, the little y's for the customer-satisfaction score (Y_1) in a restaurant chain might be

Customer satisfaction = function of (service quality, culinary satisfaction, restaurant availability, price, . . .)

These business-level little y's will become the operations-level big Y's. Operations-level big Y's are useful for Six Sigma project selection criteria because they are the operational parameters that are perfectly aligned with the business-level metrics.

The operations-level little y's for service quality of the restaurant chain may be written as

Service quality = function of (wait time, friendliness of staff, cleanliness of facility, order accuracy, . . .)

Each of the operations-level little y's may be broken down further into their components in the process-level matrix. For example,

Wait time = function of (cycle time for cooking, number of staffed registers, time of day, . . .)

This resulting function then can be used to

- Establish conditions necessary for process optimization and/or variation reduction
- Provide process-level Six Sigma project metrics
- Define critical metrics for ongoing process control

These transfer or flow-down functions, which relate the big Y's to their corresponding little y's, are determined through regression and correlation analyses. Data are collected through designed experiments, data mining, surveys, focus groups, and critical-incident techniques. The functions allow process-level metrics to be linked to both customer requirements and business strategy.

An example for a software company is shown in Figure 1.6. For each of the key stakeholder groups (i.e., customers, shareholders, and employees), metrics were established at the business level (ovals), operations level (diamonds), and process level (rectangles). At the business level, for example, the retention rate for customers is tracked on a monthly basis as a general indicator of overall

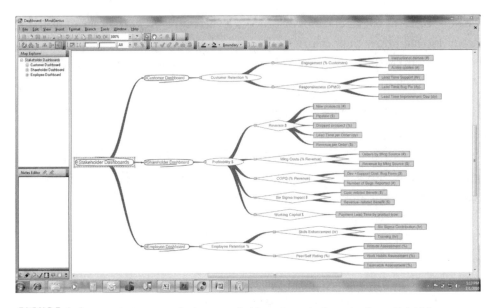

FIGURE 1.6 Example Six Sigma deployment dashboard metrics from the Green Belt XL/ MindGenius application.

existing-customer satisfaction. Predictors of customer retention were developed as part of an organizational DMAIC project that included customer support staff as well as actual customer feedback. At the operations level, the percent of customers engaged by staff is tracked each month based on the observed correlation between effective customer engagement and longer-term customer retention. Similarly, the responsiveness of the company's systems to customer inquiries is tracked using a defect rate relative to an established baseline standard for each type of customer inquiry. Feeding into each of these operations metrics is the process-level metrics. For engagement, the company tracks both the number of instructional demonstrations provided by sales, service, and support staff for existing customers, as well as the number of quotes provided for additional products and services. This last metric, while seemingly related to shareholder rather than customer concerns, was added based on data suggesting that engaged customers added substantially to the bottom line: They were more likely to be using the software for real benefit, and their relative engagement fed the need for additional products and services (a real win-win for the organization and its clients). The responsiveness of the organization, measured at the process level by quickly responding to issues or suggestions for improvement, contributes to this improved engagement.

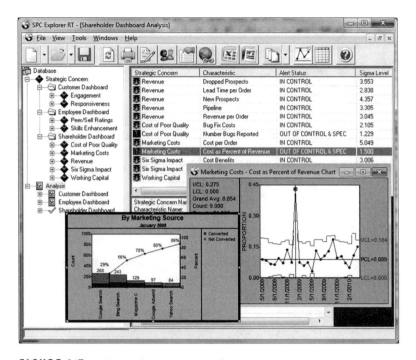

FIGURE 1.7 Example Six Sigma dashboard displays with filtering and drill down to lower levels using Quality America's *SPC Explorer* software.

These analyses are facilitated by software that allows filtering by operating unit or product family and drill-down to the lower-level drivers at the operations and/or process levels. Figure 1.7 shows an example of meaningful drill-down and analysis available by right-mouse menus for rapid feedback. The software links to operational data within quality management, customer resource management (CRM), accounting, or human resources software, so there is no need for costly reentering of data into the dashboard reporting software. The reporting software filters and groups the data as necessary for the monthly (or real-time) business- and operations-level analyses.

Chapter 5 provides further discussion of metric selection for quality, schedule, and cost focuses. Methods for understanding how metrics relate to customer needs are discussed in Chapter 3.

The result of effective measurement and feedback to the organization, when coupled with the other requirements for successful deployment, is empowerment. Rather than waffling with indecision, these data provide the critical link for action (i.e., data-driven decision making) for operational personnel and local management. With clear vision forward and feedback to confirm direction, the elements are in place for a successful journey.

CHAPTER 1 QUIZ

1. **As the sigma level for a process increases,**
   A. the number of opportunities for error decreases.
   B. the cost of quality as a percent of sales increases.
   C. the DPMO increases.
   D. the DPMO decreases exponentially.

2. **Practical uses of the Six Sigma methodologies**
   A. can be found only in Fortune 100 companies.
   B. are limited to companies that manufacture products.
   C. are limited to Fortune 100 companies that manufacture products.
   D. are found across many industry sectors and company sizes.

3. **A typical organization with a 3σ level of quality spends approximately**
   A. 50 percent of its revenues on quality-related activities.
   B. 15 to 25 percent of its revenues on quality-related activities.
   C. 1 to 2 percent of its revenue on quality-related activities.
   D. none of its revenues on quality-related activities.

4. **Four fundamental pillars of a successful Six Sigma deployment include**
   A. plan, do, check, and act.
   B. plan, do, study, and act.
   C. organizational support/resource allocation, management leadership, data-driven decision making, measurement, and feedback.
   D. failure modes and effect, cause and effect, statistical process control, and designed experiments.

5. **If you estimate your cost of quality as 2 percent of sales and your overall DPMO is about 20,000, then**
   A. your sigma level is about 3.5.
   B. you are probably underreporting the cost of quality.
   C. you should look for evidence of a hidden factory.
   D. All the above are true.

6. **Management can take a leadership role for Six Sigma deployment by**
   A. defining goals and objectives for the program based on key customer requirements and market conditions.
   B. defining and tracking business-level metrics for key stakeholder groups.
   C. allocating and training resources and advocating the merits of the program to the workforce.
   D. All the above are true.

7. **Developing and implementing an employee awareness plan for the Six Sigma program are important**

   A. so that employees understand the program's motives and objectives.
   B. so that customers realize that you're trying to solve persistent problems.
   C. so that employees become more conscientious, with a resulting improvement in quality levels.
   D. only when employees are distrustful of management.

8. **Examples of management's commitment to data-driven decision making might be evidenced by**

   A. responding only to quality concerns that are documented by large numbers of customer complaints.
   B. monthly bonuses to sales personnel linked to monthly sales revenue.
   C. project selection criteria based on strategic objectives.
   D. applying statistical confidence intervals to sales reports.

9. **In considering the resource allocation necessary for a successful Six Sigma program,**

   A. management needs to demonstrate its commitment by training everyone in the organization as soon as possible.
   B. the deployment plan should balance expenditures for training and project deployment with the expected savings achieved.
   C. management should allow only resources that aren't needed for daily operations to participate in Six Sigma projects.
   D. a mature Six Sigma program usually has about 10 percent of its workforce committed as black belts.

10. **Data-driven decision making**

   A. is necessary for management to demonstrate its commitment to the Six Sigma principles.
   B. often takes longer than making decisions based on gut feelings.
   C. reduces the subjectivity of a decision and results in improved buy-in across the organization.
   D. All the above are true.

2

Developing the Training and Deployment Plan

> Six Sigma is the most important management training thing we've ever had. It's better than going to Harvard Business School; it teaches you how to think differently.
> —*Jack Welch, April 1999 interview (Slater, 2000)*

It's been said many times that a company's most valued resource is its employees, and this is certainly the case in a Six Sigma organization. Employees provide the critical link to customer satisfaction and loyalty and ensure that the organization is consistently aligned with dynamic customer needs. Training provides the means of instructing employees on the necessary practices to meet those needs.

A starting point for many organizations is executive overview training, which allows senior executives and managers to understand the deployment strategy and resource requirements necessary to begin a Six Sigma program. Once senior management has decided on the overall strategy, it should train an initial wave of Six Sigma personnel. The necessary elements of the first wave training include

- Executive overview training
- Champion training, including project selection
- Black belt/green belt training

Each of these elements is further defined below, with the intended objectives for each training also defined. These objectives collectively constitute the *deployment plan*. The timeline necessary for each training element differs greatly depending on the size and motivation of the organization. Smaller organizations with sufficient motivation can complete the first-wave training in as few as six months; larger organizations with more resistance may take up to two years. Realistically, regardless of size, you'll need some lag time between activities to accommodate schedules and accomplish the intermediate goals and objectives (discussed below).

The schedule streamlines the deployment to expedite projects for and quickly realize project savings. This immediate payback is a great incentive to establish management commitment for further projects, including development of the feedback systems necessary to make the program a longer-term success.

Initial projects can be based on internal feedback (bottom-up projects) or well-known customer issues that are prioritized by local champions as part of their training. There is usually an abundance of potential projects at this stage. As deployment training continues, organizational *define, measure, analyze, improve,* and *control* (DMAIC) projects will create the systems necessary to detect other project opportunities, as discussed in the "Executive Overview Training" section below.

Training at each level is completed on a just-in-time (JIT) basis: Employees are trained only when they will be involved directly in pending projects. Broad-based training of employees is discouraged because training effectiveness drops off considerably (as frustration increases) when employees do not have an opportunity to use the tools and techniques immediately. Instead, additional black belts, green belts, and champions will be trained as the Six Sigma program matures and expands to other functional areas, and previously trained personnel are shifted to management positions. Additionally, black belts may need refresher courses in some topics. Frequently, an external consultant provides the initial training for the first one or two waves of employees. The role of trainer thereafter is often assumed by internal master black belts. The program will need an established protocol, resources, and budget for this continuing training.

Training Needs Analysis

Since each organization is different, the training plan should reflect the particular needs of the organization or even groups within the organization. Each organization has established a culture, either by management design or by management inattention. Recognizing and responding to these needs will increase the organizational buy-in to the Six Sigma program.

In defining the training needs, it is important to understand the knowledge, skills, and abilities (KSAs) required for each group of participants, notably the black belts, green belts, and champions. KSA requirements are covered in detail in the "Champions" section. Potential candidates for each group can be evaluated by their peers and through testing of the subject matter. Peer analysis may use confidential surveys or structured evaluations.

The results of these evaluations and the testing can be compiled using matrix diagrams. A gap analysis can be performed on individuals or the summarized results to highlight deficiencies in the current level of the KSAs.

Once an understanding of current KSAs is available, classes can be formed that group students with similar training needs. For a given group, it's best to target the instruction to the minimum level of KSAs. When employees have been exposed to similar training in the past, management may be tempted to assume that additional training on the same topic is unnecessary. Often, however, the prior training may have neglected to focus on one or more of the critical elements necessary for success, which at least partially explains the lack of success of the prior training. Even worse, the organizational environment may have provided little opportunity for application of the skills, so they were quickly forgotten.

It is important therefore to conduct posttraining assessments to gauge improvement in KSAs. The certification processes discussed in the black belt and green belt sections below provide a means of evaluating the knowledge acquired. Regular renewal of the certification, such as every three years, evaluates retention of the material. While testing may provide some indication of an individual's knowledge, the best estimate of a person's skills and abilities is often reflected in behavior, which can be monitored using employee dashboards (discussed in Chapter 1).

In addition to the KSAs, attitude is often a significant factor for consideration. Organizational assessments provide an indication of the current level of satisfaction and trust among employees. Even when trained properly, employees with a poor attitude will be unwilling to apply their KSAs in a productive fashion to truly change behavior. Poor attitude is often a reflection of distrust in management's motives or abilities, resulting from previous real or imagined blunders or slights.

Unfortunately, a bad attitude can be difficult to overcome, especially when it is deeply ingrained from years of neglect. Nonetheless, it is imperative to address these obstacles to build organizational buy-in. Successful approaches for consensus building are discussed in Chapter 4. Employees need to hear a consistent message, so the training of champions should ensure commitment at all levels of management. Perhaps most important, data-driven decision making must be at the forefront of all policy and procedures, with open communication from and to employees on these decisions. Breaking down these walls takes time and persistence, with the results monitored in employee dashboards.

Executive Overview Training

Six Sigma training should begin with the managerial ranks of the organization so that managers are prepared to lead the effort. Motorola's director of training and education estimates that the company wasted $7 million training from the bottom up. General Electric (GE) learned from this mistake, to Jack Welch's credit.

Initially, Welch required that anyone seeking promotion to a management position be trained to at least the green belt (if not black belt) level. A year later (effective January 1999), all professional employees should have begun green belt or black belt training. Considering that this directive encompassed 80,000 to 90,000 employees, it sent a clear signal that all levels of management would be leading the Six Sigma effort (Slater, 1999).

Other firms have since adopted this model as an effective way to reinforce the Six Sigma methodology throughout the organization. Studies have shown that employees are much more likely to use specific business tools if their direct management uses the tools. Employees want to speak a common language. Conversely, if management won't use specific techniques, employees are likely to abandon their use as well, feeling that the tools have been discredited or misunderstood by management.

The overall objective for senior management training is an understanding of the link between program success and business success. Managers should integrate the program into the business strategy so that completion of each Six Sigma project leads toward achievement of particular business goals. Likewise, they need to continuously promote and sponsor projects that strive for these goals.

If all levels of management do not see the vision laid out for the Six Sigma program, then deployment becomes stagnated or undermined. These are the hidden signals of a doomed Six Sigma deployment. Upper levels of management can help to overcome these problems when trained properly as Six Sigma champions.

Lower levels of management also need to clearly understand the methodology. As first- or second-line department managers and supervisors, they have to see how they and their personnel fit into the deployment scheme. Resource reallocation will have perhaps the greatest impact at their level: Personnel will be reassigned from their departments to become full-time black belts; many of the remaining employees will be diverted for week-long green belt training and then to participate as project team members; processes will be disrupted for experimentation, data collection, or process redesign.

Departmental managers must not think of themselves as mere "victims" of the Six Sigma deployment. In fact, their functional areas will show measurable improvements through deployment of the Six Sigma techniques, if they are applied properly. This improvement can only occur through strong leadership at these local levels. Thus first- and second-line managers (and their functional areas) will benefit greatly from "getting onboard" through green belt training, which will offer the deployment skills needed for success. Eventually, all employees should be trained to a green belt level so that they can participate effectively in Six Sigma teams.

An effective executive leadership course includes agenda items and workshops to develop immediate and longer-term outcomes, as shown in Table 2.1: An initial three- to five-day course will be sufficient to identify potential hur-

TABLE 2.1 Executive Training Objectives & Outcomes		
Training Agenda Item	**Objective**	**Outcome**
Elements of successful Six Sigma programs	Establish general goals for lean Six Sigma leadership team	Implementation schedule to satisfy goals
Deployment strategies	Identify and address potential stumbling blocks to the lean Six Sigma deployment	Proposed remedies incorporated into implementation schedule; initiate DMAIC project to further investigate as necessary
Stakeholder focus	Identify shareholder, employee, and customer metrics and data-collection schemes to track metrics	Initiate DMAIC project to develop metrics and data collection schemes for each stakeholder group
Resource and training requirements	Identify human resources challenges and organizational cultural issues	Initial communication plan; initiate DMAIC project to further identify and address issues
Management systems for project sponsorship and approval	Define methods for project sponsorship, approvals, and verification of gains	Project sponsorship and approval procedures
Project selection methods	Align project selection criteria with critical strategic business objectives	Weighted project selection criteria for use by champions

dles and to develop detailed plans for outstanding issues (as required). Generally, organizational-level Six Sigma projects will be deployed to develop the detailed metrics and data capture needed to track the customer, employee, and stakeholder issues. Each project is championed by the appropriate executive and led by an organizational master black belt (or consultant) whose project team includes the relevant management stakeholders in the process.

Champions

Champions are middle- to upper-level managers who are responsible for supporting the Six Sigma program and ensuring that it is aligned with the overall business strategy. Training an initial group of high-profile champions provides excellent exposure for the program and complements the ongoing marketing effort. This first wave of champions will develop and sponsor the first wave of black belt training projects. This first wave of champions should include managers who are excited about the benefits of Six Sigma, are well respected, and have good visibility across the organization. Their involvement builds credibility, and their success attracts others for subsequent waves.

As discussed in Chapter 1, choose the A team, the best and brightest of employees, for the initial waves of training. This sets a firm tone that success is the priority and that nothing will be spared.

KSA Requirements for Champions

The primary role of a champion is to ensure that organizational systems are in place to support the Six Sigma deployment. Champions are strong, vocal advocates of the Six Sigma program. Because of their standing in the organization at managerial levels, they provide critical exposure of the program to their functional reports and endorsement of the program as a management initiative.

As members of management, champions bestow authority on Six Sigma project teams. Through program development, project selection, and resource allocation, champions ensure that the organizational ground is fertile for project growth and success. Through continuous involvement in the Six Sigma initiative, champions send a clear signal to the organizational masses that management's commitment is unremitting. Dispelling the notion that the program is a "flavor of the month" is an ongoing but necessary challenge to overcome unproductive subcultures that may exist. Effective champion training provides an awareness of these roles, responsibilities, and challenges.

The attributes of a champion can be summarized as follows (Slater, 1999):

- Champions display energy and passion for the job.
- Champions excite and mobilize others.
- Champions relate Six Sigma to customer success and the bottom line.
- Champions understand the technical and financial aspects of Six Sigma.
- Champions deliver bottom-line results, not just technical solutions.

In many ways, the first two attributes are inherent to an individual's personality, although they may be dormant from lack of use. In such a case, individuals can be nurtured so that these qualities resurface, provided that there is strong upper-management commitment and support for the Six Sigma initiative. If support begins to deteriorate, then the excitement expected from champions will be either short-lived or unaccepted by the masses.

Champion and Management Training

Champions begin their training with a two- to three-day class that emphasizes their role in program development and as project sponsors. The course material should include the topics presented in Part 1 of this book. A suggested agenda for a two-day session is provided in Table 2.2. Particularly in smaller organizations, the champion and executive training may be directed toward the same staff, although the outcomes are as outline in each section regardless of the audience.

Workshops are a key part of champion training, providing an opportunity to build ownership of the Six Sigma program in the managerial ranks. The workshops support the key outcomes of the training, including

- Establishing an understanding of and commitment to the managerial role, responsibilities, and project sponsorship necessary for success of the Six Sigma project teams
- Selecting green belt and black belt candidates
- Selecting suitable Six Sigma projects using the selection criteria

An important component of champion training is to get the middle-level managers onboard because they exercise direct control over the operational resources that will be critical for project success. The project selection exercises will give managers ownership of the projects and commitment to team sponsorship.

Six Sigma champions also may attend green belt training to learn the basic techniques used by Six Sigma teams. The goal of this training is to foster an

TABLE 2.2 Suggested Agenda For Champion Training

Order	Duration	Topic	Subtopics	Workshop
1	3 hours	Deployment strategy	What is Six Sigma?	Issues contributing to successful deployment
			Comparison with total quality management (TQM)	
			Elements of successful deployment	
			DMAIC problem solving (overview)	
2	3 hours	Personnel and training requirements	Training needs analysis	Understanding training needs
			Selecting personnel	Methodology for selecting black belts
			Training regimen	
3	3 hours	Customer focus	Customer requirements	Increasing customer focus
			Feedback mechanisms	
4	3 hours	Project selection and sponsorship	Potential benefits	Project selection
			Selection criteria and methods	
			Sponsor responsibilities	

awareness of the tools and techniques so that champions know the tools' limitations as well as their strengths. This keeps champions from pushing for the impossible and also encourages them to strive for new possibilities from their project teams. When serving as project sponsors, champions who are familiar with the techniques can ensure that their project teams maintain rigor in their analyses. This serves as a useful checkpoint for sustainability of project successes.

Black Belts

Black belts generally are full-time change agents, removed from the operational responsibilities of the organization to maximize the resources available for deploying Six Sigma projects. Some organizations prefer to train an initial wave of green belts before the black belts; this can be a mistake because it delays effective use of the training by the green belts until the black belts are available for project teams. A better approach is to merge the green belt training into the first week of black belt training. This provides a cost benefit as well as a shared experience between the black belts and green belts assigned to their teams. Team members assigned to the initial projects thus are exposed to the Six Sigma principles as the projects begin.

KSA Requirements for Black Belts

An important but not comprehensive role of a Six Sigma black belt is that of technical expert in the area of Six Sigma methods. This expertise allows a black belt to understand the link between complex customer needs and the critical internal process elements designed to achieve them.

While Six Sigma black belts generally are given credit for their expertise in analytical, statistical, and problem-solving techniques, successful black belts must be much more than technical experts. The advancement of an organization from a nominal 3σ to a Six Sigma level of performance represents a vast operational and organizational (read *cultural*) change. As such, black belts are primarily *change agents*.

Knowledge of company systems and culture is often required for successful change management in an organization. For this reason, many organizations find it better to train black belts from within than to hire them from the outside. It's not uncommon for experienced black belts to later become key operational members of the management team. Their experience working on projects throughout the organization, with customers and suppliers, makes them extremely valuable in strategic positions.

Effective change agents are (Keller, 2001)

- *Positive thinkers*. Black belts need to have faith in management and in the direction of the business and its Six Sigma program. They must be upbeat and optimistic about program success, or they risk undermining management or the Six Sigma initiative. They need to exude self-confidence without the pitfalls of being overbearing, defensive, or self-righteous. Proper management support and vision allow black belts to both believe in and experience their potential as change agents.

- *Risk takers*. Black belts need to be comfortable as change agents. While ineffective change agents agonize over implementing change, effective change agents relish it. They enjoy the excitement and challenge of making things happen and "grabbing the bull by the horns." They know that change is necessary for the company's and the customers' sake, and they know that it is inevitable, given the competitive market. Only by leading the change can its outcome be steered. The effective change agent wants to lead the charge.

- *Good communicators.* An effective black belt needs to be capable of distilling a vast amount of technical material in an easily comprehensible fashion for team members, sponsors, champions, and management. Many of these personnel will have only minimal training (green belt or champion level) in statistical techniques, if any at all. The black belt who can clearly and succinctly describe to the team why, for example, a designed experiment is better than one-factor-at-a-time experimentation will strengthen the team and shorten its project completion time.

- Of course, being a good communicator is much more than just being capable of distilling technical material. An effective communicator also must comprehend and appreciate others' concerns. These concerns must be addressed in a thorough, respectful, and thoughtful manner. Through use of Six Sigma statistical techniques, data can be used to predict the merits of various improvement strategies and address the concerns of others. The effective change agent will enlist people with concerns to participate in these efforts, either as team members or as project sponsors. Through participation, such employees learn to understand the nature of the problem and the most viable solution. Buy-in, a necessary part of sustainability, is greatly enhanced through this participation.

- *Respected by peers.* It is often said that a title can be either earned or granted but that true power must be earned. Effective change agents have earned the respect of others in the organization by their hard work and effective communication. Those new to an organization or those who have not gained respect from others will find it harder to implement change.

- *Leaders.* Black belts often will serve as team leaders; other times, they need to show respect to others (and true leadership) by allowing them to assume the leadership roles. First-wave black belts also will serve as role models and mentors for green belts and subsequent waves of black belts.

Many of these change-agent skills are facets of one's personality, but they can be supported through awareness training, management policy, and coaching and mentoring by master black belts and champions. The best black belts are individuals who demonstrate a balance between these softer attributes and the technical skills discussed elsewhere in this book. Many firms expect experience with these change-agent skills, documented through work history and personal recommendations, as a prerequisite for black belt candidates. Depending on the business and functional area, a technical college degree also may be required. For example, a BS in engineering may be required for manufacturing areas, whereas a business degree may be required for sales or business development areas.

Black Belt Training

A classic model for black belt training consists of one week per month of classroom training spread over four months. It integrates classroom learning with hands-on project implementation. Black belts are assigned a project for this training, which allows them to successfully apply the skills they are taught in training to the three weeks between each class session. The trainers, aided by master black belts, serve as coaches for these projects.

A newer model for training, which has proved even more successful, is a blended approach that employs online self-study training with on-site classroom review and mentoring sessions. Based on reviews and feedback, students enjoy the flexibility offered by the online format. The clearest benefit of an online class over the classroom setting is the self-paced nature of the online class. Students progress through the material at their own pace, based on their experience, skill set, and learning objectives. For students with busy work or home lives, this often allows them to better balance their time. Online unit quizzes are often provided to test the acquired knowledge for each topic. The online materials are supplemented with workshops and review sessions to discuss questions from the online materials and apply the materials to the ongoing student projects.

A key aspect of black belt training is successful completion of a project. Projects prove training. Projects are completed successfully only when the financials have been certified by the accounting department and the project has been accepted and closed by the sponsor. In addition to the usual criteria of bottom-line impact and customer focus, training projects usually are selected that will use many of the technical skills in an area of the business in which the black belt candidate has some experience (and comfort).

Each black belt should arrive for the first week of training with several potential projects, allowing that some of the projects may not meet selection criteria defined by management (usually as part of champion training). Workshops are incorporated extensively throughout the training to provide hands-on experience to the attendees. Project data are used in the workshops wherever possible so that students can effectively apply the subject matter to real-world examples. Since open discussions of confidential process data are not well facilitated in a public seminar, effective black belt training often is limited to in-house courses (blended with online training, as discussed earlier).

The flow of the course material roughly follows the DMAIC process so that the appropriate tools and concepts are taught and applied at each stage of project deployment. The black belt training requires the use of suitable Six Sigma software, such as shown in the examples throughout this book. Because of the availability of software, the course material may concentrate on the application and use of statistical tools rather than on the detailed derivation of the statistical methods.

A suggested schedule of training topics is provided in Table 2.3. While there is a credible argument that many Six Sigma projects will require use of only a handful of tools and that a portion of these will require only rudimentary statistical knowledge, black belts nonetheless need to learn these skills. Black belts should be taught to think critically and challenge conventional thought. Successful breakthrough thinking requires rigorous analysis. Black belts must be taught to accept ideas and opinions as just that, with their limitations, and to use the power of the analytical tools to prove the solutions and their assumptions. This applies equally to manufacturing and service applications. The statistical tools allow black belts to prove concepts with minimal data and process manipulation so that great advances can be made in a short amount of time. Problems that have gone unsolved for years can be attacked and conquered. Data-driven decision making becomes the rule, not the exception.

Six Sigma certification demonstrates an individual's knowledge, skills, and dedication to achieving a high level of competency in the Six Sigma process. The certification criteria are varied. For some companies, completion of a course and a single project suffices. The American Society for Quality (ASQ) applies a rather simple scheme: passing a written exam, with a signed affidavit attesting to completion of either two projects or one project and three years' experience in the body of knowledge. While the exam offers some proof of the skills learned by the black belt, the completion of two projects certifies successful application of the skills.

The International Quality Federation (IQF, www.iqfnet.org) provides an online certification exam that can be used by an organization as part of its certification process. While the ASQ exam prohibits the use of a computer, the IQF certification mandates its use. In this way, the IQF certification testing is much

TABLE 2.3 Suggested Schedule for Black Belt Training

Week 1	Week 2	Week 3	Week 4
Elements of successful Six Sigma programs Deployment strategy	Measurement systems analysis	Defining the new process	Standardizing on the new methods
Managing projects	Value-stream analysis, including lean tools	Lean practices for error and cycle-time reduction Assessing benefits of the proposed solution	Measuring bottom-line impact
Stakeholder focus Teams and change management	Analyzing sources of variation, including statistical inference	Evaluating process failure modes, including FMEA	Documenting lessons learned
Consensus-building methods	Determining process drivers, including designed experiments	Implementation and verification	
Project definition			
Process definition			
Six Sigma goals and metrics			
Process baselines, including control charts and process capability analysis			

more realistic than certification exams that do not allow for the use of statistical software. With only the use of a calculator, it's quite difficult to have a realistic estimate of a black belt's technical skills. The IQF provides a form for use by the employer's certification committee that identifies three main components of certification: change-agent skills, application of tools and techniques, and ability to achieve results. It also provides a change-agent checklist that is completed by sponsors and team members and submitted to the committee for review.

Green Belts

Green belts are employees trained in basic Six Sigma concepts to work as part of a team assigned to a given project.

KSA Requirements for Green Belts

The role of green belts is to provide local process expertise to a team and to facilitate the brainstorming and data-acquisition activities of the team. Unlike black belts, who leave their operational duties behind, green belts "keep their day job." Likely green belt candidates include process supervisors, operators or clerical staff, technicians, and any other individual who may wish to serve on a project team. Eventually, most employees will achieve green belt status.

For the initial waves of training, select green belts who can provide the necessary process expertise to the previously selected black belt projects. These green belt candidates should be respected by their peers and capable of critical thinking in a positive fashion with a diverse team.

Green Belt Training

Green belts will learn the basics of the tools used by the project team. Their training will be "a mile wide and an inch deep." While they will rely on project black belts for problem-solving skills, it is important that they understand at least the need for the tools, if not the general DMAIC problem-solving methodology. For example, as process supervisors, they may be under pressure by the project team to conduct designed experiments to learn about significant process variables. If they have no experience with designed experiments, they may resist these necessary analysis steps.

The green belt training typically is a one-week course that provides an overview of the Six Sigma concepts and tools. It allows the green belts to speak the language of the black belts so that they understand the need for and application of the various tools. Perhaps most important, green belts learn how to function effectively on a team. These team-building skills will ensure that the project team stays focused and maintains momentum.

A suggested schedule for green belt training is shown in Table 2.4. Workshops are used, rather than detailed instruction, to demonstrate data-analysis methods.

Green belts also can be certified using a simple evaluation of their KSAs relative to the training discussed earlier. Rather than having a detailed understanding of the application of tools, green belts are required only to recognize the need for such analysis. Being an active member of two or more Six Sigma projects generally is required to demonstrate successful application of the KSAs.

In some organizations, green belts are designated project leaders, responsible for completing one to five projects per year. This is not a preferred approach for the following reasons:

1. Green belt training does not include the full breadth or depth of the technical tools and techniques required to complete projects.

2. Green belts retain their operational duties, so they lack the time required to devote themselves completely to a project.

TABLE 2.4 Suggested Training Schedule for Green Belts

Day 1	Day 2	Day 3	Day 4	Day 5
Elements of successful Six Sigma program deployment strategies	Managing projects	Data-collection workshop	Analyze-stage objectives	Improve-stage objectives, including lean practices for error and cycle-time reduction
Project definition	Teams and change management	Process baseline and measurement system analysis workshop	Value-stream analysis, including lean tools	Control-stage objectives, including standardizing on methods
Process definition	Measure-stage objectives		Determining process drivers workshop	

Organizations choosing to increase the number of projects by using green belts as Six Sigma project leaders will need to address these concerns to prevent an inordinate number of failed projects either because processes are not fully optimized (from lack of proper analysis) or because projects are not completed in a reasonable time (owing to a lack of available project leadership resources). Green belts can serve as effective Six Sigma project leaders when

1. The green belt is a professional, college-educated staff member with experience in project management.
2. An experienced black belt is assigned to the project team to lend technical problem-solving expertise at all stages of DMAIC.
3. Management is committed to free the green belt from his or her operational duties as needed to meet the project schedule.

This last issue is often difficult to address in practice because operational responsibilities often take precedence. For these reasons, a preferred strategy is for full-time black belts to lead projects.

CHAPTER 2 QUIZ

1. **The most effective strategy for training in a Six Sigma deployment**
   A. emphasizes broad-based training at the grass-roots effort to build buy-in of lower-level employees.
   B. begins with executive staff to ensure that program leadership is established.
   C. requires that all employees understand statistical analysis of data.
   D. All the above are true.

2. **Training at the executive level emphasizes**
   A. development of a training plan, project selection criteria, and systems for tracking critical top-level stakeholder issues.
   B. DMAIC for process improvement.
   C. Consensus-building tools.
   D. Statistical analysis tools.

3. **First-wave training is best direct toward**
   A. a group of lower-level employees who can be easily resourced away from critical daily operations.
   B. new employees, who require the most extensive training.
   C. your best employees, who can be assigned projects immediately to achieve optimal results and send a strong signal of management's commitment.
   D. suppliers who can correct most of the problems experienced internally.

4. **Champion training emphasizes**
   A. selecting personnel (black belts, green belts) for the initial deployment.
   B. defining initial project-rating criteria and selecting potential projects.
   C. methods for communicating program goals and strategy throughout the organization.
   D. All the above are true.

5. **When an organization selects a green belt as a project leader,**
   A. the project has the best chance of success because the green belt retains an operational role and so is involved in the process on a daily basis.
   B. the green belt should be willing to learn as many of the black belt skills as necessary and do the training on his or her own time so that his or her other responsibilities are not neglected.
   C. the green belt needs to be given ample time away from his or her operational duties and needs support from an active black belt for the more technical aspects of the project.
   D. it demonstrates the company's commitment to success by having all employees lead projects.

6. During the initial wave of Six Sigma deployment, a suitable project will

   A. focus on well-known yet achievable issues.

   B. involve as many departments as possible.

   C. address major issues that, although large in scope and potentially taking a long time to accomplish, will provide the most visibility.

   D. be selected randomly so as to avoid conflicts from competing groups.

7. Departmental managers and supervisors

   A. need to clearly understand the program deployment, including its methodology and objectives.

   B. are a key component of success because they control the local resources needed for process improvement.

   C. should actively participate in the deployment through project sponsorship.

   D. All the above are true.

8. The overall objective(s) for senior management training include(s)

   A. being able to analyze processes using statistical software.

   B. understanding the link between program success and business success.

   C. communicating to lower levels of the organization that they are the most important part of program success.

   D. All the above are true.

9. The true measure of the effectiveness of training is a(n)

   A. passing score on a test of knowledge.

   B. high scores on peer evaluations.

   C. change in behavior reflective of the course materials.

   D. increase in pay.

10. Black belt training

   A. should focus primarily on statistics because the rest of the body of knowledge reflects the "soft tools" that black belts either know or won't ever know.

   B. should emphasize the skills needed for success, including project management, communication, building buy-in, statistics, and problem solving.

   C. should be limited to students with advanced degrees in engineering.

   D. All the above are true.

$$S = \sqrt{(1.3s_1)^2 + (1.3s_1)^2 + (1.3s_1)^2 + etc.}$$

$$S = \sqrt{n(1.3s)^2}$$

$$= \sqrt{10(1.3*0.00333")^2}$$

$$S = 0.037"$$

chapter **3**

Focusing the Deployment

Customer Focus

Customer expectations must be evaluated continually, often for the simple reason that customer needs change over time. In many cases, internal estimates of customer needs do not align directly with actual customer needs. It is not uncommon to discover that many long-held assumptions regarding customer needs are simply wrong. Cost savings and improvement of customer relations are realized through a proper understanding of actual customer needs and wants. Where internal estimates do not match customer realities, Six Sigma projects even may result in a *widening* of the internal specifications, reducing operational costs as well as complaints about late deliveries. All aspects of the customer experience (the value stream) should be considered, including design, use, delivery, billing, and so on, not just the obvious operational processes that constitute revenue generation.

In many business-to-business (B2B) transactions, customers express their requirements by stating a desired *nominal*, or target, value and an upper and/or lower specification. The upper and lower specifications provide the maximum and minimum values (respectively) that will be tolerated in any given instance of product or service delivery. For example, a part may have a nominal length of 2 inches, with an upper specification of 2.005 inches and a lower specification of 1.995 inches. Parts exceeding these values (i.e., shorter than 1.995 inches or longer than 2.005 inches) will not be acceptable for use. These *defects* typically would be returned to the supplier for replacement or credit, resulting in potential delays (waiting for replacement parts) and other additional costs. The returned parts, in turn, cost the supplier in the short term (through the credit it issued, the rework of the long pieces to finish them to an acceptable length, and the scrap in discarding of the material, labor, and lost capacity associated with the short pieces that cannot be used by the customer). From a longer-term perspective, many customers prudently monitor their suppliers so that those with consistently poorer records of performance will be replaced eventually by suppliers who can meet the requirements consistently.

In many business-to-consumer (B2C) transactions and in some B2B transactions, specifications may not be stated so clearly. Instead, expectations tend to dictate perceptions of performance. Various customers may have different expectations; a given customer's expectations even may change depending on external considerations. For example, what is an acceptable queue time waiting for a teller at a bank? Do business customers who visit each day for deposits have different expectations than nonbusiness customers visiting twice a month for deposits? Is the acceptable queue time influenced by your personal schedule for that day or whether you have a small child pulling on your arm? Unstated expectations clearly are more challenging in many ways, yet they offer great potential for market differentiation and resulting revenue enhancement.

Whether detailed specifications have been provided by customers or are developed internally to meet perceived but unstated customer expectations, they tend to become the focus. Even customer-conscious personnel will define customer needs in terms of specifications: "As long as we meet their requirements, we'll be fine." These product specifications are viewed as goalposts: "Anywhere within the requirements is fine." Often, service attributes aren't that important: "The main thing is to deliver what they want, even if it's a bit late."

When customer requirements are perceived as goalposts, as shown in Figure 3.1, there is equal value for all products or services within the specifications, so there is no perceived advantage in improvement beyond this point.

In most cases, the goalpost approach does not maximize customer satisfaction because it does not represent the customer's preference accurately. Instead, customers tend to think in terms of optima. For bilateral specifications (where upper and lower specifications are provided), the optimal value for the product or service typically lies midway between the requirements, with deviations from that point less desirable. Customers value predictability, or minimum

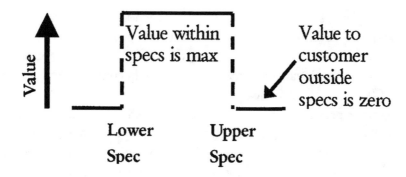

FIGURE 3.1 Perceiving customer requirements as goalposts assumes constant maximum value within specs.

variation, so that their processes are affected to a minimal degree. This enhances their ability to plan, regardless of their environment. If your organization makes a product, customers want to use your product in a consistent manner, with few adjustments of their equipment to compensate for variation between products. If your organization provides a service, your customers want that service to be consistent so that they know what to expect and when to expect it.

These concepts are illustrated in the Kano model (developed by Noritaki Kano) shown in Figure 3.2, where quality is represented on the *x* axis and customer satisfaction is represented on the *y* axis. The expected quality is shown on the diagonal line, indicating that an ambivalent level of satisfaction (neither

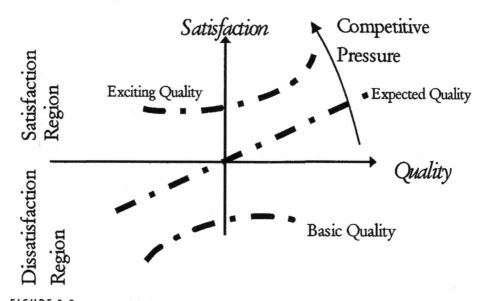

FIGURE 3.2 Kano model of customer satisfaction and quality.

satisfied nor dissatisfied) should be expected when the quality has risen from the basic quality level to the level expected for the given product or service.

Basic quality levels tend to produce dissatisfaction, and satisfaction is improved above ambivalence only as customers become excited about the quality of the product or service.

Competitive pressures tend to move the expected quality line in an upward direction. There are countless examples of this phenomenon, including phone service, home building, computer technology, car safety, and so on, especially when viewed over the course of a generation or more. In each case, a product or service that was once exciting quality became expected quality and then basic quality. Competitive pressures continue to "raise the bar."

The Kano model moves the focus from specifications to real customer needs. When the focus is on specifications and defects, only expected levels of quality will be met, which soon become basic levels of quality in a competitive market.

When the focus is on customers, their businesses, or even the needs of *their* customers, exciting levels of quality can be delivered through innovation. Consider the lessons of Polaroid: While the company focused internally to become more efficient, its customers switched to digital cameras in place of Polaroid's (once award-winning) products. Lessons such as these were not lost on Jack Welch, who remarked that the "best [Six Sigma] projects solve customer problems" (Slater, 1999).

Welch was not suggesting that companies merely reduce defects delivered to the customer or improve the perceived quality of a product or service delivered to the customer. Instead, Welch said that a Six Sigma project should investigate how the product or service is used by the customer and find ways to improve the value to the customer of that product or service.

This clearly demands involving the customer in the business needs analysis. Customer needs must be defined in larger terms than simply product specifications. Understanding how the customer uses the product or service can produce breakthrough changes in design or delivery. While initial design of a product or service process may have considered this, changes in the customer's business may not have been communicated effectively, leaving an unaddressed opportunity. As additional aspects of the customer's business are understood, changes in that customer's business climate or market that could upset your business are appreciated, if not anticipated.

In this way, maintaining customer focus is an ongoing activity. Processes for serving customers must be identified, and mechanisms must be maintained for real-time feedback from customers to these internal processes. The metrics and dashboards discussed earlier are integral to this strategy.

Internal process objectives must be defined in customer terms, and the everyday focus must be kept on the needs of the customer's operations. This visibility is a key aspect of the lean techniques used throughout Six Sigma deployment. The linkage of internal process objectives is mapped effectively using quality function deployment (QFD) techniques. Operationally, we strive to understand how internal processes drive the customer response. To facilitate this understanding, critical-to-quality (CTQ), critical-to-cost (CTC), and critical-to-schedule (CTS) metrics are measured and tracked on a continual basis. These metrics allow internal estimates *before* errors reach the customer and come back as nonconformance reports (or, in the absence of complaints, interpreted as improvement). This proactive approach fosters an ongoing attack on non-value-added (NVA) activities so that resources can be shifted to value-added customer *exciters* (in the Kano terminology).

An interesting and well-documented example is found in the book *Moments of Truth*, written by Jan Carlzon, former president of SAS Airlines. In the late 1970s and early 1980s, the company was losing vast sums of money because its market had changed drastically with the advent of deregulation. While the most prevalent idea was to cut costs across the board or cut costs in recoverable expenses such as labor, instead the company set an ambitious objective to become the frequent business traveler's first choice for travel. Each expense and resource was evaluated for its contribution toward serving the frequent business traveler. Whole business units and functions were dropped, as were a host of operations and procedures that didn't serve the target market (the business customer). Practices that contributed to the service of the target frequent business traveler actually were expanded so that a large portion of the money saved was reallocated to expand the business. As the company struggled with significant loss in revenue, it spent $45 million to improve its customer service, including projects focused on punctuality, turnaround times, and service quality. The company eliminated the detailed marketing reports that took months to create by staff disconnected from customers, replacing them with empowerment of the front-line employees who had direct customer contact for analysis and action based on real-time feedback.

The elimination of NVA activities is a lean practice used in Six Sigma to concentrate the always-limited resources on the customer. Quick feedback mechanisms using key service metrics is a fundamental Six Sigma approach. QFD techniques can be used to identify practices that contribute to customer satisfaction.

In any organization, the leadership sets the vision and the strategy. As Carlzon put it, "A leader . . . creates the right environment for business to be done." A soccer coach can neither dribble down the field for the team nor provide constant and immediate instructions to players on shooting, passing, and defense. Instead, the coach needs to develop skills in the players and then empower them to exercise judgment in the use of those skills.

As on the soccer field, responsibility in a customer-focused organization must be delegated down the line. Rather than tightened oversight to achieve adherence to customer requirements, bureaucracy must be reduced and the organizational hierarchy flattened to increase the communication between organizational levels, particularly communication *to* and *from* the front-line personnel with access to customers.

Through empowerment, the responsibility, focus, and authority of front-line personnel are shifted toward doing what is necessary to win customer loyalty—*without the need for additional management approval*. This empowerment demands flexibility, sharing of information, and an understanding of the business operations, which is afforded by cross-training. The ultimate result is what Carlzon called "moments of truth" in customer relations, where customers realize the commitment of the organization to solving their problems (see Figure 3.3).

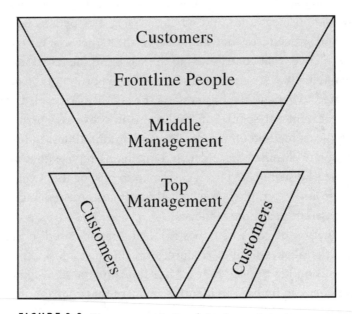

FIGURE 3.3   The new organizational structure puts customer contact at all levels of the organization. (*Pyzdek and Keller, 2009.*)

A new organizational structure results, where commitment toward the customer is shared across the organization. There still may be a sales force, but they no longer need (or want) exclusive rights to communicate with customers. (Note that the same can be said of the relationship between suppliers and purchasing agents.) As the customer becomes a more critical element of each employee's responsibilities, the relationship between the organization and the customer becomes more of a shared partnership with mutual benefits.

These real-time data at the point of delivery provide immediate feedback, which empowered employees can act on. While this is both necessary and useful, it is not sufficient. Some customers may not be open to sharing information. When the end user is several layers down in the supply chain, or when products are held in inventory, dissatisfaction may not be realized until much later, removing possibilities for immediate notification and remedy. Fortunately, additional sources of customer data are available, with varying degrees of usefulness.

Nonconformance reports or complaints are a typical source of customer feedback; however, they often include only a small percentage of all problems. Many problems go unreported. Since the complaints are generally only communicated based on a failure to meet basic customer expectations, they are at most useful for moving to basic or expected quality levels. For some organizations, particularly those at the 3σ level, this is a worthwhile and necessary place to start. These problems cannot be ignored, and their significance to the customer is highlighted by their insistence on reporting them. Prompt analysis of these reports and resulting action sends an important message to the customer. Studies have shown that when customers are made aware of these corrective actions, they tend to become more loyal customers despite the initial incident. When analysis indicates systematic deficiencies, these must be addressed, either through management policy changes or through process improvement using Six Sigma projects. These persistent problems will undermine even the best attempts at problem resolution.

In many cases, broader, more immediate feedback of customer experiences is obtained using simple phone surveys of a random sample of recent customers. More detailed information may be gathered using the critical-incident techniques described by Pyzdek and Keller (2009). The aim is to define moments of truth in customer terms and qualify key customer perceptions. Even customers who may not take the time to complain may be willing to provide quick feedback in this manner.

Customer surveys provide a useful means for collecting a fair amount of broad-based information. Information gathered from the phone surveys, critical-incident interviews, and nonconformance reports or complaints is useful input for survey development. The survey will provide a means to statistically validate the information received from these other sources. Surveys also can be used as a continuous feedback mechanism, particularly for the service aspect of processes. For example, surveys can be sent to all customers, or survey cards can be provided at the point of service or in delivery notification e-mails.

The construction of a useful customer survey is more science than art. The wording of questions, the topics addressed, and the use of open-ended versus multiple-choice responses are but several of the issues that need to be considered. Surveys that lack depth may be useful for feel-good marketing campaigns, but they do little to provide input to Six Sigma operations or process-level teams that can use the survey responses to make dramatic improvements in customer satisfaction, retention, and growth. For example, production-oriented businesses may tend to focus on the product in their improvement efforts, failing to realize how important service is to their customers. An effective customer survey can help to redirect these efforts.

When dealing with a consumer market, it's useful to provide an incentive to encourage customers with positive experiences to participate because often only customers who are upset about something will take the time to complete the survey cards. Incentives include discounted products or services, entry into a raffle for free products or services, or complimentary dinners for participants. In B2B dealings, incentives may be forbidden or even illegal, but generally in this environment the customers are more than willing to provide feedback on what they like or dislike about the product or service. When a broad sample of customers, with both positive and negative experiences, is included in the survey response, then statistical bias can be avoided in the analysis results.

Pyzdek and Keller (2009) offer these guidelines for developing the form of the survey questions:

- Format a question based on its purpose. The way the question is asked is relevant to the information required by the survey group.

- Ask only relevant questions. Respect your respondents' time by asking only questions that are truly important. Ask yourself, "How are we going to use the information from this response?" If you're unsure of the value of the information, don't bother asking.

- Use clear, concise language that is familiar to the respondent. Use the terminology and language level of the respondents so that they can provide answers that are truly relevant to the questions.

- Offer complete, mutually exclusive choices. When choices are offered, the list must be complete (all options provided) and mutually exclusive (one choice cannot conflict with another).

- Ask unbiased questions by presenting all (and only) relevant information. Including irrelevant, inflammatory, one-sided, or subjective information will bias the response.

- Quantify response measures. Use a common scale for the question responses, such as the Likert scale, which provides a convenient and familiar indication of the strength of opinion (for example, strongly disagree, disagree, agree, or strongly agree).

- Order questions in a logical and unbiased way. The survey flow should prevent confusion as to the target of the question. Don't jump around by asking about different topics, because this confuses respondents.

Site visits to business clients also can show how products are used or service received. In visiting your customers, their customers, and so on, you experience the expressed and latent customer demands that otherwise may be hidden. You even may understand how to solve customer problems, as Jack Welch had suggested.

Competitor analyses are also useful in business-level projects because of the competition's inherent influence on sales and profitability. Again, the focus is on the customer as you seek to understand market niches that you currently fill and wish to remain competitive in or new niches that you can take advantage of to increase revenues. Measuring your competitors' strengths and weaknesses, as well as your own strengths and weaknesses, allows you to generate a credible plan of attack.

It's not unusual to find certain issues that can be addressed rather quickly, whereas others may require more detailed strategies. Immediate action represents quick payback for the effort and often can sustain (through improved profitability and morale) the larger effort necessary to achieve further improvements along the path to Six Sigma.

Project Selection

Six Sigma projects are the means by which improvements are realized in a Six Sigma deployment. These improvements are achieved in the areas of quality, cost, or schedule to address the needs of customers, employees, and shareholders. Six Sigma projects must be clearly defined and managed for these improvements to be realized.

Projects must be linked directly to the strategic goals of the organization. As mentioned earlier, GE's Jack Welch considered the best projects those which solved customers' problems.

What constitutes a Six Sigma project? Juran defines a *project* as "a problem scheduled for solution" (Juran and Gryna, 1988). Snee (2002) defines a *Six Sigma project* as "a problem scheduled for solution that has a set of metrics that can be used to set project goals and monitor progress." Snee further differentiates between problems with known solutions, such as the deployment of a manufacturing resource planning (MRP) system, and those with unknown solutions. Snee suggests that projects with known solutions are best led by project managers, whereas projects with unknown solutions are best defined as Six Sigma projects.

The Snee definition notably adds the concept of quantifiable metrics to projects, which is certainly a useful addition. Organizations need to track the progress of a project, as well as to select projects that have the greatest potential for the organization relative to the time and cost of deployment. Intrinsic to these metrics is a link to organizational performance. The metrics must provide a tangible measure of benefit to the company, its customers, or its shareholders. Implementing statistical process control (SPC) on a production line, for example, would not offer this benefit directly. While deploying SPC would allow us to understand the nature of the variations in the process, improvement may not be realized for the customer or the organization unless, for example, the special causes of variation were eliminated. Although an SPC analysis would provide a useful measure of the before and after performance of a process undergoing a Six Sigma improvement project, the analysis is a means to an end rather than the end itself.

Since most businesses beginning their Six Sigma programs are at the 3σ or 4σ level, spending 15 to 25 percent of their revenue on cost-of-quality issues, they have ample opportunities for improvement. There are, however, limited resources available for project deployment, as represented by their trained black belts and green belts. Project selection thus takes on an important role in determining the magnitude of success of a Six Sigma deployment.

Six Sigma projects should be selected based on a suitable cost-benefit analysis. A simple yet effective metric for evaluating projects is the Pareto priority index, or PPI (Pyzdek and Keller, 2009):

$$\text{Pareto priority index (PPI)} = \frac{\text{savings} \times \text{probability of success}}{\text{cost} \times \text{completion time}}$$

Note that the PPI increases as the probability of success or the dollar savings increases and decreases as the implementation cost or completion time increases. The units used for each of these terms should be consistent across projects to provide a valid comparison.

Inclusion of the "probability of success" points out a simple fact: Not all Six Sigma projects will be successful. Six Sigma projects are usually not tasked for simple problems but more often for problems that have persisted despite prior attempts at solution. A number of reasons may be behind this lack of success: lack of resources, lack of management commitment or authorization, and/or lack of sufficient analysis to understand the true causes of the problems (including treating the symptoms rather than the causes). A proper Six Sigma project definition and deployment strategy [i.e., adhering to the rigors of the *d*efine, *m*easure, *a*nalyze, *i*mprove, and *c*ontrol (DMAIC) methodology] will address these issues, resulting in a successful project conclusion.

However, other issues also can prevent success. In some cases, the solution is too costly to be justified by the market. In others, the technical knowledge is lacking, and until further research and development are undertaken, a solution is not feasible. It is important that these issues be recognized as soon as possible so that project resources can be redeployed to solvable problems.

The cost to deploy is fairly easy to calculate, including costs such as labor, materials, work stoppage for data collection, and so on. Initial estimates documented on the project charter should be updated as the project proceeds to ensure that they do not overwhelm the savings. It is the project team leader's responsibility to update these budgets as the project proceeds so that the project sponsor can manage the resources effectively.

It is important that the cost and benefit estimates are accepted by the organization as fair and accurate. For this reason, the accounting and finance functions within the organization are responsible for defining the true costs and benefits for each project based on predetermined methods of cost estimation. This allows consistency across projects and removes any bias that might be perceived toward the black belt or sponsor.

The potential savings and benefits include the following, which can be applied only if and when they are actually realized by the organization's bottom line:

- Decreased material costs.
- Increased sales owing to a capacity increase. Note that this produces a benefit only if the process is currently capacity-constrained [i.e., the cur-

rent process is operating at its full output volume (capacity)] and there is market demand for the increased capacity.

- Increased sales owing to improved customer loyalty.
- Decreased labor costs. Labor savings come from either a reduction in total task time and/or a diversion of tasks to lower-paid staff (or automated systems). In either case, this benefit is realized only if the labor is reassigned or eliminated (such as through attrition). If the process is capacity-constrained, then reduced task time increases capacity and may provide additional sales, as noted earlier.
- Decreased carrying costs for work-in-process (WIP) inventory, including reworked parts and other parts in common assembly.
- Decreased accidents associated with WIP storage.
- Decreased incidental material usage. This includes the use of glues, paper, office equipment, coolants, and so on that decreases when the process runs more efficiently.
- Decreased maintenance costs and/or capital expenditure based on decreased material usage. When the process runs more efficiently, new equipment is not needed, additional offices or plants are not needed, and the cost for maintaining the existing infrastructure is reduced.
- Decreased time to deliver to customers, including decreased penalties for late shipment and/or expediting, decreased costs for communicating shipment status to customer, and decreased costs associated with customer dissatisfaction.
- Increased employee morale, with a subsequent decreased employee turnover and training expense.

As a general rule, most companies expect minimum annualized savings of $50,000 to $100,000 from each Six Sigma project. Many projects will yield much higher savings. What may seem surprising is that the per-project savings do not necessarily depend on the size of the business, so even a $100 million company can save $1.5 million on a project. Recall that a 3σ company is spending approximately 25 percent of its revenue on cost of quality, so a 3σ company with $100 million in sales is spending approximately $25 million per year on poor quality. Using a rule-of-thumb measure of 0.5 to 1 percent of employees as black belts, however, the number of projects can effectively scale the total financial return from the Six Sigma deployment for each business.

The PPIs for a group of potential projects are shown in Table 3.1. Although

TABLE 3.1	Pareto Priority Index Calculationss				
Project	Saving ($000)	Probability of Success	Cost ($000)	Completion Time	PPI
PO cycle time	220	90%	5	3.5 months	11.3
Shipping damage	40	70%	9	6 months	5.2
Design change	770	50%	30	10 months	1.28

the first project, PO (purchase order) cycle time, has the lowest projected savings, it is the preferred project, receiving the highest PPI score. This reflects its overall reduced risk (with higher probability of success and lower cost to deploy).

Although the PPI is relatively easy to use, it ignores many potential project benefits, such as the ability to meet shipment schedules, reduce inventories, or contribute to strategic business- or customer-valued objectives.

A prioritization matrix for selecting projects is shown in Figures 3.4 through 3.6. A company's project selection committee used customer input to weigh the projects. While customer surveys, interviews, and focus groups could be used to provide valuable input at this point, the company recently had received detailed feedback on its performance from a high-profile client. An internal review of the feedback determined that the client's findings were accurate and fairly representative of some key operational shortcomings. These were summarized as follows:

- Qualification of new or revised processes
- Design reviews
- Incorporation/control of engineering changes

	Qualification of new or revised processes	Design reviews	Incorporation/control of Engineering Changes	Reality-based scheduling	Work procedures/training	Benefit/Cost ratio	Time to Implement	Probability of Success	Criteria Total	Criteria Weight
Qualification of new or revised processes	-	5	1	1	10	1	10	1	29	0.17
Design reviews	1/5	-	1	1/10	10	5	5	1	22 3/10	0.13
Incorporation / control of Engineering Changes	1	1	-	1/10	1	1/5	1/5	1/5	3 7/10	0.02
Reality-based scheduling	1	10	10	-	10	5	5	5	46	0.27
Work procedures / training	1/10	1/10	1	1/10	-	1/10	1/10	1/10	1 3/5	0.01
Benefit/Cost ratio	1	1/5	5	1/5	10	-	5	5	26 2/5	0.16
Time to Implement	1/10	1/5	5	1/5	10	1/5	-	5	20 7/10	0.12
Probability of Success	1	1	5	1/5	10	1/5	1/5	-	17 3/5	0.11

FIGURE 3.4 Criteria weighting matrix. (*Quality America GreenBeltXL.*)

- Reality-based scheduling
- Work procedures/training

The company added three more criteria for project selection: benefit-cost ratio, time to implement, and probability of success. All these objectives were compared with one another and rated for relative importance by senior management. The results are shown in the criteria weights matrix in Figure 3.4. A value of 1 means that the two criteria are equal in importance, a value of 10 implies that the row is significantly more important than the column, and a value of 5 implies that the row is somewhat more important.

The project selection committee then rated each project relative to these criteria, as shown for one such criterion (benefit-cost ratio) in the options rating matrix in Figure 3.5.

A combined score then is summarized, as shown in Figure 3.6, to determine the ability of each project to fulfill the defined business objectives. The project that provides the best overall benefit relative to the weighted criteria is the row with the number one rank: "ECO Cycle Time Reduction" project. .

A similar yet simpler approach is afforded by the matrix diagram, where each candidate project can be compared directly with the criteria in a single matrix. The assumption for the matrix diagram would be that all criteria are of equal weight. The prioritization matrix and the more general matrix diagram are discussed in more detail in Part 3 of this book.

Criteria: Benefit/Cost ratio	Cell 12 Scrap Reduction	Proposal Cycle Time Reduction	ECO Cycle Time Reduction	Supplier A Reject Reduction	Option Total	Option Weight
Cell 12 Scrap Reduction	-	10	5	1/5	15 1/5	0.33
Proposal Cycle Time Reduction	1/10	-	1/5	1/10	2/5	0.01
ECO Cycle Time Reduction	1/5	5	-	1/10	5 3/10	0.12
Supplier A Reject Reduction	5	10	10	-	25	0.54

FIGURE 3.5 Options rating matrix. (*Quality America GreenBeltXL.*)

Summary Matrix	Qualification of new or revised processes	Design reviews	Incorporation / control of Engineering Changes	Reality-based scheduling	Work procedures / training	Benefit/Cost ratio	Time to Implement	Probability of Success	Option Rating	Option Rank
Cell 12 Scrap Reduction	0.043	0.005	0.001	0.003	0.001	0.052	0.059	0.051	0.215	3
Proposal Cycle Time Reduction	0.043	0.024	0.006	0.161	0.002	0.001	0.021	0.018	0.277	2
ECO Cycle Time Reduction	0.043	0.096	0.015	0.072	0.007	0.018	0.040	0.034	0.326	1
Supplier A Reject Reduction	0.043	0.008	0.001	0.039	0.000	0.086	0.002	0.002	0.182	4
Criteria Met Rating	0.17	0.13	0.02	0.27	0.01	0.16	0.12	0.11	1	
Criteria Met Ranking	2	4	7	1	8	3	5	6		

FIGURE 3.6 Summary matrix. (*Quality America GreenBeltXL.*)

CHAPTER 3 QUIZ

1. **Customer expectations are**
   A. always stated in advance as a specification.
   B. equally satisfied anywhere within the defined specifications.
   C. maximized for a bilateral specification at the midpoint of the specification.
   D. ensured if the process is in control.

2. **Repeat customers value**
   A. predictable variation within the requirements.
   B. low cost at the expense of all other criteria.
   C. customer service that will correct all problems after they are detected.
   D. competitive pressures.

3. **Focus on customer-supplied specifications**
   A. ensures a long-term relationship with the customer.
   B. may lead to loss of customer loyalty if unstated expectations are not met.
   C. provides the best metric for Six Sigma projects.
   D. is preferred to focus on internal specifications that may not apply.

4. **Failure to deliver products or services that meet customer specifications**
   A. results in delays as the customer awaits replacement products or services.
   B. affects the supplier through near-term costs for credit, rework, or scrap.
   C. affects the longer-term potential for a positive relationship between supplier and customer.
   D. All the above are true.

5. **Which of the following levels of quality tends to produce longer-term loyalty in customers?**
   A. Basic quality
   B. Expected quality
   C. Exciting quality
   D. Competitive quality

6. **Which of the following interpretations of the Kano model is *most accurate*?**
   A. Customer satisfaction is determined solely by the quantity of the product or service delivered.
   B. Customer wants can be determined once and for all and used to design high-quality products and services.
   C. Customer wants, needs, and expectations are dynamic and must be monitored continuously. Providing products or services that match the customer's expectations is not enough to ensure customer satisfaction.
   D. Customers will be satisfied if you supply them with products and services that meet their needs at a fair price.

7. In terms of project focus, Jack Welch felt that the best projects

A. attacked internal process inefficiencies.

B. solved problems experienced by customers or the end users of the customer's products or services.

C. corrected supplier issues that permeated throughout GE.

D. were micromanaged by the project sponsor to ensure that the desired solution was implemented.

8. The Pareto priority index (PPI, expressed in unit per day) for a project saving $125,000 at a deployment cost of $6,200 over a 100-day project deployment with an expected 75 percent probability of success is

A. 5.0.

B. 0.21.

C. 6.6.

D. 0.15.

9. The reduced cost of labor is an acceptable project benefit

A. in any competitive market.

B. only when labor is in tight demand.

C. whenever labor cost exceeds the cost to train new employees.

D. only if the labor is reassigned or eliminated or if the resulting capacity increase results in higher sales.

10. The preferred method for evaluating projects when there are several criteria, each of which has a different relative weight, is a

A. Pareto priority index.

B. matrix diagram.

C. prioritization matrix.

D. DMAIC project.

Part II

DMAIC
Methodology

4

Define Stage

The starting point for the *define*, *measure*, *analyze*, improve, and *control* (DMAIC) problem-solving methodology is the define stage.

Objectives

The key objectives within the define stage of DMAIC are

- *Project definition.* To articulate the project's scope, goal, and objectives; its team members and sponsors, its schedule, and its deliverables.
- *Top-level process definition.* To define its stakeholders, its inputs and outputs, and its broad functions.
- *Team formation.* To assemble a highly capable team and focus its skills on a common understanding of the issues and benefits of the proposed project plans.

These objectives should be satisfied before the team progresses to the measure stage.

Project Definition

The key project details are documented in the project charter and are updated regularly (with approval as necessary) as additional information is uncovered by the team during the DMAIC cycle. The key tasks for developing the project charter can be summarized as follows:

- Define the problem statement and the business need for doing the project.
- Define the project scope using preliminary data (which usually must be collected and analyzed).
- Develop deliverables, the useful output of the project, stated in financial terms accepted by finance and management as legitimate estimates.
- Develop an initial schedule for the project milestones.
- Define the project stakeholders, and assemble a team.
- Conduct a project kickoff meeting. In this meeting, the team agrees to the project scope, its deliverables, and the schedule.
- Map the process at its top level.
- Secure the approval of the updated project charter from the project sponsor.

Project charters provide a means to control and manage Six Sigma projects. They serve as a contract between the project sponsor and the project team. Unlike legal contracts, they are "living documents" in the sense that they are updated as new information is discovered in the DMAIC process. In this regard, they are used to actively manage and continuously focus the project over its life.

Through its sponsorship by the appropriate level of management, a project charter helps the organization avoid projects that (1) deal with unimportant issues, (2) overlap or conflict with other project objectives, (3) target soon-to-be-obsolete processes or products, (4) have poorly defined or overwhelming scope, (5) study symptoms instead of root causes, (6) provide poorly defined deliverables, and (7) lack management authority and responsibility.

An example project charter is shown in Figure 4.1. Each element of the project charter is described in detail. The example used was introduced by the author in the *Six Sigma Handbook*, third edition (Pyzdek and Keller, McGraw-Hill, 2009). Readers with both texts may notice some slight enhancements in materials in this book that reflect revisions to the charter resulting from measure-stage data. This is intentional, to further illustrate use of the charter as a living document and communication tool for project stakeholders.

Project Charter: Order Processing Efficiency

Start Date: 9/17/07	Planned End Date: 3/17/08

Problem/Project Description: Current capacity in Sales is constrained, while there are untapped opportunities for increased sales. Sales involvement in order processing should be limited to free up resource for lead follow-up and revenue generation. Errors and omissions in Order Processing data increases time to generate marketing & software renewal emails to clients and prospects, further draining Sales resources. Data correction requires senior sales staff, who might otherwise be engaged with clients, marketing efforts, or product development. Lost opportunity cost is significant.

Project Scope: Limited to order processing of software products.

Project Objectives & Goals:	Metric	Baseline	Goal	Benefits
Impact cycle time & costs	Cost/Order	$40	$20	$27,000
➤ Reduce Order Processing cost 50%	Campgn. Cost	$500	$10	$24,000
➤ Reduce email marketing costs 98%	% Renewal	x %	1.2x%	$50,000
➤ Increase renewal rate 20% ➤ Increase renewal revenue 20%	Renewal $	$250,000	$300,000	$50,000

Business Need

Customer Impact: Improved notification rate for renewals & upgrades; reduction in order processing cycle time.

Shareholder Impact: Reduced costs for order processing and marketing to existing clients; Increased capacity in sales and marketing; Increase in renewal rates.

Employee Impact: Clearer responsibilities; Less interruption in process flow.

Project Sponsor:	Stakeholder Group:	Signature / Date
Peter Keene, VP	Sales & Operations	Peter Keene
Team Black Belt: Patrick Killihan	Operations	Patrick Killihan
Team Members: Don Debuski	Sales	Don Debuski
Helen Winkleham	Shipping & Packaging	Helen Winkleham
Anne Sheppard	Accounting	Anne Sheppard

Resources: Programming/IT Support; CRM database

DEFINE		MEASURE		ANALYZE		IMPROVE		CONTROL	
Objective	Date	Objective	Date	Objective	Date	Objective	Date	Objective	Date
➤ Project Def.	9/17/07	➤ Process Def.	10/03/07	➤ VSA		➤ New Process		➤ Standardize	
➤ Process Def.	9/19/07	➤ Metric Def.	10/03/07	➤ Var Sources		➤ Benefits		➤ Control	
➤ Team Form	9/19/07	➤ Baseline	12/27/07	➤ Drivers		➤ FMEA		➤ Lessons	

FIGURE 4.1 Example project charter for order processing.

Problem Statement

The problem statement summarizes the problems to be addressed. It also should state the current or historical conditions, such as the defect rate or dollars wasted as a result of poor performance.

As is evident in the following example, the problem statement should provide quantifiable estimates of the issue and its impact. While data supporting these estimates may not be available in the very early stages of project charter development, the project team (or usually the black belt leading the project) must gather preliminary data in the define stage to provide justification for allocation of resource to the project. These preliminary data will be further substantiated (or not substantiated) in the measure stage. If the data in the measure stage do not support the data from the define stage, the project may be reevaluated at that point in time to consider reallocation of resource to other projects.

PROJECT EXAMPLE: Problem Statement

Current capacity in sales is constrained, while there are untapped opportunities for increased sales. Sales involvement in order processing should be limited to free up resources for lead follow-up and revenue generation. Errors and omissions in order processing data increase the time needed to generate marketing and software renewal e-mails to clients and prospects, further draining sales resources. Data correction requires senior sales staff, who otherwise might be engaged with clients, marketing efforts, or product development. Lost opportunity cost is significant.

Business Need Addressed

The business-need-addressed statement should indicate the business case for implementing the project and reference key metrics of cost [e.g., financial benefit or return on investment (ROI)], schedule (e.g., cycle time), and/or quality [e.g., sigma level or defects per million opportunities (DPMO)]. This answers the "Why should we care?" question. A good project should be linked directly to the strategic goals of the organization. This *alignment* is critical for program and business success.

Jack Welch commented that the best projects solve a customer problem. An example he cited was invoicing for appliances shipped to Wal-Mart (Slater, 1999). The initial problem was defined as something akin to "late payments from Wal-Mart." While this seemed accurate from General Electric's (GE's) perspective, from the customer perspective, GE was doing a poor job of filling orders, making it difficult for the customer to close out and pay the invoice.

PROJECT EXAMPLE: Business Need Addressed

The example order processing efficiency project charter breaks the business need addressed statement into separate entries for each of the three main stakeholder groups:

Customer impact: Improved notification rate for renewals and upgrades; reduction in order processing cycle time.

Shareholder impact: Reduced costs for order processing and marketing to existing clients; increased capacity in sales and marketing; increased renewal rates.

Employee impact: Clearer responsibilities; fewer interruptions in process flow.

TIP: *Use matrix diagrams to ensure that project objectives are aligned with business objectives.*

Objective

The objective is a more specific statement of the outcome desired. GE used the following as a guideline:

- If the process is operating at or less than a 3σ level of performance, then the project objective should be a 10 times reduction in defects. For example, if the current DPMO is 10,000, then the goal is for the improved DPMO to be 1,000 or less.
- If the process is operating at greater than the 3σ level, then a 50 percent reduction in defects is warranted. For example, a process operating at 1,000 DPMO should be brought to a level of 500 DPMO.

While DPMO can be useful, it also can lead to somewhat arbitrary definitions of defects and opportunities. Since the Six Sigma deployment effort should be directly related to financial benefits, cost savings provide the most useful indication of project benefit.

PROJECT EXAMPLE: **Objective**

Affect cycle time and costs associated with sales:

Reduce order processing costs by 50 percent.

Reduce e-mail marketing costs to existing clients by 98 percent.

Increase renewal rate by 20 percent.

Scope

The scope is the specific aspect of the problem that will be addressed. Many projects have too broad a scope initially, such as when objectives are too ambitious to reach a conclusion in a reasonable time frame, or the impact is too large, affecting too many stakeholders.

As the project cycle time increases, the tangible cost of the project deployment, such as the cost owing to labor and material usage, will increase. The intangible costs of the project also will increase: frustration owing to lack of progress, diversion of personnel away from other activities, and delay in realization of project benefits, to name just a few. When the project cycle time exceeds six months or so, these intangible costs may result in loss of critical team members, causing additional delays in project completion. These "world peace" projects, with laudable but unrealistic goals, generally serve to frustrate teams and undermine the credibility of the Six Sigma program.

A critical aspect of a Six Sigma project is that of providing a measurable benefit in terms of cost, schedule, and/or quality. A project whose benefit is not realized in a reasonable amount of time generally would not be acceptable as a Six Sigma project. While this may seem short-sighted, it merely reflects the reality of resource allocation. Since resources for Six Sigma projects are limited, they should be spent on projects that provide the best benefit relative to the cost to deploy.

For these reasons, Six Sigma projects assigned to black or green belts should be scoped for completion in a three- to four-month period. This tight schedule allows team members to commit themselves for the full length of the project. Projects that are too large to be completed in this length of time usually can be divided into several potential projects whose merits can be compared with those of other projects competing for project resources.

In many cases, projects can be scoped properly before assignment, but in some cases the project team, in its problem-solving effort, will uncover a much larger project than initially suspected. In such cases, the team should work with the project sponsor to update the project charter with a redefined project scope, timetable, and deliverable. The newly defined project then should be reevaluated relative to the criteria established for project selection, as outlined in Chapter 3.

The work breakdown structure for the order processing efficiency project example is shown in Figure 4.2, where the process is broken down by product and then by fulfillment type.

Breaking the process into its components forces a recognition of the subprocesses requiring separate improvement strategies. Limiting the project to one or only a few closely related categories will lead to a better chance of project success given an adequate financial return.

The Pareto diagram is useful to show the relative impact from each of these subprocesses, often to further break down the project scope. The Pareto diagram shown in Figure 4.3 displays the relative volume of orders for each product, by fulfillment type, for the order processing efficiency project example. Products B and C represent 79 percent of the total software orders, implying that the project could focus on these two products to achieve a large portion

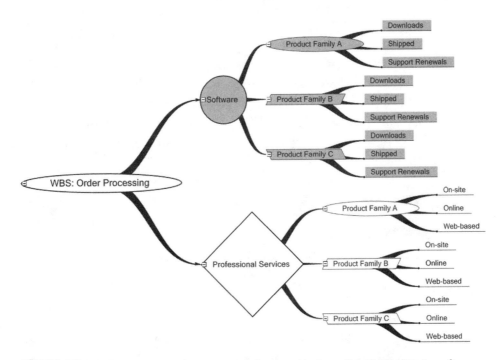

FIGURE 4.2 Example work breakdown structure developed in Green Belt XL/MindGenius software. (*From Pyzdek and Keller, 2009, by permission.*)

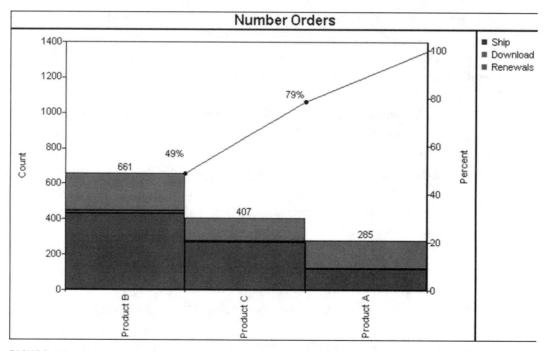

FIGURE 4.3 Example Pareto diagram for project breakdown developed in Green Belt XL software. (*From Pyzdek and Keller, 2009, by permission.*)

of the savings in order processing costs. Nonetheless, since product A has the largest share of the renewals and the campaign costs associated with renewals, the team decided to include all three products. The team also felt that the order processing changes would have an impact on all three products, with only subtle differences in processing required. Note that the Pareto diagram also can be displayed with cost data, which might produce a different result. Generally, cost data are more relevant, where available.

PROJECT EXAMPLE: Scope

Limited to software products.

Stakeholders, Team Members, and Sponsor

The term *stakeholders* refers to the departments, customers, and vendors who will be influenced by the project activities or outcome. A top-level process map is useful for determining which departments are affected by the process being studied so as to effectively determine stakeholders for the project.

The term *team* refers to the specific members of the stakeholder groups who will play an active role in the project problem solving, data collection, and analysis, including the assigned black belts, green belts, subject-matter experts, operational personnel, and facilitator (if any). Typically, one black belt is assigned to a given project. One or more green belts may be assigned from a given stakeholder department. Since black and green belts are trained in basic facilitation skills, facilitators should be needed only in exceptional situations, such as if hostility exists between team members. Ad hoc team members also may be identified to provide assistance, expertise, or background information on request but not necessarily participate as regular members of the team.

These concepts are covered in more detail in the "Team Formation" section later in this chapter.

The *sponsors* are the middle- to upper-level managers who support the project. Sponsors fund the project, allocate resources, and develop the initial charter. As a member of management, the sponsor builds support for the project in the managerial ranks of the organization. The sponsor's managerial position in the functional area that is the subject of the improvement project helps to build awareness and support for the project in the operational ranks, as well as to clear roadblocks that might inhibit timely progress of the project. When stakeholders are from different functional areas, the sponsor may be at the level above the functional area of management so that resource allocation and departmental commitment are achieved. To prevent the top levels of the organization from sponsoring too many projects, cosponsors from the top ranks of the affected functional areas also may be used.

PROJECT EXAMPLE: Stakeholders

Stakeholder groups include sales, shipping and packaging, and accounting, as shown in the top-level process map of Figure 4.4. The project champion has functional authority over all these areas.

TIP: *Use process map and suppliers-inputs-process-outputs-customers (SIPOC) analysis to determine stakeholder groups.*

Resources

Resources refer to the processes, equipment, databases, or labor (not included as team members) that may be needed to keep the project on schedule and provide the data necessary for conclusive analysis.

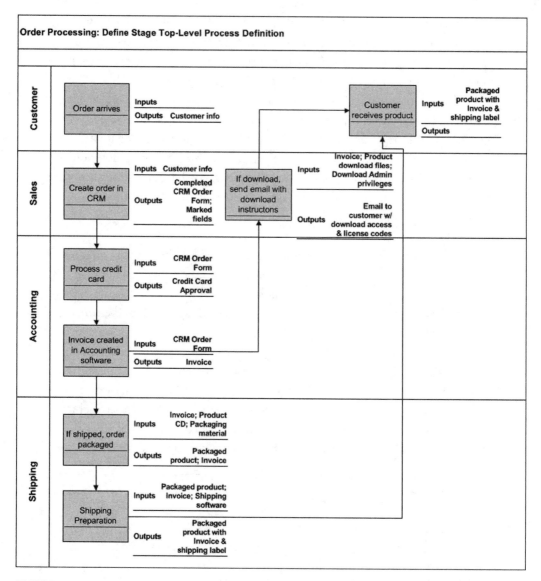

FIGURE 4.4 Top-level process map for order processing efficiency project example developed in MS Visio software.

PROJECT EXAMPLE: Resources

Resources include programming/information technology (IT) support; customer relationship management (CRM) database.

Deliverables

Deliverables include all measurable benefits from implementing the project. Properly defined deliverables will answer the question: "How do we define project success and completion?"

There are many types of project deliverables, as discussed in the section on project selection in Chapter 3.

Often, project teams are tempted to include some of their analysis results as a deliverable. Even the implementation of statistical process control (SPC) charting in a process is not a deliverable because it is not itself a direct financial benefit to the organization or customer (although it provides indirect benefit through improved product quality and reduction of unnecessary project tampering).

PROJECT EXAMPLE: **Deliverables**

In the order processing efficiency project example, the deliverables are broken down by metric:

Order processing annual savings at current order volume: $27,000.

E-mail marketing costs: The total cost of the campaigns would be reduced by $24,000 annually, and additional sales potentially could be generated, especially for renewals.

Software renewal rate: At the current (product-specific) renewal rate, this would increase revenue $50,000 annually.

Renewal revenue: The renewal rate appears to depend on the marketing campaigns, which to date have been limited to product A. If the other product families achieved renewal rates matching product A's, $250,000 in additional revenue would be realized. While the project team thought that this could be achieved over a longer term, they thought that a 20 percent increase in revenue for the first year was achievable.

Time Frame

The project charter should list the charter date (i.e., the date approved by the sponsor), the start date, and the expected completion date based on an attached project schedule (see Gantt charts in Part 3). In addition, a phase-gate review section is provided to indicate dates when objectives for each DMAIC stage have been completed. As described in the scope discussion, the duration for most Six Sigma projects should be limited to three to six months. The review for each phase is conducted as part of the status reports discussed below.

TIP: *Critical-path and/or program evaluation and review techniques (PERT) analyses are used to develop the completion date.*

The project schedule generally is in the form of a Gantt chart detailing the activities and milestones associated with the project. The Gantt chart should clearly identify tasks, their precedents, and their required resources. It should allow the project leader to manage the project's critical path.

Each stage of the DMAIC methodology is broken down into activities and milestones. The define stage is broken down into its activities, as are measure, analyze, improve, and control. Milestones are established at the conclusion of each stage that highlight the opportunity to communicate project status to the sponsor and stakeholders. Figure 4.5 shows the DMAIC schedule for the example order processing efficiency project.

Project Status Report

The project status report should be provided on a weekly or biweekly basis and at the conclusion of each DMAIC stage milestone. Weekly reports can be provided to the team and its sponsor; milestone reports additionally can be circulated to other stakeholders. As mentioned previously, this communication helps to build buy-in, which is critical for project success.

In addition to an updated project schedule and a verbal description of progress, status reports should include the following sections:

- *Action items.* Issues assigned to specific team members for completion by a stated date.

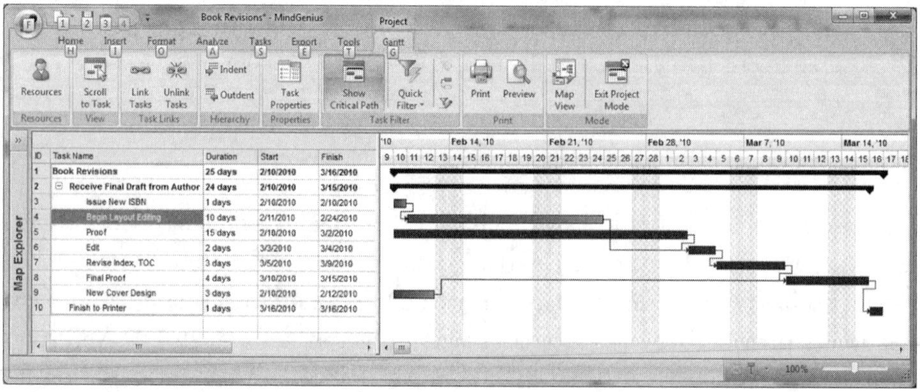

FIGURE 4.5 Example project schedule for the order processing efficiency project developed in Green Belt XL/MindGenius software.

- *Outstanding items.* Past-dated action issues.
- *Roadblocks.* Issues that are stalling the project, for which an immediate action item cannot be assigned.
- *Conclusions.* Findings from each stage of DMAIC, supported with data in their analyzed form.

Communication helps to reduce future problems: When sponsors and stakeholders see progress as it occurs, they understand the direction of the project and can see natural solutions to issues. Reducing surprises is important because surprises create confusion and roadblocks, which can slow down or permanently stall a project.

Project Conclusion

At the end of the project, in the control stage, the financial benefits are confirmed by the accounting or finance department. The project sponsor approves the findings and its control strategy. This control plan provides a monitoring scheme for tracking the financial and operational benefits gained and the process-level metrics associated with the project deliverables.

It is also important in this stage to document the "lessons learned" during the project cycle. These often provide valuable input to future projects or to the master black belt responsible for the Six Sigma program deployment. These issues are discussed in further detail in Chapter 8.

Top-Level Process Definition

There are several useful tools available for defining the as-is process:

- Flowcharts historically have been the preferred tool for documenting process activities. The graphic approach is appealing to operational personnel, who may find reading text in paragraph form laborious. The simple branching scheme of flowcharts easily highlights process complexities.
- Process maps have become the preferred choice recently for documenting process activities because they provide an additional level of detail (beyond the flowchart) to indicate functional responsibilities for each process step. An example top-level process map is shown in Figure 4.4.
- SIPOC analysis is a tool for identifying the process inputs, outputs, and stakeholders. It is particularly useful at this stage to ensure that all the

relevant stakeholders are included in the process. The process map in Figure 4.4 includes the suppliers, inputs, outputs, and customers for each top-level process item.

Generally, these tools will be used in conjunction with one another. The top-level definition of the process provides only a broad view of the process, with little of the details necessary for a complete understanding of the day-to-day process mechanics. At this stage, we are most concerned with the process boundaries and stakeholders to aid in project and team definition. Details on the application and use of each of these tools is provided in Part 3.

Team Formation

Effective team formation is a crucial step for building stakeholder buy-in. After identifying the stakeholders in the project (in the top-level process definition), the stakeholders can be categorized as either key (necessary for success) or nonkey (not necessary for success) stakeholders.

Once the key stakeholder groups have been identified, team members are selected from each of the stakeholder groups. Each representative should be credible within each stakeholder group as well as among the other stakeholder groups. These representatives should have the support of local management, be enthusiastic for the change, and be capable and willing to serve on the team. In some cases, a team member skeptical of the change may be selected if he or she has all the other characteristics, particularly those of credibility and capability. Selection of skeptical representatives is a technique that attempts to build buy-in within the stakeholder group.

Effective teams generally are limited to five to seven full-time members. Larger teams are more difficult to manage, and members may lose a sense of responsibility to the team. Additional team members may be ad hoc members from nonkey stakeholder groups, who participate only as needed, such as for process expertise.

Team Member Responsibilities

Team leaders must clearly communicate personal responsibilities to team members in initial meetings and fairly enforce these responsibilities in subsequent meetings. Each member must take responsibility for team success or failure. No one should blame the team leader, other members, or the sponsor for failure of the team, nor should anyone take personal credit for a project's success.

Team members need to follow through effectively on commitments in a timely manner. They must contribute to discussions, which includes active listening, offering constructive and nonjudgmental feedback, and active sharing of ideas. Team leaders can be given feedback regarding what seems to be working and not working.

Team Leader Responsibilities

Team leaders must accept their responsibilities for leadership:

- *Keep the team focused.* Use the charter's goal, objectives, and scope statements to focus the team. Stick to the DMAIC structure: Don't try to analyze or improve until you've defined and measured.

- *Enforce ground rules.* Ground rules provide important protocol to teams, ensuring consistency and fairness for members. Typical ground rules include respectful and inviting communication, consensus-based decision making, and prompt completion of action items.

- *Ensure that conflicts are resolved in a positive manner.* Actively listen to concerns raised by interested parties, and then address the concerns. Concerns cannot be ignored or maligned. Data should be collected so that concerns can be understood and addressed properly. While this may take "extra" time, the cost of not addressing these concerns is often a failure to achieve project buy-in, which can be fatal to a project's objectives.

- *Schedule, facilitate, and manage team meetings.* Meetings should have a defined agenda, and the leader should ensure that the team sticks to it.

- *Report regularly to project sponsors and stakeholders* (as discussed previously).

- *Ensure that barriers are removed* (if necessary by the sponsor). When roadblocks are encountered in a project, it is especially important for the team leader to use his or her consensus-building skills effectively. The project sponsor has the ultimate authority to clear roadblocks but should exercise authority to clear roadblocks only when all other options have been unsuccessful.

- *Develop team member skills.* Within each stage of DMAIC, use brainstorming tools to expand the team's thinking, followed by data-analysis tools to focus on a solution.

In an initial team meeting, the team leader should review and circulate the ground rules. The team should agree (through consensus) on the project purpose and scope, as documented in the project charter. Of course, if the scope changes as the project progresses through DMAIC, the team and sponsor again should reach consensus on the revisions.

The project plan and timeline should be reviewed, and meeting times and locations should be established. Generally, it's best to meet only when necessary, although default times can be established for meetings to help members allocate time.

Teams require ongoing management to be effective. Ideally, teams should meet only as needed to discuss or resolve issues or to follow up or assign action items. When meetings become a waste of anyone's time, then the team will begin to lose commitment and momentum. Agendas should be distributed beforehand so that members are prepared to discuss planned items. Action items should be assigned at the end of each meeting and reviewed at the start of the meeting for which they are scheduled. The project schedule should be updated regularly to reflect changes as they occur, with regular reports to the project sponsors and stakeholders.

Change Agents

To drive change in an organization, you will need to accept a basic fact of human nature: Change scares most people. Organizational change requires adoption of new policies or procedures. Personnel often will need to learn new skills, particularly in a Six Sigma deployment. This is unsettling to some, nerve-wracking to others. This fear of the unknown is a barrier to change.

To make the matter more complicated, those of us who do not fear change are usually skeptical of it. Change is not always for the better, at least in everyone's eyes. Some people will long for the "good old days."

Finally, there are those who know that change could be for the better but still won't be behind it. Why? They don't believe management is committed to make it happen! "Been there, done that, got the T-shirt. Next!"

Effective change agents will address these concerns because change cannot occur without buy-in from those responsible for change. The following DMAIC steps are useful to achieve buy-in within the organization:

- *Define* key stakeholders. These are the individuals or groups who can make or break the change initiative.
- *Measure* the baseline level of buy-in for each key stakeholder. How committed are stakeholders to change?

- *Analyze* buy-in reducers and boosters for each key stakeholder or stakeholder group. Understand the concerns of stakeholders, which may vary from one stakeholder to another.
- *Improve* buy-in by addressing issues.
- *Control* with a plan to maintain buy-in.

Bear in mind that these steps for achieving buy-in may be used several times for different issues within a given project and even applied informally within a team meeting.

The SIPOC approach to the top-level process definition discussed earlier will allow a clear definition of the stakeholder groups (required to define buy-in). Levels of buy-in (Forum Corporation, 1996) from a given stakeholder or stakeholder groups then can be assessed either formally through surveys or informally through team or individual discussions. The lowest level of buy-in, *hostility*, may be the easiest to recognize. The second level, *dissent*, may go unnoticed until stakeholders are questioned (i.e., measured) about the change initiative, such as through discussion or survey. *Acceptance*, the third level, is the lowest level of buy-in that should be considered for proceeding with the change initiative, but often it is not sufficient unless *support*, the fourth level, is achieved from a majority of the critical stakeholder groups. True *buy-in*, the fifth and highest level, is a level above support, in that stakeholders are enthusiastic in their commitment for change. As a team leader, you will want to lead individuals with true buy-in.

To analyze and improve the buy-in reducers, the issues that typically reduce stakeholder buy-in must be clearly understood (Forum Corporation, 1996):

- *Unclear goals.* The project charter serves as the communication vehicle to clearly present the goals throughout the stakeholder groups.
- *No personal benefit.* Goals, stated in terms that provide a clear link to personal benefits for stakeholders (such as decreased intervention or improved working conditions), should be enumerated in the project charter.
- *Predetermined solutions.* Projects of this type are not suitable for Six Sigma deployment. Adherence to the principles of data-driven decision making prevents subjective solutions from taking root.
- *Lack of communication.* Analyses and results are communicated throughout the stakeholder groups in the project charter.
- *Too many priorities.* The project charter, with its authorized scope, focuses the team on achievable results.

- *Short-term focus*. The linking of the project metrics with business-level priorities ensures the long-term benefits of the project.
- *No accountability*. Clearly defined project sponsors, stakeholders, and team members provide accountability.
- *Disagreement on who the customer is*. Clearly defined stakeholder groups are required in the project definition.
- *Low probability of implementation*. Formal project sponsorship and approvals provide a clear implementation channel.
- *Insufficient resources*. Project sponsorship by management ensures financial support.
- *Midstream change in direction or scope*. Changes in the project charter must be authorized by the sponsor and communicated to stakeholder groups.

On a personal level, good communication skills can assist in the buy-in process psychologically (Forum Corporation, 1996). First, show confidence in your ideas by maintaining eye contact and smiling (when appropriate). Second, present your ideas in a direct and concise manner, painting a positive yet realistic picture of your idea. Third, show interest in the ideas of others by allowing equal time for all points of view. Ask pointed questions, and use appropriate body language such as sitting up, leaning forward, or nodding to show that you are listening and understand what others are saying (even if you don't agree with them).

Communication always should be respectful and inviting for all members to participate. Toward this end, team members should "leave their badge at the door," meaning that there are no managers or seniority in a team meeting. The team leaders never should consider themselves senior to anyone on the team, nor should they feel as if this is their personal project. Rather, the project is owned by the sponsor, and all team members are serving at the sponsor's request. Leading never should imply seniority or an executive privilege.

Critical to buy-in is establishment of the criteria for team decisions. Consensus is the preferred approach to team decision making. Consensus is a prerequisite for achieving sustained change. Consensus does not mean that everyone is in absolute agreement, nor that everyone thinks the proposal is the preferred approach. Rather, consensus implies that the parties are willing to accept the proposal despite the differences of opinion that might exist. A good question to ask stakeholders in order to gauge the level of consensus is, "Can you live with it?" Differences in viewpoint are accepted and can be reconciled with Six Sigma's analytical tools. In this way, achieving consensus allows the team to move forward so that the merits of the proposal can be proven through sound data-driven analysis. Alternatives to consensus such as majority voting, arbitrary flipping of a coin, or exchanging of votes for reciprocal votes (bartering) undermine the team's results and must be avoided.

The easiest way to achieve consensus is through the proper use and analysis of data. This so-called data-driven decision making removes the subjectivity of decisions. Opinions are replaced by supported facts. Of course, gathering and analyzing data take time, so management must give teams enough time to be thorough. Fortunately, every decision does not require extensive fact finding, and proper use of DMAIC tools will provide guidance.

Three tools that are useful for building consensus (and which are further discussed in Part 3) are

- *The affinity diagram* provides a means to generate a collection of ideas about a proposal and then to summarize the ideas in terms of categories.
- *The nominal group technique* is simply a means of reducing a large collection of ideas into a workable number of key ideas.
- *The prioritization matrix* allows a team to prioritize its options according to weighted criteria.

Each of these tools helps to obtain consensus by systematically reducing a large number of disparate ideas into a smaller group of items that can be managed or analyzed.

Team Development

There are four common stages of team development: forming, storming, norming, and performing.

In the *forming stage*, team members are polite to one another. Procedures and ground rules are emphasized and respected. The team hasn't really gotten into the heart of problem solving, so there is little friction.

In the *storming stage*, the team begins to work on the problems at hand, using brainstorming, data collection, and analysis. At this point, conflicts begin to develop between opposing views. Team members establish roles within the team. This role playing undermines the authority of the team leader and circumvents the team's progress. It is important for the team leader to enforce the ground rules effectively during this stage. Failure to enforce the ground rules can prevent the team from moving forward to the norming stage, and it can result in project failure.

In the *norming stage*, the team begins to make some progress. Team members allow themselves and each other to reach a stage of independent thinking, which allows them to collaborate effectively on problem solving and analysis.

In the *performing stage*, the team has realized gains and feels confidence and pride as a result. Team members are performing as a lean, mean team.

Within the group dynamics, it is not uncommon for team members to periodically, even subconsciously, assume counterproductive roles, such as those shown in Table 4.1 (Pyzdek and Keller, 2009). The team leader and members should be aware of these easily recognizable roles, which are often prevented through enforcement of the ground rules discussed previously.

Team leaders should concentrate on practicing effective facilitation techniques, particularly when disagreements arise. Emotions must be kept in check. Facilitators must foster respectful communication among team members. Facilitators also need to remain neutral so that they continue to have the trust of all team members. Avoid judgmental language, sarcasm, or nonverbal gestures that might insult or intimidate others. Effective facilitators will ensure that all participants have an opportunity to contribute. Sometimes real effort is required to draw out the quiet participants or to quiet the overbearing participants.

Black belts learn a variety of focusing tools to lead teams from disarray and disagreement to order and consensus. Focusing on data, rather than opinions, is particularly helpful.

To maintain neutrality when discussion becomes heated, it is sometimes

TABLE 4.1 Counterproductive Team Roles

Role	Description
Aggressor	Attacks values, feelings, or ideas
Blocker	Persists on resolved issues; resists consensus
Recognition seeker	Boasts
Confessor	Airs personal opinions
Playboy	Shows lack of commitment, jokes around
Dominator	Asserts authority, manipulates
Help seeker	Evokes sympathy
Special-interest pleader	Shows interest in own group only

helpful to slow the frenzy and ensure that the points of disagreement are clear to all. In this way, misinterpretation can be resolved or minority voices heard. An effective method of doing this is to help the team develop a clear list of advantages and disadvantages for each option. Keep the focus on the specific problem at hand. Help team members to remove opinions and attitudes that cloud or prejudice the issues. At the least, develop a consensus on the points that need to be addressed for the issue to be resolved.

When team authority is not recognized, usually by those outside the team, then stakeholders may not have been identified properly. Often team authority is questioned by groups or individuals who feel that they are not represented on the team and refuse to contribute as a result. It may be that they are indeed represented, but they have not been brought up to speed on the team's mission. These problems can be prevented through proper communication throughout the stakeholder groups. When stakeholders refuse to contribute or actively block progress, sponsors may need to discuss these issues with the individuals outside the team setting.

Power struggles also can occur in teams, usually when more senior members of an organization decide to "flex their muscle" or if two groups in the organization have competing interests. The ground rules, discussed at the initial meeting, should be referenced and enforced to prevent escalation of these struggles. Data-driven consensus-based decision making often undercuts these power struggles. Creating an environment where all members participate prevents certain team members from dominating the discussions.

It may sound silly, but too much agreement also may be a bad thing. Conflict can be good. A healthy dose of skepticism may find a problem before it becomes a headache. Respectful differences of opinion can help the brainstorming process uncover new methods or discover old problems that haven't been addressed.

In summary, the following issues regarding team development and consensus building should be recognized:

- Projects cannot succeed without a team effort by the affected stakeholders.
- Team members have the responsibility to ensure team performance.
- The team leader must establish and enforce ground rules.
- Buy-in is crucial; consensus builds buy-in.
- Responsible team management leads to successful project management.

Recommended Tools

The following tools (discussed in detail in Part 3) are applicable to the define stage of DMAIC:

Project Selection and Definition

- *Matrix diagrams* and *prioritization matrices* are used to select projects that are aligned with company goals and objectives.
- *Work breakdown structure* is used to define a manageable project scope.
- *Pareto diagrams* help to identify significant opportunities.
- *Process maps* provide a visual means to define the process and identify stakeholders.
- *SIPOC analysis* identifies the process activities, key inputs and outputs, and stakeholders.

Project Scheduling

- *Gantt charts* manage the project milestone dates and are used to calculate a deterministic critical path.
- *PERT analysis* allows critical-path determination, assuming variation in time estimates.

Consensus Building

- *Affinity diagrams* provide a means to generate a collection of ideas about a proposal and then converge on useful categories of issues.
- *Nominal group technique* reduces a large collection of ideas into a workable number of key ideas.
- *Prioritization matrices* prioritize options according to weighted criteria.

CHAPTER 4 QUIZ

1. **The define stage of DMAIC achieves which of the following goals?**
   A. A good understanding of the various factors that influence the process
   B. A definition of the project's objectives and scope so as to understand what will be investigated and why
   C. Proposal of the likely solution to the problem being investigated
   D. All the above

2. **A useful tool to reduce a large project into a more realistic project that can be achieved in a reasonable time period is a**
   A. flowchart.
   B. Gantt chart.
   C. work breakdown structure.
   D. matrix diagram.

3. **Project charters help to prevent the occurrence of which of the following reducers to stakeholder buy-in?**
   A. Unclear goals
   B. No accountability
   C. Insufficient resources
   D. All the above

4. **If an affected department that had no representation on a project team begins raising objections to a project's proposed changes, then**
   A. the project champion should advise the department to accept the solution and learn to live with it.
   B. the department members probably are afraid of change, and there's not much you can do to help people like that.
   C. the department should have been identified as stakeholders early on and included in the project team or the team's problem-solving sessions.
   D. Choices a and b are true.

5. **Team leaders who are having trouble getting team members to accept their proposals should**
   A. ask the project champion to replace the team members.
   B. work on their communication skills, listen carefully to other team members' input, and use data to build buy-in to the best ideas regardless of their source.
   C. work closely with the more agreeable team members to get them on board with their ideas and then take a vote so that those who disagree will see that their ideas aren't popular enough to do.
   D. Choices a and c are true.

6. **When a team is unable to come up with ideas during a brainstorming exercise and a few people are dominating the discussions, the team leader should**
   A. cancel the meeting and come up with some ideas on his or her own.
   B. report the impasse to the sponsor and suggest that the team meet again in a month or two when members have a fresh perspective.
   C. use brainstorming tools such as affinity diagrams to encourage wider participation from the group.
   D. form a new team with process experts who have more ideas.

7. **A conflict of ideas between various members in a team meeting, even if done respectfully,**
   A. doesn't happen often because most people are business savvy enough to know not to disagree with others in public.
   B. is common when team members are becoming involved and committed to finding the best solution.
   C. generally indicates that the team leader is not enforcing the ground rules.
   D. should be reported to the project champion.

8. **As the time to completion for a project increases beyond 10 or 12 months,**
   A. the cost of the project increases.
   B. frustration of team members is likely to increase.
   C. diversion of resources is likely to occur.
   D. All the above are true.

9. **If, during the analyze stage, a team discovers that the project is actually much larger than originally thought when it was scoped, the team should**
   A. continue on by addressing all aspects of the increased scope, because a larger scope also will mean better deliverables to exceed the champion's expectations.
   B. select one aspect of the scope that seems easiest to address, and continue the project to its completion, focusing on that problem.
   C. select one aspect of the scope that provides the best benefit, and continue the project to its completion, focusing on that problem.
   D. consult with the champion regarding the findings to determine the best balance of resource versus potential benefit for the project.

10. **A Pareto diagram is useful in developing the scope of a project by**
    A. determining the correlation between the different categories of the problem.
    B. providing a baseline of the process.
    C. identifying the critical few issues or categories on a cost or count basis.
    D. defining the metrics to be evaluated.

chapter 5

Measure Stage

The objectives of the measure phase are explained and illustrated in this chapter.

Objectives

The objectives of the measure stage include

- Process definition at a detailed level to understand the decision points and detailed functionality within the process.
- Metric definition to verify a reliable means of process estimation.
- Process baseline estimation to clarify the starting point of the project.
- Measurement system analysis to quantify the errors associated with the metric.

Process Definition

In the measure stage of the *define, measure, analyze, improve,* and *control* (DMAIC) problem-solving methodology, a detailed process-level map of the current (i.e., as-is) process is developed. This detailed map clearly defines the activities subject to the improvement efforts. The top-level process map developed in the define stage serves as a starting point. While the top-level map shows the general flow of the process, it lacks the detailed decision points that truly characterize the process complexities.

A *process* consists of repeatable tasks carried out in a specific order. Process personnel responsible for implementing the process on a daily basis should be enlisted to develop the detailed process map. Their perspective on the process is likely to be quite different from that of their supervisors or the support personnel who originally developed the process flow (if that exists). It's not uncommon to find that operational workers have customized the process to address real-world situations they see in practice. This information may not get communicated to all the relevant stakeholders in the process, including their immediate supervision or even fellow line workers.

By enlisting the input of these process personnel, their experiences with the process, specifically in the steps they see as necessary and sufficient, are uncovered. At this time, judgment is reserved on whether these are desirable or undesirable customizations. It's likely that they are the source of significant variation to customers, and their effect can be evaluated in the analyze stage. The main concern at this phase is to develop a realistic picture of the as-is process.

The as-is process map then can be used to visualize the decision paths that are encountered in the process. Often much more complexity is built into the process than expected or needed, and much of this complexity is non-value-added. This complexity will be reviewed in the analyze stage.

It is critically important that changes not be introduced at this point so that baseline estimates taken later in the measure stage reflect the historical process that is being studied. If the baseline estimates are not predictive of the process performance levels that qualified the process for improvement, then either the project should be reevaluated to verify that the performance levels are in fact as understood in the define stage or the analyze stage will be burdened with disrupting the process further to attempt to replicate the historical process performance levels.

PROJECT EXAMPLE: Process Definition

The as-is process map for the example order processing efficiency project is shown in Figure 5.1.

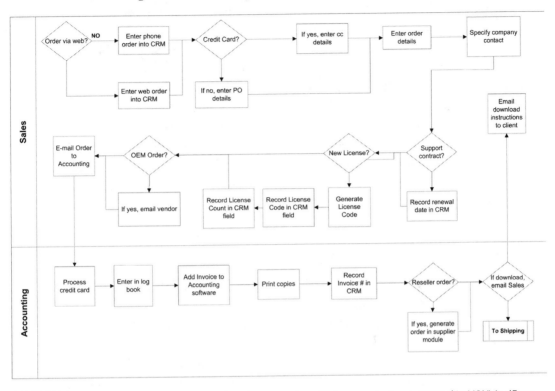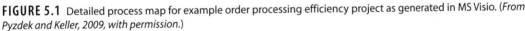

Order Processing: Measure Stage Process Definition

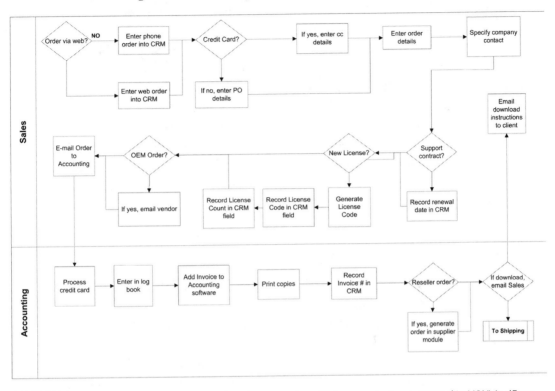

FIGURE 5.1 Detailed process map for example order processing efficiency project as generated in MS Visio. (*From Pyzdek and Keller, 2009, with permission.*)

Metric Definition

In general terms, a *process metric* is simply a measured parameter from a process that provides some indication of the process state or condition. For a given process, several metrics may be useful to operational personnel. Some of these operational metrics also may be useful in Six Sigma improvement projects.

Six Sigma metrics focus on one or more of the following three critical factors: cost, quality, and schedule. Factors critical to cost (CTC) include parameters that have an impact on work in progress (WIP), finished goods inventory, overhead, delivery, and materials and labor, even when the costs can be passed on to the customer. Critical-to-quality (CTQ) factors are perhaps most familiar to operational personnel because they have a direct impact on the functional requirements specified by the internal and external customers. Critical-to-schedule (CTS) factors affect the delivery time of the product or service.

Recall the earlier recommendations for metrics: The metric should be customer-focused, integrated with the business strategy, and developed collaboratively. It should indicate performance over time in a direct fashion so that it can be processed immediately. As discussed earlier, immediate feedback is most useful for process control, particularly when employees are empowered to respond directly to the information.

The usefulness of the data, however, is not merely a function of their availability. A reliable, repeatable, and reproducible measurement system is needed, as described in the "Measurement System Analysis" section of this chapter. The measurements must have sufficient resolution to detect changes in the process effectively and differentiate between real changes and process noise, as discussed in the following sections.

CTQ Metrics

Many production processes are evaluated by their yield or, similarly, their scrap rate. *Yield* is calculated for production applications by dividing the amount of product finishing the process by the amount of product that started the process. For example, if 1,000 units started production, and of these, 980 units completed production successfully, then the yield is calculated as 980/1,000 = 98 percent. The *scrap rate* refers to the units that could not be sold (in this case, 2 percent).

Note that once the customer requirements have been determined, any process can be defined in terms of its yield. For example, if 380 clients surveyed in a random sampling of 400 clients of a customer call center indicated that the service level was satisfactory or better, then the yield of the process can be calculated as 380/400 = 95 percent.

A problem with the yield metric is that it does not provide enough detail on the nature of the errors. As an example, consider the following three processes, each with a 95 percent yield:

- *Process A:* Of 4,000 units started and 3,800 completed, 200 defective units each had a single defect.
- *Process B:* Of 4,000 units started and 3,800 completed, 200 defective units had a total of 600 defects.
- *Process C:* Of 4,000 units started and 3,500 completed with no defects, 300 units were reworked for 420 defects, and 200 units were scrapped for 580 defects.

These processes have different outcomes, yet the yield metric fails to discriminate between them. In this production process, some units initially with errors can be *reworked* and sold as new. For example, units with unacceptable paint finish might be repaired and repainted. Likewise in a service process, a customer initially dissatisfied with the service may be directed to a manager for repair of the situation, resulting in an ultimately satisfied customer.

In terms of the metric, if the reworked units are treated the same as nonreworked units, information is lost. This simplistic yield metric obscures the "hidden factory" responsible for rework and process variation. While the hidden factory provides a useful and necessary service to the customers, its use comes at the price of increased process cycle times and costs.

A solution to this limitation is offered in the throughput yield metric. *Throughput yield* measures the ability of the process to produce error-free units (or error-free service) in the first attempt: the average percentage of units (or instances of service) with no errors. Throughput yield Y_t is calculated by subtracting the defects per unit (DPU) percentage from 100 percent.

For example, process A (described above) has a DPU of 200/4,000 = 0.05, so its throughput yield is 95 percent, the same as the yield calculated earlier. Process B has a DPU of 600/4,000 = 0.15 (a throughput yield of 85 percent). In this case, the throughput yield reflects the cost of the multiple errors in some of the sample units. Finally, process C has a DPU of 1,000/4,000 = 0.25 (a throughput yield of 75 percent). In each case, the throughput yield is considerably less than the calculated first-pass yield.

Rolled throughput yield Y_{rt} is calculated as the expected quality level after multiple steps in a process. If the throughput yield for n process steps is Y_{t1}, Y_{t2}, Y_{t3}, ..., Y_{tn}, then

$$Y_{rt} = Y_{t1} \times Y_{t2} \times Y_{t3} \times \cdots \times Y_{tn}$$

For example, suppose that there are six possible CTQ steps required to process a customer order, with their throughput yields calculated as 0.997, 0.995, 0.95, 0.89, 0.923, and 0.94. The rolled throughput yield then is calculated as

$$Y_{rt} = 0.997 \times 0.995 \times 0.95 \times 0.89 \times 0.923 \times 0.94 = 0.728$$

Thus only 73 percent of the orders will be processed error-free. It's interesting to see how much worse the rolled throughput yield is than the individual throughput yields. As processes become more complex (i.e., involve more CTQ steps), the combined error rates can climb rather quickly. This should serve as a warning to simplify processes, as suggested in Chapter 4.

Conversely, the normalized yield may be used as a baseline for process steps when a required rolled throughput yield is defined for the process series. The *normalized yield* is calculated as the *n*th root of the rolled throughput yield. For example, if the desired rolled throughput yield is 73 percent for a process with six steps, then the normalized yield for each step of the process is $(0.73)^{1/6} = 0.95$ because 0.95 raised to the sixth power is approximately equal to 0.73. The normalized yield provides the minimum throughput yield for each step of the process to achieve a given rolled throughput yield. Of course, if some process steps cannot meet this normalized yield level, then the rolled throughput yield could be less.

From a quality perspective, these throughput yields are an improvement from the simple first-pass yield, but they still lack a fundamental quality: They cannot provide immediate information to *prevent* errors. Each of these metrics relies on *attribute* (i.e., count) data, where the numerical value of the attribute count is incremented based on the property of each sample relative to a quality specification. For example, the metric may be the count of errors in a given sample of deposits from a banking process: The count is incremented only when an error is observed in one of the deposit records. Attribute data have less resolution than measurement (*variables*) data because a count is registered only if an error occurs. In a health care process, for example, the number of patients with a fever (attributes data) could be counted or the measured temperature of the patients (variables data) recorded. There is clearly more informational content in the variables measurement because it indicates *how good* or *how bad*, rather than just good (no fever) or bad (fever). This lack of resolution in attributes data will prevent detection of trends toward an undesirable state.

In addition to the lack of resolution, the data are tainted by the criteria from which they were derived. The count of errors is based on a comparison of the process measurement relative to a specification. The customer specification may be unilateral (one sided, with either a minimum or maximum) or bilateral (two sided, with both a minimum and a maximum). All values within the specifications are deemed of equal (maximum) value to the customer (i.e., they pass), and all values outside the specifications are deemed of zero value to the customer (i.e., they fail), as discussed in Chapter 3.

In most industries, the specifications provide reasonable guidelines, but they are hardly black-and-white indicators of usability or acceptability of a product or service. As a unit of product or service approaches a specification, the usability becomes gray and is subject to other mitigating concerns such as delivery dates and costs of replacement. This practicality is not surprising, considering the rather subjective manner in which specifications are often developed. Even in the best of worlds, when frequency distributions are applied to derive probabilistic estimates of requirements, there is uncertainty in the final result. In service industries, specifications are often similar to desirability levels: We may say that we want to be seen by the doctor within 45 minutes of arrival, but we're not likely to walk out at that moment if we think service is pending in just a few more minutes. Rather, we'll start complaining after 30 minutes, which will build to irritability and then disgust (at least for some of us).

Taguchi (1986) expressed this notion in terms of a loss function, where the loss to society (the inverse of customer satisfaction) is maximized at some value within the customer requirements and then minimized outside the range of acceptable values. For example, with a bilateral specification, the maximum value of the product or service may be at the midpoint between the specifications. As you move in the direction of either specification limit, the value is reduced in some fashion, typically exponentially, as shown in Table 5.1. For example, a five-day delivery is undesirable, but a two-day delivery is preferred over the four-day delivery.

Although the specifications provide reasonable guidelines on acceptability to the customer, they are not absolute. Tainting the data by removing the objectivity of a measured value (or choosing a somewhat subjective attribute data over a more objective measured value) represents a loss in informational content that is not warranted or desired.

Rather, the statistical value of the data improves as the resolution increases, at least until a resolution is reached that can reliably estimate the variation in the data. For a proper statistical analysis, the standard deviation must be estimated, which requires enough information (i.e., resolution) to the right of the decimal point to measure the variation. For example, using the data in the "Measure A" column of Table 5.1, the standard deviation is calculated as 0.548. The data in this column have been rounded up or down owing to poor resolution of the measurement system. How accurate is this estimate of variation? The data in the "Measure B" and "Measure C" columns of the table represent two possible sets of data that, when rounded, would result in the "Measure A" data. In one case, the variation is overestimated by "Measure A"; in the other, variation is underestimated. Note that there are many other possible data sets that would result in the same rounded data shown by "Measure A," but in all cases the rounding produces an inaccurate result. These inaccuracies would increase the probabilities of rejecting when the hypothesis is true, a false-alarm error, or accepting when the hypothesis is false, a failure-to-detect error. Practically, the value of the improved estimates must be balanced against the cost of obtaining the increased data resolution.

TABLE 5.1	Example of How Rounding of Data Affects Results		
	Measure *A*	Measure *B*	Measure *C*
Observation 1	9	9.4	8.6
Observation 2	10	9.8	10.4
Observation 3	9	9.3	9.3
Observation 4	10	10.1	10.1
Observation 5	10	9.7	9.6
Standard deviation	0.548	0.321	0.704

CTC Metrics

CTC metrics are used to track factors contributing to substantial cost when they vary significantly from their target value. CTC factors also may be critical to quality or schedule.

When costs are considered, the true costs of errors in the process, including unreported hidden factory costs, must be included. Examples include

- Capacity loss owing to reworks in system and scrap
- Stockpiling of raw material or in-process material to accommodate poor yield
- Engineering or management approval times
- Rush deliveries
- Lost orders owing to poor service or poor quality

Those in service or transactional businesses should not be disturbed by the wording. *Scrap, rework,* and *stockpiling of in-process material* occur in these businesses as well. Think of clients who need to come back, call back, or talk to multiple people to get the results they seek. Stockpiling occurs any time orders sit waiting for someone to process them, usually in a batch mode. While boarding in groups may work to optimize an airline's processes, it usually doesn't serve the individual customer's interest too well. Similarly, monthly meetings by health maintenance organizations to decide if a given patient's request for services may be scheduled or will be denied may optimize the scheduling of the meeting attendees but comes at the cost of delay (as well as pain and even death) for the patient desperately awaiting the treatment.

The cost of quality tends to increase as errors in a product or service move downstream. It bears repeating that if it costs $1 to fix a problem in the design of the product or service, it costs $10 to fix it in manufacturing or service delivery and $100 after delivery to the customer. Consider the costs owing to faulty tires, food poisoning, or software bugs. The sooner problems are detected and resolved, the cheaper is the solution.

In this way, failures are low-hanging fruit, providing a quick return on investment (ROI). Understanding the causal systems leads to improvement in efforts at appraisal and, eventually, prevention.

While financial metrics such as cost of quality are useful for identifying areas of potential improvements and tracking project savings, there is too much lag in their response to identify process changes requiring action. Instead, CTC or CTS metrics are defined that contribute to cost yet are quick to respond to changes in process conditions.

A review of the potential savings and benefits outlined in the "Project Selection" section in Chapter 3 helps to quantify the costs captured by the response of the particular metric.

CTS Metrics

The most often used metric for CTS issues is the cycle time metric or some derivation of cycle time such as order processing time, delivery time, queue time, or downtime. As with costs, problems in quality also can affect the schedule. For this reason, process improvement focused on CTQ metrics also may improve CTS issues. Consider the delays associated with rework or the reprocessing of orders after mistakes in a quality parameter have been detected. Preventing the errors by concentrating on the CTQ metrics results in improved CTS response.

In addition to these quality-related issues, there are many other opportunities for improvement in cycle times. In the analyze stage, lean value-stream analysis provides techniques for differentiating between value-added and non-value-added process steps. *Process efficiency* and *velocity* can be calculated, each of which indicates a process's relative value-added cycle time. While these metrics are useful for comparing processes or for comparing *before-improvement* and *after-improvement* states of the process, they are not as useful as tracking metrics for identifying changes in process conditions. Calculated values tend to dampen the signal of a cycle time change and be less intuitive to process personnel who must respond to changes, decreasing their value as metrics for immediate information.

Nonetheless, cycle time metrics are valuable tools in achieving improvement in Six Sigma projects. Even when the focus of the project is on quality or cost, the value-stream analysis offers an opportunity for cycle time reduction through elimination of non-value-added activities. As the drivers of a process become clear in the analyze stage, some activities thought necessary for process control will be found to have little effect. These can be eliminated, reducing the total process cycle time.

Conversely, when CTS metrics are the primary project focus, it is often recommended to also baseline the process relative to CTQ metrics. It can happen that efforts to reduce cycle times result in a detrimental effect on quality. At times, there can be a perception of this effect, whether it exists or not. To avoid this real or imagined impact, a baseline of key quality metrics performed in the measure stage, prior to any improvement effort, will provide a sound basis for evaluation of the cycle time reductions. This baseline is particularly well deserved in regulated industries or any industry where quality levels are contractual in nature.

PROJECT EXAMPLE: Metric Definition

For the order processing efficiency example introduced previously, the team focused on two metrics related to project objectives: order processing time and order processing errors. Referring to the top-level process map, order processing encompassed activities performed by members of the sales, accounting, and shipping departments. The team decided to baseline only the time required by the sales staff because reduction of sales staff time was a primary focus of the project, and this greatly reduced the data-collection effort. There were no available data to baseline this aspect of the process, so the team, working with the sales department manager, developed a simple means to collect the data using a spreadsheet. This was slightly complicated by the intervention required for each order by the accounting department and for download orders by the shipping department. In consideration of these necessary activities, the time metric was defined to include up until the order was passed to accounting; the time to e-mail the download order was recorded separately and added into the metric for analysis.

The metric for order processing errors was envisioned as a means to baseline the errors affecting the marketing campaign costs and the subsequent renewal rate and renewal revenue. Recall from the project define stage that the marketing campaigns were time-intensive (and thus costly) because of missing data associated with any given order in the customer relationship management (CRM) system. The senior sales staff initiating the project (one of whom served as the sponsor and another as a team member) had identified several key errors or omissions that would increase the campaign costs: e-mail address incorrect or missing, license count incorrect or missing, and renewal date incorrect or missing. Referring to the detailed process map developed earlier in the measure stage, the team confirmed that each of these was included in the process flow for the sales department's activities. The team was able to identify where the data should reside within the CRM system and use these historical data to analyze the errors. The data analysis is shown in the next section.

Process Baseline Estimation

A process baseline provides an estimate of the current state of the process and its ability to meet customer requirements. The baseline estimate typically is made of the process metric used in operations and accepted within the organization as a reliable indicator of the process under study. The baseline will allow the stakeholders to validate the costs associated with current process performance (as calculated in the preceding section).

The context of the process baseline estimate must be clearly understood. How much variation is there between the samples? Would additional samples yield better, worse, or similar results? Do the samples provide a reliable estimate of future samples?

Enumerative Statistics

The classical statistics most of us have been exposed to are enumerative techniques, used to compare samples randomly drawn from populations. Using hypothesis-testing procedures, samples can be tested for the likelihood that they came from a known population. Similarly, two samples can be compared to gauge the likelihood that they came from the same population. The term *population* simply refers to a group of data that meet a defined condition, such as all customers purchasing a specific product. A key assumption is that the samples are each representative of the population. A *representative sample* implies that there is no bias in selection of the data: Each observation has an equal chance of selection.

In a similar fashion, *confidence intervals* on point estimates may be constructed that will provide bounds (an upper and a lower bound) on the expected

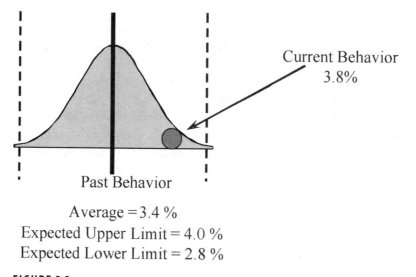

Current Behavior
3.8%

Past Behavior

Average = 3.4 %
Expected Upper Limit = 4.0 %
Expected Lower Limit = 2.8 %

FIGURE 5.2 An improper use of confidence intervals to detect process changes.

value of the statistic based on the data, an assumed distribution (such as the normal, Poisson, or binomial distribution), and a confidence level (usually 95 percent) (see Figure 5.2).

For example, the average error rate can be calculated over a six-month period for a telemarketing process. If this calculation, based on a sample of 5,000 telemarketing calls, indicates an average process error rate of 3.4 percent, then the lower and upper bounds on the 95 percent confidence interval can be calculated at 2.9 and 3.9 percent, respectively (based on techniques described later in this book). If a current sample is taken and has an error rate of 3.8 percent, then the current sample could have come from the same population as the prior samples because it falls within the 95 percent confidence interval.

When these classical statistical methods of analysis are applied, the prior data are assumed to be from a fixed population: The population does not change over time. Fixed populations may be represented graphically by a distribution curve such as that shown in Figure 5.2. Note that in this case a normal distributional curve was assumed for convenience, as is often the case in hypothesis tests and confidence intervals.

Analytical Statistics

A process, however, is different from a population because it occurs over time. In a process, variation may be due to causes that are persistent or to causes that come and go. A persistent cause, usually referred to as a *common cause*, tends to influence all data in a relatively uniform fashion. Common causes of variation are inherent to the process itself, by design. A given reason (the actual cause) often can't be assigned to a specific amount of variation, but the total level of variation is considered typical for the process owing to the influence of these (unknown) common causes. This amount of variation should be expected in the process.

Common causes of variation reflect our ignorance of process dynamics. So long as the amount of variation is acceptable, the ignorance can be tolerated. Since the variation is persistent, the process can be considered stable and can be predicted with the appropriate statistical tools.

In contrast, *special causes* of variation are sporadic in nature: They come and go, generally in an unpredictable fashion. This sporadic occurrence causes the process to behave differently in their presence, resulting in process instability. In the presence of special causes, the process outcome cannot be predicted accurately because the process is not stable.

While logic, reason, or scientific and engineering principles instinctively may be used to differentiate between common and special causes of variation in a process, this is a mistake: Only a properly designed statistical control chart can distinguish correctly between common causes and special causes of variation. A statistical process control (SPC) chart, developed by Walter Shewhart in the 1920s, provides an *operational definition* of a special cause.

SPC uses the element of time as one of its principal axes. Samples are collected over a short period of time. This sample is referred to as a *subgroup*. Each subgroup indicates two things about the process: its current location and its current amount of variation.

Once enough subgroups have been collected over a period of time, the short-term estimates (i.e., the subgroups) can be used to predict where the process will be (its location) and how much the process is expected to vary over a longer time period.

Figure 5.3 displays an SPC chart calculated from the same data used to calculate the confidence interval seen earlier. The control chart reveals something hidden in the distributional curve in Figure 5.2—the element of time. There is a predictable variation inherent to the process evident for the first 40 or so samples. During this period, the process variation was relatively stable.

The most recent sample at 3.8 percent looks different from the earlier 40 samples but is much like those seven months immediately prior to it. These last eight samples apparently represent an unknown shift in the process. The "prior

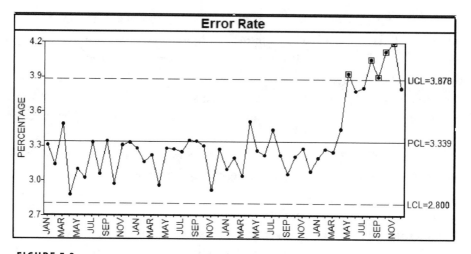

FIGURE 5.3 Using an SPC chart to properly detect process changes, employing Green Belt XL software.

defect rate" of 3.4 percent calculated using the enumerative statistical approach was inflated owing to the pooling of this unknown shift in the process with the earlier stable process. The element of time, lacking in the distributional curve and all other enumerative statistical tools, is clearly a critical parameter for investigating process characteristics because processes are, by definition, occurring over the course of time.

Baseline Estimates Using Enumerative or Analytical Statistics

For Six Sigma projects, it is important to baseline a process using a control chart to investigate whether the process is in a state of statistical control. In at least some cases, out-of-control processes make poor candidates for Six Sigma projects.

Consider a process such as the one shown in Figure 5.4. An out-of-control condition occurs for a period of time and then goes away. This is not at all uncommon in practice, and it might occur for any number of reasons (depending on the metric tracked), including inexperienced personnel filling in for someone on vacation, different material from a supplier, incorrect process settings, change in competitor offerings, and so on.

If a control chart were not used in this analysis, the existence of the special cause would remain unknown. The enumerative estimate would include the effect of the special cause as variation in the population. A fundamental error

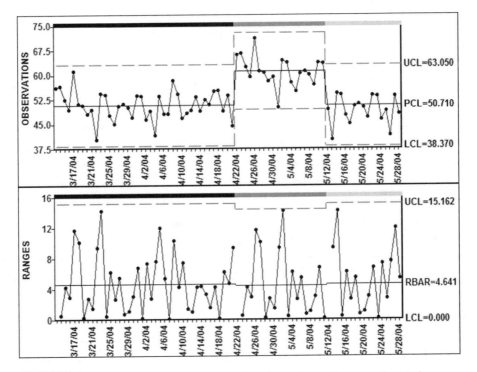

FIGURE 5.4 Without the use of a control chart, baseline estimates from out-of-control processes will be biased.

has been made because the population was not defined adequately. There are actually multiple (or at least two) populations, as evidenced by the special cause.

Even if no improvement were made to the process, subsequent estimates of the new process would show improvement if the special cause failed to reappear on its own accord. Furthermore, the "improvements" made were wasted effort or could even degrade the process performance through tampering (as explained in the "Statistical Process Control (SPC) Control Charts" section of Part 3).

This scenario is likely to have occurred in many historical improvement attempts. When processes are improved and then return to their previous level of performance, a probable explanation is a special cause that was not affected by the improvement. (The other likely explanation is that an effective control plan was not deployed to institutionalize the process change and train employees on its use.)

In at least some cases, special causes are poor candidates for Six Sigma projects because of their sporadic nature. The project investment has an unsure payoff, unlike the predictable nature of common-cause variation. Until the underlying root cause of variation is defined, the economic benefit of the improvement is questionable.

The benefit of an improvement on a special cause depends on the underlying process condition at the root of the special-cause variation. For example, out-of-control conditions on a control chart can occur when multiple process streams are shown on the same chart, as will be shown in an example later in this section. In cases such as this, the process itself is not necessarily out of control; it is our improper use of the control chart that provides the inaccurate estimate of control. When the products are charted properly (on separate control charts or using short-run standardization techniques), the focus of the Six Sigma project can be directed properly and its financial benefit calculated.

When out-of-control conditions are truly due to sporadic, unpredictable root causes, the financial benefit of improvement can be known only when the root cause of the behavior has been identified in process terms. While historical evidence of the occurrence of similar patterns of behavior may be justification to investigate the process, once an underlying cause is determined, an analysis needs to link the cause to the past behavior because this past behavior may be due to other (unidentified) root causes. Nonetheless, if there is financial burden from the special causes, it would tend to justify a proper investigation, such as a designed experiment as part of a Six Sigma project, into the causes.

Statistically, we need to have a sufficient number of data observations before we can calculate reliable estimates of the common-cause variation and (to a lesser degree) the average. The statistical "constants" used to define control-chart limits (such as shown in Appendix 6) are actually variables and approach constants only when the number of subgroups is "large." For a subgroup size of 5, for instance, the d_2 value, used to calculate the control limits, approaches a constant at about 25 subgroups (Duncan, 1986). When a limited number of subgroups are available, short-run standardization techniques may be useful.

To distinguish between special causes and common causes, there must be enough subgroups to define the common-cause operating level of the process. This implies that all types of common causes must be included in the data. For example, if the control chart is developed over a short time frame, such as an eight-hour period, then the data do not include all elements of common-cause variation that are likely to be characteristic of the process. If control limits are defined under these limited conditions, then it is likely out-of-control groups will appear owing to the natural variation in one or more of the process factors.

DPMO and Sigma Level Estimates

When the process is in a state of statistical control, then the process is predictable, and short- and long-term defect levels can be estimated. Unstable (i.e., out-of-control) processes, by definition, are the combination of multiple processes. Their instability makes prediction of defect levels unreliable.

For controlled processes, the *process capability index* provides a comparison between the calculated process location and its variation with the stated customer requirements.

When the process is unstable (i.e., not in statistical control) or control cannot be established because of lack of data, a *process performance index* may be used as a rough estimate to compare observed variation with customer requirements. Generally, many more samples are needed to reliably estimate process performance when the process is unstable. Furthermore, as discussed earlier, there is no reason to believe that the process will behave in this same fashion in the future.

The calculated process capability or process performance metric can be converted to corresponding defects per million opportunities (DPMO) and sigma level using Appendix 8. Let's see how these numbers are derived.

Assuming that the normal distribution is an adequate model for the process, the normal probability tables (Appendix 1) are used to estimate the percentage of the process distribution beyond a given value, such as a customer requirement (usually referred to as a *specification*). z values at $x = $ USL and z_L at $x = $ LSL are calculated, where

$$z = (x - \mu)/\sigma$$

USL refers to the *upper specification limit*, the largest process value allowed by the customer. LSL refers to the *lower specification limit*, the smallest allowed value.

The z value indicates how many σ units the x value is from the mean (or average, μ). For example, if the USL for a process is 16, and the process average and standard deviation are calculated as 10.0 and 2.0, respectively, then the z value corresponding to the upper specification is $z = (16 - 10)/2 = 3.0$, implying that the upper specification is 3σ units from the mean.

Using the normal tables of Appendix 1, a z value of 3 equals a probability of 0.99865, meaning that 99.865 percent of the process distribution is less than the x value that is 3σ sigma units above the mean. This implies that $1 - 0.99865 = 0.00135$ (or 0.135 percent) of the process exceeds this x value (i.e., lies to its right in the distribution curve). The 0.00135 decimal value may be converted to parts per million by multiplying by 10^6, resulting in 1,350 DPMO.

This is shown graphically in Figure 5.5. Note that a similar approach is used to estimate the DPMO for nonnormal processes, where the properties of the fitted nonnormal distribution are used in place of the normal approximations.

Recall that the DPMO-to-sigma-level conversion includes a 1.5σ shift. The Six Sigma process is one that will achieve a long-term error rate of 3.4 DPMO rather than the 2 DPBO (defects per billion opportunities) suggested by a z value of 6. When sigma levels are estimated based on internal process estimates, such as a process capability index, the estimate is termed a *short-term estimate*. External failure rates actually will be higher owing to the longer-term 1.5σ process shift. Use Appendix 8 to estimate the long-term sigma level from short-term process capability data.

When sigma levels are estimated based on external process estimates, such as through field data or customer surveys, the observed defect rate already includes the 1.5σ shift. These are long-term estimates by their very nature. Use Appendix 9 to estimate sigma level from field data.

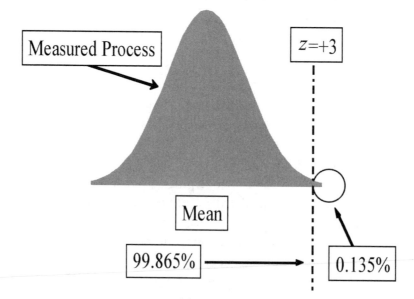

FIGURE 5.5 A calculated *z* value directly corresponds to a percentile of the normal distribution.

PROJECT EXAMPLE: Process Baseline

A control chart of the order entry time (as defined earlier in the metric discussion) is shown in Figure 5.6. The data were collected over a six-week period. An initial analysis using a moving-average chart indicates that no groups are out of control. A significant lack of fit to a normal distribution (K-S value = 0.002) prompts the use of a nonnormal Johnson distribution curve fit (K-S value = 0.935). Seeking to explain the wide common-cause variation (technically part of the analyze phase), the data were stratified by product. The team feels that this stratification suggests evidence of variation between products, as shown by the differences between the diamonds, filled circles, and triangles in Figure 5.6. Separate control charts for each product revealed relatively in control yet skewed processes for each product. The causes for the few out-of-control subgroups (4 of the total 300) will be further considered in the analyze stage; a discussion with the process personnel yielded no suggested causes. The average order processing time across all products was calculated as 21 minutes, which corresponded well to the baseline costs noted in the charter. (Note that although the median is the preferred statistic for describing central tendency of a nonnormal distribution, the average provides a more direct indication of total costs because the average cost times the number of orders equals the total cost. Use of the median cost for estimating total cost is not so straightforward.)

A control chart for the errors is shown in Figure 5.7. In this case, a *U* chart was used to plot the total errors each month. The team felt that this was the relevant

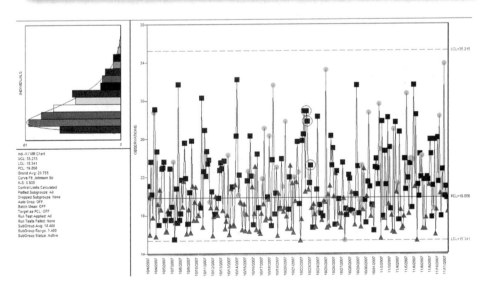

FIGURE 5.6 Control chart baseline for example project's order processing time stratified by product.

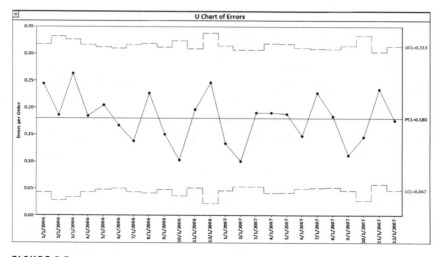

FIGURE 5.7 Control chart baseline for example project's order processing errors.

baseline metric because any of the included errors would cause delay and cost for the marketing campaign. The *U* chart was appropriate because each sample (a given order) could have multiple errors, and the number of orders varied month to month. Over the 24-month period, there were 381 errors in 2,118 orders. Since there are three opportunities per order (e-mail error, license-count error, and license-code error), the DPMO is calculated as

$$DPMO = 10^6 \times 381/(3 \times 2,118) = 59,962$$

Using Appendix 8, the sigma level is approximately 1.6.

Measurement Systems Analysis

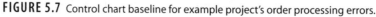

Preceding sections have discussed the need for adequate data resolution in terms of both data type (attributes versus variables) and precision (lost information when data are rounded up or down owing to the measurement method). Even when a measurement method provides adequate data resolution, the measurement may be subject to significant error from a number of sources, which can be further quanti-fied in a measurement system analysis. This measurement error affects estimates of service acceptability as well as product inspections and dispositions, process stability estimates using control charts, and their resulting effect on profitability.

A familiar form of measurement error is *bias*, also known as *accuracy*. Bias is an estimate of the systematic error in the measurement system. A measurement system that is purely consistent, with no variation in its estimate for a given unit, still may have bias because it may be consistently wrong! Bias is a simple, consistent offset in the estimate, and it can be corrected through calibration of the measurement system, much like watches are synchronized for accuracy. Measurement systems need to be analyzed for *stability* to ensure that their accuracy does not degrade over time. While this is often not a concern during the short time period of a Six Sigma project, it may become a concern for future control of the process improvements.

Another concern is that of *linearity*: Does the measurement system provide the same level of accuracy across its full range of use? If the error is higher for larger measurements, then the estimates of variation in these cases are inflated, which will have an unfavorable effect on improvement and control efforts.

Unfortunately, even a regularly calibrated measurement system may be subject to additional sources of error.

When measurements are taken of a process or population, the variation estimated between the samples includes both the actual variation between the sample units and measurement error. Mathematically, the total variance is composed of the actual variance between the items and the variance, or error, of the measurement:

$$\sigma^2_{total} = \sigma^2_{item} + \sigma^2_{measurement}$$

The measurement error appears as variation between repeat samples of a given sample unit. Bias does not affect this measurement error because bias alone will cause the measurement system to measure each sample unit consistently.

When the variance of the measurements is known, a gauge discrimination ratio can be calculated to provide a practical estimate of the measurement system resolution. The *discrimination ratio* is the number of distinct categories discernible by the measurement equipment. A value of 2, for instance, indicates that the gauge is useful only for attribute analysis because it can only effectively classify the parts as being in one group or the other (e.g., good or bad). A discrimination ratio of 8 or more is suitable for statistical analysis of the data.

A primary tool to estimate the variance of the measurements is *R&R analysis*, which categorizes the error as either a *repeatability* or a *reproducibility* error. Repeatability error is associated with the equipment and procedures, whereas reproducibility error is associated with the differences between personnel use of the measurement equipment. Repeatability is estimated by comparing multiple measurements of the same sample unit. Reproducibility is estimated by obtaining measurements of the same sample units by multiple personnel. Categorizing the error in this manner allows one to address and reduce the error.

Considering that the measurement system is used to determine acceptability of the process relative to customer requirements, it should be apparent that as the error increases, so does the chance that

- Products or service truly outside requirements could be measured as being within requirements and subsequently considered acceptable.
- Products or service truly within requirements could be measured as being outside requirements and subsequently rejected as unacceptable.

Measurement error also influences control charting and process capability analysis. The calculation of statistical control limits and the estimation of process capability require a sound estimate of the process variation. As measurement error increases, so does the chance that

- Subgroups from a controlled process will be determined to be out of control.
- Subgroups from an out-of-control process will be determined to be from an in-control process.

In some projects, the use of R&R studies has detected this measurement system variability as the most significant source of common-cause variation. In such cases, the remainder of the project addresses improvement and control of the measurement system. Of course, the loss to the organization (before this was determined) was quite real, so significant savings were achieved by the project team in eliminating these measurement errors.

R&R analyses can be performed on variable or attribute (count) data. In the case of attribute data, measurement error is often the result of the subjectivity of the inspector, which ultimately results from requirements that have been poorly defined. For example, if five inspectors are asked to classify a painted sample as having a color imperfection, then, unless proper standards are established, error often will result from the subjectivity of that assessment. How much variation in color is acceptable? Over what distance of painted part? As viewed under what lighting and optical conditions? An excellent discussion of attribute gauge analysis is provided in *The Six Sigma Handbook*.

Examples of the use of R&R analysis may be found in Part 3.

PROJECT EXAMPLE: Measurement Systems Analysis

The process metrics are cycle time, measured in minutes, and errors, measured as a count by error type. The precise start and end points for the cycle time measurements were established to eliminate potential error between personnel, so no R&R analysis was performed on the cycle time metric.

Likewise, each error type was clearly defined to avoid discrepancies. Yet the team acknowledged that the baseline data conceivably could be compromised by inaccurate count of error owing to simple miscounts or an error in interpreting the correct license count, for example. The team did a quick study using two team members to review 50 orders. Each came to the same conclusions, with no observed differences in estimates.

Recommended Tools

The following tools (discussed in detail in Part 3) are applicable to the measure stage of DMAIC:

Process Definition

- *Flowcharts* and *process maps* to define the process-level activities necessary

Process Baseline Estimates

- *SPC control charts*, including *C, Np, P, U, individual-X, X-bar*, and *EWMA charts*, for investigating process stability and evaluating process capability
- *Histograms* to graphically display the process output relative to the requirements
- *Confidence intervals on mean* and *confidence intervals on proportion* for estimating process performance when the process is not in statistical control
- *Goodness-of-fit tests* to verify the statistical distributions assumed in the various statistical tools

Measurement Systems Analysis

- *R&R studies* to quantify the measurement error associated with the equipment, personnel, and procedures
- *Linearity analysis* and *regression analysis* to understand the measurement system error as a function of measurement size

In addition, the consensus-building tools noted at the end of Chapter 4 are also applied as needed.

CHAPTER 5 QUIZ

1. **In developing a process flow diagram of the current process, the team should involve**
   A. representatives from each of the process stakeholder groups.
   B. only the engineers responsible for designing the process because they know how it's supposed to be done.
   C. only the process personnel because they know how it is actually done.
   D. only the project sponsor because he or she is paying the bill for the project team's work.

2. **If the baseline estimates in the measure stage do not match the performance levels used to justify the project in the define stage, then**
   A. verify that the process personnel conducted the baseline study using the same procedures employed in daily practices.
   B. verify the performance levels used to justify the project in the define stage.
   C. the differences should be investigated in the analyze stage to determine potential process factors that would replicate the define-stage behavior.
   D. all the above should be evaluated.

3. **If 1,000 units start a process and 100 units are scrapped owing to a total of 300 defects, the throughput yield of the process is calculated as**
   A. 90 percent.
   B. 70 percent.
   C. 97 percent.
   D. 81 percent.

4. **If 1,000 units start a process and 100 units are effectively reworked owing to a total of 300 defects, the throughput yield of the process is calculated as**
   A. 90 percent.
   B. 70 percent.
   C. 97 percent.
   D. 81 percent.

5. **A simple process yield estimate, calculated by dividing the number of units completing the process by the number of units starting the process,**
   A. is a simple and effective metric for evaluating the true performance of a process.
   B. provides a good indication of the impact of the "hidden factory."
   C. fails to reflect reworks or other corrections internal to the process.
   D. All the above are true.

6. **If the rolled throughput yield for a three-step process is 92 percent, then an acceptable target throughput yield for each step of the process is**
   A. 92 percent.
   B. 81 percent.

C. 98 percent.

D. 95 percent.

7. **Specification limits for a process**

    A. provide the best estimate of the process output—all output naturally will be produced within the specification limits.

    B. are often arbitrary goalposts that don't adequately express the real voice of the customer, who values consistency.

    C. naturally optimize the process by providing realistic goals.

    D. were devised by Taguchi to replace his loss function.

8. **Process control charts**

    A. are interchangeable with enumerative statistical methods such as confidence intervals.

    B. provide the same results as confidence intervals but are preferred because of the easy in interpreting the graph.

    C. provide results similar to confidence intervals but are inferior owing to their simple graphic approach.

    D. provide different results than confidence intervals by indicating whether a process is stable over a period of time.

9. **Special causes of process variation**

    A. can be predicted through effective brainstorming sessions with the responsible process personnel.

    B. can be eliminated by frequent calibrations of the measuring device.

    C. are not worth investigating because they happen infrequently.

    D. can be identified only by a properly constructed control chart.

10. **When defining the baseline for a Six Sigma project,**

    A. a control chart should be used to reduce bias effects from special causes.

    B. the process histogram is the best tool for showing variation in the process.

    C. the presence of sporadic process shifts has no impact owing to their spontaneity.

    D. a large sample will ensure that the confidence interval picks up the special causes.

Analyze Stage

Objectives

The objectives within the analyze stage of the *define, measure, analyze, improve,* and *control* (DMAIC) problem-solving methodology include

- Analysis of the value stream, the necessary steps that produce value for the customer
- Analysis of the sources of variation
- Determination of the process drivers, the little *y*'s that correlate with the stakeholder requirements and significantly influence the process output

Value-Stream Analysis

Value-stream analysis is a key contribution to Six Sigma, borrowed from the lean methodology. (For more details on the lean methodology, refer to that section in Part 3.) The term *value stream* refers to the necessary activities that contribute value to the product or service, as determined by the customer.

Once a process has been mapped, each process step can be categorized as one of the following:

- A step that creates value for the customer. These steps are classified as *value-added* (VA) activities.

- A step that creates no customer value but is required by one or more required activities (including design, order processing, production, and delivery). These steps are termed *type 1 waste* and are classified as *business-value-added* (BVA) activities to reflect the necessity of their use given the current business process.

- A step that creates no customer value and represents the proverbial low-hanging fruit. These steps can and should be eliminated immediately. These are termed *type 2 waste* and are classified as *non-value-added* (NVA) activities.

Quality function deployment (QFD) and simpler matrix diagrams are useful tools for comparing the contribution of each process step to value, as defined by the customer. To identify NVA activities, it is sometimes useful to ask these questions:

- Is this something the customer is willing to pay for?
- Does this step change the form, fit, or function of the product? Or does it convert input to output?

If the answer to both questions is no, then it is likely that the activity does not create value in the customer's eyes. Inspection and review activities, such as monitoring of sales calls or management signoffs on exceptions, are examples of NVA waste. They do nothing to change the product (or service) and are necessary only to address the poor quality associated with the underlying process. Unfortunately, if their removal would degrade the quality of the delivered product or service, such as for out-of-control or incapable processes, then they are necessary type 1 waste and properly classified as BVA activities.

Taiichi Ohno of Toyota defined the first five of the following six types of waste. Womack and Jones (1996) added the sixth.

1. Errors requiring rework. *Rework* refers to any operation required to fix or repair the result of another process step. In service processes, management intervention to resolve a customer complaint is an example of rework.

2. Work with no immediate customer, either internal or external, resulting in work in progress or finished goods inventory.

3. Unnecessary process steps.

4. Unnecessary movement of personnel or materials.

5. Waiting by employees as unfinished work in an upstream process is completed.

6. Design of product or processes that do not meet the customer's needs.

Reducing Process Complexities

One common method for decreasing cycle times is to reduce the process or product complexities. The process is simplified by reducing the number of "special items" that are processed. By simplifying to one product or one type of service customer, then efforts can be concentrated on achieving higher efficiencies. It should be obvious that the more options offered, the higher is the process complexity, and the longer is the cycle time. By standardizing, cycle time can be reduced.

Henry Ford, in offering the first affordable automobile, realized the efficiency advantages provided by standardization. His motto, "Any color you want, so long as it's black," exemplified the notion of standardization. While the modern approach to standardization at times may limit options, it tends to emphasize the advantages of simplified processes. It seeks to remove activities or product designs that provide little extra value at the cost of increased cycle times, processing complexity, or inventory levels. For example, the costs of approvals and upset customers may be enough to offset the cost of standardizing on second-day shipments for all orders instead of only those orders with approval. Likewise, the additional design, processing, and inventory costs of offering a wide assortment of similar products with slightly different feature sets on each product may not be justified if (for less total cost) the enhanced features could be offered on all products. I was shopping recently for a laptop computer, and one of the vendors had close to 10 product lines of laptops, each of which had 10 to 20 models. If the manufacturers are building the computers to order and have designed their processes properly using this concept of standardization, then they may well be competitive in offering such a varied product line. On the other hand, if they are building for inventory, I suspect that they could simplify the product line and save enough in design, processing, and inventory costs such that their least expensive models could include many of the features found only on their higher-priced models. By grouping parts or services into families, common methods can be applied, thus simplifying processes and reducing overall cycle times and design, processing, and inventory costs.

Yet standardization need not result in reduced choices for your customers. In some cases, processes can be shared among one or more product families, allowing all the benefits of simplification, with customer-specific modifications added at later stages. When these modifications can be provided quickly, this allows overall inventory levels to be reduced with no disruption to supply.

Decision points and subsequent parallel paths on flowcharts provide indication of process complexities that sometimes can be avoided. The Six Sigma process-optimization tools discussed in Chapter 7 provide another method for decreasing cycle times. Rather than simply reducing errors, these tools allow the process to operate at an improved level with respect to customer requirements. For example, the cycle time may be reduced to a point that goes beyond the elimination of complaints to the level of customer delight. These optimization tools include designed experiments, response surface analysis, process simulations, and failure modes and effects analysis (FMEA).

Reducing Non-Value-Added Activities

Reducing or eliminating NVA cycle times often provides the clearest and easiest methods to reduce cycle time and achieve better velocity (see Part 3 for a further discussion of velocity). It's not uncommon for more than 50 percent of a process's cycle time to consist of NVA activities.

The first step for cycle time reduction should be to identify and eliminate the type 2 waste—the process steps that simply are not necessary. These may include such activities as routine authorizations or approvals or information and data collection that is not necessary or even used. After eliminating these activities, the process flow often must be redesigned.

Significant cycle time reduction is achieved through a reduction of errors requiring rework. Practices for reducing rework include standardization of procedures, mistake-proofing (using FMEA), and improvement of process capability. (These last two items are discussed in Chapter 7; standardization procedures are discussed in Chapter 8.) As errors requiring rework are eliminated, the NVA inspections and approvals currently necessary may be reduced or eliminated.

Unnecessary movement of materials or personnel is also an NVA activity. Reducing movement typically affects the physical space in which the process takes place: Offices may be redesigned, departments may be moved or reassigned, and even entire facilities may be moved closer to customers. Movement analysis is aided by the use of spaghetti diagrams. Improvements can be realized through application of the 5S tools, which are discussed in Part 3.

The outcomes of movement and space reduction include

- *Decreased distance from supplier to customer.* Both internal and external suppliers and customers are affected. This relocation reduces the wastes of unnecessary movement and wait time associated with the movement.

- *Less departmentalization and more multifunction work cells.* Within company walls, you may reassign individuals so that they work within multifunctional work cells rather than functional departments. In small companies, cross-training may eliminate the need for some specialized functions. For example, instead of a customer-service representative forwarding an order to accounts payable, customer-service representatives could create and e-mail a completed invoice to the customer while the customer is still on the phone. This improves the flow of the process (whether a physical product, paperwork, or even ideas) so that work is not batched up at each department. Multifunction work cells reduce the waste of waiting and improve the visibility of slowdowns, barriers, or inefficiencies that occur in the preceding or following steps.

- *Reduced overhead costs and reduced need for new facilities.* As space is used more efficiently, overhead costs are reduced, as is the need for new facilities if new equipment or labor is acquired.

Level loading, to match the production rates of the process steps, also reduces NVA cycle times. *Level loading* of serial processes will remove all work in progress. The flow becomes batchless, with a shorter cycle time, increased flexibility, decreased response time, and an increase in the percent of VA activities. "Start an item, finish an item" is the mantra.

Batches are not nearly as efficient as they appear from either a systems' or a customer's perspective. As ironic as it may seem, a major reason processes contain waste is because of historical attempts to drive efficiency. One commonly accepted fallacy is that processes become more efficient by creating specialized departments that process work in batches. These departments become efficient from a process standpoint, with economic lot quantities designed to minimize setup time or material delivery costs, but they lack efficiency relative to specific product value streams. Waste is created in waiting for the batch to begin its departmental processing, and waste is additionally created when particular units of product, for which customers are waiting, must wait for the remainder of the batch to be processed.

The attempts to improve the departmental efficiency can create additional waste in the product value stream if the departmental efficiency produces outcomes that do not serve the customer's needs or require inputs that increase costs for suppliers without adding value. While standardization of product components makes the individual processes more efficient, this efficiency can come at the cost of customer value. Think about the typical experience of purchasing a new car. You buy "the package," which includes features paid for but not needed, because it is more efficient for the production and delivery processes.

This batch-imposed waste is compounded if changes occur in design or customer needs because the work-in-process (WIP) or final-good inventories require rework or become scrap. Note that these concepts are not limited to manufacturing; businesses in the service sector also can generate waste. Think of the hamburgers cooked in advance, waiting for an order, or checking account statements that come at the end of the month, long after they potentially could prevent an overdraw.

Three common reasons for considering batches are

- When the cost of movement of material is significant
- When the setup time dominates the per-item cycle time
- To accommodate processes designed for multiple product or service types

An example of the first case is shipping a batch of items when a particular customer really wants only one or a few items. Because of the perceived cost of shipment, the customer has to make the choice of paying for and receiving inventory that will not be used immediately (or perhaps ever) or of waiting to place the order until he or she needs more than one of the items. A remedy for this particular type of waste is to reduce the space between the supplier and the customer so that shipping charges are reduced. The efficiencies of offshore production may be less than perceived if the true costs of the supplier shipping to consumer, the consumer holding unused inventory, and the consumer waiting for delayed shipments are considered. On a more personal level, think of the extra pantry, cupboard, and freezer space needed since the advent of warehouse shopping. Consider also its impact on cash flow and the waste associated with the unavailability of funds for other purposes.

Some processes are designed to accommodate processing of multiple items. For example, most modern ovens are designed with large capacity. This allows us to cook the turkey, the stuffing, and the potatoes at the same time on Thanksgiving Day. But what if we only want to bake a few cookies? We might as well cook a full batch to use the oven efficiently, even though we really would prefer to eat only a few freshly baked cookies tonight, then a few freshly baked cookies tomorrow, and so on. What we really would like is a small oven that could quickly cook only the number of cookies we want to eat *now*! Since we need the same oven for Thanksgiving and for tonight's cookies, we are forced to bake the full batch and eat them before the inventory gets stale (or throw out the unused inventory). Fortunately, the process can be redesigned with smaller batch sizes by using a smaller toaster oven for tonight's cookies.

When setup time dominates a process, it seems natural to process as many items as economically feasible so as to spread the setup costs across the batch. Until 1990 or so, the printing presses used for producing textbooks required elaborate setup procedures, taking several hours per book title. For this reason, publishers and resellers were economically forced to order large quantities to keep the unit price affordable. Often this resulted in excessive inventories, which served as a disincentive to revise the book with new material. When the setup times were reduced, smaller batch sizes become efficient, as is now commonly practiced in the book printing industry.

Setup time can be defined as the time to change from the last item of the previous order to the first good item of the next order (George, 2002). Setup includes four main activities: preparation, replacement, location, and adjustment.

Preparation refers to the tasks associated with getting or storing the material or information needed for the process—obtaining the raw material from the warehouse, pulling up the process instructions from the computer, moving completed items to the next process step, starting up the software needed to process the order, and so on.

Some suitable actions to reduce the time associated with preparation include

- Convert from departments to work cells to minimize the time required to move the finished product to the next process step.
- Store tools and materials locally, such as advocated by the 5S principles.
- Convert to "always ready to go." Make the software or instructions instantly accessible.

Replacement refers to the tasks associated with adding or removing items or tools, for example, moving test fixtures, loading new material into a hopper, or loading paper in a copy machine. Actions to reduce replacement times include

- Simplify setups. Reduce the number of steps required, such as through a redesign of fixtures.

- Commonality of setups for product families. When the same setup procedures are established for multiple items, there are naturally fewer instances of change required, reducing the setup time. This is the 5S principle of standardization.
- The 5S tools of sorting and straightening also help to reduce movement and wait times.

Location tasks are those associated with positioning or placement during setup. Examples include setting temperature profiles for heating, adjusting cutoff length for a specific product, and placing the chunk of deli meat in the slicer. Actions to reduce the time associated with location include

- *Poka yoke* (the Japanese term for mistake-proofing the process), as discussed in Chapter 7
- Commonality of setups, as mentioned previously (the 5S tool of standardization)

Adjustment refers to tasks associated with ensuring correct process settings. Examples include monitoring the temperature of a furnace, checking cutoff length, and proofing copy before printing. A suitable action to reduce adjustment time is process control. If the process is more repeatable, then adjustments are not necessary. Often this is achieved though robust design methods, as discussed in Chapter 7.

A Pareto diagram can be useful to prioritize the setup-time categories. In the example shown in Figure 6.1, location and preparation dominate the setup and thus are natural targets for improvement.

George (2002) recommends the following four-step approach to reduce setup times:

- Classify each setup step as either internal or external. *Internal steps* are those which are done while the process is inactive. *External steps* are done while the process is operating.
- Convert as many internal steps as possible to external steps.
- Reduce the time for the remaining internal steps.
- Eliminate adjustments.

In converting as many internal steps as possible to external steps, the non-operational process time is reduced. For example, if money is collected from customers while they are waiting for their burgers to be cooked rather than

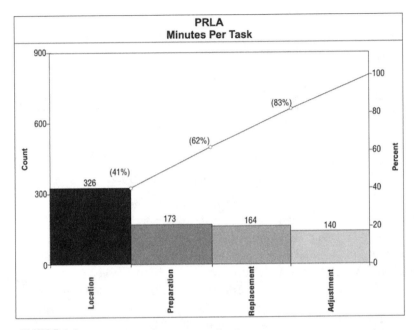

FIGURE 6.1 Pareto approach to setup reduction.

after they have been handed to the customer, then the total cycle time is reduced. The serial activities of payment and cooking are converted to parallel activities, reducing the overall cycle time.

There are some internal steps that cannot be done while the process is operational. Efforts should concentrate on the time required to complete the steps that delay the process. Here, it is necessary to understand which activities are on the critical path, as determined using the Gantt chart discussed in Part 3. If activity times not on the critical path are decreased, there is no subsequent reduction in total process time.

Adjustments can be reduced through effective process control. Statistical process control charts and designed experiments may be used to understand the causes of process variations that precede the adjustment. These causes then can be eliminated or controlled.

PROJECT EXAMPLE: Value-Stream Analysis

Referring to the as-is (i.e., current state) process map for order processing shown in Figure 5.1, many of the steps were initially considered business value-added (BVA), two steps were considered non-value-added, and five steps were considered value-added.

The value-added steps were as follows:

1. Generate license code.

2. Process payment.

3. Add invoice to accounting software (customers require an invoice, so this is value-added).

4. Generate order to reimburse reseller (if any).

5. Send invoice with download e-mail or shipment to client.

Step 2.01, *Enter Web order into CRM*, is identified as non-value-added (NVA) because the data already were available elsewhere, and entering the data into the customer relationship management (CRM) system served no useful purpose in the currrent process. Likewise, step 4.2, *Record Invoice # in CRM*, required data entry that was not being used. At one time, the process allowed for invoices to be sent directly from the CRM system. The process had been revised many times over the years, and invoices no longer could be created within the CRM system, yet this step had not been removed during these edits.

Using a sample of 50 representative orders, the processing time associated with the five value-added steps was 25 minutes. The average cycle time was 168 minutes, including an average wait time of 117 minutes. Over half the wait time was associated with the accounting processes. Accounting preferred to batch-run the credit cards, which then naturally led to batch entry into the accounting software for invoice generation. With an average of four orders in queue, the process lead time was calculated as $4 \times 168 = 672$ minutes; the process cycle efficiency was estimated at 4 percent (calculated as 25 minutes of value added divided by 672 minutes of lead time).

As the team considered the process further, team members realized that the CRM data-entry steps they classified as BVA actually were NVA for orders placed on the Web as long as that information could be made readily available to order processing and support staff. This realization, achieved through discussion of the BVA versus the NVA of each step, later would prove critical to the process improvement plans.

Analyzing Sources of Variation

In the measure stage (described in Chapter 5), a process baseline is established to quantify the current process conditions. In most cases, a control chart is used to differentiate between the variation owing to special causes and the variation owing to common causes. This provides valuable input in analyzing the sources of variation.

Special causes of variation are evidenced by out-of-control points. The time-ordered nature of the control chart provides an indication of *when* the process was influenced by a special cause to aid in an understanding of *what* happened (in process terms). Since the control chart will not detect all shifts, nor necessarily detect shifts as soon as they occur, neighboring subgroups within the control limits also could result from the assignable (special) cause under investigation. Bear this in mind when you try to associate the timing of the special cause with possible changes in process factors. Table T.19 in the section "Statistical Process Control Charts" of Part 3 provides an indication of the number of subgroups required (on average) to detect a process shift of a given magnitude.

The common-cause variation (represented by the control limits) is due to all elements of the process. These sources of variation cannot be easily associated with the point-to-point variation because they represent a combination of factors common to all the subgroups. There are likely to be several sources of variation that contribute to that common-cause variation, and a subgroup's specific value is a reflection of the combination of those sources.

Teams brainstorm to understand potential sources of variation for a process. Sources of variation are found in a process's *methods*, its *materials*, the *manpower* or personnel involved in the process, the *machines* or equipment used, the *measurement* techniques, and the surrounding *environment*. Collectively, these potential sources of variation are sometimes referred to as the *5M's and E*. In service processes, the *4P's* may be more useful—*policy, procedures, plant,* and *people*.

Categorizing the potential sources of variation using one of these techniques aids the team in brainstorming. Each of the categories provides a focus to ensure that potential causes are not ignored. As in any brainstorming exercise, individual responses should not be critiqued or criticized. The purpose of the brainstorming is to develop a comprehensive list of all possible sources, not just the likely ones. A typical *cause-and-effect diagram* provides a fishbone layout for displaying these root causes, as shown in Figure 6.2. The actual format of a cause and effect can take any form so long as the hierarchal structure is maintained, with causes and subcauses grouped by an appropriate classification scheme.

The *nominal group technique* described in Part 3 also can be used to reach consensus on the list of causes to investigate. In this approach, each team mem-

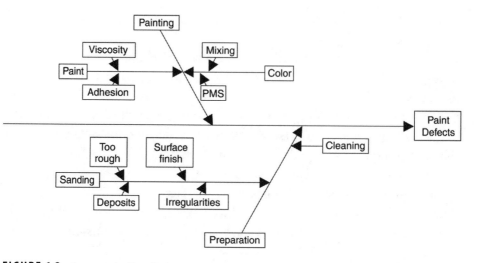

FIGURE 6.2 Cause-and-effect diagram.

ber selects and ranks his or her choice of the top several items. The choices with the most votes or most weighted votes are included in the subsequent analysis, subject to the consensus of the team. Of course, if the analysis fails to attribute the variation to any of the choices, further analysis will be needed to look for other significant factors. In this case, the team will take another look at the original list of potential sources on the cause-and-effect diagram.

During the measure stage, the team may have collected samples from the process belonging to the populations defined by these potential sources of variation. The samples can be tested to see if they are statistically different from each other. In the order processing example introduced in Chapter 4, error rates were observed for each of the errors under investigation. Different rates were observed for each product type. Were these error rates consistent with the different order volumes observed for each product, or did one or more product have an increased error rate for one or more of the error types?

How different do the true error rates by product have to be for the difference to be detected with these samples? A *hypothesis test* can be performed to test the samples to determine if the error rates by product are essentially the same or different. Minitab and Excel have many of these tests built into their functionality. The tests result in a p value indicating the probability that sample rates this extreme are likely to come from the same population. A value of 0.05 or less typically is used to reject the null hypothesis that the rates are equal. When the p value exceeds 0.05, the null hypothesis cannot be rejected—using these samples, the rates may be the same.

There are some predictable problems that can occur with hypothesis testing that should be considered, as outlined in the "Hypothesis Test" section of Part 3. Notably, samples must be random and representative of the population under investigation. In surveys, low response rates typically would provide extreme value estimates (i.e., the subpopulation of people who have strong opinions one way or the other) that are not representative of the total population. Samples must be from a stable population. If the population is changing over time, then estimates will be biased, with associated increases in alpha and beta risk. Statistical process control (SPC) charts provide an indication of statistical stability. Many of the hypothesis tests, as well as their associated alpha and beta risk, depend on the normality of the population. If the population is significantly nonnormal, then the tests are not meaningful. Goodness-of-fit tests are used to verify this assumption. Nonparametric tests can be used if the populations are significantly nonnormal.

Some tests additionally require equal variance, which can be tested using equality-of-variance tests. If the populations do not have equal variances, then the data can be transformed (see "Transformation" in Part 3).

It's important to note that a failure to reject a null hypothesis is not an acceptance of the null hypothesis. Rather, it means that there is not *yet* ample proof that the hypothesis should be rejected. Each of the tests uses a stated alpha value, where *alpha* is the probability of observing samples this extreme if the null hypothesis is true. In most situations, an alpha value of 0.05 is used, providing a small chance (5 in 100) that samples this extreme (or worse) would occur if the null hypothesis is true. Since we reject the null hypothesis, then we also could state that there are 5 chances in 100 of incorrectly rejecting a true null hypothesis. Furthermore, if n investigators are independently researching the issue, the probability that at least one researcher (incorrectly) rejects the null hypothesis is $1 - (1 - \alpha)^n$. For example, the chance that 1 of 10 researchers (i.e., $n = 10$), each with an alpha risk of 0.05, will (incorrectly) reject the true null hypothesis is 40 percent! Consider this the next time the headlines in your newspaper report the "surprising results of a new study." Would the unsurprising results of the other nine researchers warrant a headline? The alpha risk demonstrates the need for independent replication of analysis results.

The *beta risk* is the probability of not rejecting a false null hypothesis. Usually, the *power* of the test (the probability of correctly rejecting the false null hypothesis) is more interesting. It provides a quantitative reminder that even though the test is not rejected, the null hypothesis still may be false.

What influences the ability to correctly reject the false null hypothesis? Larger differences between the null and alternative means make it easier to detect the differences statistically. Smaller population sigma or larger sample sizes cause the distributions to become more narrow, and hence there is less overlap between the null and the actual mean, making the difference easier to detect. A large *significance level* alpha implies that the tail regions (which may tend to overlap) will have less influence in our decision to accept or reject. This is shown in Figure 6.3.

If we fail to reject the null hypothesis, we haven't proven the null hypothesis. Larger sample sizes may be required to detect the difference, depending on the population sigma and alpha values. When the alpha value (the significance level) of the test is defined, the beta risk has (perhaps unknowingly) been defined as well. Unfortunately, the beta risk is not known precisely because the true condition is unknown.

Operating characteristic (OC) curves (which provide beta risk) and power curves (which provide power estimates) are analogous methods to determine beta (or power) given sample size, delta (the difference), sigma, and alpha. OC and power curves are sometimes provided in statistical textbooks.

Some software (including Minitab) and Web sites will provide estimates of: power based on a stated sample size, the difference to be detected, the standard deviation of the population, and a stated alpha value. Conversely, sample size may be provided to detect a stated difference at a given alpha and power value or even the optimal sample size to minimize alpha and maximize power.

Nonparametric tests also may be used, particularly when distributional

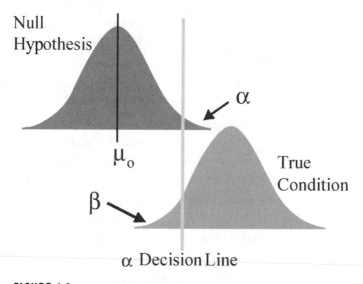

FIGURE 6.3 A stated alpha level defines the beta risk given the sample size, sigma, and difference between the null and the true conditions.

assumptions cannot be met. A *nonparametric test* is one in which there are no distributional requirements, such as normality, for the validity of the test. Typically, nonparametric tests require larger sample sizes than parametric tests.

When there are more than two populations to compare, general analysis of variance (ANOVA) techniques are applied. ANOVA provides a means of comparing the variation within each subset (or treatment) of data to the variation between the different subsets of data. The between-subset variation is a reflection of the possible differences between the subset averages. The within-subset variation, for each subset, is a reflection of the inherent variation observed when sampling from the subset repeatedly.

The null hypothesis tested by ANOVA is that all the subset averages are equal. The *F* statistic is used to compare the mean square treatment (the average between subset variation) with the mean square error (the sum of squares of the residuals). The assumptions in the test are that the distribution for each subset is normal and that the subsets have equal variance (although their means may be different). The null hypothesis that the subset means are equal is rejected when the *p* value for the *F* test is less than 0.05, implying that at least one of the subset averages is different.

The techniques described in this section provide a means of determining statistical differences between sets of observed data. The results of these types of analysis are interesting yet not compelling. The observational data used in the analysis may be biased owing to the manner in which they were collected or confounded (coincident) with other factors that were not measured or recorded during data collection. These confounding factors, rather than the factor under investigation, which appears significant, may be the underlying cause for the statistical difference.

As a result, the findings from these analyses should serve as input to more rigorous techniques for understanding causal relationships—specifically designed experiments.

PROJECT EXAMPLE: Analyze Sources of Variation

The errors observed in the measure-stage baseline data were reviewed. A Pareto diagram of error type (shown in Figure 6.4) indicated that 58 percent of errors were associated with renewal date, an additional 27 percent to license count, and the remaining 19 percent to e-mail. The vast majority of each error type was associated with missing data rather than incorrect data (as indicated by the relative size of the stacked bars in the figure).

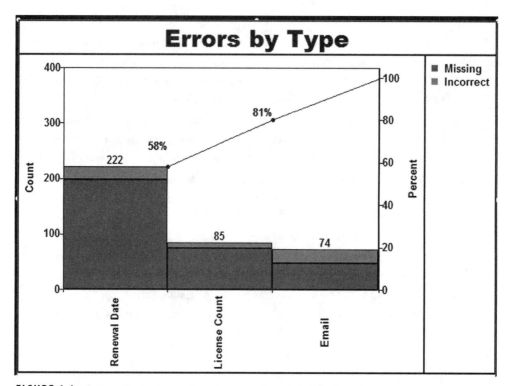

FIGURE 6.4 Pareto analysis of errors by type (using Green Belt XL software).

The error data also were analyzed by product family, where it was determined that approximately 52 percent of the errors were for Product *A*, 33 percent for Product *B*, and the remaining 16 percent for Product *C*. A contingency table analysis (discussed in detail in Part 3) was performed to investigate whether the observed error rates were consistent with the percent of total orders in the baseline trials. The relatively high *p* value (>0.05) shown in Figure 6.5 indicates that the null hypothesis of equal percent error cannot be rejected (i.e., there is no statistically significant difference between the expected and observed error rates between the products).

The team constructed a cause-and-effect diagram to brainstorm the possible sources of variation in cycle time. Their discussion included effects on both process time and wait time because the team had evidence that as the total cycle time increased (owing to the wait time), the call volume also increased as customers became anxious about the status of their orders. (The team separately collected some data on this effect and over a five-day period observed that about 10 percent of the order-related correspondence addressed by the sales staff was re-

Chi-Square Test: Product A, Product B, Product C

```
Expected counts are printed below observed counts
Chi-Square contributions are printed below expected counts

        Product A  Product B  Product C  Total
   1         197        124         60     381
          182.65     130.81      67.54
           1.128      0.355      0.842

   2        1001        734        383    2118
         1015.35     727.19     375.46
           0.203      0.064      0.151

Total       1198        858        443    2499

Chi-Sq = 2.742, DF = 2, P-Value = 0.254
```

FIGURE 6.5 Contingency table of errors by product (using Minitab).

lated to confirmations of receipt or status inquiries.) A large number of potential sources was listed, and then the team used the nominal group technique (discussed in Part 3) to quickly reach consensus on the following areas for further investigation:

- Product family
- Person entering order
- Number of line items in order
- Call volume (time of day/day of week)
- Number of available staff

These potential factors will be evaluated in the next section.

Determining Process Drivers

Designed experiments are a critical part of many successful improvement projects. While SPC provides a view of the past performance of the process, designed experiments provide a view of the process potential. They allow an understanding of the sources of the common and special causes of variation seen on the control chart or the variation between subsets of a population.

In a designed experiment, each of the factors suspected of being significant is varied, several at a time over a wide range, and the process responses are measured. Manipulating the factors over a wide range provides the best chance of detecting a change in the process that otherwise may be too subtle to detect. (A detailed discussion of these techniques is presented in the "Design of Experiments" section in Part 3.)

Consider the case of the villainous cartoon arch nemesis seeking to accurately propel a rock of sufficient size at our hero using yet another fine product from the ACME Corporation. There are several factors that may be varied to affect the slingshot's accuracy, including the size of the rubber band, the drawback distance, and the weight of the boulder to be hurdled through the air. The response variable to be measured is the distance from the large bull's-eye (sold separately).

For most designs, and especially in the early stages of the analysis, we can conveniently limit the design to two levels of each factor. Once we determine which factors are significant, we can expand the design as necessary, depending on our objectives.

How does a designed experiment differ from the traditional (sometimes called *one factor at a time*) experiments often first taught in grade school? In traditional experiments, each factor is varied one at a time, such as shown in Table 6.1. An initial trial (trial 1) is run with each of the factors set at its initial level. The response (distance from the target) is measured, establishing a baseline.

A second trial then is run to measure the effect of the first factor (rubber band size). The difference between the baseline response (trial 1) and the observed response for trial 2 is assumed to be the effect of the manipulated factor. In this case, increasing from the small rubber band to the large rubber band results in a smaller distance from target of 14 units.

Likewise, the effect of the drawback distance is estimated by comparing trials 3 and 1, and the effect of boulder weight is estimated by comparing trials 4 and 1. In this way, the effect of the drawback distance is estimated as a

TABLE 6.1 Example Traditional Experiment

Trial	Rubber Band	Drawback Distance	Boulder Weight	Distance from Target
1	Small	Short	Light	35
2	Large	Short	Light	21
3	Small	Long	Light	28
4	Small	Short	Heavy	27

decrease in distance from the target of 7 units, and the effect of boulder weight is estimated as a decrease of 8 units in distance from the target.

Based on these observations, distance from the target is minimized by setting the factors as follows: rubber band: large; drawback distance: short; and boulder weight: light.

The problem with this traditional one-factor-at-a-time experiment is that it ignores the possible effects of interactions between the three factors. The interaction plot shown in Figure 6.6 is from a designed experiment of the same process. At the high rubber band setting (shown by the line labeled 330), a distance from the target of 21.0 is observed at the *short* condition of drawback. This is trial 2 from Table 6.1. Trial 3 is shown on the line labeled 210 at the *long* condition of drawback distance.

On the 210 rubber band size setting, there is very little change in the distance from the target moving from a *short* to a *long* condition of drawback distance (left to right along the line). This implies that drawback distance makes little difference when a small rubber band is used.

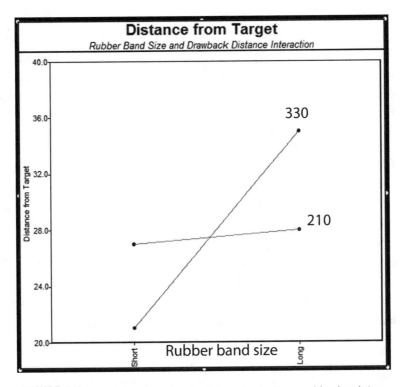

FIGURE 6.6 Interaction chart showing interaction between rubber band size and drawback distance.

However, on the 330 rubber band size setting, there is a very large change in distance from the target moving from a *short* to a *long* drawback distance (left to right along the line). This implies that drawback distance is a significant contributor to the change in distance from the target when a large rubber band is used.

The estimate of the drawback distance effect changes depending on whether the effect is measured for small or large rubber bands. This implies that there is an *interaction* between the drawback distance and rubber band size. This interaction is revealed by the nonparallel lines on the interaction plot, such as shown in Figure 6.6.

When interactions are ignored, improvement efforts may achieve haphazard results:

- Significant factors may appear unimportant when other factors are not manipulated at the same time, as shown in the one-factor-at-a-time example above.

- Process improvement may be realized only when other factors remain constant. The improvement may seem to "disappear" as the process returns to a prior level of performance for unknown reasons.

- The possibility of reducing the effect of a factor by minimizing variation of another will not be realized. This Taguchi approach to robust design of processes can be seen in the above example. If, for example, variation in rubber band size is costly to control, using a short drawback distance will dampen the impact of variations in rubber band size.

Historical data often are analyzed with ANOVA and multiple regression techniques to investigate patterns or significance of process factors. This so-called data mining has some usefulness, but it also lacks many of the key properties of designed experiments.

Designed experiments estimate parameter effects with fewer data than data mining by using an orthogonal array of data. An *orthogonal array* is a minimum set of data conditions designed to independently estimate specific factors and their interactions. The data are collected over a relatively short period of time, allowing the experimenters to control the conditions under which the data are collected. Casual factors such as environmental conditions and personnel are observed or controlled, and anomalies are recorded.

Historical, or happenstance, data often are incapable of detecting interactions. The effects of interactions can be estimated only when the data include the necessary combinations of factors, randomized to remove bias from main effects. The data may not include sufficient variation in each factor or interaction to statistically estimate a significance of the parameter. The uncontrolled nature of the data collection may allow other factors (often unrecorded) to contribute to noise in the data that may cloud the effects of each factor or be confounded with factors that seem important (as described at the end of the preceding section). Since the data are not run in random order, it is possible for unrecognized factors that vary over time to bias the results.

ANOVA may be applied to the results of the designed experiment to determine the significance of factors. In this way, a seemingly complex process with many variables can be reduced to only its few significant factors. *Regression analysis* will be used to construct an equation for predicting the response given the settings of the significant process factors (defined by the ANOVA).

For example, the results of an eight-run designed experiment are shown in Table 6.2. Four main factors (*A*, *B*, *C*, and *D*) and their six two-factor interactions (*AB*, *AC*, *AD*, *BC*, *BD*, and *CD*) are estimated with an eight-run experiment, leaving one run to estimate the overall mean (i.e., the average response). (This is discussed further in the "Factorial Designs" section in Part 3.) A fourth factor can be added by aliasing it with the three-factor interaction (i.e., *D* = *ABC*), on the assumption that three-factor interactions usually are not significant. *Aliasing* allows more factors to be included in the experiment or, conversely, allows a given number of factors to be estimated with fewer experimental runs because a 16-run experiment normally would be needed to fully estimate four factors and their interactions.

TABLE 6.2 Example Designed Experiment

Factor *A*	Factor *B*	Factor *C*	Factor *D*	Response
10	200	45	12	49
10	200	15	2	42
10	20	45	2	88
10	20	15	12	87
5	200	45	2	67
5	200	15	12	64
5	20	45	12	80
5	20	15	2	75

The effect of aliasing factor *D* with the *ABC* interaction is that the aliased parameters are *confounded* with one another. This implies that the parameters cannot be estimated independently of one another. When factor *D* is aliased with the *ABC* interaction, when we estimate the effect of factor *D*, we cannot be sure whether the effect is due to factor *D*, the *ABC* interaction, or a linear combination of the main factor *D* and the three-factor *ABC* interaction.

The intended aliasing also creates some unintended confounding between all the other possible combinations of the aliased pair. We construct the confounded pairs by moving the equal sign through the *ABC* = *D* equation.

If *ABC* = *D*, then *A* = *BCD*; *B* = *ACD*; *C* = *ABD*; *AB* = *CD*; *AC* = *BD*; *AD* = *BC*

Thus this eight-run experiment will estimate each of the main factors *A*, *B*, *C*, and *D*, each of which will be confounded with a three-factor interaction and the 6 two-factor interactions (confounded with each other). The analysis provided by this experiment is scant because there are no additional runs added for estimating error. An effects plot, shown in Figure 6.7, displays the absolute value of the (coded) effects in a Pareto chart. Larger coded effects have higher

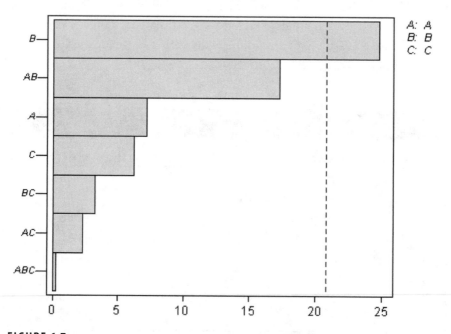

FIGURE 6.7 Pareto chart of effects showing significance of factor *B*.

significance. A line of significance, such as provided in Minitab software, provides the criteria for parameter selection. A normal or half-normal plot of the effects provides similar results.

In this screening design, there were no extra runs to estimate error, so the ANOVA table is of little value. Recall that at least one run (i.e., unique design condition) is needed to estimate each parameter, including main effects (main factors), their interactions, the overall mean (or intercept), and error. An eight-run experiment can estimate at most seven factors and interactions. If estimates are required for only six factors and interactions, then one run is available for estimating error. There are two choices to resolve this problem: Either remove one or more of the required parameters from the analysis or add more runs to the design. For example, the initial analysis in Figure 6.7 suggests that the interaction AC (confounded with BD) is insignificant, so it is perhaps a good candidate for removal. Removing it from the analysis would free up a run to estimate error. Instead, this particular design was extended by folding the design.

Folding the design is a technique for extending the design by repeating one or more randomly selected runs or by replicating the entire design. In either case, the additional trials should be run in random order and treated statistically as a block (see "Factorial Designs" in Part 3). Of course, each additional run increases the time and resources, and hence the cost, needed for the experiment. On the other hand, each replicate also improves the ability to detect the statistical significance of a given effect.

A design is folded by replicating the design and substituting the low values with high values and the high values with low values for one or more of the factors. If we fold on just one factor (i.e., substitute the plus and minus signs for one of the factors), then that factor and its two-factor interactions will be free of confounding. If we substitute the plus and minus signs for the entire design, then all main factors will be free of confounding with other main factors and two-factor interactions.

In this case, the design was extended by folding on the entire design. The ANOVA table for the complete design is provided in Table 6.3. As described in more detail in the "Regression Analysis" section of Part 3, the ANOVA table provides an estimate of the regression significance (using the F statistic), provided that there is at least one extra run to calculate error. The regression for this example is highly significant. The adjusted R^2 value is 0.97, which indicates that most of the variation in the data is accounted for by the regression model.

TABLE 6.3 Example ANOVA for Folded Design of Experiment (DOE)

	df	SS	MS	F	Significance F
Regression	8	4318.5	539.8125	65.22006	6.94E—06
Residual	7	57.9375	8.276786	42	
Total	15	4376.438		49	

Note: df = degrees of freedom; SS = sum of squares; MS = mean square

The significance of the individual parameters (i.e., main factors, interactions, and the blocking factor from the fold) can be estimated using the Student's t statistic. The graphic techniques for effects plotting just discussed should agree with these t-test results. Parameters with a p value greater than 0.1 may be removed from the model. Moreover, p values between 0.05 and 0.1 are marginal, and these parameters may be left in the model until more data are obtained.

The regression results for the folded design are shown in Table 6.4. Factors B and AB appear highly significant, and factor D is highly insignificant (because the p value is much greater than 0.1). As a result, factor D can be removed from the analysis and the analysis redone to refine the model. (Recall that factors or interactions should be removed only one at a time.) Subsequent regression

TABLE 6.4 Regression Results for Folded DOE

	Coefficients	Standard Error	t Stat	p Value
Intercept	68.1875	0.719235	94.80558	3.83E – 12
A	−2.4375	0.719235	−3.38902	0.011615
B	−14.5625	0.719235	−20.2472	1.8E – 07
C	1.5625	0.719235	2.172447	0.066377
D	−0.0625	0.719235	−0.0869	0.933186
AB = CD	−6.9375	0.719235	−9.64566	2.71E – 05
AC = BD	−0.8125	0.719235	−1.12967	0.295833
AD = BC	0.0625	0.719235	0.086898	0.933186
Block	0.8125	0.719235	1.129672	0.295833

TABLE 6.5 Regression Results for Folded DOE (After Removal of Terms)

	Coefficients	Standard Error	t Stat	p Value
Intercept	68.1875	0.670767	101.6559	1.04E − 17
A	−2.4375	0.670767	−3.6339	0.00393
B	−14.5625	0.670767	−21.7102	2.21E − 10
C	1.5625	0.670767	2.329421	0.03991
AB	−6.9375	0.670767	−10.3426	5.27E − 07

analyses were performed by removing BC, then AC, and then finally the blocking factor (one at a time). The final analysis is shown in Table 6.5. The final adjusted R^2 value is 0.975.

The predicted regression model (rounded to the first decimal) is shown in the "Coefficients" column as

$$\text{Response} = 68.2 - 2.4 \times A - 14.6 \times B + 1.6 \times C - 6.9 \times A \times B$$

This equation can be used to predict the response at any condition within the range of the data by substituting values of factors A, B, and C. The effect of a unit change in any given factor (when all other factors remain constant) is obtained directly from the coefficients. For example, an increase of one unit in factor A causes a decrease of 1.4 units in the response.

A number of tests can be applied to the residuals (the error between the predicted model and the observed data). Any abnormality of the residuals would be cause for concern about the model. Outliers indicate problems with specific data points, and trends or dependence may indicate issues with the data-collection process as a whole (as discussed in the "Residuals Analysis" section of Part 3).

The factors and their interactions can be analyzed further by breaking down the total error (represented by the residuals) into its components: pure error and lack of fit. *Pure error* is experimental error, the differences between repeated runs of the same condition. The remaining error is due to a poor fit of the model to the data. Error due to *lack of fit* is caused by either a curvature in the response surface that is not estimated with the fitted first-degree model or main factor or interaction effects that were not included in the experiment.

The ANOVA for the final model is shown in Table 6.6. The sum of squares (SS) residual term (79.1875) includes both pure error and lack-of-fit (LOF)

TABLE 6.6 ANOVA for Folded DOE (After Removal of Terms)

	df	SS	MS	F	Significance F
Regression	4	4297.25	1074.313	149.2336	1.67E – 09
Residual	11	79.1875	7.198864		
Total	15	4376.438			

Note: df = degrees of freedom; SS = sum of squares; ms = mean square

error. Pure error is calculated as 68.5 using the sum-of-squares deviations between each observation and the mean at that condition. The lack-of-fit error is calculated as 10.6875 using the difference between the total (residuals) error and the pure error. The F statistic is calculated as

$$F = \frac{SS_{LOF}/(n - p)}{SS_{PE}/(N - n)} = \frac{10.6875/(8 - 5)}{68.5/(16 - 8)} = 0.42$$

The calculated F value for the lack of fit is less than the critical value $F_{0.05,3,8}$ of 4.07, so the null hypothesis that the model is adequate cannot be rejected. In this case (failing to reject that the model is adequate), the significance of the fitted model can be tested using the F statistic applied to the residuals, as in Table 6.6. If the residuals are small (as demonstrated by significance of the regression term) and pass the other general tests described in the "Residuals Analysis" section of Part 3, then the model would seem to fit the data adequately and can be used to determine optimal combinations for the response.

If the lack-of-fit test is rejected, then the model should be updated with additional main factors and interactions or higher-order terms. A quick test for surface curvature (described in Part 3) helps to rule out higher-order terms.

Recall that the *power* of a statistical test is the probability of rejecting the null hypothesis when the null hypothesis is false. In this case, the null hypothesis is that the coefficients of the regression are zero; the alternative hypothesis is that at least one of the coefficients is nonzero.

Minitab provides a convenient way to test our ability to estimate effects of given magnitude or, conversely, to estimate the number of design replicates needed to detect effects at a given power for a given experimental design.

For example, how many design replicates are needed to estimate an effect with a magnitude 20 for a two-level factorial design with 5 factors, 8 corner points, and no center points when sigma is 17 (using $\alpha = \beta = 0.05$)?

Using Minitab's Stat/Power & Sample Size/2 Level Factorial Design function (alpha is entered using the "Options" button), five replicates, or 40 runs, are needed.

The various parameters can be manipulated in the Minitab dialog box to estimate their impact. For example, a larger effect, such as 25, would require only four replicates. If the power of the experiment is reduced to a 75 percent chance of detecting an effect with magnitude 25, then only three replicates are needed.

The purpose of this discussion is to emphasize the limitations of an experiment, which can be overcome by replicating the results before proceeding to implementation in the improve stage.

PROJECT EXAMPLE: Determine Process Drivers

The team proposed an experimental design to determine the significance of the proposed process factors (from the brainstorming exercise discussed previously). The response variable selected is the process time, calculated as the difference between the recorded start time and the recorded end time for each order less any wait time experienced during the process order. Actual orders will be selected from previous orders to match the experimental conditions (further defined below). The process under study will be conducted just as in current operations until the pass-off to accounting (and limited to nonreseller orders). The personnel entering each order will be removed from any operational responsibilities during the experiment so as to prevent any uncontrolled interference with the experiment.

The team established factor level settings that would represent the best and worst cases, assuming that the factor was significant:

- *Product family.* The baseline data indicated that Product A had the highest cycle time and Product C the lowest. (Note that this doesn't mandate that Product A be the low level for that factor, because the relative impact on the response is assumed to be unknown, so it does not determine the factor levels.)

- *Person entering order.* Don, who is on the team, was chosen to represent the more experienced order taker, whereas Karen is less experienced yet comfortable with the current procedures.
- *Number of line items.* The minimum possible number of items per order is one; the maximum usually experienced is four to five items, so five was chosen.
- *Time between call arrival.* After some discussion, the team decided that this single factor would adequately address the intended effects of *Time of Day/Call Volume* and *Number of Available Staff* factors given the manner in which the experiment would be conducted. After a brief review of phone records, the maximum incoming call rate for a single staff member was set to six calls per hour, with the minimum set to zero. During the experiment, these values would be used to interrupt the order processing (to simulate a new call) for seven minutes (an average sales inquiry call length) every 10 minutes (equivalent to six calls per hour).

A standard half-factorial (eight-run) experiment for the four factors was replicated in random order (for a total of 16 experimental runs using 16 different orders selected to match the design conditions). Using a 0.05 level of significance for each parameter, only the *Number of Line Items*, the *Time Between Call Arrival*, and the interaction of these two factors were found to be significant. The regression accounted for nearly 80 percent of the total variation (using the calculated R^2 adjusted statistic). No anomalies were discovered in the residuals analysis.

The results suggested two pieces of information that the team found interesting:

1. The order processing time is influenced not only by the number of line items but also by the number of interruptions. Furthermore, the impact of interruptions is larger for more line items. Recall that the actual wait time associated with each interruption was removed from the response. These results suggest that the process proceeds at a slower rate in the presence of interruptions than it does when there are no interruptions.

2. The product family was not significant. This seemed to contradict the baseline data, where the three products had very different cycle times. In discussing these results, the team wondered if perhaps the differences in baseline data actually were a reflection of the number of line items, which might be correlated with product family to some extent. A review of the baseline data confirmed this result.

Recommended Tools

The following tools (discussed in detail in Part 3) are applicable to the analyze stage of DMAIC:

Value-Stream Analysis

- *Flowcharts* and *process maps* help to discover process complexities that contribute to variation or longer cycle times.
- *Program evaluation and review techniques (PERT) analysis* and *Gantt charts* help to identify the critical path for cycle time reduction.
- *Spaghetti diagrams* help to identify unnecessary movement of material or personnel.
- *Velocity* is determined to prioritize cycle time improvement opportunities.

Analyzing Sources of Variation

- *Box-whisker chart* help to graphically compare the location and variation of various processes or categories of products or services.
- *Cause-and-effect diagrams* help in brainstorming potential underlying process factors, which can be investigated in a designed experiment.
- *Confidence interval on mean, confidence interval on proportion,* and *contingency tables* help to compare the means of samples from different process conditions.
- *Failure modes and effects analysis* (FMEA) helps to define high-risk activities.
- *Hypothesis testing of two samples* and *nonparametric tests on the equality of means* help to compare sample means from different conditions.
- *Statistical process control (SPC) charts,* including C, Np, P, U, Individual-X, X-bar, and *EWMA charts,* help to differentiate between special and common causes of variation.
- *Multi-vari plots* help to categorize variation and investigate interactions among factors.
- *Pareto charts* help to focus on areas with greatest opportunity.
- *Histograms* help to graphically display the process output relative to requirements.

- *Goodness-of-fit tests* help to verify the statistical distributions assumed in the various statistical tools.
- *Work breakdown structure* helps to break down a problem into its potential components, to be addressed in the improve stage.

Determining Process Drivers

- *Design of experiments, factorial designs,* and *evolutionary operations* help to define efficient data-collection experiments.
- *Regression analysis, residuals analysis,* and *scatter diagrams* help to identify significant process factors.
- *Transformations* help to stabilize variance or calculate meaningful responses.
- *Interaction plots* help to graphically depict the relationship between two factors' effect on the mean.
- *Process decision program charts* help to understand root causes of problems.

In addition, the consensus-building tools noted at the end of the define stage (see Chapter 4) are also applied as needed.

CHAPTER 6 QUIZ

1. **When process tasks in a value-stream analysis are classified, inspection of parts before they are shipped to a customer is often considered**

   A. value-added because we have to do it to ensure that the customer receives only good product.

   B. non-value-added because it does nothing to change form, fit, or function and is needed only because of our poor process quality.

   C. business-value-added because it does nothing to change form, fit, or function and is needed only because of our poor process quality, yet random sampling inspection ensures that the customer receives only good product.

   D. business-value-added for processes considered incapable (i.e., out of control or $C_{pk} < 2$) and non-value-added for in-control and capable processes.

2. **From the lean viewpoint, design of products or services that do not fully meet customers' needs is considered**

   A. best practice.

   B. waste.

   C. value-added.

   D. just in time.

3. **Standardization is an effective strategy to**

   A. simplify a process by removing as much of the "special cases" as possible.

   B. reduce the number of items needed in inventory.

   C. reduce the cost of delivery.

   D. All the above are true.

4. **Process cycle times can be reduced through**

   A. reducing the need for rework.

   B. reducing the movement of material.

   C. level loading to reduce batches and waiting.

   D. All the above are true.

5. **Impact(s) of level loading a process include**

   A. reduction or elimination of work-in-process inventories.

   B. increased flexibility to respond to change in demand.

   C. reduction of batches and downstream waiting associated with batches.

   D. All the above are true.

6. **Setup time can be reduced effectively with a corresponding reduction in total cycle time for a unit of production by**

   A. redesign of processes so that tasks that currently require process shutdown instead can be performed while the process is operational.

   B. increasing the batch size to reduce the number of setups.

C. making setups for each product as unique as possible to avoid confusion between different products.

D. All the above are true.

7. **Reducing cycle time by reducing setup time is a practice that is applicable**

A. only to manufacturing operations.

B. only to manufacturing operations that produce in batches.

C. only to manufacturing operations that produce in batches and are expensive to operate.

D. to many manufacturing and nonmanufacturing operations.

8. **In analyzing setup practices, the terms** *internal* **and** *external* **refer to**

A. tasks performed by internal personnel or external suppliers, respectively.

B. tasks performed within the department or outside the department, respectively.

C. tasks performed when the process is nonoperational or while the process is operational, respectively.

D. tasks required by internal management or external customers, respectively.

9. **In a statistical hypothesis test, failing to reject implies that**

A. the null hypothesis is true.

B. the null hypothesis is false.

C. the alternative hypothesis is true.

D. there are insufficient data to reject the null hypothesis.

10. **In trying to determine which of several possible factors might influence a process, a team decides to take data from the process while changing all of the factors one at a time. This method**

A. is the clearest method to demonstrate which factors have a significant impact on the process.

B. is the best way to quickly eliminate factors that don't have an impact.

C. will ignore any interaction between the factors.

D. All the above are true.

chapter **7**

Improve Stage

After the types and sources of variation in the analyze stage are understood, the improve stage of the *d*efine, *m*easure, *a*nalyze, *i*mprove, and *c*ontrol (DMAIC) problem-solving methodology can begin to define and implement changes necessary for process improvement.

Objectives

There are several issues to be completed within the improve stage of DMAIC:

- New process operating conditions are determined.
- Failure modes for the new process are investigated and addressed.
- Benefits associated with the proposed solution are estimated by the team and approved by the sponsor.
- Process improvement is implemented and verified.

The outcome of each of these steps may cause a reconsideration of the assumptions from prior steps, forcing further analysis of the proposed improvement. This diligence is often necessary for sustained improvement.

This stage is where the rubber meets the road. It defines the improvements and cost reductions that sustain the program. It forces the team to strive for new levels of performance and become true agents of change. Management

147

support at this point is critical, as is management buy-in. The team must work closely with its sponsor to seek direction, authority, and approval before change can be implemented.

Defining the New Process

The most obvious outcome of the improve stage is the definition of new practices to replace the current operating procedures. This change can be realized as a new process flow or as a change in operating conditions for the existing process. In some cases, the change in operating conditions mandates a new process flow, or vice versa, so both types of change are necessary.

Redefining Process Flow

The results of the value-stream analysis provided insight on the non-value-added activities that can be reduced or eliminated in the improve stage. The following techniques should be reviewed from the analyze stage for use in cycle time reduction:

- Reduce process complexity, such as through standardization.
- Remove unnecessary process steps and unnecessary movement of resources.
- Optimize the process.
- Level-load the process.
- Reduce setup times.

Also see the "Recommended Tools" found at the end of this chapter. As mentioned in Chapter 5, when improvements are made to cycle time or, for that matter, any change occurs in the process dynamics, it is critical for the team to evaluate the effects of such changes on quality. A baseline of the key critical-to-quality (CTQ) metrics from the measure stage will serve as the comparison for the data obtained in the improve and control stages, discussed later in this chapter.

Benchmarking can provide useful input for redesigning the process flow. *Benchmarking* is a means to evaluate the best in class for particular industries, processes, or even process types. Benchmarking does not require detailed analysis of a competitor's process on the mistaken assumption that your processes should be designed the same way as that of a competitor. In such a case, your organization can never exceed the values provided by your competition and never achieve recognition as an industry leader. It also will be impossible to reach breakthrough levels of improvement necessary for Six Sigma quality. Rather, similar or even dissimilar industries may be evaluated to learn techniques new to your organization. For example, a good model for improving an assembly operation can be a fast-food restaurant specializing in the rapid assembly of hamburgers.

PROJECT EXAMPLE: Redefining Process Flow

The key points realized thus far that guide the team in defining a new process include

1. The two primary project objectives are
   a. Reduce order processing time required by sales staff.
   b. Reduce errors in order entry that affected marketing campaigns.

2. Sales processing time is influenced by the number of line items and number of interruptions.

   a. The line items are an indirect measure of the complexity of the sale (each line item represents additional products or services purchased). Reducing the line item count per order by grouping products into single line items would not reduce the complexity of the sale but would increase the complexity of the order and the resulting likelihood of order errors (such as picking the wrong grouped item). The team did not consider there to be any opportunities relative to this factor.

   b. Minimizing interruptions is possible but may increase customer wait time because sales staff are taken offline to process orders.

Total cycle time consists of processing time plus wait time. Wait time does not affect sales department costs directly; however, it does affect customers directly and affects sales costs indirectly because order status inquiries from customers increase with increased wait time.

The errors are primarily errors of omission rather than incorrect data entry. The occurrence rate is consistent across products and relatively small (94 percent of opportunities for a defect resulted in no defect). The only possible reason for the omissions is "I forgot," which has many possible subcauses, including distraction and interruptions.

The vast majority of sales staff data entry is business-value-added (BVA; type 2 waste) and would be considered non-value-added (NVA) for Web orders as long as the data are available to sales and support personnel.

Item 3, regarding the prevalence of human error, suggests benefits in mistake-proofing the process. Controlling human behavior by other means, such as written procedures, often produces less than desirable results (as is evident in this example). In the case of software data entry, error prevention is often a matter of automating data entry to remove or reduce human influence or adding prompts, warnings, and/or required fields into the data-entry forms. Unfortunately, the current process uses a mass-market customer relationship management (CRM) system for storing these data that does not provide data-entry customization.

Item 4 had particular resonance among team members: If the Web order data are available to order-entry personnel, the additional data entry is limited to the license codes. The license codes are generated from internal software, which could be easily modified to write to the Web-order database. If all orders could be entered directly into the Web-order database, then order entry into the CRM system could cease immediately.

The team developed a revised flow assuming use of the Web-order database and received the sponsor's approval for information technology (IT) support to implement these changes to the Web-order database.

Simulations

When a process model is known, either from experimentation or by design, then process simulations can be used to find optimal solutions. While a regression model is *deterministic* in nature, in that the factors in the model are fixed values, factors in processes are random variables. Simulations provide a means of using probability estimates for the random variables to discover the impact of their joint probabilities.

Simulations have several advantages over experimentation. They certainly are cheaper in almost all cases, allowing the test of many more conditions than is practically possible with experiments. This makes them very suitable for "what-if" scenarios to test the response under worst-case circumstances. Simulations also can be used for planning, such as in a design for Six Sigma (DFSS) approach to estimate the effects of increased business activity on resources or for new-product processing.

Key uses of simulations include (Pyzdek and Keller, 2009)

- Verifying analytical solutions
- Studying dynamic situations
- Determining significant components and variables in a complex system

- Determining variables' interactions
- Studying effects of change without risk, cost, and time of experimentation
- Teaching

Simulations can be used to investigate alternative process scenarios for a given improvement strategy, allowing estimation of the solution's robustness to variation in input parameters. Proposed changes in resources, such as afforded by cross-training or staff reallocation, can be analyzed quickly with respect to cycle time. The effects of task prioritization, task order, and multitasking also can be measured.

The input parameters for the simulation include a model of the process and a suitable probability distribution (with parameters such as the mean and standard deviation) for each random variable. In some cases, it will be more convenient to approximate the distribution with an alternate distribution. For example, the normal distribution provides a reasonable approximation to the binomial distribution for large samples.

The simulation, sometimes referred to as a *Monte Carlo simulation*, will generate a frequency distribution for the resulting process response. In a Monte Carlo simulation, a large number of trials (5,000 or more) are run. Each time a trial is run, a random number is generated for the response. The result is calculated and stored as the *forecast* of the result. After generating a large number of forecasts, the distributional parameters of the response may be estimated.

Of course, the outcome is only as good as the prediction model, so actual data should be used to verify the model either at the onset (if the model is based on the current conditions) or at deployment of the improvements (if the model is developed to predict performance of a new process).

A number of software tools are available for process simulations. Minitab provides for random number generation in its Calc menu. Microsoft Excel provides its random number generation feature in the Tools/Data Analysis menu. These random number generators form the basis for process simulations. The common distributions and their properties and uses are shown in the "Distributions" section of Part 3.

An example simulation may be modeled for the four steps of the critical path shown in Table 7.1. The model in this case is a simple addition of the cycle times for each of the four steps in the process. Excel or Minitab may be used to generate a set of data of the appropriate distribution for each of steps 1 through 4. (Note that in Excel the exponential data for step 4 are generated from a separate set of uniform data, as described in the "Distributions" section of Part 3.)

The total cycle time, the sum of the cycle times for the process steps, is shown in Figure 7.1. The resulting distribution is nonnormal, which can be verified using the normal probability plot and the Kolmogorov-Smirnov (K-S) goodness-of-fit test. If the data are assumed to come from a controlled nonnormal process, the *capability index* indicates that the process will not meet the requirements for a 45-hour cycle time.

The effect of cycle time reduction for each of the process steps then can be evaluated. What is the effect of reducing the variation in step 1 by 50 percent? How much will total cycle time be reduced if the average cycle time for step 2 is reduced to 5 hours? If it costs twice as much to reduce the variation in step 2, is the reduction in step 1 preferred? The effect of each of these scenarios can be easily estimated using the simulation tool.

In a similar way, the effect of process variation on more complicated regression functions can be easily estimated. The effect of tightly controlling temperature on the consistency of product purity can be evaluated without first having to implement an expensive temperature-control mechanism.

It should be clear that simulations offer a relatively simple and cost-effective method of evaluating process improvement schemes. Since the simulation is a direct reflection of the assumed model and its parameters, the results of the simulation always must be verified in realistic process conditions. Regardless, the cost of data acquisition is greatly reduced by the knowledge gained in the process simulations.

Simulations allow the process flow to be easily revised "on paper" and evaluated for flow, bottlenecks, and cycle times. These "what-if" scenarios save the time and expense of actually changing the process to measure the effect. Once the process is modeled, the before and after states can be compared easily for resource allocation, costs, and scheduling issues.

TABLE 7.1 Example Cycle Time Reduction		
Step	**Distribution**	**Parameters**
1	Normal	Mean = 12.1; SD = 1.9
2	Normal	Mean = 7.3; SD = 0.5
3	Uniform	Mean = 3
4	Exponential	Mean = 5.1

SD = standard deviation.

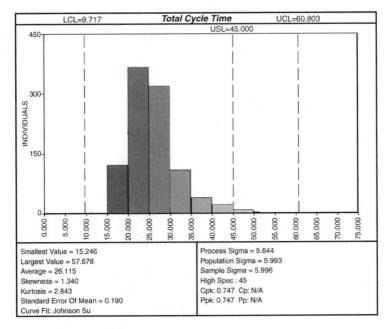

FIGURE 7.1 Example simulation results for cycle time.

The first step for using simulations begins with modeling of the process. The flowcharts, process maps, and *s*uppliers, *i*nputs, *p*rocess, *o*utputs, and *c*ustomers (SIPOC) analyses introduced in the define stage are useful now to develop the flow and responsibilities for the new process.

PROJECT EXAMPLE: Simulation

The team constructed a simulation in Excel to test the effect of taking the order taker offline while processing the order. This was accomplished in a number of steps:

1. The call arrival rate was estimated using phone records. An exponential distribution using λ equal to the mean call arrival rate was used to model call arrival. (Note that the team also could have defined one or more periods of increased call volume within the eight-hour period.)

2. Using order history data, the number of line items per order was modeled using a Poisson distribution.

3. The following columns were constructed within Excel to model the process. See "Distributions" in Part 3 for reference to the construction of random data models.

a. Column A contains a set of uniform distributed random variables between 0 and 1.

b. Column B contains the time between order arrivals, calculated using an exponential distribution at the specified arrival rate applied to the uniform distributed data of column A. For example, if the average time between order arrivals is 60 minutes (i.e., one order per hour), then row 2 of column B contains the expression "=60*(-LN($A2))."

c. Column C contains the order arrival time, expressed in minutes since the start of the eight-hour work day. Row 2 contains the value "0"; row 3 contains the expression "=IF(C2+B3>480,0,C2+B3)." An order received after the end of the business day (time exceeding 480 minutes) is assigned a value zero, indicating the first order to process the following day.

d. Column D contains the order arrival day. Row 2 contains the value "1"; row 3 contains the expression "=IF(C3=0,D2+1,D2)."

e. Column E contains the order start time, expressed in minutes since the start of the eight-hour workday. Row 2 contains the expression "=IF(K2>K1,0,IF(K2>D2,J1,IF(C2>J1,C2,J1)))" based on the following logic:

   (1) If the order is processed on the arrival day and arrives after the prior order was completed, then the arrival time is the start time; if the prior order is still in progress, the order is started once the prior order is completed.

   (2) If this order is the first order for the next day (based on comparison of the current and prior values in column K), its start time is 0; if it is processed the day after it arrives (based on comparison of columns D and K) but is not the first order, its start time is the end time of the last order; otherwise, its start time is the prior order completion time.

f. Column F contains the number of line items (random numbers based on a Poisson distribution).

g. Column G contains another set of uniformly distributed random variables between 0 and 1.

h. Column H contains the call arrival rate (calls per hour), calculated with an exponential distribution. If the call arrival rate is 3, then row 2 contains the expression " =3*(-LN(G2))."

i. Column I contains the order process time, calculated using the regression equation from the designed experiment, based on the call arrival rate and the number of line items.

j. Column J contains the order completion time; for example, row 2 contains the expression "=E2+I2."

k. Column K contains the order processing day. Row 1 contains the value "1"; row 2 contains the expression "=IF(J2>480,K2+1,IF(D3>K2,K2 +1,K2))," which increments the day count when the order completion time in column J exceeds 480 minutes or the order arrival day has been incremented.

l. Column L contains the order wait time (exclusive of that portion of waiting owing to incoming calls, which is included in the regression model), calculated as the difference between the order start time and arrival time. Row 2 contains the expression "=IF(K2>D2,E2+(480-C2), E2-C2)."

m. Column M contains the order cycle time, calculated as the sum of the process time and the wait time. Row 2 contains the expression "=I2+L2."

4. The simulation provided the following information, based on 5,000 simulated trials:

a. Using the model developed in the designed experiment, the team verified that the simulation provided a reasonable estimate of the original baseline data. Since the baseline data did not include the two main factors, the team reviewed a subset of the data and, using the records of the actual orders, noted the number of line items in the order and estimated the call arrival rate using the phone records for the particular date and time of the order. The model approximated the data fairly well, based on a residuals analysis. The average process time, including the wait time associated with incoming calls, was 36 minutes, of which the actual processing time (excluding the incoming call wait time) was 22 minutes. All orders were processed on the same day, averaging 72 minutes of total cycle time, including 35 minutes of wait time not associated with incoming calls. Although this model for the as-is process will not be used to estimate the processing time for the suggested process, it will be used as a baseline to estimate the improvement potential for the suggested process.

b. Using the design of experiments (DOE) model, the impact of various changes in the process inputs can be estimated relative to the baseline:

   (1) If the order arrival rate increased by 50 percent (from 1 order per hour to 1.5 orders per hour), the total order cycle time increased 93 percent, with 2 percent of the orders exceeding eight hours.

(2) If the call arrival rate increased by 50 percent, the total order cycle time increased by 68 percent.

(3) If both the order and call arrival rates increased by 50 percent, the total order cycle time increased by over 600 percent, with 56 percent of orders exceeding eight hours of total cycle time.

(4) These results indicate a process with little capacity to handle process disruptions, such as increased volume.

c. The proposed change to remove the order processing person from the call queue is estimated to reduce the total cycle time to less than 30 minutes, including 7 minutes of average wait time. All orders are completed within 90 minutes; only 4 percent exceed 60 minutes. This aspect of the proposed change likely would reduce customer order status inquiries and improve the overall order processing efficiency but would not greatly reduce the actual order processing time (or cost).

d. Reducing the order processing time by 50 percent results in a 68 percent reduction in total cycle time because average wait time is reduced to 5 minutes. All orders were processed in less than 100 minutes, with only 3 percent beyond 60 minutes.

(1) If the order processing person also was taken offline, the cycle time was reduced by a total of 83 percent, with only 1 percent of orders' cycle times exceeding 30 minutes. This process performance was unchanged if the order arrival rate increased by 50 percent

(2) If the order processor remained in the call queue and the incoming call rate increased by 50 percent, the total cycle time was reduced by 58 percent from baseline.

5. The simulation results indicated substantial benefit in taking the order processor offline as the order is processed. A secondary simulation to estimate the effect of taking the order processor offline on the call queue also was performed.

Redefining Operating Conditions

To truly drive a sustained reduction in process variation, process improvements must concentrate on controlling the underlying factors that predict future outcomes. This helps to prevent problems before they occur. In the analyze stage, process drivers were identified that contribute to process variation. In the improve stage, these process drivers will be investigated further to define the settings necessary to achieve optimal process performance.

There are two aspects, or objectives, of optimization. Traditionally, *optimization* involves finding the best combination of factor levels to maximize (or minimize) the response. For example, it may be important to investigate the specific concentrations of reagents and temperature of reaction necessary to achieve the highest degree of product purity. In a service process, the optimal allocation of staffing and services may be needed to minimize the cycle time for a key process.

More recently, perhaps owing to the influence of Taguchi, there is an increased interest in variation reduction. In this scope, optimization leads to the best combination of factor levels to produce the least variation in the response at a satisfactory average response. For example, the chemical process customer may be most interested in a consistent purity level. This is often the case when customers can make adjustments to their process over the long term, but short-term adjustments to deal with batch-to-batch variation are costly. This happens in service processes as well. An oil-change service that provides a consistent two-hour service is often preferred to one that occasionally delivers with half-hour service but sometimes makes the customer wait several hours. Consistency enhances the ability to plan, which improves resource utilization. Inconsistency mandates complexity, which comes at a cost, as is often discovered in the earlier stages of DMAIC.

When optimal solutions to problems are sought and the process model is not clearly understood, the response surface methods generally are the most useful. *Response surface* designs are special-case-designed experiments that allow optimal regions to be located efficiently with usually only a few iterations. The first-order regression model developed in the analyze stage serves as the starting point. This first-order model is a good assumption because the starting point is usually far enough away from the optimum that it is likely to be dominated by first-order effects, and a detailed mapping of the response region far away from the optimum is not needed. Data are collected through experimentation to determine the path toward optimality using the first-order model. Tests for curvature indicate when a local minimum, maximum, or saddle point (a combination of the two) is reached.

Using three- or five-level central composite designs, the response surface can be mapped using a higher-order model. Although response surface plots such as the one shown in Figure 7.2 are visually appealing, the classic contour plot (such as the one shown in Figure 7.3) is often more useful because of its direct approach.

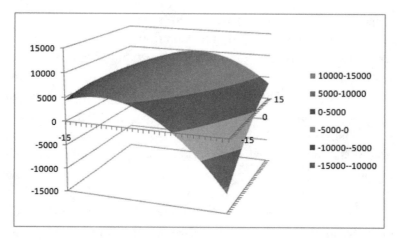

FIGURE 7.2   Example response surface plot from MS Excel.

Although these plots can display only two process factors at a time, the mathematics behind the analysis extends to additional factors. Software allows these techniques to be readily applied and then verified with additional process trials.

Evolutionary operation (EVOP) offers another approach for iteratively finding an optimal solution. The advantage of EVOP is that the process does not need to be shut down, as in a designed experiment, to run conditions that generally would be outside the normal operating region for the process. Instead, the EVOP slowly moves toward an optimum by gradually extending the operating region in the direction of improvement. As such, EVOP takes many more iterations than a response surface design to find the optimal solution, yet it is simple enough to allow process personnel to make the adjustments and monitor the results as part of daily operations.

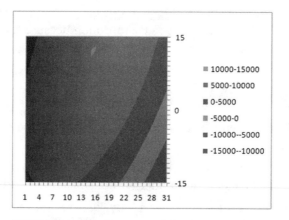

FIGURE 7.3   Example contour plot from MS Excel.

Evaluating Process Failure Modes

Once the process flow is established, it can be evaluated for its failure modes. Understanding process failure modes allows one to define mitigation strategies to minimize the impact or occurrence of failures. These mitigation strategies may result in new process steps, optimal process settings, or process control strategies to prevent failure. In some cases, where failure cannot be prevented economically, a strategy can be developed to minimize the occurrence of the failure and contain the damage.

Cause-and-effect diagrams used in the analyze stage are again useful for brainstorming the potential causes of failures. This brainstorming activity will provide necessary input to process decision program charts and failure modes and effects analysis (FMEA).

The *process decision program chart*, also known by its acronym *PDPC*, is a tool for identifying problems that can occur in a project or process and developing contingencies (either a solution or work-around) to deal with each problem.

The PDPC has the same general format as a tree diagram. For each process step shown in the first level, potential problems ("what-ifs") are identified in the second level. Countermeasures provide the contingencies for each problem.

The intent of the analysis is to confront problems that otherwise might not have been addressed. Forcing the team to anticipate problems before they occur helps team members to uncover issues or solutions that otherwise would be ignored. Additionally, this process allows team members to discuss points that they may find troublesome without feeling like they are being unduly negative. Once the potential problems are identified, the next step is to think of measures to counter-act those problems. When more than one countermeasure is available, note each of them, and prioritize the solutions using the methods discussed earlier.

For instance, suppose that the anticipated problem is resistance to change among process personnel. The possible counteractive measures include an incentive program to boost morale and an education program to inform work-ers of the need for change. You then can weigh the costs and benefits of each alternative to decide on your course of action. Of course, it is much easier to make these decisions in the calm of the planning room than in the heat of the project when you suddenly discover an unanticipated problem.

Failure modes and effects analysis (also known by its acronym *FMEA* or *failure modes, effects, and criticality analysis*) is a more detailed approach to the prob-lem. It is used to determine high-risk functions or product features based on the impact of a failure and the likelihood that a failure could occur without detection. The methodology can be applied to products or processes, although the application to processes is most useful in the improve stage of DMAIC.

The FMEA process (described in detail in Part 3) begins by defining the functions for each process step. Table 7.2 provides an example for some of the key steps in the order processing project.

TABLE 7.2 FMEA for Example Order Processing Efficiency Project

Process Step	Function	Failure Mode	Severity	Likelihood of Occurrence	Detection Method	Likelihood of Detection	RPN
Enter company contact e-mail	Communicating order status and details, as well as for ongoing support/ updates	Not entered	5	7	Unable to send e-mail	1	35
		Incorrectly entered	5	6	Returned e-mail	1	30
Record renewal date in CRM system	Indicates if client is entitled to free upgrade when revision released	Not entered	8	8	Customer complaint	9	*576*
		Incorrectly entered	8	6	Customer complaint	9	*432*
Generate license code	Provides licensing for features	Wrong software features enabled	7	4	Customer complaint	7	*196*
		Incorrect license count	7	4	Customer complaint	8	*224*
Record license code in CRM field	Used if customer lost code	Not entered	3	3	Detected on inquiry	3	27
		Incorrectly entered	3	1	Customer complaint	6	18
Record license count in CRM field	Used for pricing upgrades and renewals or to reissue code	Not entered	2	7	Detected on inquiry	3	42
		Incorrectly entered	4	6	Customer complaint	6	*144*

The severity, likelihood of occurrence, detection method, and likelihood of detection are determined, and a resulting risk factor (risk priority number, or RPN) is calculated. The likelihood of occurrence and likelihood of detection are based on historical data, where available.

The results of the FMEA will indicate activities prone to failure or likely to cause serious consequences if they do fail. These failure modes must be addressed, either through elimination or via a mitigation strategy. Improvements in detection are stopgap measures with increased cost of quality. Reducing the risk often demands a reduction in the rate of occurrence, such as through the process optimization techniques described earlier. Prevention methods can achieve satisfactory results, particularly in reducing the rate of occurrence of human errors.

Figure 7.4 displays a PDPC analysis of the key process steps, as indicated by the RPN calculated in the FMEA for each process step. The contingency plans noted for each step result in a corresponding decrease in RPN noted in the figure.

Prevention of Human Errors

It is useful to categorize process failures according to their origin. Many failures are due to human error, particularly in service processes. While some solutions will focus on the performance of individuals, most failures resulting from human error will be prevented by process or system-level solutions.

There are three main categories of human errors: inadvertent errors, technique errors, and willful errors. *Inadvertent errors* otherwise may be termed *mistakes*. *Technique errors* are related to the process procedure and often are due to poor training. *Willful errors* are deliberate attempts to sabotage the process.

Inadvertent errors typically are characterized by a low incidence rate, with little or no advance knowledge that a failure is coming. There is no predictable pattern to an inadvertent error.

Inadvertent errors can be prevented in a number of ways. *Foolproofing*, also called *poka yoke*, is one of the lean tools for preventing errors. A fundamental change is incorporated into the design of the part or the process to prevent the error from occurring.

For example, modern hypodermic needles now have been designed to prevent the needle from being used more than once to avoid possible instances of cross-contamination between patients. To prevent holes from being drilled in the wrong place on a production part, the part and the fixture used to secure the part could incorporate a pin with a mating slot so that the part will not fit correctly into the fixture unless it is aligned properly.

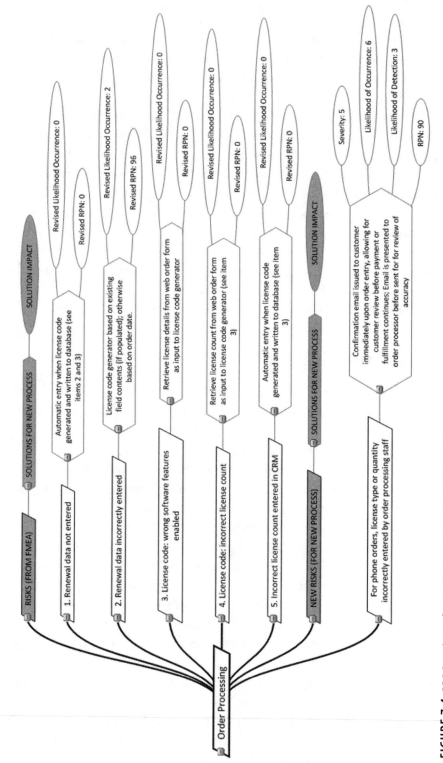

FIGURE 7.4 PDPC analysis of revised process based on FMEA results.

Automation is a common way to minimize the occurrence of inadvertent errors by removing the human element. Bar-code readers are simple devices used in many industries to prevent product numbers, customer information, or product data from being incorrectly typed into a database.

Another approach that has proven helpful is an ergonomic approach to improving the work environment. For example, a simpler keyboard, easily accessible to the clerk, might help to reduce data-entry errors.

Technique errors are characterized as being unintentional, usually confined to single characteristic or class of characteristics (e.g., cracks) and isolated to a few workers.

Technique errors can be minimized by using the same methods as for inadvertent errors (i.e., foolproofing, automation, and ergonomics) or through training. Training is perhaps the most common method of reducing technique errors and can be combined with visual aids and documentation at the process level for easy access by the workforce.

Willful errors are characteristically nonrandom and difficult to detect. Fortunately, they usually involve only a single disgruntled worker and are extremely rare in practice. Only 100 percent inspection can hope to detect these types of errors, and even 100 percent inspection is not 100 percent accurate, so errors still can be undetected. An engaged and empowered workforce is perhaps the best prevention.

PROJECT EXAMPLE: Evaluating Process Failure Modes

The team used FMEA to evaluate the risks associated with the current process, a portion of which is shown in Table 7.2. The severity, occurrence and detection level codes are based on the corresponding tables shown in Part 3; the failure rates for the occurrence table are based on the actual baseline error rate data.

The FMEA places heightened risk on the following process failure modes (ranked by RPN in Table 7.2):

1. Renewal data not entered

2. Renewal data incorrectly entered

3. License code: wrong software features enabled

4. License code: incorrect license count

5. Incorrect license count entered in CRM system

Each of the key risks identified in the FMEA then were evaluated in a PDPC based on the proposed process changes, as shown in Figure 7.4. The team's proposed use of the Web-order database permitted automated entry of the information for all Web orders, which constituted the majority of orders. The license code generator would automatically write the license details to the database using the input from the Web-order database as entered by the customer. This would prevent inconsistencies in both input and output: The license codes, counts, and renewal dates would be naturally consistent with the order payment.

The smaller percentage of orders received via phone would be processed using the same Web-order form, necessitating manual data entry by the order processor for these orders. The team added this function to the PDPC, requiring a confirmation e-mail to the customer to confirm order details. This e-mail would be presented to the order processor, forcing review of the order before the e-mail is sent or the data committed to the database. The calculated risk for this additional step was below the threshold of 120 established by the organization, which satisfied the team and its sponsor.

Assessing Benefits of the Proposed Solution

It's not uncommon for a team to reach the improve stage with several possible methods of process improvement. These potential techniques must be evaluated using objective, data-driven methods to maximize buy-in of the solution and ensure that stakeholders receive their optimal return on the project investment.

The *prioritization matrix* (introduced in Chapter 4) can be used to compare the proposed solutions against the criteria defined as critical in the define stage of the project.

Financial analysis tools are used to estimate the cost savings associated with the proposed solutions. To quantify financial value (and risk) associated with a proposed solution, variable costs must be differentiated from fixed costs. As shown in Figure 7.5, fixed costs (or fixed benefits) are constant regardless of volume (i.e., the number of orders filled, customers processed, or units produced), such as the costs associated with building and support personnel. Variable costs and benefits depend on volume and include such items as materials, direct labor, and shipping.

If fixed and variable costs and benefits are known, the earnings before inter-

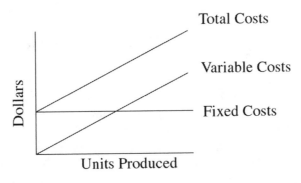

FIGURE 7.5 Variable and fixed costs.

est and taxes (EBIT) calculation provides the potential profitability of each particular solution. The benefit of a solution is calculated as the difference between the EBIT before and the EBIT after the solution:

$$\text{EBIT} = \text{volume} \times (\text{price per unit} - \text{variable cost per unit}) - \text{fixed cost}$$

It often happens that the benefits and costs come in specific time windows rather than in lump sums at the beginning or end of the term. A net present value (NPV) analysis allows us to calculate the current benefit of a project for each window of time and over the total time period. The internal rate of return (IRR) is the equivalent interest that is gained by the project if the NPV of the cash flow were invested for the time period. The IRR allows us to compare projects, with higher IRR values associated with projects yielding a better return. MS Excel provides a convenient formula for determining NPV and IRR when the cost and benefits are tabulated.

These deterministic estimates of process savings can be further enhanced using the simulation approach outlined earlier in this chapter. The cost savings for a project can consider the distributional properties of the random variable inputs:

- *Percent reduction in defects (affecting material savings, capacity, and labor).* Simulate the baseline and postimprovement distributions. Calculate the difference in error rate between the results.

- *Production volume (affecting material savings, capacity, and labor).* Simulate effects of increasing (or decreasing) sales volume.

In this way, annualized cost savings estimates may be stated in percentiles. For example, solution *A* will provide a 90 percent likelihood of saving $500,000 and a 99 percent likelihood of saving $150,000.

PROJECT EXAMPLE: Assessing the Benefits of the Proposed Solution

The automated solution using the Web-order database almost entirely removed the human interaction necessary to process the order because the CRM system was no longer necessary for even a business-value-added consideration. For Web orders (approximately 70 percent of the total), this reduced processing time by sales staff from the 21-minute average to approximately 3 minutes. Manual entry into the Web-order form also was streamlined (relative to the CRM), and with integration of the code generator and automated e-mails to accounting, the order processing time for these orders was reduced to an average of 7 minutes per order.

The simplification of the process also enabled consideration of transferring the order processing to a less expensive cost center: the order fulfillment team, which currently handles the shipping aspects of the order. This possibility pleased the team member representing that department because the department staff levels had been reduced over the past five years owing to reductions in shipments (corresponding to the increase in downloads and changes in business models). The sponsor, who also supervised the area, supported the recommendation.

The deliverables are broken down by metric:

- Cost per order (calculated in the order fulfillment department based on 30 percent of orders manual data entry) = $0.70 \times (2 \text{ minutes} \times \$1 \text{ per minute}) + 0.30 \times (7 \text{ minutes} \times \$1 \text{ per minute}) = \$3.50 \text{ per order} \times 1{,}350$ orders per year = $3,780. Annual savings are $40,000 − $4,725 = $35,275.

- E-mail marketing costs: Errors leading to increased marketing costs are expected to fall to zero, meeting the project goals of $24,000 annual savings.

- The impacts of the improved marketing on the software renewal rate and resulting renewal revenue will be monitored in the control stage.

Implementation and Verification

Once the improvement methodology and new process levels have been determined, they can be implemented. Even in the simplest of improvements, caution and diligence must be exercised at this point.

One of the most obvious—yet still overlooked—reasons for problems at this point is lack of communication. Previous chapters have discussed the need for regular updates with the stakeholder groups to avoid surprises at the improve stage. These updates allow a vision of the solution to be formed over time by stakeholders, increasing the likelihood of buy-in to the solution. Through proper communication, stakeholders will understand the need for a solution in the define stage, appreciate the extent of the problem in the measure stage, and realize its complexity through the analyze stage. Exercising rigor during the improve stage brings clarity to the solution for each of the stakeholder groups.

Nonetheless, even when the solution is evident, the project team must focus on proper communication to ensure support through implementation of the solution. Starting with the project sponsor, each step of the solution, with a contingency plan in the event of failure, must be presented in a clear and orderly fashion to the stakeholder groups. The sponsor must convey the specific authority to the project team, properly communicated through the organizational hierarchy, to implement the specific solution beginning at a specific date and time. Process personnel and their immediate management must be cognizant of the authority vested in the project team in implementing the solution and provide the necessary support to ensure its proper implementation.

Process personnel must be provided with clear instructions on their new procedures, especially with regard to process failures. While the control stage includes detailed training on the new process procedures, at this point, the procedures still may be somewhat in flux until the solution has been deployed. Depending on the extent of the solution, in-depth training of all personnel could be premature until the process and its procedures have been stabilized. This state of transition requires oversight by the project team and/or process personnel (under the direction of the team) to ensure that the process output meets the expectations of the authorized solution. The goal is to quickly establish the merits of the solution so that the project team can move to the control stage, where in-depth training can be conducted. Until this training takes place, the project team must work closely with process personnel to communicate proper action and understanding of the process conditions.

Statistical analysis of these conditions, generally using control charts, is needed to verify the results. As discussed in Chapter 8, statistical control of the process is necessary if project success is to be measured. Hypothesis tests on the difference in means may be used to compare the process before and after implementation of the solution.

Recommended Tools

The following tools (discussed in detail in Part 3) are applicable to the improve stage of DMAIC:

Defining the New Process

- *Gantt charts* and *program evaluation and review techniques (PERT) analysis* help to verify the reduction in process critical-path cycle time.
- *Five S tools* help to reduce non-value-added cycle times owing to movement, search time, ineffective use of floor space; to improve inventory management; or to reduce accidents and improve working conditions.
- *Level loading* helps to balance the flow of orders.
- *Box-whisker charts* help to graphically compare before and after states of process improvement.
- *Cause-and-effect diagram* help to generate a list of potential failure modes that should be addressed in the solution.
- *Designed experiments, factorial designs, regression analysis, residuals analysis, response surface analysis, evolutionary operations, interaction plots,* and *contour plots* help to determine where a maximum or minimum response is expected within or close to the data range.

Assessing Benefits of the Proposed Solutions

- *Matrix diagrams* and *prioritization matrices* help to ensure that process solutions are aligned with customer needs.

Evaluating Process Failure Modes

- *Procession decision program charts* and *failure modes and effects analysis (FMEA)* help to determine high-risk process activities or product features in the proposed improvement.

Implementation Verification

- *Flowcharts* and *process maps* help to define the process-level activities necessary.
- *Hypothesis testing of two samples* and *nonparametric test on the equality of means* help to compare process averages after improvements versus baseline estimates.

- *Statistical process control (SPC) charts*, including C, Np, P, U, *Individual-X*, *X-bar*, and *EWMA charts* and the *process capability index* help to verify the effects of the improvement.

- *Goodness-of-fit tests* help to verify the statistical distributions assumed in the various statistical tools.

In addition, the consensus-building tools noted at the end of Chapter 4 are also applied as needed.

CHAPTER 7 QUIZ

1. **Lean improvements, such as standardization, setup reduction, and removal of unnecessary steps,**
   A. will always have a positive impact on quality.
   B. will always have a negative impact on quality but will reduce cost.
   C. may have a negative impact on quality, suggesting that the process should be evaluated for an impact on quality.
   D. are not related to process quality.

2. **Process simulations are useful**
   A. to provide some useful data for training.
   B. to test how the process operates under a wide variety of conditions.
   C. if it is costly to run real experiments on the process.
   D. All the above are true.

3. **Before a simulation can be run,**
   A. one should find a master black belt who is well versed in stochastic processes.
   B. one will need to obtain access to a computer capable of running millions of calculations.
   C. one will need to estimate the process model and its operating conditions.
   D. All the above are true.

4. **Simulation results**
   A. are usually not useful in preventing errors but often are useful to predict errors.
   B. can be more exact than process data when real distributions are modeled.
   C. should be verified using process data.
   D. All the above are true.

5. **Process optimization can be achieved**
   A. by finding the best settings for each significant factor to maximize or minimize the response (as needed).
   B. by finding the best settings for each significant factor to minimize the variation in the response.
   C. Both A and B are true, depending on the need.

6. **If a process is so critical to daily operations that management is unwilling to shut down the process for investigation, yet the process is in need of improvement, the process improvement team might consider**
   A. a Taguchi experiment.
   B. a classical designed experiment.
   C. evolutionary operation.
   D. one-factor-at-a-time experimentation.

7. **In evaluating the RPN of an FMEA, activities with the highest RPN**
   A. have the highest risk and should be of greatest concern.
   B. have the lowest risk and should be of least concern.
   C. are of equal concern because RPN is unrelated to risk.

8. **Inadvertent errors can be prevented by**
   A. automation.
   B. *poka yoke* (foolproofing).
   C. ergonomic design.
   D. All the above are useful approaches, depending on the circumstances.

9. **Increasing the likelihood of detection**
   A. increases the RPN.
   B. usually increases cost and is useful only as a temporary strategy until the errors can be prevented.
   C. is synonymous with reducing the occurrence rate.
   D. All the above are true.

10. **A team attempting to reduce the risk associated with a process failure usually should concentrate on**
    A. prevention of the errors leading to failure.
    B. a system for operating personnel to detect errors after they have occurred.
    C. reducing the severity of errors when they occur.

chapter **8**

Control Stage

The final stage of *define*, *measure*, *analyze*, *improve*, and *control* (DMAIC) problem-solving methodology is the control stage.

Objectives

There are several objectives to be completed within the control stage of DMAIC:

- The new methods must become standardized in practice.
- The predicted impact of the improvements, the project deliverables, must be continually verified, especially the financial return.
- Lessons learned should be documented.

Standardize on the New Methods

In the improve stage, changes are made to the process. Frequently, the process procedures will be changed. The old way of doing things is replaced with new and improved methods.

Process variation may have been reduced by controlling the variation in one or more key input variables or by redefining more appropriate levels for these parameters. These changes may result in reallocation of personnel to adjust for peak demand at certain times of the day or control of the variation in key parameters, such as room temperature, to control the size of a key dimension.

The natural response of process personnel may be to gradually or even abruptly return to past practices. This may occur the first time the process experiences a shift in behavior, when personnel return from vacation and fall into old habits, or when you're just not looking.

There are several practices that are useful for standardizing on the new process methods:

- Process control is used to monitor process variation. The most effective methods often minimize process variation by precision control of the input parameters.

- Control plans are used to define the methods of control and to ensure that all potential sources of variation are addressed.

- Work instructions, flowcharts, and process maps are used to document process procedures and responsibilities.

- Training is essential for process personnel to understand their new responsibilities. The communication of these methods, procedures, and responsibilities should be integrated into a training program for process personnel.

Process Control

How do we prevent the process from deviating from its improved state, including returning to past performance levels? There are two main strategies for achieving process control, stemming from the work done in the failure modes and effects analysis (FMEA):

- Prevent or greatly reduce the occurrence of errors.
- Detect the occurrence of the error and correct its effect before the customer experiences the undesirable effect.

Of course, if the cost to implement were the same, prevention always would be preferred to detection owing to

1. The increased costs of remedying the error
2. The delay experienced by the customer as the error is remedied
3. The uncertainty in detecting all errors even when all product output is sampled

Unfortunately, prevention is at least *sometimes* more costly to implement than detection, although once the cost of failure is factored in, then the true cost of a detection-based control system often exceeds the cost of prevention-based control. Recall the costs associated with "hidden factories," and it is clear that control systems for a Six Sigma organization should be prevention-oriented in almost all cases.

As a result of designed experiments, we often discover input variables that drive the process output. When we apply control schemes to these variables, we can prevent errors from occurring. For example, if the number of incoming orders drives the cycle time for order shipment, then a statistically significant increase in the number of incoming orders is a clue to increase the number of personnel in shipping. In this way, the cycle time for shipping (the process output variable) is unaffected because of the previous effort.

The methods for process control include statistical process control (SPC), engineering process control (EPC), and operational procedures. *Statistical process control* refers to the statistical tools that detect process instability. SPC is used to monitor output or input variables so that any lack of stability is detected. When the process is statistically capable of meeting the requirements, characterized by a process capability index Cpk of 1.5 or better (as defined in Part 3), a control chart of the process output will provide a means for detecting whether the process output at the Six Sigma level exceeds the requirements. When run-test rules are applied, or if the process is highly capable at or above the Six Sigma level, the control chart also will serve as a prevention tool because it is likely to detect process shifts before out-of-control conditions are experienced.

While SPC is often applied to process output, it is much better to apply SPC to the key input variables. This was a focus for the experimentation used in the analyze and improve stages of DMAIC. Establishing and monitoring statistical control of the process drivers that determine the process output serves as a prevention-oriented method of controlling the process.

Engineering process control refers to automated devices designed to respond to process variation by adjusting one or more process input variables. A simple example of this approach is the thermostat found in most homes. When the air temperature inside the house reaches a set level, the air conditioner (or heater) turns on to respond to the undesirable condition and control the temperature within a set tolerance (usually determined by the manufacturer). Although a household thermostat has rather simple programmable controls, industrial processes often use more sophisticated algorithms with multiple input parameters and even multiple outputs. The inputs are often sampled at high frequencies, and once an acceptable model is discovered, the process can be controlled to a high level of precision.

Since EPC makes changes to the process based on the current state of the process, the data are inherently autocorrelated, or dependent on earlier observations. This serial correlation violates the assumption of data independence required for standard SPC control charts and must be addressed if control charts are to be used to monitor process output. This is discussed in more detail in the "Auto Correlation" charts section of Part 3.

Operational Procedures

As with EPC and, to some extent, SPC, operational procedures seek to control the output of the process using operational guidelines for the human inputs to the process. Rather than automatically controlling temperature using a feedback control such as a thermostat, operational procedures would instruct a process operator to turn on the heater or air conditioner when the temperature reached a particular setting. It should be clear that detection of the condition, as well as the response to the condition, is not as repeatable as when using automated control. The procedures are subject to human error, as discussed in Chapter 7.

Nonetheless, procedures offer the most cost-effective means of control for many circumstances. Particularly in transactional processes, procedures may be used effectively to

- *Standardize the process.* For example, using flowcharts or decision trees, each of the order-processing clerks will process the orders in the same fashion. Simple software also can be created to facilitate the process.

- *Divert resources.* As a matter of procedure, personnel are instructed that if the wait for their service is more than five minutes, then additional resources should be requested immediately. For example, if there are more than three people in your checkout line, request additional cashiers to the front of the store.

- *Channel orders by types.* Certain customers or types of orders are routed to a standardized process line for improved efficiency. For example, at an automotive service department, the oil-change customers are routed to a special line for expedited service. At a bank, an express lane is provided for merchant accounts.

Operational procedures must be documented and controlled to ensure their use. *Control* of procedures refers to revision control, where operational personnel have access only to current (not outdated) procedures that have been approved by the appropriate stakeholders. The ISO 9000 provisions for document control are an effective means of ensuring proper revision control.

Effective procedures may be documented in paragraph form, with flowcharts or process maps, with pictures, or with any combination of these. The documentation method and terminology should be appropriate for the audience. Bear in mind the objective: to effectively communicate the proper procedure. For personnel who have a limited command of the local language, procedures in paragraph form may be completely ineffective. Simple pictures showing the correct and incorrect methods may be the most effective way to communicate the procedure to that audience, whereas paragraph form may be used for another audience for the same procedure.

Each of these process control techniques (SPC, EPC, and operational procedures) requires a necessary standard of performance, feedback to the process, and a method of changing the process. These parameters should be specified in a control plan.

Control Plans

A *control plan* provides an overview of the strategies that will be used to ensure that key process or part characteristics are controlled through either detection or prevention strategies or a combination of the two.

Key inputs to a control plan include the results of designed experiments and FMEA. Designed experiments are fundamental tools in determining process drivers. Robust designs in particular tell us which process factors must be controlled to reduce variation in the process response. By controlling these input factors, we can prevent errors from occurring in the process. As shown in Chapters 6 and 7, these methods can be applied effectively to transactional processes.

FMEA [and its risk priority number (RPN)] determines the failure modes that are the most critical to control. This is a valuable input in construction of the control plan. The assumptions used to determine the detection level in the FMEA must be incorporated into the control plan.

A portion of a control plan is shown in Table 8.1. For each key characteristic, the following information is defined:

- *Specification.* What is the definition of good and bad for this characteristic?
- *Measurement technique.* How will the characteristic be measured? The control plan should reference more detailed measurement procedures, where needed, to instruct personnel on the proper use and interpretation of the measurement equipment.
- *Sample size.* How many measurements are required at each point in time?
- *Sample frequency.* How often should a new set of measurements be taken?
- *Analytical tool.* How are the measurements evaluated? In this case, audio alarms are installed to monitor characteristics thought to have high process capability. Other characteristics are monitored via control charts to detect process trends leading to undesirable conditions.
- *Reaction rules.* What is the proper response to the alarms (audio or from control chart)? Who should be notified?

TABLE 8.1 Example Control Plan

Characteristic	Specification	Measurement Technique	Sample Size	Sample Frequency	Detection Method	Analytical Tool
Finished diameter	1.250 ± 0.0002	Johannson	5	1 subgroup	X-bar chart with run rules	If other characteristics in control, adjust
Local ambient temperature	70 ± 5	Thermocouple	1	Continuous	Alarmed	Stop production; adjust cooling control; resume production once temperature is okay
Cooling temperature	120 ± 5	Thermocouple	1	1 sample/ min	Alarmed	Stop production; adjust cooling control; resume production once temperature is okay
Coolant viscosity	0.88–0.94	Viscometer	1	1 sample/ month	X chart	Purge system

Training Requirements

While an effective document revision and control scheme is useful for communicating new methods and procedures, it is often not sufficient, especially when procedures undergo the significant changes often resulting from the DMAIC process. Even when procedural changes are relatively narrow in scope, training is quite beneficial in communicating the changes and preventing problems or misinterpretations of the new procedures. This training can be as simple as a quick meeting with operational personnel at their workstations or a detailed multisession training, such as may be required for new equipment or to teach customer-friendly communication skills.

Topics for training include the lessons learned during the DMAIC process, the key process factors, and their interactions, in addition to the new procedures themselves. Including these lessons learned is really helpful to stakeholders, particularly operational personnel, so that they understand *why* the changes were necessary and how the conclusions were developed.

The training should include operational personnel, process owners, and other stakeholders (including suppliers, if appropriate). Most, if not all, of these stakeholder groups were represented on the team and included in data collection or analysis, so this part of the training will provide a good conclusion to their efforts.

For the training to be effective, it should be targeted to the current skill set of the audience and include a means of assessing the knowledge transfer to each individual. The format of these evaluations depends on the criticality and complexity of the subject matter. In some cases, workshops are useful for employees to practice the newly acquired skills; in cases of critical safety or quality issues, employees may have to demonstrate proficiency through written or on-the-job testing.

Participants should be evaluated immediately at the end of the training and at a stipulated time later. This posttraining evaluation gauges the longer-term retention of the material and may demonstrate a need for follow-up training or a change in training format to target the audience more effectively. Of course, the best means of evaluating the impact of the training is to measure the changes in behavior resulting from the training. Are people using the new skills? To what degree?

PROJECT EXAMPLE: Standardize on New Methods

A formal control plan was not established given that:

- The monthly marketing campaigns provided a means of regularly monitoring the error rate in order processing data entry.

> • Because the cost had been diverted away from the higher cost sales depart-
> ment, control charting of the processing time was not instituted. The actual
> processing time was less a concern, especially with the observed reduction
> in process errors.
>
> Per company policy, the cost savings would be estimated at the six month point,
> and annually for three years thereafter.
> The Order Fulfillment department was trained in the use of the new system.

Measure Bottom-Line Impact

A key part of the control stage is to continuously monitor the effects of the
process improvement. This is a critical part of DMAIC that often was neglected
in past improvement strategies.

The control plan should contain provisions for monitoring the process output either as a method of control or as a sampling audit. Generally, the process
owner (operational personnel) will be responsible for ongoing tracking of the
applicable performance metric. This activity should continue for as long as
necessary, as often as necessary, to establish the underlying process capability.
Often sampling is fairly frequent in the beginning and tapers off once the process has proven stable and capable of achieving the requirements. See the "Statistical Process Control Charts" section in Part 3 for a general discussion of
sampling frequency and the sample sizes necessary to detect process shifts.

As part of this control stage, a black belt will assume responsibility for verifying
the operational-level controls done by the process owners. In addition, the black
belt will audit the process on a regular (e.g., monthly) basis for the first year. The
audit should include observation of process procedures and controls, as well as
sampling or reviewing of the results of data samples to ensure process capability.

If the process exhibits any out-of-control behavior, the black belt should be
notified so that a further review can be made to identify its source. In such a
case, the process control should be investigated and perhaps tightened to reduce
the occurrence of further process instability. In cases of continued instability,
the process should be evaluated for a new Six Sigma project, with a critical
review of the initial Six Sigma project report for indication of its failings.

Just as crucial as process control is the ongoing tracking of the financial benefits, usually on a monthly basis, as part of cost accounting reports. The financial
reporting must include actual expenditures and savings for each of the items
used for project justification in the define stage, as well as expenditures related

to the project implementation, such as described in the improve stage. Savings are calculated based on methods agreed on in the define stage and may include actual and predicted annualized estimates. The individual responsible for tracking the cost savings should be clearly identified in the control plan.

PROJECT EXAMPLE: Measure Bottom Line Impact

No errors were experienced for the first four months; however, a new product was added that subsequently was not correctly handled by the automated system. This issue was added to the company's database of lessons learned (related to ensuring that new products and services are correctly incorporated into the order processing procedure).

Using the cost estimates form the improve stage, applied to the actual order mix, the annualized six month savings was estimated as $32,000. After twelve months the annual savings was estimated at $31,000.

The support renewal rate was analyzed for the pre- and post-project data using separate control charts for each product. Product A had the most rigorous renewal marketing program prior to the project; its renewal rate showed a monthly increase of 15 percent within the first four months of project completion. Products B and C had scant efforts at renewal marketing prior to the project. The automated data processing ensured the relevant data was included in the database, allowing increased marketing efforts. Product B's monthly renewal rate grew by 35 percent over the first six months; Product C experienced a 23 percent increase.

The renewal revenue increased by $123,000 (annualized) over the first six months. After twelve months the annual savings was estimated as $136,000.

The annualized benefits for the first six months reached $179,000. After twelve months the annual savings was estimated as $191,000.

The cost of the project included $41,000 project labor costs and $16,000 IT programming costs.

Document Lessons Learned

The results of the Six Sigma project should be documented in a project report. The project report should include the following information:

- The project charter, as a key deliverable in the define stage, introducing the reader to the project's problem statement, objectives, and plan
- A summary result of each stage of the DMAIC cycle, including the main objectives and results for each stage

- Appendices containing raw data, analysis results, and a timeline of the actual activities for reference
- A listing of the expenditures required to implement the project, including lost capacity, material, and/or labor
- The cost savings received to date and projected for the next one to three years
- The current status of the process and the control plan for the future
- Recommendations for future projects related to the process
- Recommendations for future project leaders and sponsors based on lessons learned during this project

The project report should be circulated to the finance or accounting areas for review of accuracy of the financial information. The project report (and the financial approval) must be presented to the sponsor for formal approval and project close.

In some organizations, the master black belt and senior management responsible for Six Sigma deployment also must sign off on the report. It is often a good learning experience for black belts to formally present the findings to management. When other senior management leaders are invited, it provides good exposure to the program and the work of the project teams.

Organizations should adopt some strategy for rewarding Six Sigma teams. Financial rewards, particularly a percentage of the savings, are not necessary, nor encouraged. They send the wrong message and cultivate a culture of short-sighted profiteering or inflated savings at the expense of real improvement. Instead, teams should be recognized with ceremony and appreciation from management for a job well done. Even project failures should be celebrated for their effort, in the realization that at least some of the stretch goals sought will not be achieved.

In this vein, success stories should be communicated throughout the organization. If frustrations with a process were overcome, that speaks volumes in a language that others are anxious to hear. Project failures also should be noted for their efforts, their partial success, and the lessons learned.

Many companies have found Web-based forums on the company intranet a useful venue for sharing information. Black belts should be given the opportunity to share, learn, and grow through contact with one another. The use of technical skills, as well as the softer change management skills necessary for building buy-in, will grow when practitioners have a chance to see their successful application by other teams. It's truly remarkable how one team's success can be translated into other processes, even those which seem quite different. White papers, case studies, project reports, and chat rooms are useful for spreading the word and institutionalizing the findings.

PROJECT EXAMPLE: Lessons Learned

Lessons learned for this project included:

- Add requirement to new product/service introduction procedures to update order fulfillment database with product details.
- The team also identified a few potential improvement opportunities that were outside the scope of their project.
- Add links to support renewal e-mails to encourage use of Web-order form.
- Add ability to accept purchase orders to Web-order form.

These were documented in the company's improvement opportunity database.

Recommended Tools

The following tools (discussed in detail in Part 3) are applicable to the control stage of DMAIC:

- *Flowcharts* and *process maps* help to define the process-level activities necessary.
- *Statistical process control (SPC) charts*, including *C, Np, P, U, Individual-X, X-bar,* and *EWMA charts,* and the *process capability index* help to verify the effects of the improvement.
- *Goodness-of-fit tests* help to verify the statistical distributions assumed in the various statistical tools.
- *R&R studies* help to qualify operators' proficiency on specific measurement equipment.

In addition, the consensus-building tools noted at the end of Chapter 4 are also applied as needed.

CHAPTER 8 QUIZ

1. **The best results for controlling a process are often achieved by**
   A. controlling the process outputs.
   B. controlling the process inputs.
   C. sampling inspection of supplier material.
   D. monitoring all process parameters.

2. **Effective control plans for process improvement efforts include training**
   A. process operators on the principles behind the change.
   B. to ensure that employees understand their role in the problem-solving stage of the new process.
   C. for operational employees to acquire the skills necessary to perform the new procedures or tasks.
   D. All the above are true.

3. **The control stage of a DMAIC project includes which of the following objectives?**
   A. Communicating the lessons learned to others in the organization
   B. Measuring the financial gain associated with the improvements
   C. Implementing methods to maintain the improvements
   D. All the above

4. **In comparing a preventative approach to process control with a plan that places higher emphasis on the detection of process errors,**
   A. detection is the preferred approach because it will always prevent customers from experiencing the error.
   B. prevention is always the preferred approach regardless of cost.
   C. the choice between prevention and detection should be based on the cost to implement the preventive action versus the cost to implement the detection scheme.
   D. the choice between prevention and detection should be based on the total costs, including the costs to implement and the longer-term costs, such as the costs of correction and process disruption.

5. **Engineering process control is a method to**
   A. stabilize a process by detecting process shifts.
   B. manipulate process inputs to control process output.
   C. correct for process autocorrelation using algorithmic logic.
   D. All the above are true.

6. **Statistical process control is a method to**

    A. stabilize a process by detecting process shifts.
    B. manipulate process inputs to control process output.
    C. correct for process autocorrelation using algorithmic logic.
    D. All the above are true.

7. **When considering operational procedures as a method of process control,**

    A. human error must be considered as a possible cause for lack of control.
    B. they can be considered as repeatable as automated controls.
    C. they should be considered only if the organization is ISO certified.
    D. All the above are true.

8. **Training plans**

    A. are often useful but not necessary.
    B. should be developed solely by the training department.
    C. need to consider the objectives of the organization.
    D. All the above are true.

9. **When evaluating a training session,**

    A. initial reactions are most important.
    B. initial reactions are useful, but long-term behavioral changes and results aligned with the objectives are most important.
    C. behavioral changes provide the best estimate of effective training.
    D. testing or exams to quantify the learning of each student are often not helpful.

10. **After a training session has been completed, the best way to reinforce the training is**

    A. to provide opportunities to use the new tools or techniques.
    B. through financial incentives.
    C. with examinations.
    D. with strict supervision of the employees and punishment for failing to use the techniques correctly or consistently.

Part 3

Six Sigma Tools

Affinity Diagrams

Affinity diagrams are used to take a chaotic jumble of thoughts and ideas and sort them into coherent groupings. They help you to see all aspects of a problem and to figure out how these aspects are related. This method highlights trends and patterns that otherwise might have gone unrecognized. From there, you can begin to address problems meaningfully rather than as a scattered collection of unrelated issues.

When to Use

The affinity diagram often will be your first step in a problem-solving process. Use it when you have a large number of thoughts, ideas, or facts that are not organized in any coherent manner. It is also very useful when traditional solutions to a problem have failed, and you need to find new ways to approach the problem and build consensus.

Define Stage to Control Stage

- To reach consensus on issues affecting team or project success, such as the project's objectives, scope, or data-collection strategy
- To understand perceptions of current problems and their root causes and then to categorize to focus the project's data collection

189

An affinity can be used anywhere you are trying to generate ideas and reduce those ideas to a few manageable issues.

Methodology

Start with a general problem or issue that needs to be addressed. State this as the problem, objective, or goal in a simple phrase, such as, "Develop a successful Six Sigma program," as shown in Figure F.1.

Have each team member write down one to three issues that contribute to the problem or prevent you from meeting the objective. Challenge team members to think of different issues that affect the problem or other problems that feed into it. Remember that this is a brainstorming process, which means that every idea, even the seemingly ludicrous, should be included, and criticism is not allowed. The emphasis here is on getting as many ideas out as possible. Include both general ideas and nitpicky items. This all-inclusive method can lead to the discovery of problems that may not have been mentioned otherwise. Each idea should be written down (exactly as it was suggested) onto a separate card (Post-it notes are sometimes used), represented in Figure F.1 in the lowest (rightmost) level by the software.

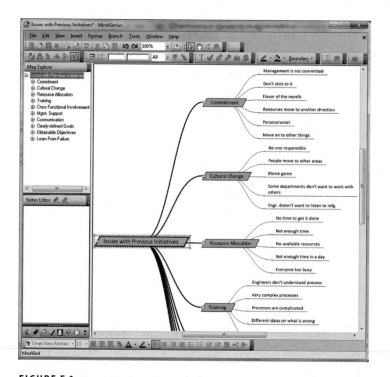

FIGURE F.1 Example of an affinity diagram showing groupings of issues using Green Belt XL/MindGenius software.

Once all the ideas are assembled, you can begin to sort them into categories of similar issues. As you might expect, it's not uncommon for there to be near replication of some of the ideas by team members because each team member is individually constructing the ideas. It's also common for some disagreement to occur in the grouping process. Because this is still a creative process, it's helpful to have team members individually group the issue cards in silence. As others disagree with the groupings, allow them to change the groupings as they see fit. As one member moves a card into a particular grouping, which is yet unnamed, another member might challenge that and silently move the card into another grouping. The lack of verbal communication can force members to silently contemplate the choices of their comembers, a coerced empathy if you will, which can be helpful. Other times, depending on the personalities involved, it may become necessary to allow verbal communication to facilitate the grouping process.

Create header cards to describe each group. Discussion can be helpful here to generate an accurate label for the grouped ideas. These group labels then become the focal point for further analysis or discussion, perhaps as input to the prioritization matrix or nominal group technique, discussed below.

Affinity Diagram

Excel

Using Green Belt XL Add-On

Open a new file in the MindGenius application.

Enter the issue as the *Map Title* in the initial dialog. Use the "OK" button to start the new branch.

With this main branch selected, simply type each new idea into the *Add Branch* dialog, and then select the "OK" button to place the idea into the *Map Editor* (drawing surface).

Once all ideas have been entered, category cards can be created, initially labeled generically as "Category 1," "Category 2," etc.

Participants then can drag and drop individual idea cards into each category branch.

Once grouped, select each category title to edit the label for each category.

Use the *Format\Map Layouts\More Layouts* option to achieve the layout in Figure F.1.

Interpretation

The end result of the affinity process is a collection of problems grouped by main ideas. These main ideas, represented by the header cards, may provide key drivers that need to be addressed for achievement of the goal.

It's important to remember that the affinity diagram uses only subjective opinions of issues. As with any of these types of tools, we can use the tool to gain focus, but we then must substantiate these ideas with objective evidence using properly analyzed data.

These issues may be further developed in other tools, such as a prioritization matrix.

ANOVA

ANOVA, the acronym for the *analysis of variance*, is a tabular presentation of the sum-of-squares (SS) variance attributed to a source, the sum of squares attributed to error, and the total sum of squares from the data. *F* statistics on the significance of the source relative to the error are included.

When to Use

Measure Stage

- To isolate sources of measurement error, particularly when Repeatability and Reproducibility (R&R) studies cannot be done (such as in destructive testing).

Analyze Stage

- To look for differences between subsets of data as a source of variation in a process
- To investigate statistical significance of a regression model to uncover potential process drivers

Methodology

ANOVA provides a means of comparing the variation within each subset of data to the variation between the different subsets of data. The between-subset variation is a reflection of the possible differences between the subset averages. The within-subset variation, for each subset, is a reflection of the inherent variation observed when sampling from the subset repeatedly.

When used to test for differences in the averages between subsets of data (or treatments), the null hypothesis tested by ANOVA (for a fixed-effects model) is that all the subset averages are equal. The F statistic is used to compare the mean square treatment (the average between-subset variation) with the mean square error (the sum of squares of the residuals). The assumptions in the test are that the distribution for each subset is normal and that the subsets have equal variance (although their means may be different). The null hypothesis that the subsets are equal is rejected when the p value for the F test is less than 0.05, implying that at least one of the subset averages is different.

For example, using the data in the Table T.1, we can use single-factor ANOVA (where the factor is the product type) to test whether the cycle times shown for the four product types are equal.

TABLE T.1 Example Single-Factor Cycle Time Data for ANOVA

Product A	Product B	Product C	Product D
159	180	167	174
161	174	163	182
164	180	160	171
166	184	165	176
158	177	161	179
162	178	158	175

ANOVA: One-Factor

Minitab

Menu: Stat\ANOVA\One-way or *Stat\ANOVA\One-way Unstacked* depending on data format.(*Note:* Data shown in the example table are in unstacked format).

Example Result

One-way ANOVA: Product A, Product B, Product C, Product D

Source	DF	SS	MS	F	P
Factor	3	1464.2	488.1	42.01	0.000
Error	20	232.3	11.6		
Total	23	1696.5			

S = 3.408 R-Sq = 86.31% R-Sq(adj) = 84.25%   *(Continued)*

Individual 95% Confidence Intervals (CIs) for Mean Based on Pooled Standard Deviation (SD)

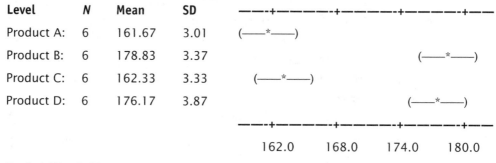

Level	N	Mean	SD
Product A:	6	161.67	3.01
Product B:	6	178.83	3.37
Product C:	6	162.33	3.33
Product D:	6	176.17	3.87

Pooled SD = 3.41

Excel

Menu: *Data\Data Analysis\ANOVA: Single Factor;* example is grouped by columns.

Result

SUMMARY

Group	Count	Sum	Average	Variance
Product A	6	970	161.6667	9.066667
Product B	6	1073	178.8333	11.36667
Product C	6	974	162.3333	11.06667
Product D	6	1057	176.1667	14.96667

ANOVA

Source of variation	SS	df	MS	F	p Value	F crit
Between groups	1464.167	3	488.0556	42.01339	8.03E – 09	3.098393
Within groups	232.3333	20	11.61667			
Total	1696.5	23				

Interpretation

The low p value indicates that the null hypothesis of equal means should be rejected: One or more of the product averages are significantly different. The confidence intervals are shown in the Minitab results for each of the products. The asterisk denotes the mean value; the parenthesis indicates the 95% confidence interval about the mean. The results indicate that the mean of product A falls within the expected range of averages for product C, and vice versa. Similarly, the mean of product B falls within the expected range of the product D average but not within the expected means of products A or C.

Autocorrelation Charts

The *autocorrelation function* (ACF) is a tool for identifying dependence of current data on previous data points. It tests for correlation (in this case, autocorrelation) between observations of a given characteristic in the data set. You may notice a similarity between the formulas used for the ACF and the correlation index calculated in the scatter diagram. The scatter diagram is used to test for correlation between observations of different characteristics, whereas the ACF tests for correlation between observations of the same characteristic.

When to Use

Measure Stage

- To investigate process autocorrelation and its effect on baseline data

Analyze Stage

- To analyze regression residuals for violation of independence assumption

Control Stage

- To develop a control strategy that considers the serial dependence of the process

Standard control charts require that observations from the process are independent of one another. Failure to meet this requirement increases the chance that the control chart will falsely indicate a process shift. Therefore, the autocorrelation function is a good tool to use to check the independence assumption. If control limits on an $\bar{X}$ chart are particularly tight, with many out-of-control points, autocorrelation should be suspected.

Many of the statistical tools, including regression, ANOVA, and general hypothesis tests, assume independence of the data observations. Failure to satisfy this assumption may result in increased type I and type II errors. Autocorrelation is inherent to many processes, including

- *Chemical processes.* Here, autocorrelation occurs because of the inertia of large batches, the continuous flow of material, and/or feedback and feed-forward process control systems.

- *Service processes.* As described in queuing theory, wait times for customers are often influenced by the wait time of previous customers.

- *Manufacturing processes.* Here, autocorrelation occurs because of computer control of production equipment and downstream pooling of multiple-stream processes.

Methodology

The ACF will first test whether adjacent observations are autocorrelated, that is, whether there is correlation between observations 1 and 2, 2 and 3, 3 and 4, and so on. This is known as *lag 1 autocorrelation* because one of the pairs of tested observations lags the other by one period or sample. Similarly, it will test at other lags. For instance, the autocorrelation at lag 4 tests, whether observations 1 and 5, 2 and 6, . . . , 19 and 23, and so on, are correlated.

In general, we should test for autocorrelation at lag 1 to lag $n/4$, where n is the total number of observations in the analysis. Estimates of longer lags have been shown to be statistically unreliable (Box and Jenkins, 1970).

Autocorrelation Function

The autocorrelation function is estimated at the given lag (w) as follows:

$$r_m = \frac{\sum_{i=1}^{n-m}(X_i - \bar{X})(X_{i+m} - \bar{X})}{\sum_{i=1}^{n}(X_i - \bar{X})^2}$$

for $m = 2, 3, 4, \ldots, n/4$, where n is the number of observations, and $\bar{X}$ is the average of the observations.

Partial Autocorrelation Function

The partial autocorrelation function (PACF) is estimated at the given lag (m) as follows:

$$\Phi_{mm} = \frac{r_m - \sum_{j=1}^{n-m} \Phi_{m-1,j} r_{m-1}}{1 - \sum_{j=1}^{m-1} \Phi_{m-1,j} r_j}$$

where r_m is the autocorrelation function.

Significance limit. The significance limit for the ACF (and the PACF) are calculated at the stated significance level, if the true population ACF (or PACF) is zero. ACFs (or PACFs) exceeding this value should be investigated and assumed to be nonzero:

$$r, \Phi = \pm \left(\frac{k}{\sqrt{n}} \right)$$

where k is the ordinate of the normal distribution at the stated significance level (determined using Appendix 1), and n is the number of observations included in the analysis.

Autocorrelation Chart

Minitab

Use *Stat\Time Series\Autocorrelation.*

Use the "Select" button to enter the data column label into the *Series* field.

Excel

Using Gree Belt XL Add-On

Use *New Chart\Autocorrelation Chart.*

Enter the data's cell references (e.g., $A\$2:\$A\$102) into the *Data Range* (step 2) dialog box.

Interpretation

If the autocorrelation is significant only at low lags (adjacent data points), you can increase the time between acquiring data points to lessen its effect. The data analyzed in the autocorrelation plot shown in Figure F.2A was sampled from a chemical process at the rate of one observation per minute. The autocorrelation is significant out to lag 5, implying that revising the sampling rate to once every five minutes (or longer) will result in an independent data set.

Autocorrelation also may be due to sampling from multiple streams in a process. For example, when order processing times are monitored, if each data point is the time taken by each of three employees operating at a different average level, then an autocorrelation would appear at lag 3, as shown in Figure F.2B.

In some cases, the effect of autocorrelation at smaller lags will influence the estimate of autocorrelation at longer lags. For instance, a strong lag 1 autocorrelation would cause observation 5 to influence observation 6 and observation

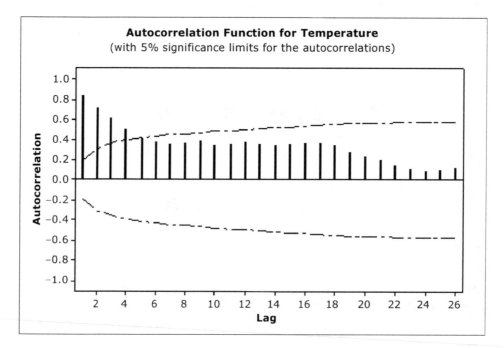

FIGURE F.2A Example of significant autocorrelation out to lag 5.

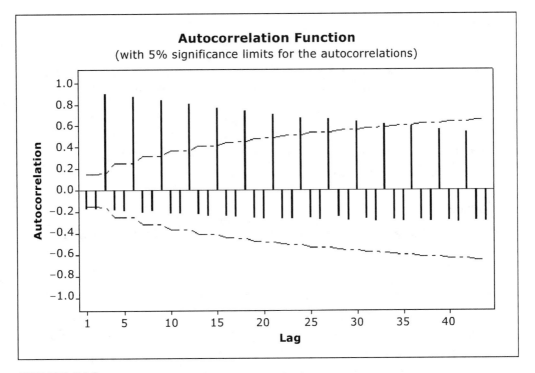

FIGURE F.2*B* Example of autocorrelation owing to mixed process streams.

6 to influence 7. This results in an apparent correlation between observations 5 and 7, even though no direct correlation exists. The partial autocorrelation function (PACF) removes the effect of shorter lag autocorrelation from the correlation estimate at longer lags. This estimate is valid only to one decimal place.

ACFs and PACFs each vary between ±1. Values closer to ±1 indicate strong correlation. Lags exceeding the confidence limits imply autocorrelation significantly different from zero.

Box-Whisker Chart

A *box-whisker chart* is a graphic tool used to compare summary data for multiple data sets. Each data set may be a unique characteristic, data unique to a given condition, or any other useful category.

When to Use

In any application, box-whisker charts are *not* control charts because they do not have statistical control limits. For this reason, they may not be used to establish statistical control of a process or to baseline a process.

Analyze Stage

- To graphically compare the location and variation of various processes or categories of products or services

Improve Stage

- To graphically compare before and after states of process improvement

Methodology

Figure F.3 of a box-whisker chart shows how cycle time varies with product. The cycle time data for each product are displayed in a box whose upper and lower edges are determined by the first and third quartiles of the data. (A quartile is 25 percent of the data, so the third quartile is at 75 percent.)

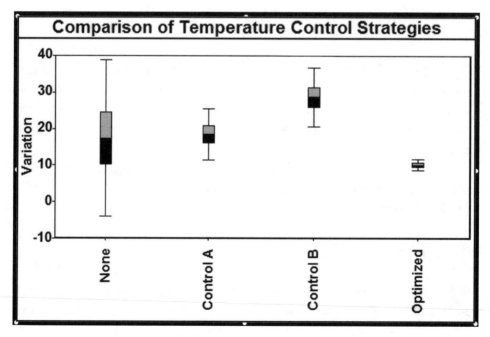

FIGURE F.3 Example of box-whisker chart.

Protruding up and down from each box are "whiskers," the lengths of which are defined by the following formula:

$$\text{Lower limit} = Q1 - 1.5 \times (Q3 - Q1)$$

$$\text{Upper limit} = Q3 + 1.5 \times (Q3 - Q1)$$

Note that quartiles typically are used because they are nonparametric (not dependent on the distribution of the data). If normality can be assumed, the box-whisker plot instead may use the mean and standard deviation (SD) to define the box and whisker lengths: the edges of the box defined at ±1 sample SDs with the whiskers extending to ±3 sample SDs.

Extreme values also may be shown, usually as dots beyond the whiskers.

Box-Whisker Chart

Minitab

Use *Stat\EDA\Boxplot* (use the *Simple* option for the result as shown in the figure).

Excel

Using Green Belt XL Add-On

Use *New Chart\Box Whisker Chart* (use *Each Column will create a Box-Whisker* option for the ANOVA data shown in Table T.1).

Interpretation

The analysis shown in Figure F.3 might be useful to understand the differences in process variation observed when each of four control strategies are employed for a given process. Categorizing the data in this way sometimes can be a good starting point for understanding the process dynamics and converging on suitable metrics.

Since this is an enumerative statistical tool, care should be taken in interpretation. Unless statistical control of the underlying process is established, the statistics presented on the box-whisker chart may not be reflective of the expected process outcome.

C Chart

The C *chart* is one of a set of control charts specifically designed for attributes data. It monitors the number of times a condition occurs relative to a constant sample size when each sample can have more than one instance of the condition. For example, a specified number of transactions each month can be sampled from all the transactions that occurred. From each sample, you can track the total number of errors in the sample on the C chart.

When to Use

Measure Stage

- To estimate, using attributes data, the process baseline (Generally, we would greatly prefer the use of variables control charts for this purpose.)

Improve Stage

- Since the number of errors tends to be quite small (even for very large samples), the use of attribute charts is limited in the improve stage.

Methodology

Samples are collected from the process at specific points each time. Each sample (at each point in time) has the same number of units, each of which may have one or more errors.

Plotted statistic: The count of occurrences of a criterion of interest in a sample of items

Centerline:

$$\bar{c} = \frac{\sum_{j=1}^{m} (\text{count})_j}{m}$$

where *m* is the number of groups included in the analysis. UCL and LCL are the upper and lower control limits:

$$UCL = \bar{c} + 3\sqrt{\bar{c}}$$
$$LCL = \max(0, \bar{c} - 3\sqrt{\bar{c}})$$

where *n* is the sample size and $\bar{c}$ is the average count.

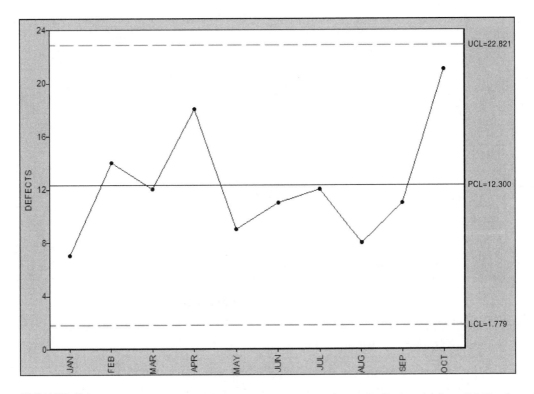

FIGURE F.4 Example of C chart for a controlled process. (*Created using Quality America Green Belt XL software.*)

For example, we observe 500 telemarketing calls each week, and we record the total number of errors in each call, where each call may have more than one error. Ten months of data were observed, with the following number of errors in each sample: 7, 14, 12, 18, 9, 11, 12, 8, 11, and 21. The control chart is shown in Figure F.4.

C Chart

Minitab
Use *Stat\Control Chart\Attribute Charts\C*.

Options:
Use *Options\Display* to specify plotted subgroups.

Use *Scale\Time\Stamp* to set the column for *x*-axis labels.

(*Continued*)

Use *Options\Parameters* for predefined centerline and control limits.

Use *Options\Estimate* to omit subgroups from calculations.

Use *Options\Stages* to define control regions.

Use *Options\Test* to apply relevant run-test rules.

Excel

Using Green Belt XL Add-On
Use *New Chart\C Chart*.

Options:
Use *Data Range* to specify plotted subgroups.

Use *Options\Title|Label* to set the column for *x*-axis labels.

Use *Options\Control Limits* for predefined centerline and control limits, to omit subgroups from calculations, and to define control regions.

Use the *Options\Analysis\Auto Drop* checkbox to automatically remove out-of-control groups from the control-limit calculations (they are still displayed on the chart).

Use *Options\Run Test* to apply relevant run-test rules.

Interpretation

The upper and lower control limits indicate the bounds of expected process behavior. The fluctuation of the points between the control limits is due to the variation that is intrinsic (built in) to the process. This variation is due to "common causes" that influence the process. Any points outside the control limits can be attributed to a "special cause," implying a shift in the process. When a process is influenced by only common causes, it is stable and predictable.

If there are any out-of-control points, then special causes of variation must be identified and eliminated. Brainstorm and conduct designed experiments to find the process elements that contribute to sporadic changes in process location. To predict the capability of the process after special causes have been eliminated, remove the out-of-control points from the analysis. This has the effect of removing the statistical bias of the out-of-control points by dropping them from the calculations of the average and control limits.

Note that some statistical process control (SPC) software will allow varying sample sizes for the C chart. In this case, the control limits and the average line will be adjusted for each sample. Many times it is less confusing to use a U chart for these data because only its control limits will vary (the average line will remain constant). See "Statistical Process Control (SPC) Charts" and "Run-Test Rules" for more detail.

Cause-and-Effect Diagram

Cause-and-effect diagrams are graphic brainstorming tools. Listing all the causes for a given effect in a clear, organized way makes it easier to separate out potential problems and target areas for improvement. These charts sometimes are referred to as *fishbone diagrams* because of their form: Causes are listed on lines that branch off from the effect in much the same way a fish's ribs branch from its spine. They are sometimes called *Ishakawa diagrams* in reference to a Japanese engineer who popularized their use for quality improvement.

When to Use

Analyze Stage

- To brainstorm potential underlying process factors that can be investigated in a designed experiment

Improve Stage

- To generate a list of potential failure modes that should be addressed in the solution

Methodology

Begin by brainstorming the potential relationships between the process and the outcome. The outcome, or effect, typically is stated in terms of a problem rather than a desired condition, which tends to help the brainstorming.

The major branches of the fishbone are chosen to assist in brainstorming or to categorize the potential problems afterwards. You may find it convenient to use the 5M's and E (manpower, machines, methods, material, measurement, and environment) or the 4P's (policy, procedures, plant, and people) to either categorize on the final fishbone or ensure that all areas are considered during brainstorming. Categorizing the potential causes (as branches off the spine) can

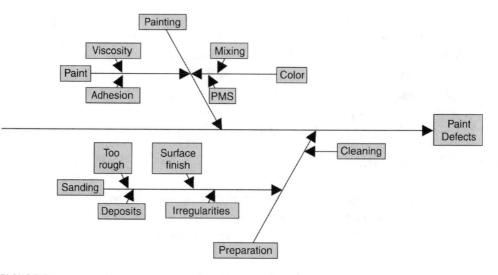

FIGURE F.5 Example of a cause-and-effect diagram.

be helpful in the data collection or analysis. Subcauses (or branches) are added as needed, and it's often helpful to go down several levels of subcauses. See Figure F.5.

Bear in mind that the causes listed are *potential* causes because there are no data at this point to support whether any of the causes really contribute to the problem. In this regard, as in all brainstorming activities, avoid judging the merits of each cause as it is offered. Only data can lead to such a judgment.

Interpretation

Use the cause-and-effect diagram to ensure that suitable potential causes are included in the data collection and analysis. If a large majority of causes are contained in a small number of categories, consider recategorizing to break down the larger categories.

Confidence Interval on Mean

Given a sample from a population, the *confidence interval about the true value of the mean* can be estimated at a given confidence level. A *confidence interval* is a tool of statistical inference, where we use sample statistics (such as a sample average $\bar{X}$ or a sample standard deviation s) to infer properties of a population (such as its mean μ or standard deviation σ).

When to Use

A key assumption is that the population has a normal distribution and is both constant (it does not change over time) and homogeneous (a given sample is representative of the sample as a whole).

Measure Stage

- To estimate process average (for baseline estimates) when insufficient data exist to establish process control

Analyze Stage

- To compare the mean of samples from different process conditions

Methodology

Two methods may be used depending on whether you have historical evidence of the population standard deviation.

Historical Standard Deviation Is Known

Calculate an average $\bar{X}$ of n sample units.
Calculate the confidence interval as

$$\bar{X} - Z_{\alpha/2}(\sigma / \sqrt{n}) < \mu < \bar{X} + Z_{\alpha/2}(\sigma / \sqrt{n})$$

Based on the assumption that the samples are from a population with a normal distribution, we use the normal distribution to determine the z values based on a confidence level. For a 95% confidence level, $\alpha = 0.05$, so for this two-sided confidence interval (above and below the mean), the significance α is split equally between the two sides of the interval. For $\alpha/2 = 0.025$, we obtain a value of $z_{\alpha/2} = 1.96$ from Appendix 1.

For example, the average waiting time in a doctor's office using a sample of 25 patients is 25.7 minutes. The population standard deviation is known to be 1.8 minutes. The confidence interval is calculated as

$$\bar{X} + Z_{\alpha/2}(\sigma / \sqrt{n}) < \mu < \bar{X} + Z_{1-\alpha/2}(\sigma / \sqrt{n})$$
$$25.7 + (-1.96)(1.8 / \sqrt{25}) < \mu < 25.7 + 1.96(1.8 / \sqrt{25})$$
$$24.99 < \mu < 26.41$$

Confidence Interval on Mean

Standard Deviation Known

Minitab

Menu: *Stat\Basic Stats\1 Sample z*

"Options" button: Set *Confidence Level* and alternative *Not Equal* (two-sided case) or > or < (for one-sided cases).

Two-Sided Example at 95% Confidence

One-Sample Z

The assumed standard deviation = 1.8.

N	Mean	SE Mean	95% CI
25	25.700	0.360	(24.994, 26.406)

One-Sided Example at 95% Confidence (Using Alternative greater than)

One-Sample Z

The assumed standard deviation = 1.8.

95% Lower

N	Mean	SE Mean	Bound
25	25.700	0.360	25.108

Excel

Calculate in cell using calculated values of $\bar{X}$, s, and n with the CONFIDENCE function (*Note:* Excel's CONFIDENCE function assumes a two-sided case and interprets entered α as $\alpha/2$).

$$\text{Upper} = \bar{X} + \text{CONFIDENCE}(\alpha, s, n)$$

$$\text{Lower} = \bar{X} - \text{CONFIDENCE}(\alpha, s, n)$$

Two-Sided Example at 95% Confidence

Upper (results in calculated value of 26.406) = 25.7 + CONFIDENCE(0.05, 1.8, 25)

Lower (results in calculated value of 24.994) = 25.7 − CONFIDENCE(0.05, 1.8, 25)

One-Sided Example at 95% Confidence

Lower (results in calculated value of 25.108) = 25.7 − CONFIDENCE(0.10, 1.8, 25)

Historical Standard Deviation Is Not Known

Calculate an average ($\bar{X}$) and the sample standard deviation s of n sample units.

Calculate the confidence interval as

$$\bar{X} - t_{\alpha/2, n-1}(s / \sqrt{n}) < \mu < \bar{X} + t_{\alpha/2, n-1}(s / \sqrt{n})$$

Based on the assumption that the samples are from a population with a normal distribution, we use the Student's t distribution to determine the t values based on a confidence level. For a 95% confidence level, $\alpha = 0.05$, so $\alpha/2 = 0.025$.

For example, the average waiting time in a doctor's office using a sample of 25 patients is 25.7 minutes. The sample standard deviation is calculated as 1.8 minutes. From Appendix 2, $t_{0.025,24} = 2.064$. The confidence interval is calculated as

$$\bar{X} - t_{\alpha/2, n-1}(s / \sqrt{n}) < \mu < \bar{X} + t_{\alpha/2, n-1}(s / \sqrt{n})$$

$$25.7 - 2.064(1.8 / \sqrt{25}) < \mu < 25.7 + 2.064(1.8 / \sqrt{25})$$

$$24.96 < \mu < 26.44$$

Both Excel and Minitab offer confidence interval calculations. Minitab requires the raw data. In Excel, you can use its other functions to calculate the required input parameters when using raw data.

Confidence Interval on Mean

Standard Deviation Unknown

Minitab

Menu: *Stat\Basic Stats\1 Sample t*

"Options" button: Set *Confidence Level* and alternative *Not Equal* (two-sided case) or > or < (for one-sided cases).

Two-Sided Example at 95% Confidence

One-Sample T

N	Mean	SD	SE Mean	95% CI
25	25.700	1.800	0.360	(24.957, 26.443)

One-Sided Example at 95% Confidence (Using Alternative greater than)

One-Sample T

95% Lower

N	Mean	SD	SE Mean	Bound
25	25.700	1.800	0.360	25.084

Excel

Calculate in cell using calculated values of $\bar{X}$, s, and n with the TINV function. (*Note:* Excel's TINV function assumes a two-sided case and interprets entered α as $\alpha/2$).

$$\text{Upper} = \bar{X} + \text{TINV}(\alpha, n-1) \times s/\text{SQRT}(n)$$

$$\text{Lower} = \bar{X} - \text{TINV}(\alpha, n-1) \times s/\text{SQRT}(n)$$

Two-Sided Example at 95% Confidence

Upper (results in calculated value of 26.443) = 25.7 + TINV(0.05, 24) × 1.8/SQRT(25)

Lower (results in calculated value of 24.957) = 25.7 − TINV(0.05, 24) × 1.8/SQRT(25)

One-Sided Example at 95% Confidence

Lower (results in calculated value of 25.084) = $25.7 - \text{TINV}(0.1, 24) \times 1.8/\text{SQRT}(25)$

Interpretation

A 95% confidence limit on the mean, for example, indicates that in 95 percent of the samples, the confidence interval will include the true population mean μ (pronounced "mu"). A true value of the population mean so large (or small) so as to fall outside the confidence interval is likely to happen only 5 percent of the time. We see from the calculation that as the number of samples n increases, the confidence interval gets smaller. That is, we have more confidence in the value of the true mean when we take a larger sample.

Notice that the confidence interval when σ is unknown (using the t tables) is wider than when σ is known (using the z tables) because we lose some statistical confidence when we estimate the standard deviation. An additional parameter of the Student's t distribution is the degrees of freedom v (pronounced "nu"), which equals $n - 1$. Statistically, we say that we have lost a degree of freedom in estimating the standard deviation using the sample data.

A given sample lying within the confidence interval does *not* provide evidence of process stability, which must be verified with an SPC chart. Confidence intervals are applicable only to static populations and not to processes.

Confidence Interval on Proportion

When we sample from a population and have historical evidence of the population standard deviation, we can estimate the confidence interval of the mean at a given confidence level. A *confidence interval* is a tool of statistical inference, where we use sample statistics (such as a sample average $\bar{X}$ or a sample standard deviation s) to infer properties of a population (such as its mean μ or standard deviation σ).

When to Use

A key assumption is that the population has a normal distribution and is both constant (it does not change over time) and homogeneous (a given sample is representative of the sample as a whole). The normal distribution provides a good approximation to the binomial distribution when the sample size is large and when np and $n(1 - p)$ are both greater than 5.

Measure Stage

- To estimate process average error rate (for baseline estimates) when insufficient data exist to establish process control

Analyze Stage

- To compare error rates of samples from different process conditions

Methodology

Calculate an average error rate $\hat{p}$ of n sample units.
Calculate the confidence interval as

$$\hat{p} - Z_{\alpha/2}\sqrt{\frac{\hat{p}(1 - \hat{p})}{n}} \leq p \leq \hat{p} + Z_{\alpha/2}\sqrt{\frac{\hat{p}(1 - \hat{p})}{n}}$$

Based on the assumption that the samples are from a population with a normal distribution, we use the normal distribution to determine the z values based on a confidence level. For a 95% confidence level, $\alpha = 0.05$, so $\alpha/2 = 0.025$. From Appendix 1, $z_{\alpha/2} = 1.96$.

For example, there were 14,248 orders processed during the third week of June. A sample of 100 orders processed during that week was randomly selected. Twenty-four orders in the sample were found to have one or more critical defects. The confidence interval is calculated as

$$\bar{p} + Z_{\alpha/2}\sqrt{\frac{\bar{p}(1 - \bar{p})}{n}} \leq p \leq \bar{p} + Z_{1-\alpha/2}\sqrt{\frac{\bar{p}(1 - \bar{p})}{n}}$$

$$0.24 + (-1.96)\sqrt{\frac{0.24 \times 0.76}{100}} \leq p \leq 0.24 + 1.96\sqrt{\frac{0.24 \times 0.76}{100}}$$

$$0.16 \leq p \leq 0.34$$

Confidence Interval on Proportion

Minitab

Menu: Stat\Basic Stats\1 Proportion

"Options" button: Set *Confidence Level* and alternative *Not Equal* (two-sided case) or > or < (for one-sided cases); by default uses exact method (not normal approximation).

Two-Sided Example at 95% Confidence

Test and CI for One Proportion

Sample	X	N	Sample p	95% CI
1	24	100	0.240000	(0.160225, 0.335735)

One-Sided Example at 95% Confidence (Using Alternative greater than)

Test and CI for One Proportion

				95% Lower
Sample	X	N	Sample p	Bound
1	24	100	0.240000	0.171348

Excel

Using the normal distribution assumption, calculate in cell using $\bar{p}$, s, and n with NORMSINV function, where

$$s = \sqrt{\frac{\bar{p}(1-\bar{p})}{n}}$$

$$\text{Upper} = \bar{p} + \text{NORMSINV}(1 - \alpha/2) \times s$$

$$\text{Lower} = \bar{p} + \text{NORMSINV}(\alpha/2) \times s$$

(Continued)

Two-Sided Example at 95% Confidence

Upper (results in calculated value of 0.324) = 0.24 + NORMSINV(0.975) × SQRT(0.24 × 0.76/100)

Lower (results in calculated value of 0.156) = 0.24 + NORMSINV(0.025) × SQRT(0.24 × 0.76/100)

One-Sided Example at 95% Confidence

Lower (results in calculated value of 0.170) = 25.7 + NORMSINV(0.05) × SQRT(0.24 × 0.76/100)

Interpretation

A 95% confidence limit on the error rate, for example, indicates that in 95 percent of the samples, the confidence interval will include the true error rate. We see from the calculation that as the number of samples n increases, the confidence interval gets smaller. That is, we have more confidence in the value of the true error rate when we take a larger sample.

In the preceding example, how many orders with defects would we expect during the third week of June? An estimate of the number of orders with defects would range from 2,280 (16 percent of 14,248) to 4,559 (32 percent of 14,248).

A given sample lying within the confidence interval does *not* provide evidence of process stability, which must be verified with an SPC chart.

Contingency Tables

Contingency tables, also known as *R × C contingency tables*, refer to data that can be assembled into tables (of rows and columns) for comparison.

When to Use

The statistical test examines whether subsets of populations are independent. For example, we may have five health care plans to choose from and wish to determine if there is a detectable difference between how these different plans are rated by hourly and salaried employees. Similarly, we may be interested to see if there is a difference between how men and women rate three different television shows or whether the repair rate for four machines is different from shift to shift.

Analyze Stage

- To compare results of sampling from different process conditions to detect if they are independent

Methodology

The methodology for analyzing the R rows by C columns involves using the chi-square statistic to compare the observed frequencies with the expected frequencies, assuming independence of the subsets. The null hypothesis is that the p values are equal for each column in each row. The alternative hypothesis is that at least one of the p values is different.

Construct the $R \times C$ table by separating the subsets of the population into the tested categories.

Calculate the expected values for each row-column intersection cell e_{ij}. The expected value for each row/column is found by multiplying the percent of that row by the percent of the column by the total number.

Calculate the test statistic:

$$\chi_0^2 = \sum_{i=1}^{r} \sum_{j=1}^{c} \frac{(o_{ij} - e_{ij})^2}{e_{ij}}$$

For example, consider a survey of 340 males and 160 females asking their preference for one of three television shows. The $R \times C$ contingency table is shown in Table T.2.

TABLE T.2 Example Data Comparing Preferences for Three Shows

Sex	Show 1	Show 2	Show 3	Total
Male	160	140	40	340
Female	40	60	60	160
Totals	200	200	100	500

The expected frequency for male and show 1 = e_{11} = (340/500) × (200/500) × 500 = 136. Similarly, the expected values for the other row/column pairs (e_{RC}) are found as $e_{12} = 136$; $e_{13} = 68$; $e_{21} = 64$; and $e_{22} = 64$; $e_{23} = 32$ (as shown in Table T.3).

The test statistic is calculated as

$$\chi_0^2 = (160 - 136)^2/136 + (140 - 136)^2/136 + (40 - 68)^2/68$$
$$+ (40 - 64)^2/64 + (60 - 64)^2/64 + (60 - 32)^2/32 = 49.6$$

TABLE T.3 Expected Preferences for Each Show Assuming Independence				
Sex	**Show 1**	**Show 2**	**Show 3**	**Total**
Male	136	136	68	340
Female	64	64	32	160
Totals	200	200	100	500

Contingency Table

Minitab

Menu: *Stat\Tables\Chi-Square Test (two-way table)*

Example

Expected counts are printed below observed counts, and chi-square contributions are printed below expected counts.

	Show 1	**Show 2**	**Show 3**	**Total**
1	160	140	40	340
	136.00	136.00	68.00	
	4.235	0.118	11.529	
2	40	60	60	160
	64.00	64.00	32.00	
	9.000	0.250	24.500	
Totals	200	200	100	500

Chi-square = 49.632; df = 2; p value = 0.000.

Excel

CHITEST(a_{ii}, e_{ii}) reports p.

Example

For actual data (excluding labels) in cells B2:D3 and expected data in cells B7:D8, CHITEST(B2:D3, B7:D8) returns a value $p = 0.00$. Since $p < 0.05$, reject the null that the percentages of males and females preferring each show are equal.

Interpretation

We reject the null hypothesis if $X_0^2 > X_\alpha^2$ for $(r-1)(c-1)$ degrees of freedom, where X_α^2 is the chi-square value at the α level of significance.

In the preceding example, the calculated p value from Excel and Minitab is less than 0.05, so the null hypothesis is rejected, and we assert that there is a difference between the male and female responses. Alternatively, the critical value of the chi-square statistic at the 0.05 level of significance, with two degrees of freedom, may be found from Appendix 3 as 5.991. Since the test statistic exceeds the critical value, the null hypothesis is rejected.

Contour Plot

A *contour plot* is made up of curves, each having a constant value of a fitted response. The curves have equally spaced values of the response. Additional factors are set at selected values (usually their mean).

When to Use

Improve Stage

- Use in response surface analysis to determine where a maximum or minimum response is expected within or close to the data range

Methodology

For example, we can generate a contour plot for the model $Y = 4.5 + 0.32x_1 - 0.63x_2$. For any value of the response (Y), we can determine x_1 given x_2 or x_2 given x_1.

When $y = 5$, then $0.32x_1 - 0.63x_2 - 0.5 = 0$. If $x_1 = 0$, then $x_2 = -0.5/0.63 = -0.794$. If $x_2 = 0$, then $x_1 = 0.5/0.32 = 1.56$.

Thus the contour line for $Y = 5$ passes through the points $(0, -0.79)$ and $(1.56, 0)$. We also can easily determine for $Y = 5$ the value of x_2 when $x_1 = +1$ and $x_1 = -1$ and the value of x_1 when $x_2 = +1$ and $x_2 = -1$. In this way, we then calculate other contour lines (for different y values).

Overlaid Contour Plots

Overlaid contour techniques provide a method for evaluating joint regions of optimality for more than one response. In this technique, we lay one contour plot over the other and look for regions that provide good compromise on optimizing both responses. The overlay requires the same factors and scaling on each contour plot.

Contour Plot

Minitab

After analyzing results of a suitable designed experiment, use *Stat\DOE\(design type)\Contour/Surface Plots* or *Stat\DOE\(design type)\Overlaid Contour Plot*.

Setup options: Select the pair of factors used for axes, or choose to create a contour plot for each possible pair. Use the "Settings" button to define the values used for other factors (not displayed on chart axes).

Excel

Construct a table of evenly incremented values of the desired pair of factors, where the first column of the table lists the values for factor A and the first row lists the values for factor B. Calculate the table contents (the row/column cell values) corresponding to each factor A–factor B value combination using the REGRESSION function (determined in the design-of-experiments analysis).

Select the table; then select *Insert\Other Charts\Surface\Contour* to draw the chart.

Interpretation

An example of a first-order model contour plot with interaction is shown in Figure F.6. The interactions produce a curvature in the contours. When there are first-order main effects only, the contour plot will have straight, parallel lines. The response surface will be a flat plane. When interaction terms are present, the contours take on an elliptical shape, and the response surface is a twisted plane.

The direction of the path of steepest ascent or descent is indicated by a line drawn perpendicular to the contour lines.

Because contours can involve only two factors, the appearance of contour plots using different factors can vary widely.

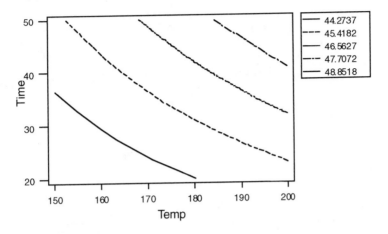

FIGURE F.6 First-order response surface with interaction using Minitab.

The contour plot for the second-order model may look as shown in Figure F.7. Note in this example how the response is a local minimum in the y direction ("PhosAcid") and a local maximum in the x direction ("Nitrogen"), indicating a saddle point.

In Figure F.8, an overlaid contour for yield and cost is shown for temperature

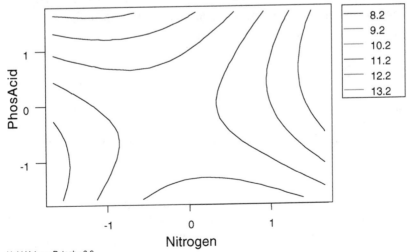

FIGURE F.7 Example of second-order contour plot using Minitab.

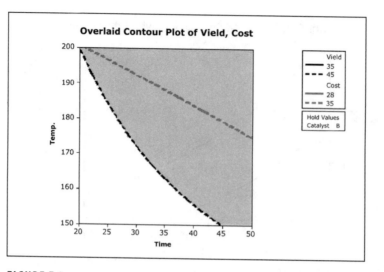

FIGURE F.8 Example of overlaid contour plot using Minitab.

and time when the third factor ("Catalyst") is held at its high condition (B). The area between the two dashed lines indicates the region of joint optimality of the response yield and cost. See also "Response Surface Analysis" below.

Control Plans

A *control plan* provides an overview of the strategies that will be used to ensure that key process or part characteristics are controlled through either detection or prevention strategies or a combination of the two.

When to Use

Control Stage

- To document the strategy for controlling the key process variables

Methodology

Key inputs to a control plan include the results of designed experiments and failure modes and effects analysis (FMEA). FMEA [and its risk priority number (RPN)] determines the failure modes that are the most critical to control. The assumptions used to determine the detection level in the FMEA must be incorporated into the control plan.

For each key characteristic, the following information is defined as shown in Table T.4:

- *Specification.* What is the definition of "good" and "bad" for this characteristic?

- *Measurement technique.* How will the characteristic be measured? The control plan should reference more detailed measurement procedures, where needed, to instruct personnel on the proper use and interpretation of the measurement equipment.

- *Sample size.* How many measurements are required at each point in time?

- *Sample frequency.* How often should a new set of measurements be taken?

- *Analytical tool.* How are the measurements evaluated? In this case, audio alarms are installed to monitor characteristics thought to have high process capability. Other characteristics are monitored via control charts to detect process trends leading to undesirable conditions.

TABLE T.4 Example Control Plan

Characteristic	Specification	Measurement Technique	Sample Size	Sample Frequency	Analytical Tool	Reaction Rules
Finished diameter	1.250 ± 0.0002 in	Johannson	5	1 subgroup/h	$\bar{X}$ chart with run rules	If other characteristics in control, adjust
Local ambient temperature	70 ± 5°F	Thermo-couple	1	Continuous	Alarmed	Stop production; adjust cooling control; resume production once temperature is okay
Cooling temperature	120 ± 5°F	Thermo-couple	1	1 sample/minute	Alarmed	Stop production; adjust cooling control; resume production once temperature is okay
Coolant viscosity	0.88–0.94	Viscometer	1	1 sample/month	$\bar{X}$ chart	Purge system

- *Reaction rules.* What is the proper response to the alarms (audio or from a control chart)? Who should be notified?

Interpretation

See example shown in Table T.4.

Design of Experiments (DOE)

A *designed experiment* consists of planned trials, where factors are set to pre-defined levels, and one or more response variables are measured. Design of experiments (DOE) provides an understanding of the sources of variation contributing to a process.

When to Use

Measure Stage

- To estimate the effect of various conditions or equipment on measurement variation

Analyze Stage

- To determine the process drivers, the sources of variation in a process

Improve Stage

- To optimize a process (using response surface designs)

Methodology

Planning

In planning for a designed experiment, one should consider the following issues:

- Why should an experiment be done?
- What responses should be measured? How will responses be measured?
- What factors and interactions will be investigated? What are suitable levels for each?

- When should the experiment be scheduled so as to minimize disruptions to the process?
- Who should specify/execute the experiment?

The project team and key stakeholders must be committed to the experimental design and its plan. Key team personnel, including the black belt, should be on hand to lead the experiment (although operational personnel will be responsible for running the process). Through monitoring the course of the experiment, it is possible the black belt will observe conditions that lead to a better understanding of process dynamics.

The experimental plan should include projections and allocation of resources, including costs for personnel, materials, and equipment. Do not commit all your resources to one design. A good rule of thumb is to spend no more than 20 percent of your total resources on any one experiment because each successive experiment will provide information that will be confirmed or expanded on in subsequent experiments. The summarized results of each experiment should provide information on what went wrong and what to do next. Critical factors may not have been included or may not have been varied sufficiently, so additional trials may be needed to collect more information.

There are several desirable characteristics of an experimental design:

- It provides distribution of information throughout the region of interest. You may begin the experimental process looking at a wide region and then narrow your focus to a particular region that looks interesting.
- It includes the necessary conditions to develop a model that predicts the response, as close as possible to the true response, at all points within the stated region of interest. This may require three or more levels of particular factors when nonlinear models are required.
- It allows the analyst to detect a lack of fit in the model.
- It may require blocking to meet the limitations of data collection or when you wish to add runs to designs (such as folding).
- It allows sequential buildup of design, such as by folding or added axial points.
- It provides an internal estimate of error variance.

The best, and most common, approach is to begin with an effective *screening design*, which will provide information on key factors and the two-factor interactions between those factors. The design can be improved sequentially with additional trials to acquire additional information.

Defining Responses

The *response* in a designed experiment is the parameter you are observing as the outcome of the experiment. For example, in a manufacturing process, you may be concerned about the density of an injection-molded part. You will change a variety of conditions within the process and measure the resulting part density. In a service process, you may seek to measure the impact of process changes on customer satisfaction or cycle time.

You often can measure more than one response in an experiment. In some cases, the responses are converted or transformed during analysis to simplify the model or to uncover factors that contribute to variation in the response. See also "Transformation" below.

In any event, the most useful responses are quantitative variables rather than qualitative attributes. You need sufficient resolution on the measured variable to use the statistical regression techniques. Before conducting the experiment, you should analyze the measurement system for error in estimating the response using measurement systems analysis (MSA) techniques. When responses are qualitative, you sometimes can convert them to quantitative scores (such as Likert scales). When conversion is not convenient or helpful, logistic regression techniques should be used for analysis.

Defining Factors

The parameters that you vary in the process to achieve changes in the response are known as *factors*. Generally, you will control these factors by setting them at specific levels for each run, or trial, of the experiment. You will run the experiment at various conditions of each of the factors so that the effect of each factor on the response can be calculated. In an injection-molding process, you may want to investigate the effect of changing furnace temperature, fill pressure, and the moisture of the raw materials. Even though you generally cannot set the moisture level of the materials in normal operations, you can sample and segregate the materials into two or more distinct levels for the experiment. Likewise in a service process, you may choose, for the experiment, to test the effect of two different process designs, such as with and without customer follow-up.

The factors that generally are not controlled in your operations are sometimes called *subsidiary factors*. Taguchi referred to these as *noise factors* or the *outer array*. Examples include ambient temperature, humidity, and vibration. As mentioned earlier, it is preferred to control these factors for the experiment.

Factors are selected for the designed experiment by brainstorming among team members. This typically will result in a long list of potential factors. For an effective yet small screening design, you'd like to limit the design to five or seven key factors. Even though this may seem "impossible" for your process, it is often the best practice. If cost and time are of little concern, then add more factors as necessary. However, when cost or time is limited, the number of factors can be reduced using the nominal *group technique* or *prioritization matrix*. Alternatively, you could decide to hold some factors constant, effectively excluding them from the analysis. Factors that are neither held constant nor included are potential *lurking factors*.

Lurking factors may be a source of bias or error in the analysis. Bias causes you to confuse the effect of a factor with that of another factor, particularly if the lurking factor happens to be coincident with another factor. In other cases, it just limits the usefulness of the results, such as if you do not include the effects of communications skills in a customer-support experiment.

You always should randomize the order of the trials to prevent any bias in the estimates. In some cases, however, you cannot fully randomize the experimental trials and, instead, run the experiments in blocks. Examples of *blocking factors* include the day of the week, a batch of material, a run of the furnace, an airline flight, and so on. In each of these cases, you may have multiple run conditions that can be randomized within the block, but these blocking factors cannot be randomized within the entire experiment.

Consider the baking of cookies. You might vary a number of parameters, such as the ingredients (margarine versus butter, chocolate chips versus M&M's), the cooking temperature, and the cooking time. While the ingredients can be varied within each batch, the time or temperature within a batch cannot be varied. In this case, time and temperature are coincident with the batch and thus are blocking factors.

In other cases, you cannot run all the sample combinations within a given batch simply because the limited size of a batch (e.g., the size of the oven) permits only so many factor combinations. In this case, the batch itself becomes a blocking factor. The differences you see between the factor combinations in batch 1 and batch 2 may be due to the factor effects or to the batch-to-batch variation.

If you have a strong suspicion that the blocking factor would interact with another factor, you might be able to include it as a main factor. In the cookie baking example, you could treat each oven cycle as a single run of the experiment and vary the temperature, time, and ingredients for each oven cycle. In this way, you could estimate interactions among temperature, time, and ingredients.

There are other factors, sometimes called *casual factors*, that may have an impact on your experimental response, such as temperature, humidity, time of day, and so on. If you think that these factors are truly important, you should make them controllable factors for the experiment. If you can't, or you choose not to because it would increase the size or cost of the experiment, you should at least measure them. You then can estimate if they are correlated with the response, which would suggest the need for additional experimental runs to analyze their effect.

Defining Factor Levels

For each factor, you must define specific levels at which to run the experimental conditions.

Factors may be either quantitative (measured) or qualitative (categorical). The qualitative factor categories are converted to coded units (such as -1 and $+1$) for regression analysis.

Qualitative factor levels may be inherent to the process or product under investigation. For example, you may have three product configurations, or you may be interested in the variation among four machining centers.

For quantitative factors, if you expect the response to be nonlinear with respect to the factor, you need at least three levels for that factor. Nonlinear effects are not addressed in initial experiments but instead are left until you can optimize in the improve stage. Earlier experiments will be used to screen out insignificant factors, which can be done with only two levels per factor. Bear in mind that more levels lead to more experimental runs. In addition, software used for generating designs may limit the design choices when there are mixed levels for the factors.

When you define the levels for each factor, you want to span the region of interest. It's helpful to think of the expected variation you are likely to see for the factor during normal operations, but sometimes this results in factor levels being too close to measure an effect. For example, if you think that temperature typically only varies from 70 to 80 degrees, you may not see much of an effect owing to temperature over that 10-degree difference. It's usually better to think of "worse-case scenarios," where the factor may vary considerably more. Generally, the wider the difference between the factor levels, the easier the effect will be to measure.

When you start moving far away from normal operating conditions, you can enter unknown terrain that even can be hazardous for some processes. In this case, it might be better to keep the factor levels at reasonable values and, if the factor is significant, perform additional experiments using the response surface or evolutionary operation techniques to find optimal factor levels.

Conducting the Experiment

When it comes time to implement the experimental design, some helpful guidelines include

- *Be there!* It's important to be an active participant in the design. The data collection is a critical part of the learning process, offering opportunities to experience aspects of the process dynamics that may not have been discussed in problem solving. For this reason, and to limit potential bias in the data, process personnel should run the process and collect the data.
- *Randomize trials.* The order of the experimental runs should be randomized across the entire design and within blocks (if blocking factors are used). This randomization limits any potential bias introduced during the experiment.
- *Independence of runs.* When each condition is run, the process should not be influenced by prior conditions. Some processes will require their setup conditions to be torn down and reset.

For specific methods of constructing designs, see "Factorial Designs" and "Central Composite Design" in the Glossary.

Interpretation

Analysis of the experiment includes many tools discussed elsewhere in Part 3. See "Regression Analysis" as a starting point.

When an experiment is run in blocks, the design isolates the effect of the blocking factor so that its contribution to an ANOVA may be estimated. As a result of this design, interaction effects cannot be estimated between the blocking factor and any of the main factors. In the regression analysis, if the blocking factor is significant, its interactions with the significant main factors can be investigated with additional runs.

Distributions

When process and population data are fit by assumed *distributions*, broad predictions can be made with minimal data. Popular statistical distributions include the binomial and Poisson distributions for discrete (count) data and the normal, exponential, and robust Johnson and Pearson distributions for continuous (measurement) data.

When to Use

Measure to Control Stages

- To estimate properties of an existing or potential process or population, including its failure rate or sigma level
- To generate random data for process modeling

Binomial Distribution

The binomial distribution is used to estimate the number of units meeting one of two possible conditions in a process or population. For example, if the population is the total number of orders shipped in July, the condition of interest might be the number of units shipped on time. Since there is only one other possible condition (the order is not shipped on time), the binomial distribution is appropriate for modeling the number of units shipped on time. It may be applied when the number of samples is fixed and trials are independent with equal probability of success.

Binomial Distributions

Minitab

Use *Calc\Random Data\Binomial* to generate random numbers using a fixed sample size and *p* value.

Excel

Use *Data\Data Analysis\Random Number Generation*.

Set *Distribution = Binomial* using a fixed sample size and *p* value.

Poisson Distribution

The Poisson distribution is used to estimate the number of times a condition occurs in a process or population, where the condition may occur multiple times in a given sample unit. For example, if the population is the total number of orders shipped in July, the condition of interest might be the number of errors on the invoices. Note how this is different from the binomial estimate of the process error rate because each invoice can have more than one error. When counting the number of occurrences within each sample unit, the Poisson distribution is appropriate for modeling the total number of occurrences. Each trial is independent of others, and the data are positive integers.

Poisson Distributions

Minitab

Use *Calc\Random Data\Poisson* to generate random numbers using a fixed λ (lambda) value (equal to the mean and standard deviation).

Excel

Use *Data\Data Analysis\Random Number Generation.*

Set *Distribution = Poisson* using a fixed λ value (equal to the mean and standard deviation).

Exponential Distribution

Used for highly skewed measurement (continuous) data, such as the time between occurrences of a condition of interest, the exponential distribution is often used to estimate the mean time between failures, which is a convenient statistic when process failures are well modeled by the Poisson distribution. The exponential distribution is suited for processes with a constant failure rate.

Exponential Distributions

Minitab

Use *Calc\Random Data\Exponential* to generate random numbers.

Use *Stat\Quality Tools\Individual Distribution Identification* to test whether sample data meet the *Exponential* distribution. Use goodness-of-fit tests (described below) to determine if an assumed distribution provides a reasonable approximation.

Excel

To generate a set of randomly distributed exponential data, use *Data\Data Analysis\Random Number Generation*.

Set *Distribution = Uniform*, and then transform the data to an exponential distribution using the formula M*(–LN(UNIFORM)), where M is the average of the exponential distribution to be constructed, and UNIFORM refers to a value in the uniform distribution. For example, if the uniform distributed data are in cells A2:A1000, to create an exponential distribution whose mean equals 20, transform the uniform data value in cell A2 to an exponential distribution using the formula 20*(–LN($A2)).

Normal Distribution

Used for measurement (continuous) data that are theoretically without bound in both the positive and negative directions and symmetric about an average (i.e., skewness equals zero) with a defined shape parameter (i.e., kurtosis equals 1), normal distributions are perhaps the most widely known distribution—the familiar bell-shaped curve. While some statisticians would have you believe that they are also nature's most widely occurring distribution, others would suggest that you take a good look at one in a textbook because you're not likely to see one occur in the "real world." Most statisticians and quality practitioners today would recognize that there is nothing inherently "normal" (pun intended) about the normal distribution, and its use in statistics is due only to its simplicity. It is well defined, so it is convenient to assume normality when errors associated with that assumption are relatively insignificant.

Normal Distributions

Minitab

Use *Calc\Random Data\Normal* to generate random numbers.

Use *Stat\Quality Tools\Individual Distribution Identification* to test whether the sample data meet the normal distribution. Use goodness-of-fit tests (described below) to determine if an assumed distribution provides a reasonable approximation.

Excel

Use *Data\Data Analysis\Random Number Generation*.

Set *Distribution = Normal*.

Lognormal Distribution

Used for measurement (continuous) data that theoretically are without bound in only the positive direction and bounded at zero (or a positive value above zero), the lognormal distribution is often applied to reliability and financial analysis. Data that are normally distributed, when transformed using the natural log function, will follow the lognormal distribution.

Lognormal Distributions

Minitab

Use *Calc\Random Data\LogNormal* to generate random numbers. Specify location, scale, and threshold.

Use *Stat\Quality Tools\Individual Distribution Identification* to test whether the sample data meet the lognormal distribution. Use goodness-of-fit tests (described below) to determine if an assumed distribution provides a reasonable approximation.

(Continued)

Excel

Use *Data\Data Analysis\Random Number Generation*.

Set *Distribution = Normal*. Transform normally distributed data to lognormal using the natural log function. For example, if cell A2 contains normally distributed data, LN(A2) contains lognormally distributed data.

Weibull Distribution

Used for measurement (continuous) data that theoretically are without bound in only the positive direction and bounded at zero (or a positive value above zero), the Weibull distribution is often applied to reliability (time to failure) and financial analyses.

Weibull Distributions

Minitab

Use *Calc\Random Data\Weibull* to generate random numbers. Specify shape, scale, and threshold (which equals zero for a two-parameter distribution).

Use *Stat\Quality Tools\Individual Distribution Identification* to test whether the sample data meet the Weibull distribution. Use goodness-of-fit tests (described below) to determine if an assumed distribution provides a reasonable approximation.

Excel

Use *Data\Data Analysis\Random Number Generation*.

Set *Distribution = Uniform*. Transform the uniformly distributed data to Weibull using the natural log function and shape and scale parameters. For example, if cell A2 contains uniformly distributed data, =15*(–LN(A2))^(1/3) contains Weibull distributed data with a shape parameter of 15 and a scale parameter of 3.

Johnson Distributions

Johnson distributions are used for measurement (continuous) data that do not fit the properties of known distributions such as the normal and exponential distribution. Quality improvement efforts often lead to nonnormal processes, such as through narrowing or constraining the distribution or moving its location to an optimal condition. Similarly, nature itself can impose bounds on a process, such as a service process whose waiting time is physically bounded at the lower end by zero. The proper design of a service process sets the process wait time as close as economically possible to zero, causing the process mode, median, and average to move toward zero. In manufacturing, concentricity or roundness is also achieved in this manner. These processes will tend toward nonnormality regardless of whether they are stable (in control) or unstable.

Johnson Distributions

Minitab

Use *Stat\Quality Tools\Individual Distribution Identification* to fit a Johnson distribution to the data. Use goodness-of-fit tests (described below) to determine if an assumed distribution provides a reasonable approximation.

Excel

Using Green Belt XL Add-On

Use *New Chart\Histogram* (*Note:* The histogram also may be displayed as an option with the $\bar{X}$ and individual-X control charts discussed later in Part 3.) Use goodness-of-fit tests (described below) to determine if an assumed distribution provides a reasonable approximation.

Methodology

Statistical distributions are characterized by up to four parameters:

- *Central tendency*. For symmetrical distributions (see "Skewness"), the average (or mean) provides a good description of the central tendency or location of the process. For very skewed distributions, such as incomes or housing prices, the median is a much better indicator of central tendency.

- *Standard deviation.* The standard deviation provides an estimate of variation. In mathematical terms, it is the *second moment about the mean*. In simpler terms, it is related to the average distance of the process observations from the mean.

- *Skewness.* The skewness provides a measure of the location of the mode (or high point in the distribution) relative to the average. In mathematical terms, it is the *third moment about the mean*. Symmetrical distributions, such as the normal distribution, have a skewness of zero. When the mode is to the left of the average, the skewness is negative; to the right, it is positive.

- *Kurtosis.* The kurtosis provides a measure of the "peakedness" of a distribution. In mathematical terms, it is the *fourth moment about the mean*. The normal distribution has a kurtosis of 1. Distributions that are more peaked have higher kurtoses.

If we know or can reliably assume the type of distribution to be applied to the process, we can estimate the necessary parameters using sample data.

The binomial, Poisson, and exponential distributions require only a known (or reliably estimated) average to define the distribution. These are one-parameter distributions, meaning that the remaining parameters (standard deviation, skewness, and kurtosis) are defined solely by its mean. The normal distribution requires two parameters (the mean and the standard deviation) because the skewness and kurtosis are defined to produce its characteristic bell shape.

The Johnson and Pearson distributions require estimates of up to four parameters for a given distribution shape. These methods are best applied using statistical software to fit the distributional curves to a set of sample data.

Interpretation

Binomial Distribution

The distributional parameter, the average proportion, is assumed for a given population or is calculated by dividing the number of items in a sample that meet the condition of interest (the count) by the total number of items inspected (the sample size). We can calculate the probability of counting x items in a sample from a population with a known average proportion using Minitab or MS Excel's statistical function BINOMDIST.

Binomial Distributions

Example

Estimate the probability of finding exactly 3 orders with one or more errors in a sample of 50 orders when the process mean is known to be 10 percent.

Minitab

Use *Calc\Probability Distributions\Binomial\Probability*. Set *Number of Trials* = 50; *Event Probability* = 0.10; *Input Constant* = 3.

Result (From Session Window)

Probability Density Function
Binomial with $n = 50$ and $p = 0.1$.

x	$P(X = x)$
3	0.138565

Note: To find the probability of 3 or less orders, use the *Cumulative Probability* option. Result = 0.25 (or 25 percent)

Excel

Enter =BINOMDIST(3, 50, 0.1, 0) into an Excel cell. The solution provided is 13.86 percent. The last parameter in the Excel formula (zero in this case) indicates whether the solution provides the cumulative result or the finite result. Use BINOMDIST(3, 50, 0.1, 1) to calculate the cumulative probability.

Poisson Distribution

The distributional parameter, the average number of instances per unit, is assumed for a given population or is calculated by dividing the number of instances that occur in a sample (the count) by the total number of items inspected (the sample size). We can calculate the probability of counting x instances in a sample from a population with a known average number of instances per unit using Minitab or MS Excel's statistical function POISSON.

Poisson Distributions

Example

Estimate the probability of finding exactly 300 typographic errors in a sample of 150 orders (i.e., 2 errors per order) when the process is known to average 4 typographic errors per order.

Minitab

Use *Calc\Probability Distributions\Poisson\Probability*. Set *Mean* = 4; *Input Constant* = 2.

Result (From Session Window)

Probability Density Function
Poisson with mean = 4.

x	$P(X = x)$
2	0.146525

Note: To find the probability of 3 or fewer orders, use the *Cumulative Probability* option. Result = 0.24 (or 24 percent).

Excel

Enter =POISSON(2, 4, 0) into an Excel cell. The solution provided is 14.65 percent. The last parameter in the Excel formula (zero in this case) indicates whether the solution provides the cumulative result or the finite result. Use POISSON(2, 4, 1) to calculate the cumulative probability. Note that the cumulative probability also may be calculated as the sum of POISSON(0, 4, 0), POISSON(1, 4, 0), and POISSON(2, 4, 0).

Exponential Distribution

The distributional parameter λ (lambda) is calculated as $1/\mu$, where μ is the average time between occurrences.

Exponential Distributions

Example

Estimate the probability of an accident within the first 31 days of the last accident if the time between accidents averages 47 days (i.e., the accident rate is 13 percent, and the plant runs 365 days a year).

Minitab

Use *Calc\Probability Distributions\Exponential\Cumulative Probability*. Set *Scale* = 47; *Input Constant* = 31.

Result (From Session Window)

Cumulative Distribution Function
Exponential with mean = 47.

x	$P(X \le x)$
31	0.482929

Excel

Enter =EXPONDIST(31, 1/47, 1) into an Excel cell. The solution provided is 48.3 percent. Conversely, the probability of being accident-free for that period is $1 - 0.4829$, which equals 51.7 percent.

Normal Distribution

The average ($\overline{X}$) of a sample can be calculated by summing the measurements and dividing by the number of measurements (N). The standard deviation of the N sample measurements can be calculated as

$$s = \frac{\sum_{j=1}^{N}(\overline{X} - X_1)^2}{N}$$

We calculate a z value to convert the given normal distribution into a standardized normal distribution, which has a mean of zero and a standard deviation of 1:

$$z = \frac{(X - \overline{X})}{s}$$

Appendix 1 provides the cumulative percentage points of the standard normal distribution. The z value allows us to estimate the probability of being less than or greater than any given x value, such as a customer requirement. For example, if we calculate that the average cycle time of an order fulfillment process is 4.46 days and the standard deviation of the cycle time is 2.97 days, we can calculate a z value for an upper specification of 10 days as follows:

$$z = \frac{(10 - 4.46)}{2.97} = 1.86$$

From Appendix 1 we find that a z value of 1.86 corresponds to a cumulative probability of 0.9686, implying that 96.86 percent of the process will be within the customer requirement. Conversely, $1 - 0.9686$ (or 3.14 percent) will exceed the requirement of 10 days, assuming that the process is modeled adequately by the normal distribution. This assumption is conveniently verified for a set of data using the tests discussed below (see "Goodness-of-Fit Tests").

Normal Distributions

Example

Estimate the probability of not exceeding a customer limit of 10 days for order fulfillment if the process average is 4.46 days and the standard deviation is 2.97 days.

Minitab

Use *Calc\Probability Distributions\Normal\Cumulative Probability*. Set *Mean* = 4.46; *Standard Deviation* = 2.97; *Input Constant* = 10.

Result (From Session Window)

Cumulative Distribution Function
Normal with mean = 4.46 and standard deviation = 2.97.

x	$P(X \leq x)$
10	0.968932

Excel

Enter =NORMDIST(10, 4.46, 2.97, 1) into an Excel cell. The solution provided is 96.9 percent. Conversely, the probability of being accident-free for that period is $1 - 0.969$, which equals 3.1 percent.

Johnson Distributions

When the convenience of known distributions such as the normal or exponential distribution cannot be applied, the more advanced curve-fitting techniques can be used to model the process data using these basic assumptions (Figure F.9):

1. The data are representative of the process during the period when the data were collected (i.e., measurement error is negligible, and the sampling process produced data reflective of the process conditions). This implies that the data have sufficient resolution to estimate variation among the data and that there are sufficient data to represent the common-cause variation in the process.

2. The data can be represented by a single, continuous distribution. A single distribution can be sensibly fit to the data only when the process is stable (in statistical control), without any influences that may shift the process in time (special causes).

3. We cannot claim that data are distributed according to our hypothesis. We can claim only that the data may be represented by the hypothesized distribution. More formally, we can test and accept or reject, at a given

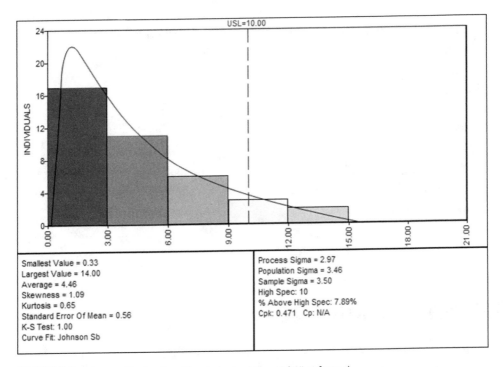

FIGURE F.9 Johnson distribution. (*Created using Green Belt XL software.*)

confidence level, the hypothesis that the data have the same distribution function as a proposed function. The Kolmogorov-Smirnov (K-S) goodness-of-fit statistic should be used as a relative indicator of curve fit.

For example, the K-S goodness-of-fit test is 0.31 for the preceding order fulfillment cycle time data, indicating a relatively poor fit for the normal distribution. Figure F.9 shows the Quality America Green Belt XL software's Johnson curve fit to the data. The predicted percentage exceeding the upper specification limit for the Johnson distribution is 7.89 percent. Note that the shape of the data differs significantly from the normal assumption, with a negative skew and bound at zero. The normal distribution would incorrectly estimate that 6.7 percent of the process would be less than zero (i.e., $z = -1.50$), which is quite impossible for the cycle time metric.

Johnson Distributions

Minitab

Use *Stat\Quality Tools\Individual Distribution Identification* to fit a Johnson distribution to the data. Use goodness-of-fit tests (described below) to determine if an assumed distribution provides a reasonable approximation.

Excel

Using Green Belt XL Add-On

Use *New Chart\Histogram*. (*Note:* The histogram also may be displayed as an option with the $\bar{X}$ and individual-X control charts.) Use goodness-of-fit tests (described below) to determine whether an assumed distribution provides a reasonable approximation.

Equality-of-Variance Tests

Equality-of-variance tests indicate whether given subsets of data have comparable levels of variation. Equal variance is a critical assumption in ANOVA.

When to Use

Analyze Stage and Improve Stage
- To test observed data used in an ANOVA
- To test residuals in a regression analysis

Methodology

A statistical test for the equality of the variance at a experimental conditions is provided by Bartlett. Minitab offers this test, as well as the Levene test, which is preferred if nonnormality is suspected. We would generally expect the regression residuals to follow a normal distribution, and ANOVA requires normality of the parameters, so Bartlett's test is adequate in these cases.

The Bartlett test tests the equality of the treatment variances against the alternative that at least one variance is unequal to the others. The null hypothesis is that of equal variances for the subsets:

$$H_0: \sigma^2_1 = \sigma^2_1 = \sigma^2_2 = \cdots = \sigma^2_a$$

The alternative is that at least one of the subsets has an unequal variance. The equality of variance test requires multiple samples from each test condition to evaluate the variance at each condition. For example, the replicated experimental data presented in the "Factorial Design" topic may be analyzed for equality of variance. In the original design, there are six factors (A through F) estimated using eight unique design conditions, replicated for a total of sixteen total experimental trials. In this original model of six factors, there would be two samples available to estimate variance at each of the eight unique design conditions. We could instead evaluate the equality of variance for the final recommended model, where four of the six factors have been removed for being statistically insignificant. This two factor model provides four samples to estimate the variance at each of the final four design conditions, summarized shown in Table T.5. It should be clear the test for equality of variance will necessarily differ for a given set of data depending on the model chosen for analysis.

Equality of Variance

Minitab

Use *Stat\ANOVA\Test for Equal Variances*. Select the response column, then select the factors that are considered significant for the model.

TABLE T.5 95% Bonferroni Confidence Intervals for Standard Deviations					
B	**E**	**N**	**Lower**	**StDev**	**Upper**
−50	−50	4	0.75935	1.54123	9.2426
−50	50	4	1.75787	3.56791	21.3964
50	−50	4	1.15265	2.33952	14.0298
50	50	4	1.44256	2.92794	17.5585

Bartlett's Test (Normal Distribution)
Test statistic = 1.81, p–value = 0.613

Excel

Using BlackBelt XL Add-On

Use *New Chart\Designed Experiment* or *New Chart\Regression*. Select the response column, then select the factors that are considered significant for the model.

Interpretation

If the condition of non-constant variance is detected, we can transform the variable to remove its effect. See "Transformation" topic elsewhere in Part 3. In the example above, the high p-value indicates the Null Hypothesis of equal variance cannot be rejected, and equal variances may be assumed.

Evolutionary Operation (EVOP)

The *EVOP strategy* involves a series of sequential 2^k fractional factorial experiments with two or three factors. Unlike designed experiments, where we purposely manipulate factor levels to cause significant changes to the process, each of the factor levels in an EVOP represents small increments to minimize the upset to the process.

George Box proposed EVOP in 1957 as a method of routine plant operation to move toward an optimal. The techniques were further defined in Box and Draper (1969).

When to Use

Analyze Stage

- To determine the significance of process factors

Improve Stage

- To define new process factor settings resulting in an improved response

EVOP has a number of disadvantages. A large number of repeat runs often are needed for each phase because the factor level changes are small, with an effect that is weak relative to process noise. The repeat runs provide a reduction in the statistical error of estimating the effects.

The experiments generally are much longer term than traditional designed experiments because only two to three factors are changed at a time. In other words, it may take weeks or months to determine the significant effects compared with days for a designed experiment on the same process.

Despite these shortcomings, EVOPs provide a number of advantages. Most important, during the course of the experimentation, the process continues to make usable product, unlike a designed experiment that requires the process be shut down to manipulate factors beyond their normal ranges.

Unlike happenstance data that are collected without specific purpose, EVOP data are collected at predefined operating conditions. In addition, the data may be collected as part of revised operating procedures by operational personnel.

Methodology

Definitions

- A *cycle* refers to a collection of data at a given experimental condition. A cycle is complete when one observation has been collected at each point in the design (the replicates for that condition). A cycle is a blocking factor for the EVOP.
- A *phase* refers to a new iteration of cycles centered about a previously defined optimal condition. After several cycles, a phase is completed when the operating conditions are changed to improve the response.

- The *change in the mean*, also known as *curvature*, refers to the difference between the edge points of the 2^k experiment and their center point. If the process is centered on the current optimum, there should be a statistically significant difference between the center point and the edge points.

- Juran suggests choosing two or three important factors to keep the EVOP manageable. Choose levels for each factor as "small steps" to avoid large changes in quality or operating conditions, and center the first experiment at the current "best operating condition" for the process.

- Run a 2^2 (for two factors) or 2^3 (for three factors) experiment with a center point. Repeat the experiment, and after the second cycle, begin to estimate the error and the significance of effects.

- Continue with this experiment for a third cycle (i.e., third replicate), and if a factor is significant after this third cycle, then begin phase 2 with a new experiment centered on the new "best condition."

- When factors are not calculated as statistically significant, consider increasing the range of the levels for these factors because it is possible that the levels were too similar to detect a statistical difference. Alternatively, consider replacing the insignificant factors with new factors that currently may be contributing to error.

- If no factor is determined to be significant after eight cycles, then either change the factor-level ranges or select new factors.

- When the optimal condition has been reached, run additional experiments with new factors or new factor-level ranges to verify the optimal condition.

Consider this example chemical process to maximize yield using two process factors—temperature and reaction time. The current process setting for temperature is 150°C. Levels are chosen at 145 and 155°C. The current process setting for reaction time is 30 minutes. Levels are chosen at 28 and 32 minutes.

The measured responses are shown in Figure F.10 for cycle 1 and Figure F.11 for cycle 2 at each experimental condition. The number in parentheses refers to the order of the trial. For example, the first data point of cycle 1 was run at a temperature of 150°C and reaction time of 30 minutes, with a resulting yield of 74 percent.

Note: See "Factorial Designs" for information on defining and analyzing the experimental runs in Minitab and MS Excel.

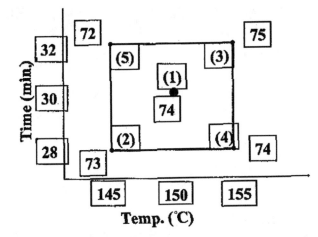

FIGURE F.10 Cycle 1 EVOP results.

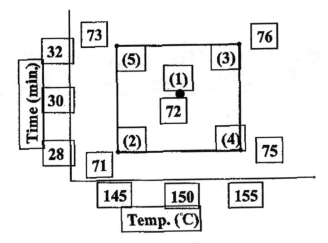

FIGURE F.11 Cycle 2 EVOP results.

Interpretation

The ANOVA results from Minitab are provided in Table T.6. Note the significance of the main-effect terms.

The estimated effects and coefficients from Minitab are provided in Table T.7. Note the significance of the temperature term.

TABLE T.6 Minitab ANOVA Results for EVOP Example: Analysis of Variance for Yield (Coded Units)

Source	df	Seq SS	Adj SS	Adj MS	F	p
Blocks	1	0.1000	0.1000	0.1000	0.07	0.799
Main effects	2	16.2500	16.250	8.1250	6.02	0.062
Two-way interactions	1	0.1250	0.1250	0.1250	0.09	0.776
Curvature	1	0.6250	0.6250	0.6250	0.46	0.534
Residual error	4	5.4000	5.4000	1.3500		
Total	9	22.5000				

TABLE T.7 Minitab Effects for EVOP Example: Estimated Effects and Coefficients for Yield (Coded Units)

Term	Effect	Coef.	SE Coef	T	p
Constant		73.6250	0.4108	179.23	0.000
Block		0.1000	0.3674	0.27	0.799
Temp	2.7500	1.3750	0.4108	3.35	0.029
Time	0.7500	0.3750	0.4108	0.91	0.413
Temp × time	0.2500	0.1250	0.4108	0.30	0.776
Center point		−0.6250	0.9186	−0.68	0.534

Based on the phase 1 results, temperature is significant. Its effect on yield is positive, meaning that to obtain an increase in yield, we should increase temperature. The suggestion for phase 2 experimentation is to center the new design (the cycle replicates) around a temperature setting of 155°C and a time setting of 30 minutes. Note that the time factor is not changed after just two cycles. If we continue to see no significance of the time factor after eight cycles, we can either increase the factor level difference (levels such as 25 and 35 minutes) or substitute a different factor.

EWMA Charts

An *exponentially weighted moving-average (EWMA) chart* is a control chart for variables data. It plots weighted moving-average values. A weighting factor is chosen by the user to determine the relative impact of older data to more recent data on the calculated moving-average value. Because the EWMA chart uses information from all samples, it detects much smaller process shifts than a normal control chart.

When to Use

Measure Stage

- To baseline a process, particularly when nonnormality of the process is suspected and rational subgroup size is one

Control Stage

- To control a process, particularly when either nonnormality of the process is suspected and rational subgroup size is one or when small shifts in the process must be detected

EWMA charts generally are used for detecting small shifts in the process mean. They will detect shifts of $\frac{1}{2}\sigma$ to 2σ much faster than Shewhart charts with the same sample size. They are, however, slower in detecting large shifts in the process mean. In addition, typical run tests cannot be used because of the inherent dependence of data points.

EWMA charts also may be preferred when the subgroups are of size $n = 1$. In this case, the alternative chart is the individual-X chart, whose standard control limits are based on the normal distribution. When processes are severely nonnormal, the individual-X chart's normal control limits may not fit the process data well. When nonnormal control limits are calculated for the individual-X chart, the data are assumed to be from a controlled process as a requirement of the curve fitting. The advantage of EWMA charts is that each plotted point includes several observations, so the central limit theorem provides that the average of the points (or the moving average in this case) is normally distributed and the control limits clearly defined.

EWMA charts are also used to smooth the effect of known, uncontrollable noise in the data. Many accounting, service, and chemical processes fit into this categorization. For example, while day-to-day fluctuations in accounting processes may be large, they are not purely indicative of process instability. The choice of λ can be determined to make the chart more or less sensitive to these daily fluctuations.

As with other control charts, EWMA charts are used to monitor processes over time. The charts' x axes are time-based so that the charts show a history of the process. For this reason, you must have data that are time-ordered, that is, entered in the sequence from which they were generated. If this is not the case, then trends or shifts in the process may not be detected but instead attributed to random (common-cause) variation.

Methodology

When choosing the value of λ used for weighting, it is recommended to use small values (such as 0.2) to detect small shifts and larger values (between 0.2 and 0.4) for larger shifts. An EWMA chart with $\lambda = 1.0$ is an $\bar{X}$ chart (for subgroups larger than 1) or an individual-X chart (when subgroup size equals 1).

Plotted statistic:

$$z_t = \lambda_1 \bar{x}_t + (1 - \lambda_1)z_{t-1}$$

where λ is the value of the weighting factor, $\bar{x}_t$ is the subgroup average for the current subgroup at time t, and the value of z at time zero (z_0) is either a target value or the overall average of the selected subgroups.

EWMA control limits:

$$CL_{EWMA} = z_0 \pm \left(\frac{3\bar{R}}{d_2\sqrt{n}}\right)\sqrt{\frac{\lambda}{(2-\lambda)}[1-(1-\lambda)^{2t}]}$$

where z_0 is the starting value (either the target value or process mean value), n is the subgroup size, d_2 is a function of n, and m is the number of subgroups selected for analysis.

The range chart $(n > 1)$ or the moving-range chart $(n = 1)$ is generally used to monitor process variation.

EWMA Chart

Minitab

Use *Stat\Control Charts\Time-Weighted charts\EWMA*.

Use the "Select" button to enter the data. Specify the λ value between 0 and 1 using the *Weight of EWMA* field.

Excel

Using Green Belt XL Add-On

Use *New Chart\EWMAChart*. Enter the data's cell references (e.g., $A$2:$A$102) into the *Data Range* (step 2) dialog box. Specify the λ value between 0 and 1 in the *Analysis* tab of step 3.

Interpretation

Always look at the range chart first. The control limits on the EWMA chart are derived from the average range (or moving range if $n = 1$), so if the range chart is out of control, then the control limits on the EWMA chart are meaningless.

On the range chart, look for out-of-control points. If there are any, then the special causes must be eliminated. Remember that the range is the estimate of the variation within a subgroup, so look for process elements that would increase variation between the data in a subgroup. Brainstorm and conduct designed experiments.

After reviewing the range chart, interpret the points on the EWMA chart relative to the control limits. Run tests are never applied to an EWMA chart because the plotted points are inherently dependent, containing common points. Never consider the points on an EWMA chart relative to specifications because the observations from the process vary much more than the exponentially weighted moving averages.

If the process shows control relative to the statistical limits for a sufficient period of time (long enough to see all potential special causes), then you can analyze its capability relative to requirements. Capability is meaningful only when the process is stable because you cannot predict the outcome of an unstable process.

Factorial Designs

Factorial designs include complete factorial designs (CFDs) and fractional factorial designs (FFDs). They serve as the basis for most design of experiments (DOE).

When to Use

Analyze Stage

- Use fractional factorial designs as screening designs to understand sources of variation and discover the process drivers

Improve Stage

- Supplement fractional factorial designs with center points to estimate curvature effects

Methodology

Refer also to "Design of Experiments (DOE)" above for a general discussion of the methodology for conducting a designed experiment.

Complete Factorial Designs

Complete factorial designs are capable of estimating all factors and their interactions. We can calculate the number of experimental runs needed to estimate all the factors and interactions using this simple formula, where b is the number of levels of each factor and f is the number of factors:

$$\text{Number of experimental runs} = b^f$$

For example, with three factors at two levels each, we calculate that we need at least eight (2^3) experimental runs to estimate the main factors (A, B, and C), the two-factor interactions (AB, AC, and BC), and the three-factor interaction (ABC). One degree of freedom is needed to estimate the overall mean.

The complete factorial design for three factors at two levels each is presented in Table T.8. Note the pattern in the design, where a positive sign indicates the high level of the factor and a negative sign indicates the low level of the factor. The actual run order of the design will be randomized when implemented, but the pattern is useful for seeing how the design is generated.

Graphically, the design would look as shown in Figure F.12. The trial numbers from Table T.8 are shown at the corners of the cube.

When we have five factors, we can estimate all the main factors and interactions using a 32-run (2^5) experiment. This will allow us to estimate 5 main factors (*A*, *B*, *C*, *D*, and *E*), 10 two-factor interactions (*AB*, *AC*, *AD*, *AE*, *BC*, *BD*, *BE*, *CD*, *CE*, and *DE*); 10 three-factor interactions (*ABC*, *ABD*, *ABE*, *ACD*, *ACE*, *ADE*, *BCD*, *BCE*, *BDE*, and *CDE*), 5 four-factor interactions (*ABCD*, *ABCE*, *ABDE*, *ACDE*, and *BCDE*), and 1 five-factor interaction (*ABCDE*).

Notice how quickly the number of runs increases as we add factors, doubling for each new factor when there are only two levels per factor. You may notice that adding a single factor at three levels would triple the number of runs required.

You may wonder: Do we really need to estimate all these three-, four-, and five-factor interactions? Fortunately, the answer is no. CFDs are rarely, if ever, used and are presented only to aid in an understanding of the benefits of fractional factorial designs.

TABLE T.8 A Complete Factorial Design for Three			
Std. Order	**Factor *A***	**Factor *B***	**Factor *C***
1	+	+	+
2	+	+	−
3	+	−	+
4	+	−	−
5	−	+	+
6	−	+	−
7	−	−	+
8	−	−	−

Fractional Factorial Designs

In most experiments, particularly screening experiments, we can ignore the effects of the higher-order (larger than two-factor) interactions. It's unlikely that these higher-order interactions are significant unless the main factors or two-factor interactions are also significant. Therefore, we can reduce the number of runs by excluding the higher-order interactions. These fractional factorial designs are constructed by *aliasing* (or substituting) the higher-order interac-

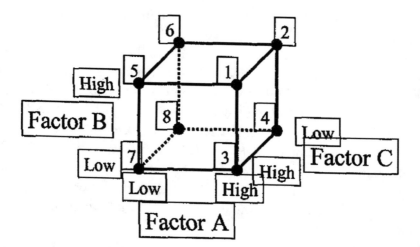

FIGURE F.12 A 2^3 design.

tion terms with main factors, as shown in Table T.9. The result is a smaller design, a fraction of the original.

Consider the two-level three-factor CFD constructed earlier. It had 8 runs to estimate the three main effects (A, B, and C), the three two-factor interactions (AB, AC, and BC), and the one three-factor interaction (ABC). If we assume that the ABC interaction is unlikely to be significant, then we can alias it with a fourth factor D. The result of this alias is a design that is half the size! Instead of requiring 16 runs, only 8 runs are needed to estimate the effect of the four factors.

Construction of the four-factor FFD is similar to the three-factor design seen earlier. The columns labeled "Factor A," "Factor B," and "Factor C" are identical to those shown in the CFD 2^3 design. The column labeled "Factor D" is constructed in the same way as its alias, the ABC interaction, is constructed—by multiplying the columns for factors A, B, and C. For example, the first row, trial 1, is the result of multiplying $(+1) \times (+1) \times (+1) = (+1)$.

Similarly,

Trial 2: $(+1) \times (+1) \times (-1) = (-1)$

Trial 3: $(+1) \times (-1) \times (+1) = (-1)$

Trial 4: $(+1) \times (-1) \times (-1) = (+1)$

And so on.

TABLE T.9   A Fractional Factorial Design for Four Factors

Std. Order	Factor *A*	Factor *B*	Factor *C*	Factor *D*
1	+	+	+	+
2	+	+	−	−
3	+	−	+	−
4	+	−	−	+
5	−	+	+	−
6	−	+	−	+
7	−	−	+	+
8	−	−	−	−

The effect of aliasing factor D with the ABC interaction is that the aliased parameters are *confounded* with one another. This implies that the parameters cannot be estimated independently of one another. For example, if factor D is aliased with the ABC interaction, then when the effect of factor D is estimated, we cannot be sure whether the effect is due to factor D, the ABC interaction, or a linear combination of D and ABC.

The intended aliasing also creates some unintended confounding between all the other possible combinations of the aliased pair. We construct the confounded pairs by moving the equal sign through the $ABC = D$ equation. If $ABC = D$, then $A = BCD$; $B = ACD$; $C = ABD$; $AB = CD$; $AC = BD$; and $AD = BC$. These can be verified in Table T.9 by noticing, for example, that the results of multiplying the columns for factor A and factor B provide the same result for all rows as multiplying the columns for factor C and factor D. This provides evidence that the AB interaction is confounded with the CD interaction.

FFDs have several uses. They are used commonly as screening designs to identify significant factors and their interactions and to remove insignificant factors and interactions. We often start the design process with many factors, brainstorm to a manageable number of key factors, and then run a relatively small screening design to reduce the number of factors and interactions even further. This allows further designs to explore the process dynamics in more detail, using fewer factors in the model.

FFDs are also used in response surface analysis to develop the initial first-order model and its factor effect estimates needed for the steepest ascent methods. When higher-order models are suspected, the FFDs can be supplemented with axial and center points.

Saturated designs refer to special cases of FFDs where only the main factors can be estimated. In a saturated design, the minimum number of experimental conditions $(1 + p)$ is used to estimate the p main factors. For example, use a 2^{3-1} design to estimate three factors in four runs, a 2^{7-4} design to estimate seven factors in eight runs, and a 2^{15-11} design to estimate 15 factors in 16 runs. In saturated designs, the main factors are all confounded with two-factor interactions. In addition, we have no "extra" runs to estimate error, so we cannot determine which parameters are significant to the regression. We can only calculate the parameter effects, which provide the coefficients of the regression equation. Generally, we will add at least one additional run (a degree of freedom) to the saturated design, resulting in $p + 2$ runs, to allow an estimate of experimental error and resulting significance of the model terms. A center point [where each factor is set to the midpoint between its high (+1) and low (−1) condition] can be used to provide a rough estimate.

It should be clear that the fewer parameters we need to estimate, the less costly the experiment will be to run. Often at least one factor in a design is statistically insignificant. If, after collecting and analyzing the data, we can remove that factor from the analysis, we are left with a replicated data set that provides an estimate of error and better estimates of the remaining factors.

See also "Plackett-Burman Designs," "John's ¾ Designs," and "Central Composite Design" in the Glossary and "Response Surface Analysis" topic elsewhere in Part 3.

Factorial Designs

Minitab

Use *Stat\DOE\Factorial\Create Factorial Design\2-level factorial (default generators)*. Specify *Number of Factors*.

Select the "Designs" button to select a design. Replicated screening designs are usually preferred, so select two corner point replicates; blocks (see "Blocking Factor" in the Glossary) are not generally needed for an initial screening design; center points are optional. Select the "Factors" button to specify *Numeric* (i.e., quantitative) or *Text* (i.e., qualitative) and real experimental values for each factor level.

Use the "Options" button to randomize experimental trials.

For example, a ⅛ fraction two-level replicated design (8 runs × 2 replicates = 16 runs) was constructed for six factors *A* through *F*. Two levels were chosen for each factor at (real) experimental units of (–50, 50). The design array is shown in standard order with experimental response column added for use in the "Interpretation" section below (data provided are generated by *IQF Six Sigma Black Certification Exam Study Guide*, available at www.qualityamerica .com):

A	B	C	D	E	F	Response
–50	–50	–50	50	50	50	–108,154
50	–50	–50	–50	–50	50	–43,493.8
–50	50	–50	–50	50	–50	–46,565.2
50	50	–50	50	–50	–50	–153,947
–50	–50	50	50	–50	–50	–43,490.4
50	–50	50	–50	50	–50	–108,146
–50	50	50	–50	–50	50	–153,947
50	50	50	50	50	50	–46,558.7
–50	–50	–50	50	50	50	–108,154
50	–50	–50	50	50	50	–43,493.4
–50	50	–50	–50	50	–50	–46,562
50	50	–50	50	–50	–50	–153,947
–50	–50	50	50	–50	–50	–43,492.8
50	–50	50	–50	50	–50	–108,149
–50	50	50	–50	–50	50	–153,942
50	50	50	50	50	50	–46,564.5

Excel

Using Black Belt XL Add-On

Use *New Chart\Designed Experiment* to generate a new design. Specify factor labels, factor type, and experimental values for each factor. Select *Terms* and then select only the main factors to generate a screening design. Choose from the list of designs, and optionally choose *Randomize Runs* and add *Design Replicates* and *Center Point*.

Using the preceding example, the fractional factorial–Taguchi L8 screening design is chosen with *Design Replicates* set to 2 to produce a design similar to Minitab's shown above.

Interpretation

The two-levels-per-factor (2^k) designs used for screening only can provide a first-order model. When saturated designs have been augmented with one or more additional runs, we can estimate the error in the model and the significance of parameters using ANOVA techniques "Regression" topic outlined earlier. Error in a regression analysis is due to two sources—pure error and lack-of-fit error. Pure error is experimental error, the differences between repeated runs of the same condition. The remaining error is due to a poor fit of the model to the data. Error owing to a lack of fit is caused by either a curvature in the response surface that is not estimated with the fitted first-degree model or main factor or interaction terms not included in the model. When center points are available, the F statistic may be used to investigate curvature in the data, suggesting the need for a higher-order model. (This technique is explained further under "Response Surface Analysis" below.)

The parameter effects, the influence each factor or interaction has on the response, can be estimated for the 2^k design by calculating the difference between the average response when the parameter is set at the high level and the average response when the parameter is set at the low level. The coefficient of the parameter in the regression model is calculated as one-half the effect.

In the fractional factorial 2^{k-x} design, the effect of the aliasing is confounding between main factors and interactions. For example, if an FFD is run where factor A and interaction BC are confounded, then the calculated parameter effect may be due to either factor A, the interaction BC, or a linear combination of factor A and interaction BC.

When the results of a screening experiment are ambiguous because of the confounding of factors, we often can *fold* the design to select additional trials to remove the confounding. A design is folded by replicating the design and substituting the low levels with high levels and high values with low levels for one or more of the factors. If we fold on just one factor (i.e., substitute the plus and minus signs for one of the factors), then that factor and its two-factor interactions will be free of confounding. If we substitute the plus and minus signs for the entire design, then all main factors will be free of confounding with other main factors and two-factor interactions.

The next step after successful analysis of the screening experiment depends on the objectives of the experimental process.

- To control the process, the successful experiment has differentiated between the significant and insignificant sources of variation. Verify by replicating the experiment, and then implement control mechanisms on the significant factors as part of the improve stage.

- To model the process for prediction, run a central composite design (described in the Glossary and applied as discussed in the "Response Surface Analysis" topic below). It's possible the screening design can be extended with just a few experimental conditions to satisfy this requirement.

- To optimize the process by relocating it to a region of maximum yield, proceed to response surface analysis (discussed below) or evolutionary operation techniques (discussed earlier).

Factorial Designs

Minitab

Enter the experimental results in a column (one result for each run), and then use *Stat\DOE\Factorial\Analyze Factorial Design* to select the column containing the response data. Use the "Terms" button to specify only first-order terms for the initial screening analysis.

(For designs not created in Minitab, select the "Factors" button, and then select the "Low/High" and "Designs" buttons to define factor levels and select a design and optional center points, as described earlier.)

For example, the initial analysis (partial results shown) for the preceding experiment are

Factorial Fit: Response versus A, B, C, D, E, and F—Estimated Effects and Coefficients for Response (Coded Units)					
Term	**Effect**	**Coef.**	**SE Coef.**	**T**	**p**
Constant		−88,038	14,337	−6.14	0.000
A	1	0	14,337	0.00	1.000
B	−24,432	−12,216	14,337	−0.85	0.416
C	3	2	14,337	0.00	1.000
D	−1	0	14,337	0.00	1.000
E	21,362	10,681	14,337	0.75	0.475
F	−1	0	14,337	0.00	1.000

$S = 57347.0$ $R^2 = 12.46\%$ $R^2 \text{ (adj)} = 0.00\%$

(Continued)

Interpreting Results

No factors are initially significant, but factors B and E were more significant than the others based on their lower p values. Terms are removed one at a time based on their p value, and the analysis is repeated after each term is removed. The resulting analysis confirms significance of factors B and E and the BE interaction. The first-order model (in coded form) is

$$y = -88038 - (12216*B) + (10681*E) + (43010*B*E)$$

Estimated Effects and Coefficients for Response (Coded Units)

Term	Effect	Coef.	SE Coef.	T	p
Constant		−88,038	0.6749	−130,445.28	0.000
B	−24,432	−12,216	0.6749	−18,100.72	0.000
E	21,362	10,681	0.6749	15,826.29	0.000
B*E	86,020	43,010	0.6749	63,728.10	0.000

This example is continued under "Response Surface Analysis" below.

Excel

Using Black Belt XL Add–On

Enter the experimental results in a column (one result for each run), and then use *New Chart\Designed Experiment* to select the response column and analyze results. Use the "Terms" button to specify only first-order terms for the initial screening analysis and to define terms in each subsequent pass, as described earlier for Minitab. Use its *Fold Design* option to complete the design and analysis process at this stage.

Failure Modes and Effects Analysis (FMEA)

Failure modes and effects analysis, also known by its acronym *FMEA* or as *failure modes, effects, and criticality analysis*, is used to determine high-risk process activities or product features based on the impact of a failure and the likelihood that a failure could occur without detection.

When to Use

Analyze Stage

- To prioritize process activities or product features that are prone to failure

Improve or Design Stage

- To determine high-risk process activities or product features in the proposed improvement

Methodology

The following steps are required for the FMEA:

- Define the function of each process step (or product feature, for designs). For example, in a sales process:

  Process step: Enter the product ID number for each purchased item.

  Function: Links to the product database to identify the item numbers necessary for the products being purchased.

- Identify the failure mode and its effect for each function. In defining failure modes and their effects, it is helpful to ask, "What could go wrong?" or "What could the customer dislike?" For example:

  Function: Links to the product database to identify the item numbers necessary for the products being purchased.

  Failure mode 1: Product ID mistyped.

  Effect of failure mode 1: Wrong product shipped.

  Failure mode 2: Item numbers not correctly defined in database.

  Effect of failure mode 2: Wrong product items shipped.

- Define the severity for each of the failure modes. Table T.10 provides a good means of identifying the severity for a given failure effect. Granted, defining a severity level is subjective. In the example that follows, a severity of 5 or 7 could have been reasonable choices; the "right" answer can never be known, but consistency within a given analysis or between analyses that compete for resources certainly is important for meaningful prioritizations. For example:

  Failure mode 1: Product ID mistyped; severity = 6. From Table T.10, severity 6 is described as "Moderate disruption to operations. Some loss of product or service may occur requiring moderate remedy. Customer will complain; product return likely."

- Define the likelihood (or probability) of occurrence. Table T.11 (AIAG, 1995) provides useful descriptions of occurrence levels from 1 to 10 based on C_{pk} and possible process defect rates. For example:

  Failure mode 1: Product ID mistyped; occurrence level = 5.

- Define the detection method and likelihood of detection. Table T.12 provides useful descriptions of detection levels from 1 to 10. For example:

  Failure mode 1: Product ID mistyped; detection = 4; detection method: Accounting clerk compares the PO with the order form as the invoice is created for shipping.

- Calculate risk priority number (RPN) by multiplying the severity, occurrence, and detection levels. For example:

  Failure mode 1: Product ID mistyped; RPN = 120 [calculated as 6 (the severity level) × 5 (the occurrence level) × 4 (the detection level)].

- Prioritize the failure modes based on the RPN.

TABLE T.10 Severity Table*

Level	Description
10	May endanger personnel without warning or violate law or regulation.
9	May endanger personnel with warning or potentially result in violation of law or regulation.
8	Major disruption to operations. Complete loss of customer goodwill or 100 percent loss of product or service may occur.
7	Significant disruption to operations. Some loss of product or service will occur, requiring significant remedy, such as product sorting, rework, or extra effort. Customer very dissatisfied.
6	Moderate disruption to operations. Some loss of product or service may occur, requiring moderate remedy. Customer will complain; product return likely.
5	Minor disruption to operations. Some loss of product or service may occur, requiring minor remedy. Customer's productivity reduced.
4	Marginal disruption to operations, requiring slight remedy. Customer experiences some dissatisfaction.
3	Marginal disruption to operations. No remedy required. Customer likely to be inconvenienced.
2	Slight disruption to operations. Discriminating customer notices the effect but is not affected. Average customer doesn't notice effect.
1	No effect noticed by customer or operations.

*FMEA severity ratings based on AIAG (1995) and Pyzdek and Keller (2009).

TABLE T.11 FMEA Occurrence Rankings

Probable Failure	Failure Rate	C_{pk}	Occurrence Ranking
Very high (inevitable)	>1 in 2	<0.33	10
	1 in 3	0.33	9
High (often)	1 in 8	0.51	8
	1 in 20	0.67	7
Moderate (occasional)	1 in 80	.83	6
	1 in 400	1.00	5
	1 in 2,000	1.17	4
Low (isolated)	1 in 15,000	1.33	3
Very low	1 in 150,000	1.50	2
Remote (unlikely)	<1 in 150,000	>1.67	1

Source: AIAG, 1995.

TABLE T.12 Detection-Level Table*

Level	Description
10	Nearly certain that failure won't be detected ($p \approx 1$)
9	Extremely poor chance of detection ($0.95 < p \leq 0.99$)
8	Poor chance of detection ($0.90 < p \leq 0.95$)
7	Highly unlikely to be detected before reaching customer ($0.70 < p \leq 0.90$)
6	Unlikely to be detected before reaching customer ($0.50 < p \leq 0.70$)
5	Might be detected before reaching customer ($0.20 < p \leq 0.50$)
4	Likely to be detected before reaching customer ($0.05 < p \leq 0.20$)
3	Low probability of reaching customer without detection ($0.01 < p \leq 0.05$)
2	Extremely low probability of reaching customer without detection ($0 < p \leq 0.01$)
1	Nearly certain to detect before reaching customer ($p \approx 0$)

*FMEA detection levels, from Pyzdek and Keller (2009).

Interpretation

The RPN will range from 1 to 1,000, with larger numbers representing higher risks. Failure modes with higher RPNs should be given priority. Some organizations use threshold values, above which preventive action must be taken. For example, the organization may require improvement for any RPN exceeding 120.

Reducing the RPN requires a reduction in the severity, occurrence, and/or detection levels associated with the failure mode. Generally:

- Reducing severity level requires a change to the design of the product or process. For example, if the process involves a manufactured part, it may be possible to alter the design of the part so that the stated failure mode is no longer a serious problem for the customer.

- Reducing detection level increases cost with no improvement to quality. In order to reduce the detection level, we must improve the detection rate. We might add process steps to inspect product, to approve product, or (as in the example) to double-check a previous process step. None of these activities adds value to the customer, and each is a "hidden factory" sources of waste to the organization.

- Reducing the occurrence level is often the best approach because reducing severity can be costly (or impossible) and reducing the detection level is only a costly short-term solution. Reducing the occurrence level requires a reduction in process errors, which reduces cost.

5 S

5S is a lean tool that originates from the Japanese words used to create organization and cleanliness in the workplace [*Seiri* (organization), *Sieton* (tidiness), *Seiso* (purity), *Seiketsu* (cleanliness), and *Shitsuke* (discipline)]. The traditional five S's have been translated into the following five English words (Revelle, 2000):

1. *Sort:* Eliminate whatever is not needed.
2. *Straighten:* Organize whatever remains.
3. *Shine:* Clean the work area.
4. *Standardize:* Schedule regular cleaning and maintenance.
5. *Sustain:* Make 5S a way of life.

When to Use

Improve Stage

- To reduce non-value-added cycle times owing to movement, search time, and ineffective use of floor space
- To improve inventory management
- To reduce accidents and improve working conditions

Methodology

Measure a particular workstation's level of 5S achievements using a rating system such as that shown below for each of the 5S criteria.

Sort

Level 1: Needed and unneeded items mixed

Level 2: Needed and unneeded items identified; unneeded items removed

Level 3: Work area clean; sources of spills removed

Level 4: Documented housekeeping assignments and schedules

Level 5: Mess prevention implemented

Straighten

Level 1: Items randomly placed

Level 2: Needed items safely stored and organized according to frequency of use

Level 3: Locations for items labeled *Level 4:* Needed items minimized and arranged for retrieval

Level 5: Needed items can be retrieved in 30 seconds with minimal steps.

Shine

Level 1: Key items not identified

Level 2: Key items identified; acceptable levels documented

Level 3: Visual controls established

Level 4: Inspection, cleaning, and restocking on daily basis

Level 5: Potential problems identified; countermeasures defined

Standardize

Level 1: Work methods not followed or documented

Level 2: Documented agreements for needed items, organization, and controls

Level 3: Documented agreements on visual controls, labeling of items, and required quantities

Level 4: Reliable methods for housekeeping and inspections documented and practiced

Level 5: Reliable methods for housekeeping and inspections shared

Sustain

Level 1: No visual measurement of 5S

Level 2: Initial 5S level determined and posted

Level 3: 5S routinely monitored by work group

Level 4: Causes and frequency of problems routinely documented; corrective action CA implemented

Level 5: Root causes eliminated; preventive action deployed

Scores from this rating can be shown on a radar chart to display a particular area's performance in the 5S rating. An example radar chart for 5S drawn using Excel's chart wizard is shown in Figure F.13. The center point designates a score of 0, and a pentagon ring is shown for scores of 1.0, 2.0, and 3.0 (the maximum score in this example). This particular workstation achieved a rating of sort 1.50, straighten 2.00, shine 1.75, standardize 3.00, and sustain 2.00.

Interpretation

These scores are useful for tracking improvement over time and identifying areas of opportunity. Higher scores demonstrate better implementation of the 5S principles.

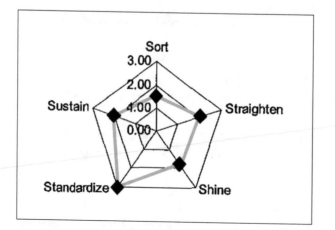

FIGURE F.13 A radar chart for 5S.

Flowchart

A *flowchart* is a simple graphic tool for documenting the series of steps necessary for the activities in a process.

When to Use

Measure Stage
- Document as-is process
- Uncover varied shareholder perceptions

Analyze Stage
- Discover process complexities that contribute to variation or longer cycle times

Improve Stage
- Communicate proposed changes

Control Stage
- Document revised process

Methodology

In a flowchart, each task is represented by a symbol. The American National Standards Institute (ANSI) provides a list of symbols that are intended primarily for computing processes but that most practitioners find useful—rectangles for most process tasks and diamonds for decision tasks. Decisions should have only two outcomes (yes or no), so decision points must be phrased in this manner.

We can use a flowchart to document the current (as-is) process. Use symbol color or shape to indicate process delays, functional responsibility for each step (e.g., yellow is customer service), or points in the process where measurements are taken.

Interpretation

A quick review of the as-is process using a flowchart usually can uncover complexities in the form of an excessive number of decision points and branches that may contribute to delays or even defects. When used to document the future (desired) process, we strive to make process flow uncomplicated, with the fewest symbols (tasks) and branches possible. This lack of complexity in the process will reduce the number of errors.

Figure F.14 is a rather simple flowchart. Notice how the diamond decision points have two outputs: One output continues down the main process flow,

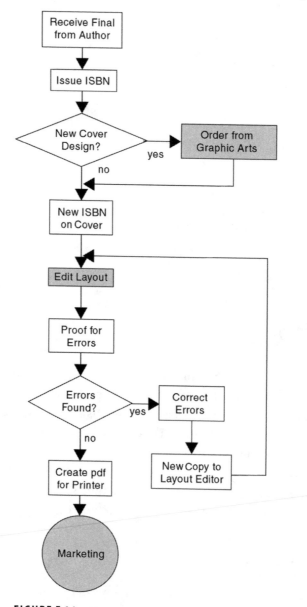

FIGURE F.14 Example of flowchart.

whereas the other diverts to a secondary path. Note that these secondary paths may result in a jump to a later point in the process (as shown in the first decision's yes path) or to a prior point in the process (as shown in the second decision's yes path). Decision paths and endpoints for processes, also may branch to other process flowcharts, as indicated by the circle in the last step of this process. In this example, the shaded symbols indicate external process steps.

Gantt Chart

The Gantt chart is a tool to define the critical path for dependent tasks in a project. The *critical path* consists of all activities, in order of occurrence, required as soon as possible to keep the project on schedule. Delay in any of the critical task activities will result in slippage to the project's completion date. Tasks that are not on the critical path do not need to be completed as soon as possible: They have *slack time* associated with them. Differentiating between tasks on the critical path and those with slack time allows us to allocate our limited resources most effectively.

When to Use

Define Stage

- To identify the critical path for cycle time reduction
- To identify project activities that determine the total project duration
- To identify and schedule all activities in the project (define through control stage)

Improve Stage

- To verify the reduction in process critical-path cycle time

Methodology

Begin by compiling a list of all the tasks that must be completed for the overall project or process. Arrange these tasks in chronological order. Next, place all the tasks in a progressing line. Depending on the project, you might be able to work on some tasks simultaneously, whereas other tasks may depend on the prior completion of tasks. Jobs that can be done simultaneously can be placed on parallel paths, whereas jobs that are dependent should be placed in series. In

Figure F.15, a book revision process begins with the receipt of a final draft from the author. There are three simultaneous paths that could begin immediately: new cover design, issue new ISBN, and proof. Notice that the edit task cannot begin until both the proof and the begin layout editing tasks are complete. Likewise, the finish to printer task cannot begin until the final proof and new cover design tasks are complete.

Gantt Chart

Excel

Using Green Belt XL Add-On

Open a new or existing file (or import an MS project file) in the *MindGenius* application.

Select the *Gantt View* from the *Project* menu.

Enter each new task using the *New Task* option in the right mouse menu.

Define task duration, priority, status, and due date (if any).

Use the *Resources* menu to assign tasks to individuals.

Link tasks (using the right mouse *Link Tasks* option) to define tasks that must be completed before subsequent tasks may be started.

Use *Hierarchy* settings to define subtasks.

Use the *Show Critical Path* option in the *Task Filter* group to identify the project/process critical path.

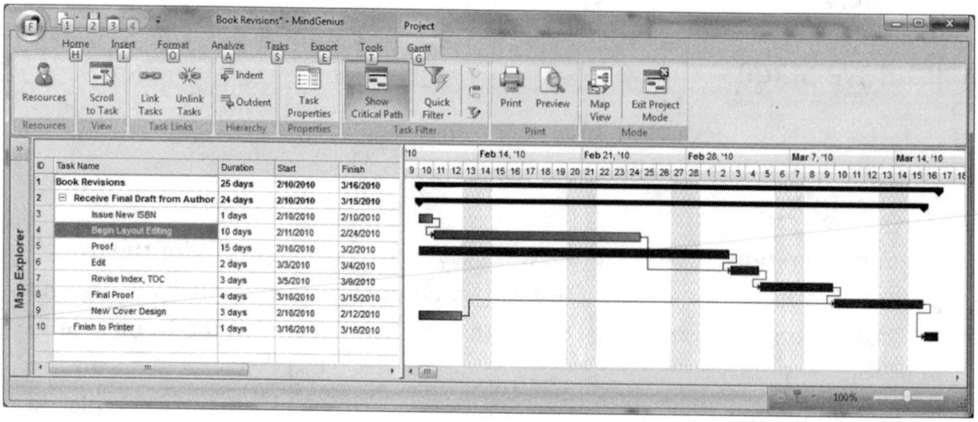

FIGURE F.15 Example Gantt chart for defining critical path using Green Belt XL/MindGenius software.

Interpretation

This method will let you see where you can afford delays. On the critical path, any delay will result in a change in the process/project completion time. Activities not on the critical path have slack time. In Figure F.15, the *Begin Layout Editing* task has a slack time of 4 days. This implies that the task does not need to begin as soon as possible (day 1, its earliest start time) but must begin by day 4 (its latest start time).

There is, by definition, no slack time on the critical path. That is, all tasks on the critical path must be completed as soon as possible (i.e., each task's earliest start time) or the project will be delayed.

Program evaluation and review techniques (PERT) analysis, discussed below, allows probabilistic estimates to be applied to a task's duration.

Goodness-of-Fit Tests

Popular goodness-of-fit tests include the chi-square, Kolmogorov-Smirnov (K-S), and Anderson-Darling tests. They are often reported with probability plots provided as a graphic aid.

When to Use

Measure to Control Stages

- To verify an assumed distribution to ensure validity of statistical tests, including confidence tests, hypothesis tests, and statistical control charts

While the chi-square test is perhaps the most frequently referenced goodness-of-fit technique in general-application statistical textbooks, its popularity in academic circles indeed may be due to its simplicity: Authors can easily describe and demonstrate the test without the need for computer software. In practice, however, data are analyzed almost exclusively using computer software, allowing the use of more sophisticated techniques that are better suited for most applications, particularly in testing continuous distributions. Two of these techniques are the Kolmogorov-Smirnov (K-S) test and the Anderson-Darling test. Both these techniques may be used to compare the fit of assumed distributions to sample data.

For the most part, probability plots offer only visual confirmation of goodness of fit of the data to the assumed distribution. A common method to interpret the probability plots predates computerization of the technique. In days past, one simply would lay a fat pencil on the graph, and if the data were obscured by the pencil, then the data fit the distribution fairly well. The statistical goodness-of-fit tests described here obviously add objectivity to the analysis.

The adequacy of the test for a given distributional fit depends on the stability of the process and the number of data points. Generally, 200 to 300 data points are recommended for testing distributional fits, although fewer data points can be used with less certainty in the results. If the process is not in statistical control, then no one distribution should be fit to the data.

Methodology

The K-S criterion is based on the expectation that there is likely to be a difference between a discrete distribution generated from data and the continuous distribution from which the data were drawn, caused by step difference and random error. As n increases, the size of the difference is expected to decrease. If the measured maximum difference is smaller than expected, then the probability that the distributions are the same is high.

Note that the K-S criterion is very demanding as n becomes large because the K-S criterion is scaled by the square root of n, reflecting an expected decrease in the step-size error. The random error and outliers then dominate, with outliers having a strong effect on the reported value for α (because K-S is a measure of maximum deviation).

The Anderson-Darling statistic is a modification of the K-S test that gives more weight to the data in the tails of the distribution. It requires a known distribution for which critical values are calculated.

Goodness of Fit

Minitab

Use *Stat\Basic Statistics\Normality Test*.

Use the reported p value for the null hypothesis that the data follow the specified distribution. Values less than 0.05 generally indicate that the fitted distribution is not a good match.

Excel

Using Green Belt XL Add-On
Use *New Chart\Normal Probability Chart*. (*Note:* The K-S value is also reported on histograms and control charts where the histogram is displayed.)

(Continued)

The K-S value reported is the p value for the null hypothesis that the data follow the specified distribution. Values less than 0.05 generally indicate that the fitted distribution is not a good match.

Interpretation

A useful graphic technique for determining whether there are too much data in the tail regions of the distribution is to look for patterns near the far-left and far-right portions of the line. Excessive data in the tails would group data above the confidence interval on the left side (small probabilities) and below the confidence interval on the right side (high probabilities). When normal-distribution plots are analyzed and the data fit the distribution well, the mean of the population can be estimated as the value of the line as it crosses the 50th percentile. The distribution standard deviation may be estimated as the difference between the x values corresponding to the points at which the normal line crosses the $y = 50$th ($z = 0$) and $y = 84$th ($z = 1$) percentiles.

In both the Kolmogorov-Smirnov and the Anderson-Darling tests, the null hypothesis is that the data follow the specified distribution. Most statistical software reports a p value, where the null hypothesis is rejected (implying that the distribution is a poor fit) if the p value is less than a predetermined α value (typically 0.05 or 0.10). Distributions also can be compared: The distribution with the larger p value is the more likely distribution.

See also "Histogram" and "Distribution" topics.

Histogram

A *histogram* is a graphic tool used to visualize data. It is a bar chart where the height of each bar represents the number of observations falling within a range of rank-ordered data values.

When to Use

Measure Stage and Analyze Stage

- To graphically display the data as an aid in fitting a distribution for capability analysis or to visually detect the presence of multiple distributions

Methodology

Rank order the data from the smallest value to the largest value. Calculate the number of bars (or cells) as approximately equal to the square root of the number of data values. The number of cells (or bars) will influence the shape of the perceived distribution, so never base it on convenience, data resolution, or anything other than the number of data observations.

The width of each bar is calculated by dividing the range of the data (the maximum value minus the minimum value) by the number of bars. Count the number of data observations in each bar. The vertical axis plots the count of observations in each bar. The horizontal axis displays the data values for each bar (usually either the starting point, ending point, or midpoint). See Figure F.16.

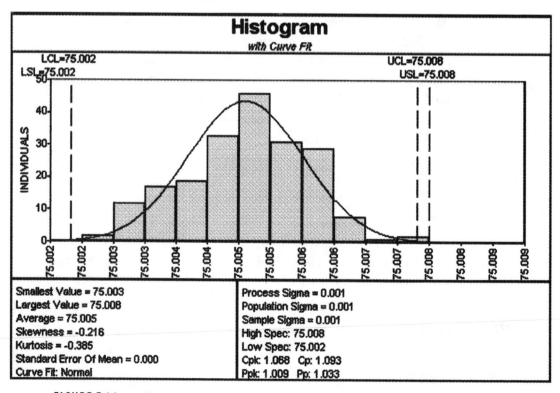

FIGURE F.16 Example of a histogram.

Histogram

Minitab

Use *Stat\Quality Tools\Capability Analysis.*

Excel

Using Green Belt XL Add-On

Use *New Chart\Histogram.* (*Note:* The histogram also may be displayed as an option with the $\bar{X}$ and individual-X control charts.)

Interpretation

An advantage of a histogram is that the process location is clearly identifiable. In Figure F.17, the central tendency of the data is about 75.005. The variation is also clearly distinguishable: We expect most of the data to fall between 75.003 and 75.007. We also can see if the data are bounded or if they have symmetry, such as is evidenced in these data.

If your data are from a symmetric distribution, such as the bell-shaped normal distribution shown in Figure F.17A, the data will be evenly distributed about the center of the histogram. If the data are not evenly distributed about the center of the histogram, the histogram is skewed. If it appears skewed, you should understand the cause of this behavior. Some processes naturally will have a skewed distribution and also may be bounded, such as the concentricity data in Figure F.17B. Concentricity has a natural lower bound at zero because no measurements can be negative. Most of the data are just above zero, so there is a sharp demarcation at the zero point representing a bound.

If double or multiple peaks occur, look for the possibility that the data are coming from multiple sources, such as different suppliers or machine adjustments.

The histogram provides a view of the process as measured. The actual output over a larger sample period may be much wider, even when the process is in control. As a general rule, 200 to 300 data observations are preferred to provide a realistic view of a process distribution, although it is not uncommon to use a

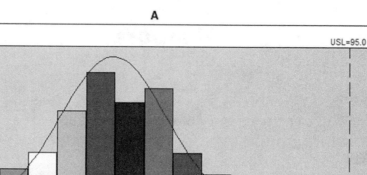

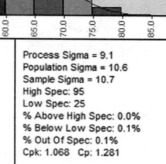

A

LSL=25.0   USL=95.0

Smallest Value = 28.4
Largest Value = 80.8
Average = 54.2
Skewness = -0.2
Kurtosis = -0.4
Standard Error Of Mean = 0.6
K-S Test: 0.1
Curve Fit: Normal

Process Sigma = 9.1
Population Sigma = 10.6
Sample Sigma = 10.7
High Spec: 95
Low Spec: 25
% Above High Spec: 0.0%
% Below Low Spec: 0.1%
% Out Of Spec: 0.1%
Cpk: 1.068   Cp: 1.281

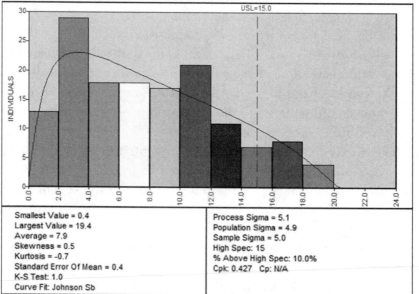

B

USL=15.0

Smallest Value = 0.4
Largest Value = 19.4
Average = 7.9
Skewness = 0.5
Kurtosis = -0.7
Standard Error Of Mean = 0.4
K-S Test: 1.0
Curve Fit: Johnson Sb

Process Sigma = 5.1
Population Sigma = 4.9
Sample Sigma = 5.0
High Spec: 15
% Above High Spec: 10.0%
Cpk: 0.427   Cp: N/A

FIGURE F.17 Two histograms: (A) Histogram of symmetric process with normal distribution fit; (B) histogram of skewed process with nonnormal distribution fit.

histogram when you have much fewer data. Bear in mind that fewer data generally imply a greater risk of error.

One problem that novice practitioners tend to overlook is that the histogram provides only part of the picture. A histogram with a given shape may be produced by many different processes, the only difference in the data being their order. So the histogram that looks like it fits our needs could have come from data showing random variation about the average or from data that are clearly trending toward an undesirable condition. Since the histogram does not consider the sequence of the points, we lack this information. Statistical process control (SPC) provides this context.

The two sets of control charts on the right side of Figure F.18 are based on the same data as shown in the histogram on the left. The only difference between the data in the top set of control charts versus the bottom set of control charts is the order of the data. It is clear that the top set of control charts is from a stable process, whereas the bottom set of control charts is from an out-of-control process. The histogram by itself fails to distinguish between these two very different processes, and it is therefore misleading in its ability to graphically depict the process distribution. In fact, there is *no* single distribution

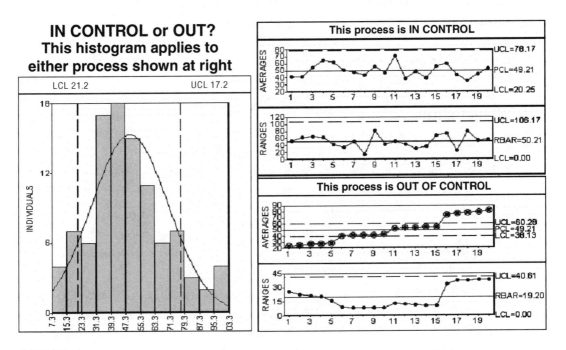

FIGURE F.18 This histogram conceals the time order of the process.

for the process represented by the bottom set of control charts because the process is out of control. By definition, then, the data are from multiple process distributions.

Thus, if the process is out of control, then, by definition, a single distribution cannot be fit to the data. Therefore, always use a control chart to determine statistical control before attempting to fit a distribution (or determine capability) for the data. Once statistical control is established, use goodness-of-fit tests (described earlier) to determine if an assumed distribution provides a reasonable approximation. Remember that a histogram provides only part of the picture and can never be used to assess process stability.

Hypothesis Testing

Hypothesis testing refers to a general class of problems where we seek to compare, at a stated degree of confidence, a sample statistic against a standard value or a statistic from another sample. Hypothesis testing is used in regression analysis and designed experiments to determine if factors included in the analysis contribute to the variation observed in the data (as discussed under "Regression Analysis" below). Hypothesis testing is a tool of statistical inference, where we use sample statistics (such as a sample average $\bar{X}$ or a sample standard deviation s) to infer properties of a population (such as its mean μ or standard deviation σ).

When to Use

Key assumptions include

1. The population is both constant (it does not change over time) and homogeneous (a given sample is representative of the sample as a whole).

2. Samples are randomly collected from the population and representative of the population under investigation. In surveys, low response rates typically would provide extreme value estimates (i.e., the subpopulation of people who have strong opinions one way or the other).

3. The hypothesis tests shown below and their associated α and β risks, depend on the normality of the population. If the population is significantly nonnormal, then the tests are not meaningful, and nonparametric tests should be used. Goodness-of-fit tests are used to test this assumption. Nonparametric tests can be used if the populations are significantly nonnormal.

4. Some tests additionally require equal variance, which can be tested using the *F* test for equality of variance (see "Hypothesis Test for Two-Sample Variances: Two-Sided Example"). If the populations do not have equal variances, then the data can be transformed (see "Transformation"). In some cases, an equivalent test assuming unequal variance may be applied (as shown below for the two-sample mean test).

Analyze Stage

- To compare the calculated mean of a sample to a desired mean value or to a calculated mean from another data set

Improve Stage

- To compare process averages after improvements versus baseline estimates

Methodology

1. *State the null hypothesis H_0.* For example, $H_0: \mu = 25$. The null hypothesis is often stated as what you would like to assert by the test. Sometimes, however, it is better to state what you'd like to disprove because the test provides only two possible conclusions: Reject the null hypothesis or fail to reject it. In other words, we can't prove the null hypothesis, but we can disprove it or fail to disprove it based on the statistical evidence.

2. *Specify the alternative hypothesis H_1.* Most authors recommend that the alternative hypothesis cover all the remaining options. For example, a null hypothesis that the mean is less than or equal to a certain value would have an alternative hypothesis that the mean is greater than that same value. Minitab does not follow these conventions; its null hypothesis always uses the "equal to" designation so that your selection of an alternative hypothesis determines the test criteria.

3. *Choose a significance level (α) or define the p value.* The significance level α, or type 1 error, is the probability of rejecting a hypothesis that is true. A significance of 0.05 is often used. Historically, an α error was assigned in advance of the hypothesis test, much the same way a confidence interval is constructed using an assigned significance. In this way, a hypothesis test can be directly analogous to (and provide the same result as) a confidence interval. The calculated statistic is compared with a tabulated value of the

standardized statistic at the stated significance, indicating whether the null hypothesis is probable given the data. Software now makes it easy to calculate the specific percentile corresponding to the calculated test statistic (see "Interpretation" below). *p* Values are more useful because we might otherwise fail to reject a null hypothesis when the test statistic is just inside the critical value or, conversely, reject a null hypothesis when we are just beyond the critical value. Using the *p* value allows flexibility in rejecting the test and input that might lead to collecting more data.

4. *Collect samples; calculate statistics.* The sample statistics and associated test statistic for the particular null and alternative hypotheses are calculated as described below. The sample size determines the type 2 error (β error): the probability of accepting a false hypothesis. The value $1 - \beta$ is the power of the test, as discussed in Chapter 6.

5. *Reach conclusion.* See "Interpretation" below.

The calculated test statistics for a variety of typical hypothesis tests are provided as follows:

Tests on One-Sample Mean

Two-Sided Test on Mean

Null hypothesis H_0: $\mu = \mu_0$

Alternate hypothesis H1: $\mu \neq \mu_0$

Test statistic: t_0

$$t_0 = \frac{(\bar{X} - \mu)}{s/\sqrt{n}}$$

Reject if $t_0 > t_{\alpha/2, n-1}$ or $t_0 < -t_{\alpha/2, n-1}$

Example: H_0: $\mu = 25$; H_1: $\mu \neq 25$

$\alpha = 0.05$; $n = 25$; $s = 1.8$; $\bar{X} = 25.7$

Test statistic: $t_0 = (25.7 - 25)/(1.8/\text{SQRT}(25))$

$t_0 = 1.94$

$$t_{\text{critical}} = t_{\alpha/2, n-1} = 2.064$$

Conclude: Fail to reject H_0; true mean may be 25.

One-Sided Test on Mean: Case 1

Null hypothesis H_0: $\mu \geq \mu_0$

Alternate hypothesis H_1: $\mu < \mu_0$

Test statistic: t_0

$$t_0 = \frac{(\bar{X} - \mu)}{s/\sqrt{n}}$$

Reject if $t_0 < -t_{\alpha, n-1}$

One-Sided Test on Mean: Case 2

Null hypothesis H_0: $\mu \leq \mu_0$

Alternate hypothesis H_1: $\mu > \mu_0$

Test statistic: t_0

$$t_0 = \frac{(\bar{X} - \mu)}{s/\sqrt{n}}$$

Reject if $t_0 > t_{\alpha, n-1}$

Example: H_0: $\mu \leq 25$; H_1: $\mu > 25$; $\alpha = 0.05$; $n = 25$; $s = 1.8$; $\bar{X} = 25.7$

Test statistic: $t_0 = (25.7-25)/(1.8/\text{SQRT}(25))=1.94$

$$t_{\text{critical}} = t_{0.05, 24} = 1.711$$

Conclude: Reject H_0; true mean $\mu > 25$.

Hypothesis Tests on One-Sample Mean

Minitab

Menu: *Stat\Basic Stats\1 Sample t*

Check *Perform Hypothesis Test*; enter μ_0.

"Options" button: Set *Confidence Level* $1 - \alpha$ and alternative *Not Equal* (two-sided case) or > or < (for one-sided case).

(Continued)

Two-Sided Example at 5% Significance

One-Sample *T*

Test of $\mu = 25$ versus $\neq 25$

N	Mean	SD	SE Mean	95% CI	T	p
25	25.700	1.800	0.360	(24.957, 26.443)	1.94	064

Conclude: Fail to reject ($p > 0.05$). Samples this extreme occur 6.4 percent of time. Consider a larger sample.

One-Sided Example at 5% Significance (Case 2, Using Alternative greater than)

One-Sample *T*

Test of $\mu = 25$ versus > 25

95% Lower

N	Mean	SD	SE Mean	Bound	T	p
25	25.700	1.800	0.360	25.084	1.94	0.032

Conclude: Reject null ($p < 0.05$); $\mu > 25$

Excel

Calculate *p* as

Two-sided: TDIST($|t_0|$,n-1,2)

One-sided Case 1: 1-TDIST($|t_0|$,n-1,1) for $t_0 > 0$; TDIST otherwise

One-sided Case 2: TDIST($|t_0|$,n-1,1) for $t_0 > 0$; 1-TDIST otherwise

Two-Sided Example at 5% Significance

=TDIST(ABS(1.94),25–1,2); $p = 0.064$; fail to reject

One-Sided Example at 5% Significance (Case 2)

=TDIST(ABS(1.94),25–1,1); $p = 0.032$; reject null

Tests on Two-Sample Means (Assuming Unequal Variances)

Null hypothesis H_0: $\mu_1 = \mu_2$

Alternate hypothesis H_1: $\mu_1 = \mu_2$

Test statistic: t_0

$$t_0 = \frac{\overline{X}_1 - \overline{X}_2}{\sqrt{\dfrac{s_1^2}{n_1} + \dfrac{s_2^2}{n_2}}}$$

Reject if $t_0 > t_{\alpha/2,\upsilon}$ or $t_0 < -t_{\alpha/2,\upsilon}$

where $\quad \upsilon = \dfrac{(s_1^2/n_1 + s_2^2/n_2)^2}{\dfrac{(s_1^2/n_1)^2}{n_1 - 1} + \dfrac{(s_2^2/n_2)^2}{n_2 - 1}}$

Example: $n_1 = 25$; $\overline{X} = 15.7$; $s_1 = 1.8$; $n_2 = 50$; $\overline{X}_2 = 21.2$; $s_2 = 2.5$

Test statistic: $t_0 = 10.90$

df $\upsilon = 63$ (always rounded down)

$$t_{\text{critical}} = t_{0.025,63} = 2.00$$

Conclude: Reject H_0; means are not equal.

Hypothesis Tests on Two-Sample Means (Assuming Unequal Variances)

Minitab

Menu: *Stat\Basic Stats\2 Sample t.*

Uncheck *Assume Equal Variances.*

"Options" button: Set *Confidence Level* $1 - \alpha$ and alternative *Not Equal* (two-sided case) or > or < (for one-sided cases).

Two-Sided Example at 5% Significance

Two-Sample *T* Test and CI

Sample	N	Mean	SD	SE Mean
1	25	15.70	1.80	0.36
2	50	21.20	2.50	0.35

(Continued)

Difference = $\mu_1 - \mu_2$

Estimate for difference: –5.500

95% CI for difference: (–6.508,–4.492)

T test of difference = 0 (versus not): T value = –10.90; p value = 0.000; df = 63.
Conclude: Reject null ($p < 0.05$); means are not equal.

Excel

Calculate p as

Two-sided: TDIST($|t_0|$,v,2)

One-sided Case 1: 1-TDIST($|t_0|$,v,1) for $t_0 > 0$; TDIST otherwise

One-sided Case 2: TDIST($|t_0|$,v,1) for $t_0 > 0$; 1-TDIST otherwise

Two-Sided Example at 5% Significance

=TDIST(ABS(10.90),63,2); $p = 0.000$; reject null.

Test on Paired Means

Note: This is a special case of the general two-sample mean test. In this case, each observation in sample 1 has a corresponding observation in sample 2 reflecting paired estimates of the same sample unit. For example, if two people inspected the same item, each of the measurements (from each person) would have a corresponding paired sample with the measurement for the second person for the same sample unit. The differences between each pair is calculated first, and then the standard test on mean is applied to the differences, using the calculated average and standard deviation of the differences.

Null hypothesis H_0: $\mu_1 - \mu_2 = 0$
Alternate hypothesis H_1: $\mu_1 - \mu_2 = 0$
Test statistic: t_0

$$t_0 = \frac{(\bar{X} - \mu)}{s/\sqrt{n}}$$

where $\bar{X}$ and s are calculated using the differences between the paired data.

Reject if $t_0 > t_{\alpha/2,n-1}$ or $t_0 < -t_{\alpha/2,n-1}$

Example: $n = 25$; average difference = 11.4; $S_{\text{differences}} = 2.1$

$$t_0 = \frac{11.4}{2.1/\sqrt{25}} = 27.14$$

$$t_{\text{critical}} = t_{0.025,24} = 2.064$$

Conclude: Reject H_0; means are not equal.

Hypothesis Tests on Paired Means

Minitab

Menu: *Stat\Basic Stats\Paired t*
"Options" button: Set *Confidence Level* $1 - \alpha$ and alternative *Not Equal* (two-sided case) or > or < (for one-sided cases).

Paired *T* Test and CI

	N	Mean	SD	SE Mean
Difference	25	11.400	2.100	0.420

95% CI for mean difference: (10.533, 12.267)

T test of mean difference = 0 (versus not): *T* value = 27.14; *p* value = 0.000.

Conclude: Reject null ($p < 0.05$); means are not equal.

Excel

Calculate p as

Two-sided: TDIST($|t_0|$,n-1,2)

One-sided Case 1: 1-TDIST($|t_0|$,n-1,1) for $t_0 > 0$; TDIST otherwise

One-sided Case 2: TDIST($|t_0|$,n-1,1) for $t_0 > 0$; 1-TDIST otherwise

Two-Sided Example at 5% Significance
=TDIST(ABS(27.14),24,2); $p = 0.000$; reject null; means are not equal.

Tests on One-Sample Variance

Two-Sided Test on Variance
Null hypothesis H_0: $\sigma_1^2 = \sigma_0^2$

Alternate hypothesis H_1: $\sigma_1^2 \neq \sigma_0^2$

Test statistic:

$$\chi_0^2 = (n-1)\frac{s^2}{\sigma_0^2}$$

Reject if $\chi_0^2 > \chi_{\alpha/2,n-1}^2$ or $\chi_0^2 < \chi_{\alpha/2,n-1}^2$

Example: H_0: $\sigma_1^2 = 25$; H_1: $\sigma_1^2 \neq 25$; $\alpha = 0.05$; $n = 15$; $s^2 = 23$

Test statistic: $\chi_0^2 = (15 - 1)/(23/25)$
$$= 12.88$$

$$\chi_{0.975,14}^2 = 5.629;\ \chi_{0.025,14}^2 = 26.119$$

Conclude: Fail to reject H_0.

One-Sided Test on Variance: Case 1

Null hypothesis H_0: $\sigma_1^2 \geq \sigma_0^2$

Alternate hypothesis H_1: $\sigma_1^2 < \sigma_0^2$

Test statistic:

$$\chi_0^2 = (n-1)\frac{s^2}{\sigma_0^2}$$

Reject if $\chi_0^2 < \chi_{1-\alpha/2,n-1}^2$

Example: H_0: $\sigma_1^2 \geq 25$; H_1: $\sigma_1^2 < 25$; $\alpha = 0.05$; $n = 15$; $s^2 = 23$

Test statistic: $\chi_0^2 = (15 - 1)/(23/25)$
$$= 12.88$$

$\chi_{0.95,14}^2 = 6.571;\ \chi_{0.05,14}^2 = 23.685$

Conclude: Fail to reject H_0.

One-Sided Test on Mean: Case 2

Null hypothesis H_0: $\sigma_1^2 \leq \sigma_0^2$

Alternate hypothesis H_1: $\sigma_1^2 > \sigma_0^2$

Test statistic:

$$\chi_0^2 = (n-1)\frac{s^2}{\sigma_0^2}$$

Reject if $\chi_0^2 > \chi_{\alpha,n-1}^2$

Hypothesis Tests on One-Sample Variance

Minitab

Menu: *Stat\Basic Stats\1 Variance*

Check *Perform hypothesis test*; enter σ_0.

"Options" button: Set *Confidence Level* $1 - \alpha$ and alternative *Not Equal* (two-sided case) or > or < (for one-sided cases).

Two-Sided Example at 5% Significance

Method	Chi-square	df	p Value
Standard	12.90	14	0.932

Conclude: Fail to reject ($p > 0.05$).

One-Sided Example at 5% Significance: Case 1 (Using Alternative less than):

Method	Chi-square	df	p Value
Standard	12.90	14	0.466

Conclude: Fail to reject null ($p > 0.05$).

Excel

Calculate p as

Two-sided:

If CHIDIST≤0.5: 2*(CHIDIST(χ_0,n-1))
If CHIDIST>0.5: 2*(1-CHIDIST(χ_0,n-1))

One-sided Case 1: 1-CHIDIST(χ_0,n-1)

One-sided Case 2: CHIDIST(χ_0,n-1)

Two-Sided Example at 5% Significance

=2*(1-CHIDIST(12.88,14)); $p = 0.928$; fail to reject.

One-Sided Example at 5% Significance (Case 1)

=1-CHIDIST(12.88,14); $p = 0.464$; fail to reject.

Test on Two Sample Variances

Two-Sided Test on Two Variances

Null hypothesis H_0: $\sigma_1^2 = \sigma_2^2$

Alternate hypothesis H_1: $\sigma_1^2 < \sigma_2^2$

Test statistic: F_0

$$F_0 = \frac{s_1^2}{s_2^2}$$

where $s_1 > s_2$.

Reject if $F_0 > F_{\alpha/2, v1, v2}$, where $v_1 = n_1 - 1$; $v_2 = n_2 - 1$; equal n not required.

Example: Using a 90% confidence level with $n_1 = 50$; $S_1 = 2.5$; $n_2 = 25$; $S_2 = 1.8$

Test statistic:

$$F_0 = \frac{2.5^2}{1.8^2} = 1.93$$

$v_1 = 50 - 1 = 49$; $v_2 = 25 - 1 = 24$

$F_{0.05, 49, 24} = 1.86$ [using Excel FINV(0.05,49,24)]

Conclude: Reject H_0; variances are not equal.

One-Sided Test on Two Variances:

Null hypothesis H_0: $\sigma_1^2 \geq \sigma_2^2$

Alternate hypothesis H_1: $\sigma_1^2 < \sigma_2^2$

Test statistic: F_0

$$F_0 = \frac{s_1^2}{s_2^2}$$

where $s_1 > s_2$.

Reject if $F_0 > F_{\alpha, v1, v2}$, where $v_1 = n_1 - 1$; $v_2 = n_2 - 1$; equal n not required.

Hypothesis Tests on Two-Sample Variances

Minitab

Menu: *Stat\Basic Stats\2 Variance*

Reports two-sided case.

Two-Sided Example

95% Bonferroni confidence intervals for standard deviations

Sample	N	Lower	SD	Upper
1	50	2.03691	2.5	3.22022
2	25	1.35868	1.8	2.63474

F Test (Normal Distribution)

Test statistic = 1.93, p value = 0.083.

Conclude: Fail to reject null ($p > 0.05$); Variances may be equal.

One-Sided Example

Calculate $p = $ (reported p)/2 = 0.083/2 = 0.0415.

Conclude: Reject null; variances are not equal.

Excel

Reports one-sided case; calculate p as

Two-sided: $2*\text{FDIST}(F_0, v_1, v_2)$

One-sided: $\text{FDIST}(F_0, v_1, v_2)$

Two-Sided Example

$=2*\text{FDIST}(1.93,49,24)$; $p = 0.083$; fail to reject; variances may be equal.

One-Sided Example

$=\text{FDIST}(1.93,49,24)$; $p = 0.042$; reject null; variances are not equal.

Interpretation

The result of the test is to compare the calculated statistics with a test statistic. If the calculated statistic exceeds the critical value of the test statistic (based on the α level chosen), then we reject the null hypothesis. If not, then we fail to reject the null hypothesis. When software is used, the calculated p value provides a direct estimate of the probability of obtaining results as extreme as (or more extreme than) the sample data if the null hypothesis is true. A small observed p value indicates that the chance of observing data as extreme as the sample data (if the null hypothesis were true) is so small that the null hypothesis should be rejected.

Rejecting the null hypothesis is known as a *strong conclusion*. For example, we have disproven that the means are equal. When we fail to reject the null hypothesis, then the means may be equal or may not be; we really can't tell based on the data. This is considered a *weak conclusion*, for obvious reasons. If the calculated p value is close to the specified cutoff (usually 0.05), we may want to collect larger samples to further test the hypothesis. See also the discussions of power and alpha error found in Chapter 6.

Individual-X and Moving-Range Charts

Individual-X and *moving-range charts* are a set of control charts for variables data. The individual-X chart monitors the process location over time based on a subgroup containing a single observation. The moving-range chart monitors the variation between consecutive subgroups over time.

When to Use

Measure Stage

- To baseline the process by quantifying the common-cause level of variation inherent in the process

Analyze Stage

- To differentiate between common and special causes of variation

Improve Stage

- To verify the results of the process improvement on the process metric

Control Stage

- To monitor the process to ensure the stability of the revised process and the continued benefit of the improvement

Individual-X and moving-range charts generally are used when you can't group measurements into rational subgroups or when it's more convenient to monitor actual observations rather than subgroup averages. Each subgroup, consisting of a single observation, represents a "snapshot" of the process at a given point in time. The charts' x axes are time-based, so the charts show a history of the process. For this reason, you must have time-ordered data; that is, entered in the sequence from which the data were generated. If this is not the case, then trends or shifts in the process may not be detected but instead may be attributed to random (common-cause) variation.

If rational subgroups can be formed, $\bar{X}$ charts generally are preferred because the control limits are calculated easily using the normal distribution. When rational subgroups cannot be formed, then we must make assumptions about the distribution of the process to calculate the statistical control limits on an individual-X chart. This can be troublesome, particularly when the process distribution is very skewed or bounded.

Individual-X charts are efficient at detecting relatively large shifts in the process average, typically shifts of 2.5σ to 3σ or larger. If $\bar{X}$ charts can be used, then their larger subgroups will detect smaller shifts much more quickly; see "Statistical Process Control (SPC) Charts" for more detail. EWMA charts also can be used at any subgroup size to increase the sensitivity to smaller process shifts.

Methodology

An important consideration for the individual-X chart is the choice of curve fit used for determining the control limits. There is a fundamental dilemma, in that a distribution should not be fit to the data unless the data are from a controlled process, yet the process distribution must be assumed to determine the control limits. Because of this limitation, you may consider using other control charts, such as the $\bar{X}$ chart or EWMA chart, to first establish process control for a set of data; then a distribution can be fit to the data.

Individual-X Chart Calculations

Plotted statistic: The observation.

Centerline: The average (normal distribution); the median of the fitted distribution (nonnormal distributions).

UCL, LCL *(upper and lower control limit):*

$$UCL_x = \bar{x} + 3\sigma_x \text{ (normal distribution)}$$

$$LCL_x = \bar{x} - 3\sigma_x \text{ (normal distribution)}$$

where $\bar{x}$ is the average and σ_x is the process sigma.
Note: Some authors prefer to write this as:

$$UCL_x = \bar{x} + E_2 \overline{MR}$$

$$LCL_x = \bar{x} - E_2 \overline{MR}$$

For nonnormal distributions, the UCL is defined at the 99.865 percentile of the fitted curve, and the LCL is defined at the 0.135 percentile of the fitted curve.

Moving-Range Chart Calculations

Plotted statistic: The moving ranges between successive subgroups in an individual-X chart (i.e., the difference between the current observation and the observation immediately prior):

$$MR = |x_j - x_{j-1}|$$

Centerline:

$$\overline{MR} = \frac{1}{m-1} \sum_{j=1}^{m} MR_j$$

where m is the total number of subgroups included in the analysis, and MR_j is the moving range at subgroup j.

UCL, LCL *(upper and lower control limit):*

$$UCL_{MR} = \overline{MR} + 3d_3\sigma_x \quad \text{(all distributions)}$$

$$LCL_{MR} = \max(0, \overline{MR} - 3d_3\sigma_x) \quad \text{(all distributions)}$$

where $\overline{MR}$ is the average of the moving ranges, σ_x is the process sigma, and d_3 is a function of n (tabulated in Appendix 6).

Note: Some authors prefer to write this as

$$\text{UCL}_{\text{MR}} = \overline{MR}D_4 \qquad \text{LCL}_{\text{MR}} = \overline{MR}D_3$$

Individual-X Chart

Minitab

Use *Stat\Control Chart\Variable Charts for Individuals\I-MR or Individuals*.

Options

Use *Options\Display* to specify plotted subgroups.

Use *Scale\Time\Stamp* to set column for *x*-axis labels.

Use *Options\Parameters* for predefined centerline and control limits.

Use *Options\Estimate* to omit subgroups from calculations.

Use *Options\Stages* to define control regions.

Use *Options\Test* to apply relevant run-test rules.

Note: When the normality assumption is not met, the data must be transformed (using *Stat\Quality Tools\Johnson Transformation*).

Excel

Using Green Belt XL Add-On

Use *New Chart\Individual-X and Moving Range Chart*.

Options

Use *Data Range* to specify plotted subgroups.

Use *Options\Title\Label* to set column for *x*-axis labels.

Use *Options\Control Limits* for predefined centerline and control limits, to omit subgroups from calculations, and to define control regions.

Use *Options\Analysis\Auto Drop* checkbox to automatically remove out-of-control groups from the control limit calculations (they are still displayed on the chart).

(Continued)

Use *Options\Run Test* to apply relevant run-test rules.

Use *Options\Format\Show Moving Range Chart* to turn on/off moving-range chart display.

Use *Options\Analysis\Curve Fit* to change to/from normal and Johnson curve fits, which are automatically applied to the control limit calculations. This allows users to see the data in raw units rather than transformed units (as in Minitab).

Interpretation

Research has shown that for processes following the normal distribution, when a special cause is detected on the moving-range chart, it also will appear on the individual-X chart, thus making the moving-range chart redundant.

Never adjust the process based on the observation's value relative to specifications because this *tampering* will increase the overall variation in the process.

If there are any out-of-control points on the individual-X chart, then the special causes must be eliminated. Brainstorm and conduct designed experiments to find the process elements that contribute to sporadic changes in process location. To predict the capability of the process after special causes have been eliminated, you should remove the out-of-control points from the analysis, which will remove the statistical bias of the out-of-control points by dropping them from the calculations of the centerline and control limits.

Look for obviously nonrandom behavior. Use the run-test rules, which apply statistical tests for trends to the plotted points.

If the process shows control relative to the statistical limits and run tests for a sufficient period of time (long enough to see all potential special causes), then you can analyze its process capability relative to requirements. Capability is only meaningful when the process is stable because we cannot predict the outcome of an unstable process.

Interaction Plots

Interaction plots are a particular form of point-and-line charts used to graphically show the relationship among three parameters, usually two factors and a response.

When to Use

Analyze Stage and Improve Stage

- In analyzing the results of multiple regression and designed experiments to graphically show the effect of two factor interaction on a response

Methodology

The plot variable is assigned to the x axis, and a second variable (usually the response) is assigned to the y axis. The levels of the interaction variable are used to form the separate lines displayed on the plot.

For example, we may be interested in seeing if there is an interaction between two process factors—cycle time and personal response—on the response satisfaction score obtained from a customer survey.

We can sort the data based on cycle time as the first field and personal response as the second. In this case, there were only two conditions for cycle time (210, 330) and two conditions for personal response (yes, no). Referring to Figure F.19, we average the response data (satisfaction score)

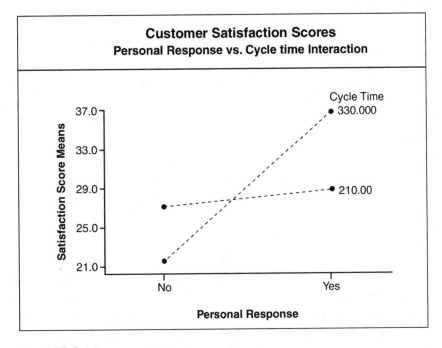

FIGURE F.19 Example of an interaction plot.

for those four conditions of cycle time, personal response [(210, yes), (210, no), (330, yes), (330, no)], and plot the average response on the interaction plot.

Interpretation

In this interaction plot, there are two lines: The line for cycle time equals 210 is relatively flat, with little change in customer satisfaction as we move from the personal response (no) to the personal response (yes) condition. The line for cycle time equals 330 is relatively steep, with a big difference in customer satisfaction between the personal response (yes) and the personal response (no) conditions. Since the effect of cycle time on satisfaction varies depending on whether there was a personalized response or not, we say that there is an *interaction* between cycle time and personalized response. Interactions are easily spotted on an interaction plot by nonparallel lines, such as shown in the figure.

Lean Methodology

Lean is a set of principles and methodologies for improving cycle times and quality through elimination of waste, sometimes known by its Japanese name of *muda*. Lean thinking allows us to distinguish between value-added and non-value-added activities. The immediate result is the removal of unnecessary non-value-added activities. The objective is to improve cycle times, reduce waste, and increase value to the customer.

Lean thinking has been shown to reap dramatic benefits in organizations. Organizations are able to sustain production levels with half the personnel, improving quality and reducing cycle times from 50 percent to 90 percent (Womack and Jones, 1996).

The lean methodology is credited to Taiichi Ohno of Toyota; it has been popularized by James Womack and Daniel Jones in *The Machine That Changed the World* and *Lean Thinking*. The methodology goes by several names, including *lean manufacturing*, when used in manufacturing applications, and the *Toyota Production System*, owing to its origins. The more recent label of *lean thinking*, used by authors Womack and Jones, applies the methodology across a broad range of businesses. While the lean methods have been a hot topic in business only since the 1970s, it is well acknowledged that Henry Ford pioneered many of these same techniques.

When to Use

Lean encompasses a variety of tools useful throughout DMAIC. Lean tools discussed elsewhere in Part 3 include 5S, level loading, process cycle efficiency, spaghetti diagrams, and velocity.

Methodology

Several of the lean methods are fairly well known in and of themselves. *Just-in-time*, for example, has been a buzzword within automotive manufacturing for over two decades. Other well-known methods include *kanban* (Japanese for cards), *kaizen* (which refers to rapid improvement), and 5S.

There may be some confusion regarding the use of lean methods and Six Sigma. Some recent practitioners of Six Sigma have struggled in their Six Sigma deployment by retaining separate functional teams responsible for lean deployment. Six Sigma is an umbrella deployment strategy for implementing value-added improvement projects aligned with an organization's business strategy. Lean provides essential methods to define *value* and *waste* to improve an organization's responsiveness to customer needs. As such, the lean methods enhance the Six Sigma strategy and can be seen as critical methods for accomplishing the Six Sigma goals.

Lean focus is on three areas: visibility, velocity, and value. *Visibility*, also known as *transparency* or *visual control*, broadens our awareness of problems. Visibility implies that problems become immediately (or very quickly) known to all stakeholders so that action may be taken. Visibility fosters an "all hands on deck" philosophy: Stakeholders stop what they're doing to help relieve the bottleneck caused by process problems.

Velocity, sometimes known as *flow*, refers to the speed of process delivery. Speed provides flexibility and improved responsiveness to customer demands. By reducing process lead times, we can quickly respond to new orders or changes required by the customer.

Value simply is the opposite of waste. Value can be defined as something for which the customer is willing to pay. If a process step does not produce value, it is a source of waste and should be removed. More detail is provided in the "Value-Stream Analysis" section of Chapter 6.

Although it may be your initial tendency, don't limit your value stream to the walls of your organization. Fantastic sums of money have been saved by evaluating value streams as they move from supplier to customer, often because of mistaken concepts of value or attempts to achieve operational savings that diminish the customer value.

Although we often think of physical inventories of product or work in process as useful for satisfying customer demands, lean thinking challenges this assumption. Instead, we should view inventory as money spent on partial work that generates no income until it is completed. Inventories hide problems, such as unpredictable or low process yields, equipment failure, or uneven production levels. When inventory exists as work-in-process (WIP), it prevents new orders from being processed until the WIP is completed. Although these concepts are most clearly identified with manufacturing processes, they persist in service processes, where inventory may refer to health-care patients, hamburgers at a fast-food counter, or an unfinished swimming pool under construction.

Interpretation

Visibility, velocity, and value are key focus points of lean. Visibility (or transparency) allows the organization to see progress and barriers to success. A focus on value forces resources to activities important to customers. Improved velocity allows us to be more responsive to customer needs. Velocity can be improved by the following means:

- Increasing completions per hour
- Removing unnecessary process steps
- Reducing movement of material and personnel
- Reducing process/product complexities
- Reducing errors that require rework
- Optimizing process
- Reducing waiting
- Reducing work-in-process

Level Loading

Level loading is a lean tool used to balance the flow of orders throughout a process.

When to Use

Improve Stage

- To balance the flow of orders through a process and reduce in-process inventories

Methodology

Some prerequisites for successful level loading include

- Standardization of work instructions
- Cross-training so that employees can be shifted to meet increased demand or address process problems
- Transparency so that operational personnel detect and respond to shifts in demand or process problems as soon as possible (Transparency, or visual control, has been found to decrease the reaction time to waste, foster responsibility, and aid in problem solving.)

To balance the process steps,

- We first calculate the *takt* time. *Takt* is the German word for "metronome," and it is used to indicate the desired rhythm of the process.
- *Takt* time = demand (units)/available resource (hours) For example, if the product has an average demand of 64 units per day, and the cell works 16 hours per day (two shifts), then the *takt* time is calculated as 15 minutes (i.e., 4 units per hour).
- The *takt* time is posted at the cell, and the resources (machines and personnel) at each step within the cell are balanced so that their cycle time equals the *takt* time.
- While we usually can design the process and allocate standard resources for any process to meet its standard *takt* time, we recognize that a shift in demand will shift the *takt* time requirements. One way to accommodate the *takt* time adjustment is to shift resources.

Interpretation

Level loading ensures that goods produced at each step are used immediately by the next step, ensuring a constant flow of items (or service) through the value stream. If a temporary increase in orders is received, the pace remains the same, but resources are moved to meet demand.

Linearity Analysis

Linearity analysis provides an indication of whether the bias error associated with a measurement system is constant throughout the operating range of the equipment. In other words, is the measurement system equally accurate for large measurements as for small?

When to Use

Measure Stage

- To evaluate the accuracy of a measurement system throughout the range of measurements required for the process

Methodology

The Automotive Industry Action Group method (AIAG, 1995) of calculating linearity is as follows: Choose two or more parts (product or service types) throughout the operating range of the gauge. Measure the pertinent characteristic using high-accuracy gauges, such as those used in layout inspections, to obtain a reference value. Using the gauge to be studied, have one or more process personnel measure the characteristic multiple times. Calculate the average of these measurements for each part. Calculate the bias for each part as the difference between the gauge average and the reference value. Using a scatter diagram, plot the reference value (x axis) versus the bias (y axis).

Linearity

Minitab

Data input: Enter columns for part/item designator, reference value, and measured value.

Menu: *Stat\Quality Tools\Gauge Study\Gauge Linearity and Bias Study*

Results: Obtain slope from plot; report as percent linearity.

Excel

Using Green Belt XL Add-On

Data input: Enter columns for part/item designator, reference value, and measured value; calculate bias for each item.

Menu: *New Chart\ Scatter Diagram*

Data range: Select column of reference values as x axis (first column in data range); select column of bias as y axis (second column in data range)

Results: Obtain slope from plot; report as percent linearity.

Interpretation

Use the coefficient of determination R^2 to determine if the linear fit is adequate. (Usually, a number such as 70 percent or higher provides sufficient linearity.) If the fit is linear, then the percent linearity is the absolute value of the slope of the regression line, reported as a percentage.

$$\%\text{Linearity} = |\text{slope}| \times 100\%$$

Matrix Diagrams

A *matrix diagram* is used to show the relationship between the various items in two or more groups. Matrix diagrams are tabular in format, where each cell contains a numerical score that indicates the strength of the perceived relationship between the row and its intersecting column.

When to Use

Define Stage

- To select projects aligned with the company's goals and objectives
- To understand how customer requirements are aligned with process metrics

Improve Stage

- To ensure that process solutions are aligned with customer needs

A matrix diagram establishes pairings between two sets of items or helps to rate an item according to its relationship to another item (or items). For instance, you might choose to make a matrix showing the relationship between all the departments in your organization and the various jobs that need to be completed. You can use the matrix to assign primary responsibility, secondary responsibility, and other levels of interest for each task. Examples of use include

- Project deliverables versus business objectives
- Customer requirements versus internal process objectives
- The foundation of quality function deployment
- Suggested projects versus project rating criteria
- Black belt candidates versus candidate rating criteria

Methodology

First, you will need to determine what groups of items you would like to compare within your matrix. (You might want to use information collected in another tool. For instance, you could use the group headings from an affinity diagram of process issues as one group of items and the project objectives as another.)

Each item in the group will be compared, one at a time, with each item in the other group. Using consensus decision rules, determine whether there is a relationship between the two items and, if so, whether the relationship is a strong or weak one. Then mark the intersection of the two items. There are several standard systems used to denote relationships.

Plus and Minus System

A plus indicates that a relationship exists. A minus indicates that no relationship exists.

Symbol System

A triangle indicates that a weak relationship exists. A circle shows that some relationship exists. A circle within a circle shows that a strong relationship exists.

Directional System

Use arrows to show that one item has an effect on another. The process of deciding which arrow to use often can lead to helpful realizations. You might have known that two things were related but never thought about the nature of the cause and effect. Some software allows these arrows to be weighted (using boldface) to show the relative strength of the relationship.

Numerical System

Analogous to the directional system, this system is intended to show the strength and direction of relationships. For example, a 10 implies a strong causal relationship, whereas 1/10 shows a strong relationship in the other direction.

Matrix Diagram

Excel

Using Green Belt XL Add-On

Use *New Chart\Matrix Diagram*. Enter the numerical score for each paired relationship.

Interpretation

An example of a prioritization matrix is shown in Figure F.20. The organization's business objectives are as follows:

- Improve profitability by 50 percent.
- Improve on-time delivery rate to 90 percent.
- Improve process efficiency (cycle time estimated to actual) to 95 percent.
- Improve process yield to the Six Sigma level.
- Increase number of inventory turns to 10.

Deployment Strategy	Financial Benefit	On-time Delivery	Process Efficiency	Quality OBA	Process Yield/Scrap	Inventory turns	Totals	Rank of Strategies
BMP Cell 12 Scrap Reduction	9	3	9	3	9	3	36	1
ADS Cell 2 Efficiency	3	9	3	1	1	9	26	3
SMT Efficiency Improvements	3	3	3	9	9	3	30	2
Totals	15	15	15	13	19	15	92	
Rank of Issues	2	2	2	6	1	2		

FIGURE F.20 Example of a matrix diagram for project selection from the Green Belt XL software.

Since these objectives conveniently summarized the primary concerns of their customers, shareholders, and employees, the executive staff decided to use them as prioritization criteria for the improvement projects.

A score of 1, 3, or 9 is applied to each of the projects for each of the criteria, with a score of 9 indicating that a given project is highly capable of meeting that requirement. A score of 1 indicates that the project is not likely to fulfill the criteria, and a score of 3 indicates that it is likely to meet the requirement.

For example, the first project ("BMP Cell 12 Scrap Reduction") was considered to be highly likely to meet the requirements of financial benefits (improve profitability by 50 percent), process efficiency (95 percent improvement in cycle time), and process yield/scrap, so the project received a score of 9 for each of these items. This project was likely to improve the on-time delivery rate to 90 percent and inventory turns (to 10 or higher), so it received a score of 3 for these items. The sum of these scores is 36, as shown in the "Totals" column.

This score then can be compared with the score for other projects, with the highest-scored projects receiving the highest implementation priority.

The "Totals" column provides an indication of how well the projects are geared to meet the criteria the organization has established. A low number indicates that few projects are likely to meet the criteria.

Multi-Vari Plots

Multi-vari plots, popularized by Dorian Shainin, are used to assign variation to one of the following:

- *Within-piece or within-sample variation.* For example, this includes taper or out-of-round conditions in a manufactured part or temperature or pH variations in a chemical sample.
- *Piece-to-piece variation.* This is what we typically think of as within-subgroup process variation—the variation we see over a short term from one sample to another.
- *Time-to-time variation.* This refers to variation changing over a period of time.

When to Use

Analyze Stage

- To categorize variation to eliminate factors
- To investigate interactions among factors

Methodology

First, decide how data will be collected for the analysis. Are multiple measurements from the same sample available (or useful) to calculate within-sample variation?

After collecting the data, construct a plot such as that shown in Figure F.21. Each sample unit will be represented with its own symbol ("Batch" as shown in the figure). The symbol length (the distance between the horizontal bars on a symbol) represents the within-sample variation.

Multi-Vari Chart

Minitab

Use *Stat\Quality Tools\Multi-vari Chart*.
Use the "Select" button to enter the response and one or more data column labels.

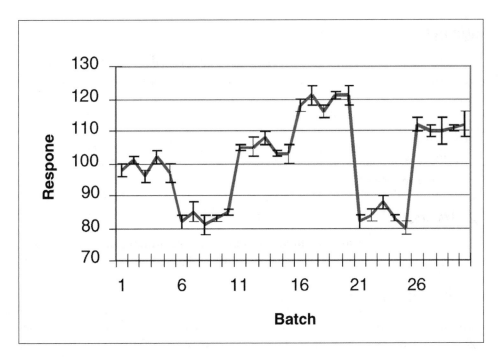

FIGURE F.21 Example of a multi-vari plot.

Interpretation

The categorizations aid in our understanding of the types of factors that cause variation in our processes. This categorization helps to reduce the number of factors. At times, we can see the effects of interactions because they contribute to one or more of the categories of variation.

It is important to understand that the multi-vari plot is not a control chart, so it cannot be used to determine if there is a statistical instability in the process.

In Figure F.21, the plot shows both the within-batch variation and the time-to-time variation. Piece-to-piece variation (the variation between batches 1–5, 6–10, etc.) is negligible, but step changes to the process are clear between batches 5 and 6, 10 and 11, 15 and 16, and so on.

Nominal Group Technique

The *nominal group technique* (NGT) is a method of ranking subjective information to build consensus. It is used to reduce a large number of ideas into a workable number of key ideas.

When to Use

The NGT can be used whenever consensus building is desired and there are no data to otherwise narrow the list. It may be used as a precursor to data collection.

Define Stage

- To reduce a large number of potential projects into a workable number of key projects

Analyze Stage

- To reach consensus on which solution, of a large number of potential solutions, should be investigated in the initial stages of analysis

Methodology

Start by handing out a number of index cards to each team member. For fewer than 20 potential options, hand out four cards per member; for 20 to 35 five options, six cards per member; and for more than 35 options, eight cards per member.

After discussion of the options, each member should choose his or her top *N* options, where *N* is the number of cards handed out per member. Write one option on each card, not repeating any option; then write the rank order on each of the *N* cards. It's best to weight using the "larger is better" criterion. For example, if there are six cards per member, then a member's top vote should be rated 6 and the least favorite selection (of the six) should be rated 1.

Based on all the rankings from all the participants, you calculate how often an option was selected and the ranked weight for each option. For example, six options for software implementation were evaluated by a team. Since the number of options is fewer than 20, each team member was provided four index cards. Each member selected his or her preferred four options and then ranked those options, with a rank of 1 being the least desirable option (of the four). See Table T.13.

Software Options	**Bob**	**Jim**	**Tim**	**Jill**	**Times Selected**	**Total Score**
Internal	2	1	4	3	7	
Existing	1	4	2	4	4	11
Vendor A				1	1	1
Vendor B	4	3	3	2	4	12
Vendor C	3	2		3	3	8
Vendor D			1		1	1

TABLE T.13 Nominal Group Technique

Interpretation

The result is that we can concentrate our efforts on the items selected most often or with the highest ranked weight.

In the preceding example, based on both the number of times an option was selected and the total score, the "Existing" software and that from "Vendor B" are the two favored options. Note that when the two evaluation methods (total score and number of times selected) do not agree, or when the scores are close, it is usually preferred to evaluate more than one leading option.

Nonparametric Test on Equality of Means

Nonparametric tests may be used in place of traditional hypothesis tests on the equality of two means when distributional assumptions cannot be met. A nonparametric test is one in which there are no distributional requirements, such as normality, for the validity of the test. Typically, nonparametric tests require larger sample sizes than parametric tests.

When to Use

Analyze Stage

- To compare the mean of samples from different conditions when normality cannot be assumed

Improve Stage

- To compare process averages after improvements versus baseline estimates when normality cannot be assumed

Methodology

State the null hypothesis H_0 using the same reasoning discussed under "Hypothesis Testing on Mean of Two Samples" above. In this case, the null hypothesis will be *the median of population 1 equals the median of population 2*. Nonparametric tests typically will use the median rather than the mean because the median is a reliable estimate of the central tendency regardless of the distribution. Recall that the average is not a reliable predictor for nonsymmetric distributions.

Specify the alternative hypothesis H_1 to cover the remaining options. In this case, the alternative hypothesis would be *the median of population 1 does not equal the median of population 2*.

Choose a significance level (α) or the p value. The significance level, or type I error, is the probability of rejecting a hypothesis that is true. A value of 0.05 is typical.

Collect samples. As the sample size is increased, the type II error (β error: the probability of accepting a false hypothesis) is decreased.

The simplest of the nonparametric tests for central tendency is the one-sample sign test, which tests that approximately half the data are above the test level.

An enhancement of this test, known as the *Wilcoxen signed rank test*, includes the magnitude and sign of the difference from the median. It assumes a *symmetric*, continuous distribution, and it can be applied to differences between paired observations as well.

The *Mann-Whitney test* may be used for testing the equality of two medians. It assumes that the distributions of the two populations have the same shape and spread. If the distributions are approximately normal, the test is 95 percent as efficient as a standard *t* test for large samples. Regardless of the distribution, the test is always at least 86 percent as efficient as a *t* test.

These tests may be performed in Minitab (use *Stat\Nonparametrics*) or other statistical software.

Interpretation

The result of the test is to compare the calculated statistics with a test statistic. For example, if the calculated statistic exceeds the critical value of the test statistic (based on the α level chosen), then we reject the null hypothesis. If not, then we fail to reject the null hypothesis. Rejecting the null hypothesis is known as a *strong conclusion:* We have disproven that the medians are equal. When we fail to reject the null hypothesis, then the medians may be equal or may not be; we really can't tell based on the data. This is considered a *weak conclusion* for obvious reasons. We may want to collect larger samples to further test the hypothesis.

Np Chart

An *Np chart* is one of a set of control charts specifically designed for attributes data. The *Np* chart monitors the number of times a condition occurs, relative to a constant sample size, when each sample can either have this condition or not have this condition. For example, we could sample a set number of transactions each month from all the transactions that occurred and from this sample count the number of transactions that had one or more errors. We then would track on the *Np* control chart the number of transactions with errors each month.

When to Use

Measure Stage

- To estimate, using attributes data, the process baseline (Generally, we would greatly prefer to use a variables control chart for this purpose.)

Improve Stage

- Since the number of errors tends to be quite small (for even very large samples), the use of attribute charts is limited in the improve stage.

Methodology

Samples are collected from the process at specific points each time. Each sample (at each point in time) has the same number of units, each of which must either match or not match some criterion of interest (such as being defective).

Plotted statistic: The number of items in the sample meeting a criterion of interest.

Centerline:

$$n\bar{p} = \frac{\sum_{j=1}^{m}(\text{count})_j}{m}$$

where m is the number of groups included in the analysis.

UCL, LCL (upper and lower control limits):

$$\text{UCL}_{np} = n\bar{p} + 3\sqrt{n\bar{p}(1-\bar{p})}$$
$$\text{LCL}_{np} = \max[0,\ n\bar{p} - 3\sqrt{n\bar{p}(1-\bar{p})}]$$

where n is the sample size, $n\bar{p}$ is the average count, and $\bar{p}$ is calculated as follows:

$$\bar{p} = \frac{\sum_{j=1}^{m}(\text{count})_j}{m \times n}$$

For example, we observe 500 telemarketing calls each week, and we record the total number of calls with one or more errors. Ten months of data are observed, with the following number of calls with errors in each sample: 7, 14, 12, 18, 9, 11, 12, 8, 11, and 21. The control chart is shown in Figure F.22.

Np Chart

Minitab

Use *Stat\Control Chart\Attribute Charts\Np*. Specify a constant *Subgroup Size* for each group.

Options

Use *Options\Display* to specify plotted subgroups.

Use *Scale\Time\Stamp* to set column for x-axis labels.

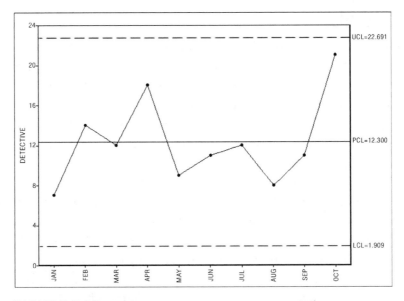

FIGURE F.22 Example of an *Np* chart created using Quality America Green Belt XL software.

Use *Options\Parameters* for predefined centerline and control limits.

Use *Options\Estimate* to omit subgroups from calculations.

Use *Options\Stages* to define control regions.

Use *Options\Test* to apply relevant run-test rules.

Excel

Using Green Belt XL Add-On

Use *New Chart\Np Chart*. Specify a constant *Subgroup Size* for each group.

Options

Use *Data Range* to specify plotted subgroups.

Use *Options\Title\Label* to set column for *x*-axis labels.

Use *Options\Control Limits* for predefined centerline and control limits, to omit subgroups from calculations, and to define control regions.

Use the *Options\Analysis\Auto Drop* checkbox to automatically remove out-of-control groups from the control limit calculations (they are still displayed on the chart).

Use *Options\Run Test* to apply relevant run-test rules.

Interpretation

The upper and lower control limits indicate the bounds of expected process behavior. The fluctuation of the points between the control limits is due to the variation that is intrinsic (built in) to the process. We say that this variation is due to common causes that influence the process. Any points outside the control limits can be attributed to a special cause, implying a shift in the process. When a process is influenced by only common causes, then it is stable and can be predicted.

If there are any out-of-control points, then special causes of variation must be identified and eliminated. Brainstorm and conduct designed experiments to find the process elements that contribute to sporadic changes in process location. To predict the capability of the process after special causes have been eliminated, you should remove the out-of-control points from the analysis, which will remove the statistical bias of the out-of-control points by dropping them from the calculations of the average and control limits.

Note that some SPC software will allow varying sample sizes for the Np chart. In this case, the control limits and the average line will be adjusted for each sample. Frequently, it is less confusing to use a P chart for these data because only its control limits will vary (the average line will remain constant). See "Run-Test Rules" and "Statistical Process Control (SPC) Charts" for more detail.

P Chart

A *P chart* is one of a set of control charts specifically designed for attributes data. The P chart monitors the percent of samples having the condition, relative to either a fixed or varying sample size, when each sample either does have this condition or does not have this condition. For example, we might choose to look at all the transactions in the month (since this would vary from month to month) or a set number of samples, whichever we prefer. From this sample, we would count the number of transactions that had one or more errors. We then would track on the P control chart the percent of transactions with errors each month.

When to Use

Measure Stage

- To estimate, using attributes data, the process baseline (Generally, we would greatly prefer to use variables control charts for this purpose.)

Improve Stage

- Since the number of errors tends to be quite small (for even very large samples), the use of attribute charts is limited in the improve stage.

Methodology

Samples are collected from the process at specific points each time. Each sample (at each point in time) may have a unique number of units, each of which must either match or not match some criterion of interest (such as being defective).

Plotted statistic: The percent of items in the sample meeting a criterion of interest.

$$p_j = \frac{(\text{count})_j}{n_j}$$

where n_j is the sample size (number of units) of group j.

Centerline:

$$\bar{p} = \frac{\sum_{j=1}^{m}(\text{count})_j}{\sum_{j=1}^{m} n_j}$$

where n_j is the sample size (number of units) of group j, and m is the number of groups included in the analysis.

UCL, LCL (upper and lower control limit):

$$\text{UCL} = \bar{p} + 3\sqrt{\frac{\bar{p}(1-\bar{p})}{n_j}}$$

$$\text{LCL} = \max\left[0, \bar{p} - 3\sqrt{\frac{\bar{p}(1-\bar{p})}{n_j}}\right]$$

where n_j is the sample size (number of units) of group j, and $\bar{p}$ is the average percent.

For example, we observe a varying number of telemarketing calls each week, and we record the total number of calls with one or more errors. Ten months of data are observed, with the following number of calls with errors in each sample: 7 of 350, 14 of 312, 12 of 125, 18 of 170, 9 of 165, 11 of 264, 12 of 254, 8 of 404, 11 of 137, and 21 of 312. The control chart is show in Figure F.23.

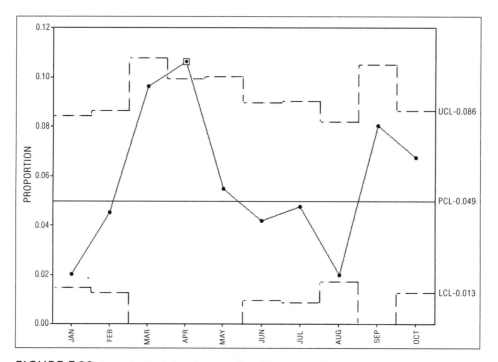

FIGURE F.23 Example of a *P* chart for examples of varying size (created using Quality America Green Belt XL software).

P Chart

Minitab

Use *Stat\Control Chart\Attribute Charts\P*. Specify a constant *Subgroup Size* or a column containing variable *Subgroup Sizes* for each group.

Options

Use *Options\Display* to specify plotted subgroups.

Use *Scale\Time\Stamp* to set column for *x*-axis labels.

Use *Options\Parameters* for predefined centerline and control limits.

Use *Options\Estimate* to omit subgroups from calculations.

Use *Options\Stages* to define control regions.

Use *Options\Test* to apply relevant run-test rules.

Excel

Using Green Belt XL Add-On

Use *New Chart\P Chart*. Specify a constant *Subgroup Size* or a column containing variable *Subgroup Sizes* for each group.

Options

Use *Data Range* to specify plotted subgroups.

Use *Options\Title|Label* to set column for *x*-axis labels.

Use *Options\Control Limits* for predefined centerline and control limits, to omit subgroups from calculations, and to define control regions.

Use the *Options\Analysis\Auto Drop* checkbox to automatically remove out-of-control groups from the control limit calculations (they are still displayed on the chart).

Use *Options\Run Test* to apply relevant run-test rules.

Interpretation

The upper and lower control limits indicate the bounds of expected process behavior. The fluctuation of the points between the control limits is due to the variation that is intrinsic (built in) to the process. We say that this variation is due to common causes that influence the process. Any points outside the control limits can be attributed to a special cause, implying a shift in the process. When a process is influenced by only common causes, then it is stable and can be predicted.

If there are any out-of-control points, then special causes of variation must be identified and eliminated. Brainstorm and conduct designed experiments to find the process elements that contribute to sporadic changes in process location. To predict the capability of the process after special causes have been eliminated, you should remove the out-of-control points from the analysis, which will remove the statistical bias of the out-of-control points by dropping them from the calculations of the average and control limits. See "Run-Test Rules" and "Statistical Process Control (SPC) Charts" for more detail.

Pareto Chart

A *Pareto chart* is a vertical bar graph showing problems in a prioritized order to determine which problems should be tackled first. The categories for the

vertical bars represent mutually exclusive categories of interest. The categories are sorted in decreasing order from left to right in the Pareto diagram
based on the value of the metric displayed in the y axis, either by count or by
cost.

When to Use

Pareto charts provide a guide to selecting opportunities by differentiating between the vital few and the trivial many. They are typically used to prioritize
competing or conflicting "problems" so that resources are allocated to the most
significant areas. In general, though, they can be used to determine which of
several classifications have the most count or cost associated with them, for
instance, the number of people using the various ATMs versus each of the in-
door teller locations or the profit generated from each of 20 product lines. The
important limitations are that the data must be in terms of either counts or
costs. The data cannot be in terms that can't be added, such as percent yields
or error rates.

Define Stage and Analyze Stage

- To focus project resources on the products, departments, issues, defects,
  or causes yielding the highest return

Methodology

Choose the categories (or problem areas) for which to collect data by brainstorming, or use existing data to look for these problem areas. The data you
analyze must be counts (attributes data) or costs, and the data must be additive.
Data as yields or percentages cannot be added, so they are inappropriate for
Pareto analysis. You also should decide the time period over which the data
should be collected.

The left vertical axis of the Pareto chart has counts or costs, depending on
the data used. Each vertical bar represents the contribution to the total from a
given problem area. The bars are placed on the graph in rank order: The bar at
the left has the highest contribution to counts or costs. The right vertical axis
has percent demarcations. A cumulative line is used to add the percentages
from each bar, starting at the left (highest cost or count) bar.

Pareto Chart

Minitab

Use *Stat\Quality Tools\Pareto Chart*. Data may be in one of two forms:

- *Summarized form.* When the count for each pareto bar is expressed in a single cell in the spreadsheet, use the *Chart Defects Table* option. The *By Variable In* option allows for separate Pareto diagrams for each group, as indicated by unique text strings in the specified column.
- *Raw form.* When a single row or column represents the instance of an occurrence, and the count for the occurrence is obtained by counting the number of times each unique numeric or text string occurs, then use the *Chart Defects Data In* option.

Excel

Using Green Belt XL Add-On

Use *New Chart\Pareto Chart* option. Select a range of numeric data (without labels), where data are entered as counts for each pareto bar (same as Minitab summarized form above). Data for each bar may span multiple rows or columns, in which case bar height is based on the sum of the counts. In the *Title\Labels* tab, specify the row/column containing the label for each bar as the *X-Axis Label* When each bar spans multiple rows/columns of data, specify a *Stack Label*, or turn off pareto stacking in the *Format* tab.

Interpretation

The bar at the left has the highest contribution to counts or cost. Thus we can see which categories contribute the most problems and, with the cumulative line, determine how much of the total problem will be fixed by addressing the highest few issues.

Remember that the purpose of the Pareto chart is to distinguish the "vital few from the trivial many." Therefore, we would like only a few bars on the left side of the Pareto chart that account for most, say, 80 percent, of the problems. Then it's clear which areas we should address. We also can look at the cumula-

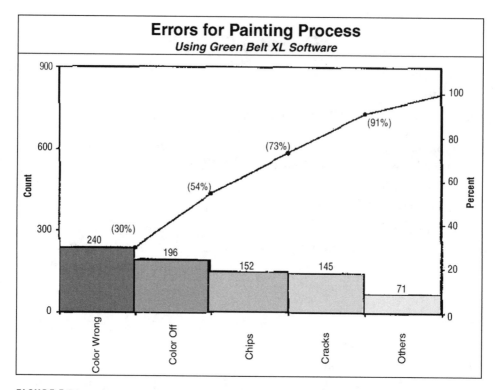

FIGURE F.24 Example of a Pareto chart.

tive line to tell us if our Pareto chart is working well. The cumulative line should be steep, with a lot of arch to it, implying that the first few problem areas rapidly add to a high percentage of the total problems. If the cumulative line is straight, it is telling us that the contribution from each successive bar (after the first) is about even. These bars then should be about the same height. This says that no problems stand out as being more bothersome than the rest, which doesn't help much for problem solving.

We can get flat Pareto diagrams just by the way we gather our data. If we separate major problem areas into many small problem areas, then each bar won't have much in it—hence a flat shape. We might consider regrouping the problems into meaningful, larger problem areas.

The goal for Pareto analysis is a clear identification of key categories requiring attention. A useful Pareto analysis should lead to five or fewer key categories. Note that key categories may differ for count or cost. That is, a problem that appears quite often may not be as costly as something that occurs less frequently but is more costly. It is generally most useful to consider cost data.

For key categories, we need to know whether the high count or high cost is due to common or special causes of variation, which is determined using a control chart. This distinction is important to understand our response to the high cost or occurrence: If it is due to common causes, then we must change the underlying nature of the process, whereas if it is due to a special cause of variation, we can respond to that particular issue.

The Pareto chart in Figure F.24 displays the number of errors of each type of error associated with a painting process. "Color Wrong" represents the largest source of errors (30 percent), followed by "Color Off" (an additional 24 percent), and "Chips" (another 19 percent), so these categories represent the best opportunities for improvement (if all errors have the same costs).

PERT Analysis

Program evaluation and review techniques (PERT) analysis allows probabilistic estimates of activity times, such as in project scheduling or cycle time analysis.

When to Use

Define Stage

- To identify project activities that determine the total project duration

Analyze Stage

- To identify the critical path for cycle time reduction

Improve Stage

- To verify the reduction in process critical-path cycle time

Methodology

Begin with activity times on the critical path, such as those determined using an activity network diagram. We assume that each activity time follows a β distribution, where a is an estimate of the optimistic time, b is an estimate of the pessimistic time, and m is an estimate of the most likely time (usually the deterministic time applied to the activity network diagram).

The estimated duration for each activity is then calculated as

$$\mu = (a + 4m + b)/6$$

The estimated standard deviation for each activity is calculated as

$$\sigma = (b - a)/6$$

Based on central limit theorem, the total time for all tasks follows the normal distribution. The total duration can be calculated by summing the task times on the critical path. Likewise, the variance of the project duration can be calculated by summing the variances for the task times on the critical path. Recall that the variance is the standard deviation squared:

Total duration = sum(task times on critical path)

Variance (total duration) = sum(variances for task times on critical path)

Standard deviation (total duration) = square root[variance(total duration)]

Upper predicted limit of duration = total duration + 1.96 × standard deviation(total duration)

Lower predicted limit of duration = total duration – 1.96 × standard deviation(total duration)

In Table T.14 we used the likely times for the critical-path tasks based on the earlier activity network example. Best and worst times were estimated, and from these, the mean, standard deviation, and variance for each task were calculated using the preceding equations. The average time of process tasks then was calculated as the sum of the mean times. The standard deviation of process tasks was calculated as the square root of the sum of the variances. In this case, the mean time is the same as that calculated using the activity network diagram (25 days), but this may not always be the case.

TABLE T.14   Example PERT Data

Task	Likely Time	Best Time	Worst Time	Mean	Sigma	Variation
Proof	15	10	20	15	1.67	2.78
Edit	2	0.6	3.4	2	0.467	0.22
TOC	3	1.8	4.2	3	0.4	0.16
Final	4	3	5	4	0.333	0.11
Finish	1	0.75	1.25	1	0.083	0.01

Interpretation

Use the upper and lower predicted limits of duration as best- and worst-case estimates of the project or process cycle time.

Prioritization Matrix

A *prioritization matrix* is a special type of matrix diagram designed especially to prioritize or rank options and build consensus.

When to Use

Define Stage

- To select projects aligned with company goals and objectives
- To understand how customer requirements are aligned with process metrics

Improve Stage

- To verify that project solutions are aligned with customer needs

Methodology

There are two methods that you can use to make a prioritization matrix: the full analytical method and the quicker consensus-criteria method. The *full analytical method* gives you a quantitative method for deciding which criteria are the most important to your project and which options best fulfill the given criteria. It is especially useful when you are unsure which criteria are the most important. The *consensus-criteria method* is somewhat simpler than the full analytical method in that the team simply decides the importance of each criterion and then ranks the options according to their ability to meet each criterion.

Full Analytical Method

The first step in any prioritization matrix is to compile a list of your options. Then compile a list of all the criteria for evaluating the options. Each criterion should be stated as a goal: short period of time, low cost, ease of use, employee satisfaction, etc.

The first matrix will compare each criterion with every other criterion. The criteria will be listed across the horizontal top of the matrix as well as down the left side of the matrix. Evaluate each criterion in relation to each other criterion, and assign a number designating their relative importance. Use the following number system:

10 = much more important/preferred/desirable

5 = more important/preferred/desirable

1 = equally important/preferred/desirable

1/5 = less important/preferred/desirable

1/10 = much less important/preferred/desirable

In Figure F.25, using Quality America's *GreenBelt XL* software, six criteria were defined for the selection of black belts—technical competence, familiarity with company systems and culture, having a positive attitude, being a risk taker, having good communication skills, and being seen as a leader by peers.

The group decided that technical competence was more desirable than familiarity with company systems and culture, so a value of 5 was placed in the "Technical Competence" row, "Familiarity with Company Systems and Culture" column. The software automatically filled in the complementary cell ("Familiarity with Company Systems and Culture" row, "Technical Competence" column) with a value of 1/5. Likewise, the group considered technical competence to be equally important as positive attitude, so a 1 was placed in those two complementary cells, and so on. The software provides an easy-to-use wizard that prompts the user for each of these comparisons.

The full analytical method then requires you to compare each of these options for a given criterion. In Figure F.26, the options are the individuals being evaluated as black belt candidates. The criterion shown is "Positive Attitude." The evaluation team apparently thought that Art's attitude was equal to Jerry's but less positive than any of the other candidates. Jessie's score of 56 (the highest) shows that her attitude is perceived as more positive than those of any of the other candidates, with Peter a close second. The percent of total, which is shown in parentheses, will be used to calculate the final scores for all criteria.

Once the options have been compared for each of the criteria, a final weighted score can be calculated by combining the matrices. Each option's score (as a percent of total) for a given criterion is multiplied by the ranking for that criterion, summed across all criteria. The options are rank-ordered in the summary matrix, with the top row being the highest ranking (i.e., best at meeting the weighted criteria). In Figure F.27, Peter, Jessie, and Adrianne are clearly distinct from the other candidates.

Criteria Weighting Matrix ▼	Technical Competence	Familar w/ Company Systems, Culture	Positive Attitude	Risk Taker	Good Communicator	Leader
Technical Competence	■	5	1	$\frac{1}{5}$	$\frac{1}{5}$	1
Familar w/ Company Systems, Culture	$\frac{1}{5}$	■	$\frac{1}{5}$	1	$\frac{1}{5}$	$\frac{1}{10}$
Positive Attitude	1	5	■	10	1	1
Risk Taker	5	1	$\frac{1}{10}$	■	$\frac{1}{5}$	$\frac{1}{5}$
Good Communicator	5	5	1	5	■	1
Leader	1	10	1	5	1	■

FIGURE F.25 Example of a criteria-weighting matrix.

Options Rating Matrix for 'Positive Attitude' ▼	Art	Peter	Mike	Carl	Jessie	Maria	Jerry	Adrianne	Row Totals
Art	■	$\frac{1}{5}$	$\frac{1}{5}$	$\frac{1}{5}$	$\frac{1}{5}$	$\frac{1}{5}$	1	$\frac{1}{5}$	2.2 (0.01)
Peter	5	■	1C	1C	1	1C	5	1C	51 (0.31)
Mike	5	$\frac{1}{10}$	■	1	$\frac{1}{10}$	1	5	1	13.2 (0.08)
Carl	5	$\frac{1}{10}$	1	■	$\frac{1}{10}$	1	5	1	13.2 (0.08)
Jessie	5	1	1C	1C	■	1C	1C	1C	56 (0.34)
Maria	5	$\frac{1}{10}$	1	1	$\frac{1}{10}$	■	5	1	13.2 (0.08)
Jerry	1	$\frac{1}{5}$	$\frac{1}{5}$	$\frac{1}{5}$	$\frac{1}{10}$	$\frac{1}{5}$	■	$\frac{1}{5}$	2.1 (0.01)
Adrianne	5	$\frac{1}{10}$	1	1	$\frac{1}{10}$	1	5	■	13.2 (0.08)
Column Totals	31	1.8	23.4	23.4	1.7	23.4	36	23.4	164.1

FIGURE F.26 Example of an option-rating matrix.

Summary Matrix ▼	Familar w/ Company Systems, Culture	Positive Attitude	Risk Taker	Good Communicator	Leader	Row Totals
Peter	0.21x0.05=0.010	0.31x0.23=0.071	0.16x0.12=0.019	0.25x0.23=0.058	0.26x0.23=0.060	0.238 (0.26)
Jessie	0.21x0.05=0.010	0.34x0.23=0.078	0.02x0.12=0.002	0.25x0.23=0.058	0.25x0.23=0.058	0.213 (0.23)
Adrianne	0.1x0.05=0.005	0.08x0.23=0.018	0.03x0.12=0.004	0.29x0.23=0.067	0.3x0.23=0.069	0.183 (0.20)
Jerry	0.13x0.05=0.007	0.01x0.23=0.002	0.37x0.12=0.044	0.07x0.23=0.016	0.02x0.23=0.005	0.081 (0.09)
Maria	0.18x0.05=0.009	0.08x0.23=0.018	0.13x0.12=0.016	0.01x0.23=0.002	0.06x0.23=0.014	0.066 (0.07)
Carl	0.11x0.05=0.006	0.08x0.23=0.018	0.25x0.12=0.03	0.03x0.23=0.007	0.01x0.23=0.002	0.064 (0.07)
Mike	0.06x0.05=0.003	0.08x0.23=0.018	0.02x0.12=0.002	0.06x0.23=0.014	0.06x0.23=0.014	0.058 (0.06)
Art	0.01x0.05=0.000	0.01x0.23=0.002	0.02x0.12=0.002	0.04x0.23=0.009	0.04x0.23=0.009	0.023 (0.02)
Column Totals	0.050	0.228	0.12	0.23	0.23	0.928

FIGURE F.27 Example of a summary matrix.

Prioritization Matrix

Excel

Using Green Belt XL Add-On

Use *New Chart\Prioritization Matrix*. Enter the *Options* and *Criteria*. Enter into the resulting *Criteria Weighting Matrix* the score for each paired comparison. Enter into each of the resulting *Options Rating Matrices* the score for each paired comparison (for the selected criterion). The *Summary Matrix* is automatically updated with the results based on the completed options and criteria matrices.

Consensus-Criteria Method

The full analytical method can be quite time-consuming, particularly as the number of options grows. The consensus-criteria method is an alternate technique that streamlines the analysis. In this method, we again start by specifying the options and the criteria, and then we compare the criteria. The criteria rating is done simply by distributing 100 percent across the criteria, with the highest weights given to more important criteria. See Figure F.28. You may find it useful to think of distributing a hundred dollars, giving the most money to the more important criterion.

Each option then is compared against the criteria with a simple weighting scale, such as 1 to 3, 1 to 5, or 1 to 10, with the largest value assigned to the best option. Figure F.29 shows the options rating matrix using the 1 to 3 scale. Peter, Jessie, and Adrianne achieved the highest scores in this example.

The final score for each option then is obtained in the summary matrix by multiplying the scores for each criterion by the criterion weight. See Figure F.30.

Interpretation

The final weighted score indicates the prioritization you should assign to each option. The higher the score, the greater is the priority.

Criteria Weighting Matrix	Rating
Technical Competence	.15
Familar w/ Company Systems, Culture	.1
Positive Attitude	.25
Risk Taker	.05
Good Communicator	.20
Leader	.25

FIGURE F.28 Example of a criteria-weighting matrix for the consensus-criteria method.

Options Rating Matrix for 'Leader'	Rating
Art	1
Peter	3
Mike	1
Carl	1
Jessie	3
Maria	2
Jerry	1
Adrianne	3

FIGURE F.29 Example of an options-rating matrix for the consensus-criteria method.

Summary Matrix	Row Totals
Peter	2.95
Jessie	2.75
Adrianne	2.7
Maria	2.15
Mike	1.7
Carl	1.45
Jerry	1.35
Art	1.1

FIGURE F.30 Example of a summary matrix for the consensus-criteria method.

Process Capability Index

Process capability indices attempt to indicate, in a single number, whether a process can consistently meet the requirements imposed on the process by internal or external customers. Much has been written about the dangers of these estimates, and users should interpret capability only after understanding the inherent limitations of the specific index being used.

When to Use

Process capability attempts to answer the question, Can we consistently meet customer requirements? Once process capability has been calculated, it can be converted into a corresponding defects per million opportunities (DPMO) or sigma level. It is important to remember that process capability indices are meaningless if the data are not from a controlled process. The reason is simple: Process capability is a prediction, and you can only predict something that is stable. In order to estimate process capability, you must know the location, spread, and shape of the process distribution. These parameters are, by definition, changing in an out-of-control process. Therefore, only use process capability indices (and resulting DPMO and sigma-level estimates) if the process is in control for an extended period.

The statistic C_p can be used when there are both and upper and lower specifications for the process. C_{pk} can be used when only one or the other or both specifications are provided.

Measure Stage

- To provide a process baseline estimate for a controlled process

Improve Stage

- To provide an estimate of the improved process and to verify that the improved process is in a state of statistical control

Control Stage

- To continuously monitor the process to verify that it remains in a state of statistical control at the desired capability level

Methodology

Since process capability is not valid unless the process is stable, always analyze the process using a control chart first. Once statistical control is evidenced, then process capability may be analyzed.

For normal distributions, the capability indices are calculated as

$$C_p = \frac{\text{high spec} - \text{low spec}}{6\sigma_x}$$

$$C_{pk} = \min(Cp_l, Cp_u)$$

$$C_{pm} = \frac{C_p}{\sqrt{1 + \frac{(\bar{\bar{x}} - T)^2}{\sigma_x^2}}}$$

where T is the process target, $\bar{\bar{x}}$ is the grand average, and σ_x is process sigma, which is calculated using the moving-range (when subgroup size = 1) or subgroup sigma (subgroup size > 1) statistic.

$$C_p = \frac{Z_l}{3} \qquad Cp_u = \frac{Z_u}{3}$$

$$Z_l = \frac{\bar{\bar{x}} - \text{low spec}}{\sigma_x} \qquad Z_u = \frac{\text{high spec} - \bar{\bar{x}}}{\sigma_x}$$

For nonnormal distributions, the capability indices are calculated as

$$C_p = \frac{\text{high spec} - \text{low spec}}{\text{ordinate}_{0.99865} - \text{ordinate}_{0.00135}}$$

$$Z_l = |Z_{\text{normal},\, p}| \qquad Z_u = |Z_{\text{normal},\, 1-p}|$$

where $\text{ordinate}_{0.99865}$ and $\text{ordinate}_{0.00135}$ are the z values of the nonnormal cumulative distribution curve at the 99.865 and the 0.135 percentage points, respectively, and $Z_{\text{normal},\, p}$ and $Z_{\text{normal},\, 1-p}$ are the z values of the normal cumulative distribution curve at the p and the $1 - p$ percentage points, respectively.

Process Capability Index

Minitab

Use *Stat\Quality Tools\Capability Analysis*. Enter the upper and/or lower specifications. Use the *Boundary* option to indicate whether the specification is a physical bound that cannot possibly be exceeded (e.g., zero is a lower boundary for cycle time data).

Excel

Using Green Belt XL Add-On

Use *New Chart\Histogram*. (*Note:* The histogram and resulting capability indices also may be displayed as an option with the $\bar{X}$ and individual-X control charts.) Enter the upper and/or lower specifications in the *Analysis* tab of step 3. If the Johnson distribution is selected, use the *Upper Bound* and/or *Lower Bound* options to indicate physical bounds that cannot possibly be exceeded (e.g., zero is a lower boundary for cycle time data).

Interpretation

Compare the nonnormal and normal indices. Capability indices are quite sensitive to assumptions of the distribution.

C_p provides the ratio of the tolerance (specification or permitted amount of variation) to the process variation. A value of 1 indicates that the process variation exactly equals the tolerance; values less than 1 indicate that the allowable variation (the tolerance) is smaller than the process variation, an undesirable condition.

C_{pk} provides a relative indication of how both process variation and location compare with the requirements.

When both C_p and C_{pk} are available (i.e., bilateral specifications), then C_p can be used to estimate the best-case process capability (assuming that the target value for the process is located exactly at the centerpoint between the specification limits).

C_{pm} is similar to the C_{pk} index but takes into account variation between the process average and a target value. If the process average and the target are the same value, C_{pm} will be the same as C_{pk}. If the average drifts from the target value, C_{pm} will be less than C_{pk}.

A comparison of capability index with sigma values is shown here. Table T.15 provides an indication of the level of improvement effort required in a process to meet these escalating demands, where DPMO refers to the average defect level measured in parts per million.

TABLE T.15 Capability with Sigma Level Conversion

C_{pk}	Long-Term DPMO	Long-Term Sigma
0.5	500,000	1.5
0.75	226,627	2.25
1.0	66,807	3.0
1.25	12,224	3.75
1.33	6,387	4.0
1.5	1,350	4.5
2.0	3.4	6

Process Cycle Efficiency

Process cycle efficiency is a metric useful for prioritizing cycle time improvement opportunities.

When to Use

Analyze Stage

- To prioritize cycle time improvement opportunities

Methodology

Process cycle time efficiency is calculated by dividing the value-added time associated with a process by the total lead time of the process.

Process cycle efficiency = value-added time/process lead time

Little's law is used to calculate the process lead time by dividing the number of items in process by the completions per hour (George, 2002).

Process lead time = number of items in process/completions per hour

For example, if it takes 2 hours on average to complete each purchase order, then there are 0.5 completions per hour. This is the denominator of the equation for Little's law. If there are 10 purchase orders waiting in queue (the numerator), then Little's law says that we need 10 divided by 0.5 equals 20 hours of lead time for the process. In other words, we can't process any new orders until the 20-hour lead time has allowed the existing work-in-process to be completed.

Interpretation

If the process consists only of value-added activities, then process cycle efficiency would reach a theoretical maximum of 100 percent. In practice, process cycle efficiencies will exceed 25 percent for processes that have been improved through the use of lean methods. Typical process cycle efficiencies are shown in Table T.16.

TABLE T.16 Typical Process Cycle Efficiencies		
Process Type	**Typical Efficiency**	**World-Class Efficiency**
Machining	1%	20%
Fabrication	10%	25%
Assembly	15%	35%
Continuous	30%	80%
Transactional	10%	50%
Creative	5%	25%

Source: George, 2002.

The key to improving (increasing) process cycle efficiency is often to reduce the lead time, the denominator of the equation. Lead time is reduced and process efficiency increased when work-in-process (WIP) is reduced.

The rationale is simple: New orders from customers cannot be started until work (or items) in process is completed. Thus the activity on new items is stalled, and efficiency (from a customer's point of view) suffers. An example from a service process is a doctor's waiting room. The patients are work-in-process. New patients aren't seen by the doctor until those who arrived earlier are processed.

Process Decision Program Charts

Process decision program charts (PDPCs) are used to delineate the required steps to complete a process, anticipate any problems that might arise in the steps, and map out a way of counteracting those problems.

When to Use

Analyze Stage

- To understand root causes of problems

Improve Stage

- To identify potential problems with the suggested solution so that contingency plans may be adopted for process control

Methodology

The top level is the project or process statement, for example, "Pool Construction" in Figure F.31. Moving from left to right in the second level are the steps required for the project or process. These steps should not be overly specific so as to avoid cluttering the chart. A third level may be used, if necessary, to display process substep detail.

The next level contains "what-if" scenarios for each step, which represent the potential problems that can occur at that step. Try to think of any problems that might arise in the execution of each process step. Each step should be examined independently.

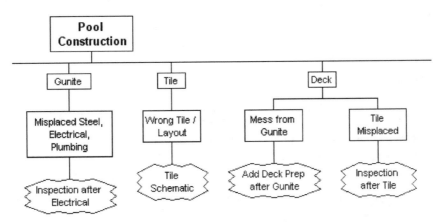

FIGURE F.31 Example of a process decision program chart.

Countermeasures (such as "Tile Schematic") provide the contingencies for each problem.

Process Decision Program Charts

Excel

Using Green Belt XL Add-On

Open a new file in the MindGenius application.

Enter the problem statement as the *Map Title* in the initial dialog. Use the "OK" button to start the new branch.

With this main branch selected, simply type each process step into the *Add Branch* dialog, and then select the "OK" button to place the idea into the *Map Editor* (drawing surface).

Select a given process step, and then type in the potential problem associated with that step. For each potential problem, enter a countermeasure.

Interpretation

In Figure F.31, a number of inspection steps have been added as well as a deck preparation step. These changes to the process flow need to be documented in the process maps discussed next. The inspection steps are not a preferred contingency because they are not value-added from a customer perspective.

Process Maps

Similar to a flowchart, a *process map* is a simple graphic tool for documenting the flow (the series of steps necessary) of a process. The process map can be used to display the value stream and even the movement of materials (including such information as in a service process) so that each step and movement can be analyzed for value creation. Often, "swim lanes" can be used on a process map to indicate movement into functional departments. Cycle times also may be included to assist in the analysis.

When to Use

Define Stage
- Document top-level process.
- Identify shareholders.

Measure Stage
- Document lower levels of process.
- Uncover varied shareholder perceptions.

Analyze Stage
- Discover process complexities, responsible agents, and locations that contribute to variation or longer cycle times.

Improve Stage
- Communicate proposed changes.

Control Stage
- Document revised process.

Methodology

As in the flowchart, each task will be represented by a symbol. ANSI standard symbols may be used, but most practitioners use rectangles for most tasks and diamonds for decision tasks. Decisions should have only two outcomes (yes or no), so decision points must be phrased in this manner.

We can use the process map to document the current (as-is) process. See Figure F.32. We can use symbol shade or shape to indicate process delays, functional responsibility for each step (e.g., the small gray inverted triangle is customer service), or points in the process where measurements are taken.

Location of process steps on the map is indicated by swim lanes, used to indicate physical layout, responsible department, stakeholder, schedule, or other condition for each process activity.

Figure F.32 is an example of a process map using Sigma Flow software. In this case, the swim lanes provide an indication of department responsible (i.e., customer service, customer processing, or production).

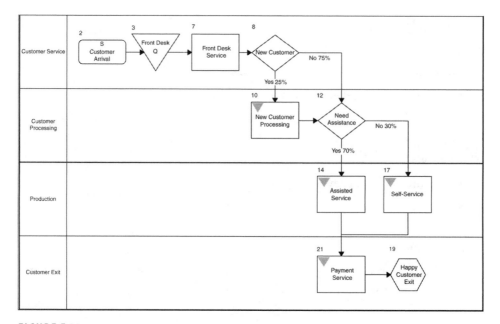

FIGURE F.32 Example of a process map showing stakeholder departments as swim lanes.

Interpretation

A quick review of the as-is process usually can uncover complexities in the form of an excessive number of decision points and branches that may contribute to delays or even defects. When used to document the future (desired) process, we strive to make process flow uncomplicated, with the fewest symbols (tasks) and branches possible. This lack of complexity in the process will tend to reduce the number of errors.

Process Performance Indices

Process performance indices attempt to answer the question, Does this sample meet customer requirements? It differs from process capability in that process performance applies only to a specific batch of material. Samples from the batch may need to be quite large to be representative of the variation in the batch.

When to Use

Process performance indices should be used only when SPC cannot be evaluated or achieved. For example, we may have insufficient data to analyze SPC

initial stages of product or process design, or in the measure stage we may have processes that lack statistical control.

The statistic P_p can be used when there are both and upper and lower specifications for the sample. P_{pk} can be used when only one or the other or both specifications are provided.

Measure Stage

- To provide a process baseline estimate for an uncontrolled process

Methodology

For normal distributions, the performance indices are calculated as

$$P_p = \frac{\text{high spec} - \text{low spec}}{6\sigma_x}$$

$$P_{pk} = \min(Pp_l, Pp_u)$$

$$P_{pm} = \frac{P_p}{\sqrt{1 + \dfrac{(\bar{\bar{x}} - T)^2}{\sigma_x^2}}}$$

where T is the process target, $\bar{\bar{x}}$ is the grand average, and σ_x is the sample sigma.

$$P_{pl} = \frac{Z_l}{3} \qquad\qquad P_{pu} = \frac{Z_u}{3}$$

$$Z_l = \frac{\bar{\bar{x}} - \text{low spec}}{\sigma_x} \qquad Z_u = \frac{\text{high spec} - \bar{\bar{x}}}{\sigma_x}$$

For nonnormal distributions, the performance indices are calculated as

$$P_p = \frac{\text{high spec} - \text{low spec}}{\text{ordinate}_{0.99865} - \text{ordinate}_{0.00135}}$$

$$Z_l = |Z_{\text{normal}, p}| \qquad Z_u = |Z_{\text{normal}, 1-p}|$$

where $\text{ordinate}_{0.99865}$ and $\text{ordinate}_{0.00135}$ are the z values of the nonnormal cumulative distribution curve at the 99.865 and 0.135 percentage points, respectively, and $Z_{\text{normal}, p}$ and $Z_{\text{normal}, 1-p}$ are the z values of the normal cumulative distribution curve at the p and $1 - p$ percentage points, respectively.

Process Performance Index

Minitab

Use *Stat\Quality Tools\Capability Analysis*. Enter the upper and/or lower specifications. Use the *Boundary* option to indicate whether the specification is a physical bound that cannot possibly be exceeded (e.g., zero is a lower boundary for cycle time data).

Excel

Using Green Belt XL Add-On

Use *New Chart\Histogram* (*Note:* The histogram and resulting capability indices also may be displayed as an option with the $\bar{X}$ and individual-X control charts.) Enter the upper and/or lower specifications in the *Analysis* tab of step 3. If the Johnson distribution is selected, use the *Upper Bound* and/or *Lower Bound* options to indicate physical bounds that cannot possibly be exceeded (e.g., zero is a lower boundary for cycle time data).

Interpretation

Process performance uses sample sigma in its calculation, so it cannot provide an estimate of process capability for the future. Since the process is not in a state of control, we cannot predict its future performance.

The calculated process performance and process capability indices likely will be quite similar when the process is in statistical control.

- A value of 1 indicates that the sample variation exactly equals the tolerance.
- Values less than 1 indicate that the allowable variation (the tolerance) is less than the sample variation.
- Values greater than 1 are desirable, indicating that the sample variation is less than the tolerance. Values greater than 1.3 or 1.5 are often recommended.

Use of performance indices is generally discouraged in favor of capability indices wherever possible.

Quality Function Deployment

Quality function deployment (QFD) is a detailed methodology for linking customer requirements with internal process and product requirements.

When to Use

Analyze Stage and Improve Stage

- To understand how customer requirements are translated into internal process and product requirements

Methodology

There are four distinct stages of a proper QFD. In service organizations, the QFD can be focused on the last two stages—ensuring that processes are designed and controlled to meet customer requirements (customer req.).

In the design stage, customer requirements (the *whats*) are translated into design requirements (design req.—the *hows*). In this way, the product planning matrix provides a means of ensuring that each customer requirement is satisfied through one or more design elements. See Figure F.33.

The customer requirements next are translated into part characteristics in

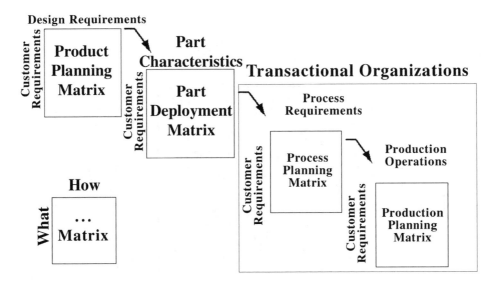

FIGURE F.33 QFD stages with associated matrices.

the part deployment matrix. This matrix thus provides insight into how specific qualities of the finished part will satisfy the needs of the customer.

In the process planning matrix, the customer requirements are translated into process requirements, determining the processing methods that will be used.

Finally, in the production planning matrix, the whats of customer requirements are translated into the hows of production operations, which determine how the process will be designed and controlled. In each matrix, the whats of the customer requirements are translated into the hows of the internal requirements.

The "house of quality" in Figure F.34 is an extended matrix used to define and rate the whats and hows at each stage. The basis for each of these elements is as follows: We start by listing the whats in rows at the left. The whats are the customer requirements—what the customer wants or desires in the product or service, the quality attributes. If there is a natural grouping of the requirements, it's often advantageous to list them by groups. For example, convenient groups could be critical to quality, critical to schedule, or critical to cost or perhaps aesthetics, performance, and function. Each what is weighted for importance. A useful scale is a rating between 1 and 5, with 5 being high importance and 1 being low importance. We then define the design requirements—the hows—depending on which matrix we are defining (i.e., product, part, process, or production), that meet the customer requirements.

In the relationship matrix, we then determine the relationship of each how

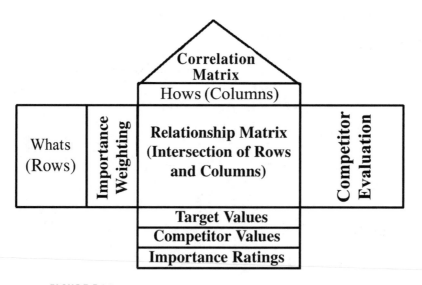

FIGURE F.34 House of quality.

to each what, recording the score in the proper intersecting cell using the following scoring index:

Strong relationship = 9.

Moderate relationship = 3.

Weak relationship = 1.

No relationship = 0.

Figure F.35 is an example of a relationship matrix. The customer requirements for a restaurant are listed for three main categories—service quality, culinary satisfaction, and pricing. Each category is broken down into more definitive requirements. For example, service quality is broken down into wait time, friendliness, and order accuracy.

Each of the subcategory items is rated for importance, shown in the column labeled "Import.," using a 1 (low) to 5 (high) scale, as discussed earlier.

Operational requirements, such as number of wait staff, number of cook staff, and so on, are rated for their influence on the customer requirements using a 1 (weak), 3 (moderate), 9 (strong) scale.

The QFD correlation matrix represents the roof of the house of quality. In this matrix, we enter an estimate of the relationships between the hows, generally using scores of 1 (low), 3 (moderate), or 9 (high).

Customer Requirements	Import.	Operational Requirements						
		No. Wait Staff	No. Cook Staff	Pre-prep	Plate Prep	Menu	Cook Training	Wait Staff Training
Service								
Wait Time	3	9	3	3	0	3	3	3
Friendliness	4	3	0	0	0	0	0	3
Order Accuracy	4	3	1	0	0	3	3	9
Culinary								
Taste	4	0	3	3	3	1	9	3
Temperature	3	3	3	1	9	0	9	3
Pricing								
Entrées<$13	3	3	3	3	0	9	0	0
Kids Menu	2	1	1	0	0	9	0	0

FIGURE F.35 Relationship matrix.

Correlation Matrix

						0	Cook Training
					3	9	Menu
				-3	3	0	Plate Prep
			3	-3	3	0	Preprep
		-3	-3	-3	9	0	No. Cook Staff
	0	0	0	-1	0	9	No. Wait Staff

Operational Requirements

No. Cook Staff	Pre-prep	Plate Prep	Menu	Cook Training	Wait Staff Training

FIGURE F.36 Example of a correlation matrix.

Each estimate can be either positive or negative in sign. Positive values indicate a supportive relationship. In this case, the how resources can be used for multiple purposes. Negative values indicate a conflicting relationship, which will require a tradeoff in resources.

In Figure F.36, the correlation matrix shown is from an Excel file. Since Excel's table structure does not permit angled cells, the shape of the roof is not triangular, as shown in the standard house of quality. Nonetheless, the inputs and results are the same.

We compare each of the hows (the operational requirements in this case) and enter the relationship, with sign, in the intersecting cell. For example, the relationship between the number of cook staff and the number of wait staff is insignificant, so a zero is entered. On the other hand, an increase in plate prep will moderately hurt the number of cook staff, so a negative 3 is entered.

Based on these entries, we can see that cook training and wait staff training will positively influence each of the other hows, whereas a more complex menu will conflict with the other operational requirements.

The competitor evaluation (on the right in Figure F.37) provides a rating of each competitor's ability to satisfy each customer requirement [i.e., the rows are the customer requirements (whats), and the columns list the competitors by name or code]. Each competitor is rated on a scale of 1 to 5, with 5 being the highest (or most likely to satisfy the customer requirements). The competitor evaluation shows where competition is strong (a challenge for you), as well as where it is weak (an opportunity).

Customer Requirements	Competitor Evaluation		
	House of Italy	Leonardo's	Mama Mia
Service Quality			
Wait Time	2	5	3
Friendliness of Staff	1	4	4
Order Accuracy	5	4	4
Culinary Satisfaction			
Taste	5	3	2
Temperature	5	4	3
Pricing			
Some Entrées <$13	1	4	3
Kids Menu	1	4	3

FIGURE F.37 Example of a competitor evaluation matrix.

Figure F.37 is an example of a competitor evaluation. Each of the competitors is rated for each customer requirement from 1 (low) to 5 (high).

Beneath the relationship matrix in Figure F.38 is the target row, where you will enter the desired value for the how. Conveniently listed beneath this is the competitor row for indicating a score for the competition's best solution for that how. The last row beneath the relationship matrix is the importance ratings. These are calculated by first calculating each cell's importance by multiplying each relationship score (the cell) by the importance rating for that what. We then sum these for each column to get the importance for that how. We also can rank order the hows, where a value of 1 is given to the highest importance rating, indicating the most important how.

In Figure F.38, the values provided above for both the target and competitor are defined using a common metric specific to each operational requirement. For example, the target value for number of wait staff is defined using a staff-to-table ratio (1 staff for every 2.5 tables), whereas the menu target is defined using an average entrée price.

The importance score for each operational requirement is also shown. We calculate the importance value for the number of wait staff using the sum of the importance times the relationship score as follows:

Customer Requirements	Import.	Operational Requirements						
		# Wait Staff	# Cook Staff	Pre-prep	Plate Prep	Menu	Cook Training	Wait Staff Training
Service Quality								
Wait Time	3	9	3	3	0	3	3	3
Friendliness of Staff	4	3	0	0	0	0	0	3
Order Accuracy	4	3	1	0	0	3	3	9
Culinary Satisfaction								
Taste	4	0	3	3	3	1	9	3
Temperature	3	3	3	1	9	0	9	3
Pricing								
Some Entrées<$13	3	3	3	3	0	9	0	0
Kids Menu	2	1	1	0	0	9	0	0
Target Value		1:2.5	1:5	30	3	$12	40	60
Competitor Value		1:2	1:4	30	3	$11:60	40	60
Importance		71	45	33	39	70	84	78
Rank		3	5	7	6	4	1	2

FIGURE F.38 Example of target, competitor, and importance scores.

$$(3 \times 9) + (4 \times 3) + (4 \times 3) + (4 \times 0) + (3 \times 3) + (3 \times 3) + (2 \times 1) = 71$$

The importance of the other operational requirements is calculated similarly. They are rank-ordered, with the largest being the highest priority. In this example, cook training was the most important operational requirement, followed by wait staff training. You can use the importance as input to the target value: The most important requirements might be best targeted at or better than the competitors' values, as shown in the example.

Interpretation

If there are no hows (or a weak relationship of hows) for a given what, then there's an opportunity for improvement, although it may be that subsequent matrices (part, process, or operational) will address this what.

Hows unrelated to any whats are candidates for removal as non-value-added activities. We should check the customer requirements to ensure that they are accurate and complete and verify this against the competitor analysis.

R&R Studies

Gauge repeatability and reproducibility (R&R) analysis quantifies the error owing to a measurement system.

When to Use

Measure Stage

- To quantify the measurement error's contribution to the variation (common and special causes) included in process baseline estimates
- To verify adequate gauge discrimination

Control Stage

- To qualify the proficiency of specific measuring equipment

Methodology

When conducting an R&R study, it is imperative to use typical samples from the operations rather than pristine reference standards or test cases. The ability of the measurement system to measure these atypical test cases precisely is not a good indicator of whether the system will measure samples precisely in daily operations. Remember the purposes of the measurement system: (1) to evaluate the suitability of the process output to meet (internal or external) customer requirements and (2) to evaluate the stability (i.e., statistical control) and capability of the process producing the output.

Using actual samples from operations allows us to estimate error associated with process equipment (such as measurement fixtures used to hold the sample or gauge during measurement), as well as variation within the sample pieces themselves. Each of these sources of error contributes to increased repeatability error on a regular basis. When operations personnel have developed improved techniques for dealing with the equipment problems or the within-sample variation, their repeatability error often will be less than that of other appraisers, providing an opportunity that, when recognized, will lead to system improvements.

These techniques are not limited to mechanical inspections or to material parts. They also can be applied to optical inspections, chemical analyses, surveys or rating systems, or any other system designed to measure process performance, its output, or its subject matter. In chemical analyses and patient care, sample preparation may be a critical component of the measurement and should be incorporated into the measurement systems analysis.

After obtaining a representative sample, process personnel (i.e., appraisers) will inspect each sample multiple times (each inspection is termed a *trial*). A typical study involves having 3 appraisers measure 10 samples, 3 trials each.

The number of samples, personnel, and trials can vary from case to case, but in any case, multiple trials are needed to estimate repeatability, and multiple personnel are needed to estimate reproducibility. Larger sample sizes provide better estimates of repeatability and reproducibility, as well as overall sample variation, but offer diminishing return given the cost of the exercise. The typical study outlined above is usually sufficient.

When you conduct an R&R study, keep these things in mind:

- Use actual samples from operations (see above).
- Randomize the order of the samples presented to each appraiser.
- Number each sample, but try to keep this "blind" to the appraiser. (Some appraisers have astounding memories!)

R&R Analysis

Minitab

Data input: Enter columns for part/item designator, appraiser name, and measured value.

Menu: *Stat\Quality Tools\Gage Study\Gage R&R Study (Crossed)*; set *ANOVA* analysis method.

Options: Enter specifications and historical standard deviation (from SPC analysis); use default $\alpha = 0.25$ to remove the interaction term.

Results

Gauge R&R Study—ANOVA Method

Two-Way ANOVA Table with Interaction					
Source	df	SS	MS	F	p
Item	2	0.0061000	0.0030500	78.4286	0.013
Operator	1	0.0002722	0.0002722	7.0000	0.118
Item * operator	2	0.0000778	0.0000389	0.3889	0.686
Repeatability	12	0.0012000	0.0001000		
Total	17	0.0076500			

Note: Alpha to remove interaction term = 0.25.

Two-Way ANOVA Table without Interaction

Source	df	SS	MS	F	p
Item	2	0.0061000	0.0030500	33.4174	0.000
Operator	1	0.0002722	0.0002722	2.9826	0.106
Repeatability	14	0.0012778	0.0000913		
Total	17	0.0076500			

Gauge R&R

Source	VarComp	%Contribution (of VarComp)
Total gauge R&R	0.0001114	18.42
Repeatability	0.0000913	15.10
Reproducibility	0.0000201	3.33
Operator	0.0000201	3.33
Part-to-part	0.0004931	81.58
Total Variation	0.0006045	100.00

Source	SD	Study Var (6 × SD)	%Study Var (%SV)
Total gauge R&R	0.0105535	0.063321	42.92
Repeatability	0.0095535	0.057321	38.86
Reproducibility	0.0044840	0.026904	18.24
Operator	0.0044840	0.026904	18.24
Part-to-part	0.0222063	0.133238	90.32
Total Variation	0.0245865	0.147519	100.00

Number of distinct categories = 2.

Excel

Using Green Belt XL Add-On

Data input: Enter columns for part/item designator, appraiser name, and measured value or enter column for part/item designator and separate columns for each appraiser containing his or her measured values.

Menu: *New Chart\ Repeatability Chart.*

Data range: Select orientation, number of trials, and number of appraisers based on data input. Select *ANOVA Method* option in the *Analysis* tab of step 3.

Interpretation

Discrimination Ratio

The discrimination ratio provides an estimate of the number of distinct categories or classes discernible by a measurement system. A value of 2, for instance, indicates that the system is useful only for attribute analysis because it can effectively classify the sample units only as being in one group or the other (e.g., good or bad). AIAG recommends a value of 3 or more, and typically a value of 8 or more is suitable for statistical analysis.

Gauge R&R

The gauge R&R statistic is usually reported as either a percent of tolerance or as a percent of the total process variation. When expressed as percent of tolerance, gauge R&R indicates the relative usefulness of the gauge system for determining acceptability of the process output. Tolerance, calculated as the upper specification limit minus the lower specification limit, indicates the amount of variation that is permitted. As measurement system error increases relative to tolerance, the chances increase that

- Output whose true value is beyond specifications could be measured as being within specifications and subsequently considered acceptable.
- Output whose true value is within specifications could be measured as being outside specifications and subsequently rejected as unacceptable.

When expressed as a percent of process variation, R&R indicates the relative usefulness of the measurement system in control charting and process capability analysis. The calculation of statistical control limits and the estimate of process capability require a sound estimate of process variation. Subgroups plotted on a control chart are subject to this measurement system error as well. As measurement error increases, so does the chance that

- Subgroups from a controlled process will be incorrectly determined to be out of control.
- Subgroups from an out-of-control process will be incorrectly determined to be from an in-control process.

Typical recommendations for R&R, expressed as either percent of tolerance or percent of process variation, are

- 0 to 10 percent: Acceptable
- 10 to 30 percent: Marginal
- Over 30 percent: Unacceptable

Interpreting a Repeatability Control Chart

Repeatability control charts are constructed by grouping each appraiser's trials for each sample unit into a single subgroup. The size of the subgroup is equal to the number of trials per sample unit. The variation within a subgroup is an estimate of the repeatability error inherent to the measurement equipment so long as the variation is shown to be statistically stable over all parts and all appraisers. This assumption may be proved by observing the range chart for repeatability.

The range chart should be in statistical control (all the plotted groups within the control limits). Each plotted group represents the variation observed between the trials by a specific appraiser for a single sample unit. If a group is out of control, the variation observed between the trials for that sample unit was larger than expected (based on the variation observed for the other sample unit). Perhaps the sample unit had an abnormality that impeded the measurement. This suspicion grows if the out-of-control condition is observed for the same sample unit in more than one appraiser's measurements.

The $\bar{X}$ chart for repeatability is analyzed quite differently from most $\bar{X}$ charts. The plotted statistic, $\bar{X}$, is the average of each appraiser's trials for a given sample unit. These $\bar{X}$ variations are an indication of variation between sample units. The control limits, however, are calculated using the average range between trials for each sample unit, providing an indication of repeatability error. Since it is desirable that the measurement system detect real differences between sample units in the presence of this repeatability error, the subgroup-to-subgroup variation (i.e., sample unit fluctuations) should be larger than the repeatability error (i.e., the control limits). Many subgroups should be out of control on the $\bar{X}$ chart if repeatability is sufficiently small relative to process variation. AIAG recommends that at least half the subgroups exceed the $\bar{X}$ control limits.

Repeatability control charts are available in two formats: combined and per appraiser. The combined charts are those typically used to analyze statistical stability of the measurement system across selected appraisers and parts. The per-appraiser charts are provided to estimate each appraiser's repeatability independently. Appraisers' repeatability then may be compared to indicate possible training benefits.

Interpreting a Reproducibility Control Chart

The $\bar{X}$ chart for reproducibility analyzes whether each appraiser's average for the selected parts is within the expected variability of these averages. In other words, it detects whether the differences between appraiser averages are an indication of appraiser bias or an expected variation owing to equipment.

If the equipment error, as represented on the combined appraiser repeatability range chart, is in control, then σ_{repeat} is an appropriate estimate of the variation from trial to trial. As long as there are not outside influences affecting the trial measurements, such as appraiser bias, trial averages should fall within the variability reflected by

$$\sigma_{repeat} \Big/ \sqrt{\text{no. of trials}}$$

This is the basis for the reproducibility $\bar{X}$ control chart.

The range chart for reproducibility analyzes the variability in appraiser averages for each part. As such, it may be used to identify whether the reproducibility is in a state of statistical control. If control is not exhibited, then the estimate of reproducibility may not be valid. Out-of-control points indicate that the variability in average measurements between appraisers is affected by part bias.

Regression Analysis

Regression analysis is used to determine if a dependent variable can be predicted adequately by a set of one or more independent variables.

When to Use

Measure Stage

- Assess the linearity of a measurement system

Analyze Stage

- Investigate the relationship of process factors to metrics

Improve Stage

- Verify the relationship of process factors to metrics after improvement

Simple linear regression analysis is often applied as part of the analysis done with a scatter diagram (described below). Multiple regression is used when there is more than one factor that influences the response. For example, cycle time for a sales process may be affected by the number of items purchased and the time of day. In this case, there are two independent variables: (1) number of items purchased and (2) time of day. We also can estimate the interaction between these factors. For example, perhaps the effect of time of day varies depending on the number of items purchased. It may be that when only a few items are purchased, the time of day makes a big difference in cycle time variation, yet when many items are purchased, time of day makes little difference to cycle time variation.

Methodology

Simple Linear Regression

The regression model used for simple linear regression is that of a straight line. You might recall this equations as $y = m \times x + b$, where y is the dependent variable, x is the independent variable, m is the slope, and b is the value of y when x equals zero (b is sometimes called the *intercept*).

$$Y = \beta_0 + \beta_1 X + error$$

Another way to write this is using the Greek letter beta, as shown above. β_0 ("beta naught") is used to estimate the intercept, and β_1 ("beta one") is used to indicate the slope of the regression line. We show the equation using the Greek letters because most statistical textbooks use this notation and it may be expanded easily to the multiple regression case discussed below.

To define the equation, we need to estimate the two parameters—slope and intercept. The statistical technique used most often is known as the *method of least squares*, which will find values for β_0 and β_1 such that the fitted line has a minimum squared distance from each of the experimental data values.

The error term is an acknowledgment that even if we could sample all possible values, there most likely would be some unpredictability in the outcome. This unpredictability could result from many possibilities, including measurement error in either the dependent or independent variable, the effects of other unknown variables, or nonlinear effects.

Multiple Regression First-Order Model

Multiple regression is used when there is more than one factor that influences the response. For example, the cycle time for a sales process may be affected by the number of cashiers, the number of floor clerks, and the time of day. In this case, there are three independent variables: (1) number of cashiers, (2) number of floor clerks, and (3) time of day.

Multiple regression requires additional terms in the model to estimate each of the other factors. If we have enough data of the right conditions, such as in an analysis of a designed experiment, we also can estimate the interaction between these factors. For example, perhaps the effect of time of day varies depending on the number of cashiers such that when only a few floor clerks are working, the time of day has a big effect on cycle time variation, yet when many floor clerks are working, time of day has little effect on cycle time variation.

The first-order model for this example is of the form

$$Y = \beta_0 + \beta_1 X_1 + \beta_2 X_2 + \beta_3 X_3 + \beta_{12} X_{12} + \beta_{13} X_{13} + \beta_{23} X_{23} + \text{error}$$

where X_1 is the number of cashiers

X_2 is the number of floor clerks

X_3 is the time of day

X_{12} is the interaction between the number of cashiers and the number of floor clerks

X_{13} is the interaction between the number of cashiers and the time of day

X_{23} is the interaction between the number of floor clerks and the time of day

The error is assumed to have zero mean and a common variance (for all runs). The errors are independent and normally distributed. These assumptions will be tested in the *residuals analysis* of the model (the next tool).

The first-order model produces a plane when viewed in three dimensions of two significant factors and the response. Interaction effects between the two factors cause a twisting, or flexing, of the plane.

First-order models work well for a great number of cases. They are often used in Six Sigma projects because so much can be learned about reducing process variation with few data. We only need to identify significant factors and two-factor interactions and may have little use for precisely defining the model or a higher-order curvilinear response surface. Over limited regions, it is not uncommon for linear effects to dominate, so higher-order models are not necessary.

Multiple Regression Higher-Order Models

Higher- order terms, such as squares (the second power), also may be added. These higher-order terms generate curvilinear response surfaces, such as peaks (maximums) and valleys (minimums). To estimate these higher-order terms, we need at least three or more experimental levels for the factor because two-level designs can estimate only linear terms.

The full model includes p parameters for k main factors, where p is calculated as

$$p = 1 + 2k + k(k - 1)/2$$

For example, a model for two factors includes one constant term plus four main factor and second-order terms $(\beta_1 X_1 + \beta_2 X_2 + \beta_{11} X_1^2 + \beta_{22} X_2^2)$ plus one interaction term $(\beta_{12} X_1 X_2)$. A three-factor model includes one constant term plus six main factor and second-order terms $(\beta_1 X_1 + \beta_2 X_2 + \beta_3 X_3 + \beta_{11} X_1^2 + \beta_{22} X_2^2 + \beta_{33} X_3^2)$ plus three interaction terms $(\beta_{12} X_1 X_2 + \beta_{13} X_1 X_3 + \beta_{23} X_2 X_3)$. To estimate these terms, at least p distinct parameter conditions are needed.

The effect of higher-order terms is generally small, unless the main factors themselves are important. In this way, initial experiments seek to discover the significance of only the main factors $(X_1, X_2, X_3,$ etc.) and their interactions $(X_{12}, X_{13}, X_{23},$ etc.) and ignore the effect of the higher-order terms. If main factors or interactions appear significant, higher-order effects may be investigated with additional experimental trials.

The shape of the resulting response surface is highly dependent on the region analyzed and the signs and magnitudes of the coefficients in the model, particularly the pure quadratic (the squared terms) and the interaction terms. The shape of the surface is *estimated* subject to errors inherent in the model-building process.

Despite their limitations, second-order models are used widely because of their flexibility in mapping a variety of surfaces, including simple maximums (peaks) or minimums (valleys), stationary ridges (such as in a mountain range), rising ridges (a ridge that increases in height), and saddles (also known as *minimax*, where a minimum in one factor meets a maximum in the other). Second-order models are used in response surface analysis to define the surface around a stationary point (a maximum, minimum, or saddle) and to predict the response with better accuracy than first-order models near the optimal regions.

In investigative analysis, second-order models are also used to understand the effect of current operating parameters on the response.

Regression Analysis

TIP: *When working with data from designed experiments, use the regression analysis tools described under "Factorial Designs" above and "Response Surface Analysis" below.*

Example Data			
Factor A	**Factor B**	**Factor C**	**Response**
14.7	101.3	352	19
44.2	51.6	300.25	35.12
14.9	51.3	317	23.29
15.3	49.5	339	21.89
44.9	99.5	310.5	34.02
14.7	50.7	213.5	35.7
15.1	99.4	200.5	13.2
45.2	101.5	203	14.26
44.7	50.3	199.75	43.16
14.8	100.3	331	21.36
45.8	102.7	221.25	10.53
15.2	51.2	210	57.34
45.3	49.9	214.75	47.13
45	100.3	332	38.22
15.4	99.8	208.25	1.78
44.9	48.7	345	40.06

Minitab

Data input: Enter columns of data for the independent (x) variables and a column of equal length for the dependent (y) variable.

Menu: *Stat\Regression\Regression.* Using the "Options" button, select *Fit Intercept, Variance inflation factors,* and *Durbin-Watson statistic.* Using the "Graphs" button, select *Standardized residuals* and *Normal Plot of Residuals,* or *Four in one.*

Results

Regression Analysis: Response versus Factor *A*, Factor *B*, Factor *C*

The regression equation is

$$\text{Response} = 45.6 + 0.288(\text{factor } A) - 0.380(\text{factor } B) + 0.0111(\text{factor } C)$$

Predictor	Coef.	SE Coef.	T	p	VIF
Constant	45.57	17.29	2.64	0.022	—
Factor *A*	0.2879	0.1981	1.45	0.172	1.003
Factor *B*	−0.3802	0.1181	−3.22	0.007	1.000
Factor *C*	0.01115	0.04863	0.23	0.823	1.003

S = 11.8641 R-Sq = 50.8% R-Sq(adj) = 38.5%
PRESS = 2964.16 R-Sq(pred) = 13.68%

Analysis of Variance

		SS	MS	F	p
Regression	3	1744.7	581.6	4.13	0.032
Residual error	12	1689.1	140.8		
Total	15	3433.8			

Source	df	Seq SS
Factor *A*	1	280.8
Factor *B*	1	1456.5
Factor *C*	1	7.4

Obs.	Factor *A*	Response	Fit	SE Fit	Residual	St. Residual
1	14.7	19.00	15.22	6.50	3.78	0.38
2	44.2	35.12	42.03	5.27	−6.91	−0.65
3	14.9	23.29	33.89	5.54	−10.60	−1.01
4	15.3	21.89	34.94	6.12	−13.05	−1.28
5	44.9	34.02	24.13	5.48	9.89	0.94
6	14.7	35.70	32.91	5.85	2.79	0.27

(Continued)

7	15.1	13.20	14.37	6.16	−1.17	−0.12
8	45.2	14.26	22.26	6.04	−8.00	−0.78
9	44.7	43.16	41.55	6.02	1.61	0.16
10	14.8	21.36	15.39	5.88	5.97	0.58
11	45.8	10.53	22.18	5.78	−11.65	−1.12
12	15.2	57.34	32.83	5.86	24.51	2.38R
13	45.3	47.13	42.04	5.75	5.09	0.49
14	45.0	38.22	24.10	6.03	14.12	1.38
15	15.4	1.78	14.39	5.94	−12.61	−1.23
16	44.9	40.06	43.83	6.56	−3.77	−0.38

R denotes an observation with a large standardized residual.
Durbin-Watson statistic = 2.22237.

Excel

Using Green Belt XL Add-On

Data input: Enter a column of data for the independent (x) variable and a second column of equal length for the dependent (y) variable.

Menu: *New Chart\Regression*. Select cell range containing dependent variable data and range containing independent variable data.

Results: Provides regression function with ANOVA.

Regression Statistics	
Multiple R	0.712811
R square	0.5081
Adjusted R^2	0.385125
Standard error	11.86411
Observations	16
Durbin-Watson statistic	2.22

ANOVA					
	df	SS	MS	F	Significance F
Regression	3	1744.711214	581.5704046	4.131728	0.031554
Residual	12	1689.086161	140.7571801		
Total	15	3433.797375			

	Coefficients	Standard Error	VIF	t Statistic	p Value	Lower 95%	Upper 95%
Intercept	45.57286	17.2869763		2.636253991	0.021723	7.907775	83.23795
Factor A	0.287911	0.198068624	1.003	1.453591774	0.171708	−0.14364	0.719465
Factor B	−0.38017	0.118088416	1.000	−3.219371735	0.007363	−0.63746	−0.12288
Factor C	0.011149	0.048634311	1.003	0.229234568	0.822547	−0.09482	0.117114

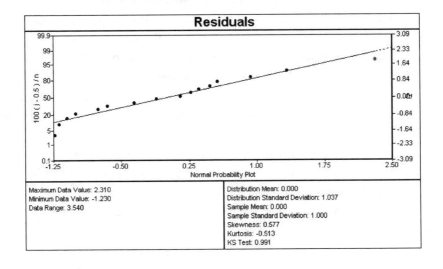

Interpretation

The statistical methods used to develop the regression model include an ANOVA table. Analysis of variation is a statistical tool for partitioning error among terms. For simple linear regressions, the ANOVA table provides an indication of the statistical significance of the regression by partitioning the variation into two components:

1. Variability accounted for by the regression line: and regression sum of squares:

$$SS_R = \sum_{i=1}^{n}(\hat{y}_1 - \bar{y})^2$$

2. Variability *not* accounted for by regression line: error sum of squares:

$$SS_E = \sum_{i=1}^{n}(y_i - \hat{y}_1)^2$$

The ANOVA table uses the F statistic to compare the variability accounted for by the regression model with the remaining variation owing to error. The null hypothesis is that the coefficients of the regression model are zero; the alternative hypothesis is that at least one of the coefficients is nonzero and thus provides some ability to estimate the response.

Although we could use the F-statistic tables in Appendices 4 and 5 to determine whether to accept or reject the hypothesis, most statistical software will provide a p value for the F statistic to indicate the relevance of the model. Most times we will reject the null hypothesis and assert that the calculated linear regression model is significant when the p value is less than 0.10. (While a p value of 0.05 or less is preferred to indicate significance, a value of 0.10 or less is accepted in preliminary analyses. The assumption is that the parameter will be retained so that additional analysis can better determine its significance.)

Bear in mind that statistical significance may or may not indicate physical significance. If we measure the statistical significance of a given factor to a response, this does not necessarily mean that the factor is in fact significant in predicting the response in the real world. Factors may happen to vary coincident with other factors, some of which may be significant. For example, if we estimate that shoe size is statistically significant in understanding the variation in height, it does not mean that shoe size is a good predictor of height, nor should it imply the causal relation that increasing shoe size increases height.

In this example, the calculated p value for the F test is 0.032, so the null hypothesis that all the coefficients are zero is rejected.

The regression model shown in the Minitab and Excel analyses above is

$$\text{Response} = 45.6 + 0.288(\text{factor } A) - 0.380(\text{factor } B) + 0.0111(\text{factor } C)$$

The regression model represents our best estimate of future values of y based on given values of each significant factor. For example, when there are 10 units of factor A, 1 unit of factor B, and 100 units of factor C, the best estimate for the response y is

$$\text{Response} = 45.6 + 0.288(10) - 0.380(1) + 0.0111(100) = 49.21$$

Similarly, we could calculate values of the response y for any value of input factors x. Recall that extrapolation beyond our data region should be done with caution.

Each coefficient β_i indicates the predicted change in y for a unit change in that x when all other terms are constant. For example, $\beta_1 = 0.288$ implies that the response increases by 0.288 units for each additional unit of factor A.

Generally, the magnitude of the β coefficients does not provide an indication of the significance or impact of the factor. In the example equation below, we cannot say that factor A is more critical than factor C simply because β_1 is larger than β_3 because the scaling (or unit of measure) of each factor may be different. Some software (such as Minitab) will provide the regression function in coded form, in which case the coefficients are applied to coded values of the factors (such as -1 and $+1$), allowing direct comparison to estimate the effects of the factors.

Once we have constructed a model, there are a number of ways to check the model, especially through the use of *residuals analysis* (discussed next) to look for patterns.

A confidence interval for the regression line may be constructed to indicate the quality of the fitted regression function. The confidence lines diverge at the ends and converge in the middle, which may be explained in one of two ways:

1. The regression function for the fitted line requires estimation of two parameters: slope and y intercept. The error in estimating intercept provides a gap in the vertical direction. The error in estimating slope can be visualized by imagining the fitted line rotating about its middle. This results in the hourglass-shaped region shown by the confidence intervals.

2. The center of the data is located near the middle of the fitted line. The ability to predict the regression function should be better at the center of the data; hence the confidence limits are narrower at the middle. The ability to estimate at the extreme conditions is much less, resulting in a wider band at each end.

Don't confuse the confidence interval on the line with a prediction interval for new data. If we assume that the new data are independent of the data used to calculate the fitted regression line, then a prediction interval for future observations depends on the error that is built into the regression model plus the error associated with future data. While our best estimate for the y value based on a given x value is found by solving the regression equation, we recognize that there can be variation in the actual y values that will be observed. Thus the shape of the prediction interval will be similar to that seen in the confidence interval but wider.

Another useful statistic provided by the ANOVA table is the coefficient of determination (R^2), which is the square of the Pearson correlation coefficient R. R^2 varies between 0 and 1 and indicates the amount of variation in the data accounted for by the regression model. In multiple regression, the Pearson correlation coefficient R^2 approaches 1 as the number of factors approaches the number of data values. That is, if we have five factors and eight data values, R^2 may be close to 1 regardless of whether the fit is good or not. R^2 always increases as factors are added, whether the factors are significant or not. An adjusted value R_a^2 is calculated for multiple regression models that are corrected based on the number of parameters in the model. R_a^2 always will be less than R^2 and provides a better approximation of the amount of variation accounted for by the model. In the preceding example, the R_a^2 statistic is calculated as 0.385: Approximately 39 percent of the variation in the response is explained by the regression function. Values near 0.7 or higher generally are considered acceptable.

A large R^2 value does *not* imply that the slope of the regression line is steep, that the correct model was used, or that the model will predict future observations accurately. It simply means that the model happens to account for a large percent of the variation in this particular set of data.

A t test is performed on each of the model parameters, with a resulting p value provided. If the p value is less than 5 percent, then it is likely to be significant and should be retained in the model. (In some cases, such as when we have limited data from an initial study, we may choose a higher threshold, such as 0.10.) In this example, it would appear that only factor B is significant; the p values for factors A and C both greatly exceed even the 0.10 threshold. The R_a^2 of 0.385 indicates a relatively poor fit, implying that the model may be missing terms.

A variance inflation factor (VIF) also may be evaluated to determine the presence of multicollinearity, which occurs when parameters are correlated with one another. Any parameter with a VIF of between 5 and 10 is suspect; those exceeding a value of 10 should be removed.

Removing Terms from the Multiple Regression Model

When reviewing the results of the t and VIF tests for the individual factors, we are considering whether the individual factors provide benefit in estimating the response. When removing terms from the model, remove only one term at a time because the error is partially reapportioned among the remaining parameters when each parameter is removed.

It is recommended to remove higher-order terms (such as third-, second-, and then higher-order interactions) first. In fact, we often don't include higher-order terms in initial studies so that we can eliminate the factors that are not significant using less data. Factors with borderline significance, such as a p value between 0.05 and 0.10, are best left in the model, particularly at the early stages.

There are two considerations for modeling. The first is *paucity*, which means that the best model is the one with the fewest number of significant parameters with the highest R_a^2 value. Basically, paucity implies doing more with less: The best model explains the data with only a few simple terms. The opposite of paucity is *overmodeling*: adding lots of terms that help the model explain all the variation in the data. This sounds great, until you collect more data and discover that there is a random component that cannot be explained by your earlier model. When we overmodel, we tend to have a poorer fit when new data are analyzed. Since there is no predictive value in the model, it is of little practical purpose.

When considering terms for a statistical model, it is helpful to recall the infamous words of George Box: "All models are wrong, but some models are useful."

The other consideration is that of *inheritance*: If a factor is removed from the model because it is insignificant, then all its interactions also should be removed from the model. Likewise, if the interaction is significant, then all its main factors should be retained. For example, if the *AC* interaction is significant, and factor *A* was borderline significant (*p* value near 0.10), it would be best to leave both *A* and *AC* in the model.

When interactions are significant, and one or more of their main factors are insignificant, then consider whether the interaction may be confounded with another interaction or main factor or perhaps even a factor not included. *Confounding* means that the factors move together, often because of the way in which the data were collected. Randomizing the data collection helps to reduce the instances of confounding.

Stepwise regression is a set of techniques for automating the removal of terms in the model based on statistical considerations. There are three basic types of stepwise regression:

- *Forward selection.* This begins with no parameters, and adds them one at a time based on a partial *F* statistic. In this case, factors are not revisited to see the impact of removing them after other terms have been added.

- *Backward elimination.* This begins with all parameters, and removes one at a time based on a partial *F* statistic. This is basically what we did manually after adding the interaction terms.

- *Stepwise.* This is a combination of forward selection and backward elimination.

Minitab provides each of these stepwise regression techniques in the *Stat\ Regression\Stepwise* menu. To further test the fitted model, we should conduct residuals analysis.

Residuals Analysis

Residuals analysis refers to a collection of techniques used to check the regression model for unnatural patterns, which may be indicative of an error in the model. A *residual* is calculated as the difference between the observed value of a response (the dependent variable) and the prediction for that response based on the regression model and the actual value of the dependent variables.

$$e_i = y_i - \hat{y}_i$$

Minitab and Excel will calculate a standardized residual. The effect of standardizing the residuals is to scale the error to achieve a variance of 1, which helps to make outliers more prominent.

Standardized residual:

$$e_i / \sqrt{s^2}$$

There are a number of tools (discussed elsewhere in this part) that are useful for finding patterns in residuals.

- *Normality test for residuals.* If the error between the model and the data is truly random, then the residuals should be normally distributed with a mean of zero. A normal probability plot or goodness-of-fit test will allow us to see departures from normality, indicating a poor fit of the model to particular data. The normal probability plot for the residuals in the preceding "Regression Analysis" topic example provides a K-S test value of 0.991, indicating that the standardized residuals approximately fit a normal distribution, supporting the premise that the regression model fits the data. The residual associated with observation 12 (marked in red in the software) was significantly beyond the variation expected of a normal distribution with mean of 0 and standard deviation of 1. Data far removed from the "middle" of the data may have a large influence on the model parameters (the β coefficients, the adjusted correlation coefficient, and the mean square error terms). When standardized residuals are greater than 2.0 for any observation (such as observation 12 in the example), they are often considered outliers that should be investigated and removed. Similarly, Cook's distance (such as provided in Minitab) provides a measure of the squared distance between the β estimate with and without the observation.

- *Residuals versus independent variable (x)*. We shouldn't see any pattern or any significant correlation when we analyze the residuals (on the y axis) and the independent variable (on the x axis) using a scatter diagram. If patterns exist, they would imply that the model changes as a function of the x variable, meaning that a separate model for particular values of x (or higher-order terms in x) should be considered.

- *Residuals versus fitted response*. A pattern here would suggest that the model does not fit well over the range of the response. When we have repeated runs at each experimental condition, we also can look for nonconstant variance of the response (shown in Figure F.39). If nonconstant variance of the response is suspected, then Bartlett's equality-of-variance test can be used to test for the condition. Reasons for nonconstant variance include an increase in measurement error for larger responses (such as when error is a fixed percentage of the measured value) and the distributional properties of the response (such as for skewed distributions where the variance is a function of the mean).

  If the data can be ordered in a time-based manner (meaning that for each datum you have a unit of time at which it occurred), then we can do some additional analysis of the model.

- *Control chart of residuals*. A control chart of the residuals would indicate whether the error changes over the time in which the data occurred. An out-of-control condition (or run-test violation) on this chart implies that another factor (that changes over time) is influencing the response.

- *Test for autocorrelation of residuals*. Significant autocorrelation of the residuals (which may be detected using the autocorrelation function) implies that the error at one period in time is influenced by earlier error. In this case, it's likely we are missing a factor that varies over time. We can use the autocorrelation function or the Durbin-Watson test (shown in the "Regression Analysis" example) for independence of consecutive residuals. The Durbin-Watson statistic tests for first-order (lag one) serial correla-

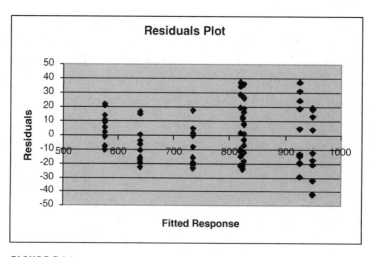

FIGURE F.39 Example of a residuals plot.

tion (autocorrelation). The null hypothesis H_0 is that there is no first-order serial correlation. The test statistic d is interpreted as follows:

$d < d_L$: Reject H_0; positive autocorrelation.

$4 - d < d_L$: Reject H_0; negative autocorrelation.

$d > d_U$: Do not reject (assume zero autocorrelation).

$d_L \leq d \leq d_U$: Test inconclusive.

Appendix 10 provides values of d_L and d_U based on the number of data observations n and the number of terms in the model p. Note the areas of inconclusive results and that the value of d also may provide information as to the nature of the autocorrelation (positive or negative).

In the "Regression Analysis" example the Durbin-Watson statistic is calculated as 2.22. Using Appendix 10, for $n = 16$ observations and $p = 3$ terms in the model (i.e., $p - 1 = 2$), $d_L = 0.98$ and $d_U = 1.54$ at a 5 percent significance. Since $d > d_U$, we do not reject the null hypothesis and assert that no autocorrelation is present.

Response Surface Analysis

Response surface analysis (RSA) refers to techniques to determine the optimal value of a response. For example, we may be interested in finding the specific concentrations of reagents and temperature of a reaction to achieve the highest degree of product purity. In a service process, we may seek optimal allocation of staffing and services to minimize the cycle time for a key process.

When to Use

Improve Stage

- To map the response surface in the region of interest to provide a prediction of the change in the response as factor settings vary
- To optimize the response, such as a maximum or minimum response or minimum variation in the response, to achieve improved process capability and yield for existing processes or best performance for new products or processes
- To select operating conditions to meet desired specifications, such as when there are multiple specifications (one for each response) that must be met simultaneously

Methodology

The general technique for RSA, sometimes referred to as the *sequential RSA technique*, involves two phases (phase 1 and phase 2) and a prerequisite (phase 0) (Myers and Montgomery, 1995).

Phase 0 is the use of screening designs to narrow the list of potential factors down to a critical set of significant factors and develop a first-order regression model. RSA should not be started until this work has been completed.

In phase 1, the steepest ascent methodology is used to define the current operating region and determine the direction of maximum response. (When seeking to minimize the response variable, the technique is sometimes referred to as *steepest descent*). Phase 1 uses the first-order model generated earlier because of its economy of data collection. The first-order model is a good assumption because the starting point is usually far enough away from the optimum that it is likely to be dominated by first-order effects, and we are not interested in a detailed mapping of the response region far away from the optimum.

Phase 2 will use a second-order model and ridge analysis techniques within a small region to locate the optimal conditions, which occur at a stationary point. A *stationary point* is the point where the slope of the second-order response surface model with respect to each of the factors is zero. A stationary point may be either a maximum, a minimum, or a saddle point (also known as a *minimax*). In *n* dimensions, a saddle point is a point where one or more parameters are at a maximum and one or more parameters are at a minimum. The stationary point may lie well outside the data range, in which case it is useful for direction only.

Phase 1: Steepest Ascent Methodology

Data are collected (either single data points or replicated runs) along the path of steepest ascent using the first-order regression equation developed in phase 0. Start at the design center: the point where, in coded units, $(x_1, x_2) = (0, 0)$. Continuing the example provided under "Factorial Designs" above, we have a first-order model developed in coded form:

$$y = -88,038 - 12,216x_1 + 10,681x_2 + 43,010x_1x_2$$

Given the levels of x_1 (factor B) and x_2 (factor E) in real terms (−50, 50) in both cases, the design center is (0, 0). This will be our first test condition.

The path of steepest ascent is a simultaneous move of β_1 (the coefficient of the x_1 term: −12,216) coded units in the x_1 direction for every β_2 (the coefficient of the x_2 term: 10,681) coded units in the x_2 direction. Sufficiently small step changes provide reasonable resolution of the response. Given a specified change of 10 (uncoded) units in x_1, for the coefficients specified in coded units, the appropriate real (uncoded) change in x_2 is calculated as

$$\text{Uncoded change in } x_2 = (\text{uncoded change in } x_1)\beta_2/\beta_1$$

$$\text{Change in } x_2 = 10 \times 10,681/(-12,216) = -8.74$$

Thus each new design condition will be calculated as a step of 10 units in the positive direction of factor B for every step of 8.8 units in the negative direction of factor E.

We also can consider steepest ascent subject to constraints imposed by the physical limitations of the system. For example, if x_2 could not exceed 50, then we proceed along the path of steepest ascent until the constraint is hit and then proceed along its path (i.e., all subsequent data have the x_2 factor set at 50).

We determine local maximum conditions by observing when the response decreases. Data preceding an observed decrease in the response are likely to be near a maximum condition.

We then conduct another experiment centered near the assumed maximum. It is sufficient to run a suitable design to obtain a first-order model with one or more centerpoints (to estimate curvature) and one or more replicated runs to estimate lack of fit.

If the lack of fit is not significant, then determine a new path of steepest ascent by varying the starting point, intervals, or direction along the first-order model. If lack of fit is significant and curvature is present, then this suggests that you are near a stationary point, which may be a local maximum, minimum, or saddle point (a maximum in one factor, minimum in another). At this point, stop the steepest ascent methodology and proceed to phase 2 ridge analysis.

Phase 2: Ridge Analysis

The graphic method for ridge analysis is as follows:

1. Use a central composite design near the optimum (defined in the RSA) to generate a second-order regression model.

2. Generate contour plots and response surface plots for each pair of factors.

3. Determine the stationary point (the local minimum, maximum, or saddle point as described earlier) from the plots.

4. Calculate the predicted response at the optimum using the second-order regression model.

5. Collect new data in the region of the optimum to verify the model.

In practice, many processes must achieve optimality with respect to more than one response. For example,

- Cost and yield in chemical, manufacturing, and health-care processes
- Cost and customer satisfaction in service processes
- Efficacy of drug and minimal side effects in pharmaceutical processes
- Timeliness of service and cost in service processes

For multiple responses, overlaid contour plots (see "Contour Plot") or desirability functions can be used.

Derringer and Suich (1980) developed an analytical approach to determining the simultaneous optima for several responses, known as a *desirability function* (Myers and Montgomery, 1995). Minitab provides a calculation of the desirability function given the input parameters discussed below. For each response, we define the goal as either a minimization, a maximization, or a specified target value. Each response is weighted with respect to meeting its goal using a desirability function d. A composite response D is generated as the simple geometric mean of each response desirability function as follows:

$$D = (d_1 \times d_2 \times d_3 \times \uparrow \times d_m)^{1/m}$$

The composite desirability function D is maximized in each case so that values of desirability near 1 (the maximum) indicate that all responses are in the desirable range simultaneously.

Minimizing the Response

The desirability function, when the goal is to minimize the response (i.e., smaller is better), requires a specified target value, which is the desired minimum (where smaller values provide little improvement) and an upper bound (a point of undesirable response).

$$d = \left(\frac{\text{response} - \text{upper bound}}{\text{target} - \text{upper bound}} \right)^s$$

Maximizing the Response

The desirability function, when the goal is to maximize the response (i.e., larger is better), requires a specified target value (the desired maximum, where larger values provide little improvement) and a lower bound (a point of undesirable response).

$$d = \left(\frac{\text{response} - \text{lower bound}}{\text{target} - \text{lower bound}} \right)^s$$

Target the Response

The desirability function, when the goal is to achieve a target value, requires a specified target value and specified lower and upper bounds. When the response is between the lower bound and the target, the desirability function is as calculated for the maximize-the-response case. When the response is between the upper bound and the target, the desirability function is as calculated for the minimize-the-response case.

Calculating the Weights

The weights s and t are determined as follows:

<1 (min = 0.1): Less emphasis on target; response far from target is very desirable.

= 1: Equal importance on target and bound (linear).

>1 (max = 10): High emphasis on target; must be very close to target for desirability.

Response Surface Designs

NOTE: *This example is a continuation of the example presented under "Factorial Designs" above.*

Collect data along the path of steepest ascent:

B	E	Response	Conclusion
0	0	8,669.2	Centerpoint establishes initial response.
10	–8.8	–986.6	Response decreased; verify with replicate.
10	–8.8	–985.0	Verified response decreases in that direction; try opposite direction.
–10	8.8	7,810	Response decreases in this direction; confirm local maximum at origin.
0	0	8,668.8	Verified local maximum near origin.

A first-order experiment then is constructed and data collected, with the centerpoint at a local maximum (0, 0), using the factor levels defined by the path of steepest ascent.

Minitab

Use *Stat\DOE\Response Surface\Create Response Surface Design*. Depending on number of factors, select either *Central Composite* or *Box-Behnken*. Generally, response surface designs are used only after the number of factors has been reduced using screening designs. One or more factors must have three or more levels to generate a response surface design.

Select the "Designs" button to select a design. Usually the default values for centerpoints and α are appropriate, as discussed earlier.

Select the "Factors" button to specify *Numeric* (i.e., quantitative) or *Text* (i.e., qualitative) and real experimental value for each factor level,

Use the "Options" button to randomize experimental trials.

(Continued)

Std. Order	Run Order	Centerpoint	Blocks	B	E	Response
9	1	0	1	0	0	8,670.25
7	2	1	1	−10	8.74	7,810.83
4	3	1	1	10	8.74	5,931.26
2	4	1	1	10	−8.74	−987.85
6	5	1	1	10	−8.74	−986.2
5	6	1	1	−10	−8.74	7,083.35
8	7	1	1	10	8.74	5,929.95
1	8	1	1	−10	−8.74	7,079.78
3	9	1	1	−10	8.74	7,806.47

The results are analyzed (see details in "Interpretation" below), with significant curvature suggesting proximity to a stationary point. Axial points are added using *Stat\DOE\Modify Design* (see also *Central Composite Design* in the Glossary):

Std. Order	Run Order	Centerpoint	Blocks	B	E	Response
10	10	−1	2	−16.8	0	4,269.41
11	11	−1	2	16.8	0	−3,950.65
12	12	−1	2	0	−14.7	3,667.12
13	13	−1	2	0	14.7	9,947.51

Using both blocks of data (all 13 runs), the quadratic effects are estimated. This analysis indicates that the block (the added axial points) is not itself significant (i.e., the second block agrees with the earlier block's data), but the quadratic terms are significant.

Excel

Using Black Belt XL Add-On

Use *New Chart\Designed Experiment* to generate a new design. Specify factor labels, factor type, and experimental values for each factor. One or more factors must have three or more levels to generate a response surface design. Select *Terms* to select the factors, interactions, and higher-order terms. Choose from the list of designs, and optionally choose *Randomize Runs* and add *Design Replicates* and *Center Point*.

A *Central Composite* or *Box-Behnken* design is chosen with *Design Replicates* set to 2 to produce a design similar to Minitab's (shown above). Use *New Chart\ Designed Experiment* to edit the existing design and add axial points.

Interpretation

In the ANOVA shown in the following example, the *F* statistic is used to compare the sum of squares variation owing to curvature with the sum of squares variation owing to pure error. The low *p* value (0.000; much less than 0.05) indicates that curvature is significant, suggesting that we are near a stationary point (such as a local minimum, maximum, or saddle point).

When the stationary point is outside the experimental region, the experimental region should be expanded with new data, where possible. When new data cannot be generated because the stationary point lies in a region where the factors cannot exist, then we can use the steepest ascent techniques with constrained optimization.

When the stationary point is a saddle point, we also can use the steepest ascent with constrained optimization techniques.

Axial points are added to the current design (at the new centerpoint), and the full results are analyzed (to make maximum use of the data). The locations (values) of the axial points are chosen to achieve rotatable orthogonal designs based on the number of parameters (see further discussion under *Central Composite Design* in the Glossary). In the following example, there are three parameters (*B*, *E*, *BE*), so the axial points are chosen at a value of 1.682, which is applied to factor *B*'s level of 10 to achieve an axial level of 16.82 and to factor *E*'s level of 8.74 to achieve an axial level of 14.7.

Once the optimal point has been defined, additional data always must be collected at this new operating region to verify the predicted results.

Response Surface Designs

Minitab

The results of the first-order design with centerpoint at local maximum are analyzed using the *Stat\DOE\Factorial\Analyze Factorial Design* option.

(Continued)

Source	df	Seq SS	Adj SS	Adj MS	F	P
Main effects	2	78,688,608	78,688,608	39,344,304	16.06	0.007
Two-way interactions	1	19,161,424	19,161,424	19,161,424	7.82	0.038
Residual error	5	12,246,657	12,246,657	2,449,331		
Curvature	1	12,246,639	12,246,639	12,246,639	2,706,955.45	0.000
Pure error	4	18	18	5		
Total	8	110,096,688				

Significant curvature is evident ($p = 0.000$), suggesting proximity to a stationary point. Axial points are added and the data analyzed. The block term was not significant ($p = 0.147$), so it is removed to achieve the following results:

Term	Coefficient	Std Error Coeff.	T	p
Constant	8,632	44.12	195.635	0.000
B	−4,152	23.27	−178.429	0.000
E	3,184	23.27	136.804	0.000
B × B	−8,496	61.78	−137.507	0.000
E × E	−1,848	61.78	−29.906	0.000
B × E	4,377	51.13	85.605	0.000

R-Sq = 99.99% R-Sq(adj) = 99.99%

Analysis of Variance for Response						
Source	df	Seq SS	Adj SS	Adj MS	F	p
Regression	5	217,645,831	217,645,831	43,529,166	16,647.44	0.000
Linear	2	13,218,2457	132,182,457	66,091,228	25,276.15	0.000
Square	2	66,301,951	66,301,951	33,150,975	12,678.37	0.000
Interactions	1	19,161,424	19,161,424	19,161,424	7,328.16	0.000
Residual error	7	18,303	18,303	2,615		
Lack of fit	3	18,285	18,285	6,095	1,347.24	0.000
Pure error	4	18	18	5		
Total	12	217,664,134				

The quadratic terms are significant. Contour and/or surface plots are generated using *Stat/DOE/Response Surface/Contour Surface Plots* to reveal a maxima in the region of the last data value ($B = 0$; $E = 14.6989$).

Use *Stat/DOE/Response Surface/Response Optimizer.* The optimal condition is predicted at ($B = -0.51$; $E = 12$), resulting in a predicted maximum response of 10,010.

Excel

Using Black Belt XL Add-On

Use *New Chart\Designed Experiment* to select the response column and analyze results. Use the "Terms" button to specify only first-order terms for the initial screening analysis and to define terms in each subsequent pass as described above for Minitab.

Select Excel's *Data\Solver* to use the regression function (from the DOE analysis) to determine an optimal condition for the response. The *Set Target Cell* references a cell containing the regression function, for example, "=8632 + (–4152*B3) + (3184*B4) + (–8496*B3^2) + (–1848*B4^2) + (4377*B3*B4)," where B3 and B4 refer to cells containing the starting value for factors B and E (respectively), which are selected in the *By Changing Cells* field. The starting values for these cells may be entered as the values of B and E that produce the optimal observed response (but often can be left empty). The *Min, Max,* and *Value of x* options are used to define the desired response as a maximum, minimum, or target.

Run-Test Rules

The Western Electric *run-test rules* add sensitivity to a control chart. These run tests, developed by Western Electric, with some improvements by statistician Lloyd Nelson, apply statistical tests to determine if there are any patterns or trends in the plotted points.

When to Use

Use tests 1 through 8 on $\bar{X}$ and individual-X control charts; use tests 1 through 4 on attribute (P, U, Np, and C) charts. Run tests cannot be applied when the underlying data or the plotted statistic is autocorrelated, such as in EWMA charts.

Methodology

The *Western Electric Statistical Quality Control Handbook* defined zones using the sigma levels of the normal distribution, as shown in Figure F.40.

Run test 1 (Western Electric): One subgroup beyond 3σ, an indication that the process mean has shifted. See Figure F.41.

Run test 2 (Nelson): Nine consecutive subgroups on the same side of the average. (*Note:* Western Electric uses eight consecutive points on the same side of the average). See Figure F.41.

Run test 3 (Nelson): Six consecutive subgroups increasing or decreasing. See Figure F.42.

Run test 4 (Nelson): Fourteen consecutive subgroups alternating up and down. See Figure F.42.

Run test 5 (Western Electric): Two of three consecutive subgroups beyond 2σ. See Figure F.43.

Run test 6 (Western Electric): Four of five consecutive subgroups beyond 1σ. See Figure F.43.

Run test 7 (Western Electric): Fifteen consecutive subgroups between +1σ sigma and −1σ. See Figure F.44.

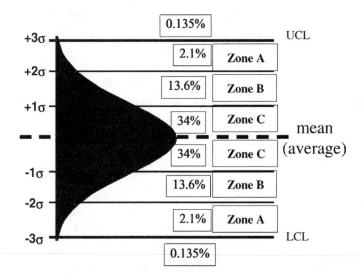

FIGURE F.40 Normal distribution zones.

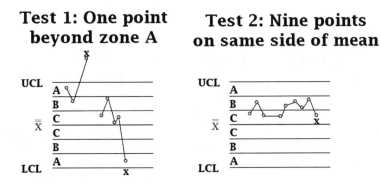

FIGURE F.41 Run tests 1 and 2. Pyzdek and Keller (2009).

Run test 8 (Western Electric): Eight consecutive points beyond $+1\sigma$ and -1σ (both sides of center). See Figure F.44.

The run tests are applied as written to m charts and individual-X charts when the normal distribution is used. When nonnormal distributions are used for individual-X charts, the average is replaced with the median, and zones are defined to provide the same probabilities as the normal curve at the stated sigma level. For example, run test 1 is interpreted as any point in the 0.135 percent tails (99.73 percent within the control limits), even though this probably would not be $\pm3\sigma$ for a nonnormal distribution.

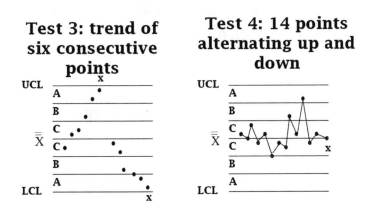

FIGURE F.42 Run tests 3 and 4. Pyzdek and Keller (2009).

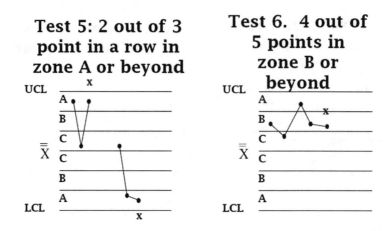

FIGURE F.43 Run tests 5 and 6. Pyzdek and Keller (2009).

Run tests 1, 2, 5, and 6 are applied to the upper and lower halves of the chart separately. Run tests 3, 4, 7, and 8 are applied to the whole chart.

Run-test rules are provided in most SPC software as an option to be applied when constructing the applicable SPC control chart. See "Statistical Process Control (SPC) Charts" below for methods of constructing each control chart in Minitab and MS Excel.

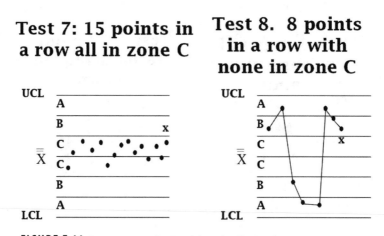

FIGURE F.44 Run tests 7 and 8. Pyzdek and Keller (2009).

Interpretation

The run tests apply statistical tests to determine if there are any patterns or trends in the plotted points. Run tests 1, 2, 3, 5, and 6 provide an indication that the process mean has shifted, whereas the others tell us something about sampling errors, inconsistent with the base premise of rational subgrouping.

> *Run test 4:* An indication of sampling from a multistream process (subgroups alternate between two or more process levels)
>
> *Run test 7:* An indication of stratification in sampling (multistream sampling within a subgroup)
>
> *Run test 8:* An indication of sampling from a mixture (multistream sampling, subgroups on each side of the center from separate distributions)

The statistical basis of the run tests is simply that if the subgroups are truly from the stated distribution and independent of one another, then there will not be any pattern to the points. The run tests increase the power of the control chart (the likelihood that shifts in the process are detected with each subgroup) but also provide an increased (yet minimal) false-alarm rate.

Keep in mind that the subgroup that first violates the run test does not always indicate when the process shift occurs. For example, when run test 2 is violated, the shift may have occurred nine points (or more or less) prior to the point that violated the run test. As another example, a process may be in control and not in violation of the run tests for a period of time, say, 50 subgroups. Then the process average shifts upward. As more and more subgroups are added at the new level, subgroups in the original 50 subgroups will start violating run tests or control limits because these points now show an unnatural pattern relative to the combined distributions of the two process levels.

Scatter Diagrams

A *scatter diagram* is an *XY* plot used to investigate the correlation of one variable with another.

When to Use

Analyze Stage

- To investigate the correlation of one variable with another

Methodology

The x axis is used to measure the scale of one characteristic (called the *independent variable*), and the y axis measures the second (called the *dependent variable*). To collect data, independently change values in x, and observe values of the y variable.

For example, we are interested in understanding the relationship between cooking time and the amount (or percent) of popcorn effectively cooked. We observe that a cooking time of 1½ minutes produces a 76 percent kernel conversion rate in a bag of popcorn, so we plot a point at an x value of 1.5 minutes and a y value of 76. We conduct additional trials at other cooking times, measure the resulting conversion rate, and then plot the (x, y) paired values. The collected data are shown in Table T.17, with the resulting scatter diagram shown in Figure F.45.

There are a few general suggestions to keep in mind when working with scatter diagrams:

- Vary the x value over a sufficient range so that you have data over the entire region of interest.

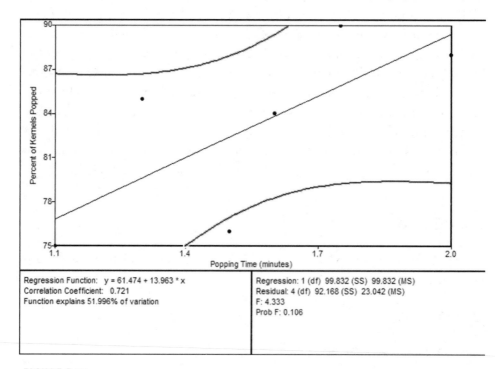

Regression Function: $y = 61.474 + 13.963 * x$
Correlation Coefficient: 0.721
Function explains 51.996% of variation

Regression: 1 (df) 99.832 (SS) 99.832 (MS)
Residual: 4 (df) 92.168 (SS) 23.042 (MS)
F: 4.333
Prob F: 0.106

FIGURE F.45 Example of a scatter diagram (created using Green Belt XL software).

- It is best to only work with data that are collected specifically for the analysis. Other so-called happenstance data may include data that are mixed over several populations. These separate populations may indicate a hidden variable or interaction that is difficult to detect after the fact.

TABLE T.17 Example Paired Data for Scatter Diagram

x: Cooking Time	y: Kernel Conversion Rate
1.5	76
1.3	85
1.1	75
1.6	84
2	88
1.75	90

Scatter Diagram

Minitab

Data input: Enter a column of data for the independent (x) variable and a second column of equal length for the dependent (y) variable.

Menu: *Graph\Scatter Plot\With Regression*

Results: Regression function with ANOVA is provided separately using the *Stat\Regression\Regression* function.

Excel

Using Green Belt XL Add-On

Data input: Enter a column of data for the independent (x) variable and a second column of equal length for the dependent (y) variable.

Menu: *New Chart\Scatter Diagram*

Results: Provides regression function with ANOVA.

Interpretation

Correlation implies that as one variable changes, the other also changes. Although this may indicate a cause-and-effect relationship, this is not always the case because there may be a third characteristic (or many more) that actually cause the noted effect of both characteristics.

Sometimes, though, if we know that there is good correlation between two characteristics, we can use one to predict the other, particularly if one characteristic is easy to measure and the other isn't. For instance, if we prove that weight gain in the first trimester of pregnancy correlates well with fetus development, we can use weight gain as a predictor. The alternative would be expensive tests to monitor the actual development of the fetus.

If the two characteristics are somehow related, the pattern formed by plotting them in a scatter diagram will show clustering in a certain direction and tightness. The more the cluster approaches a line in appearance, the more the two characteristics are likely to be linearly correlated.

The relative correlation of one characteristic with another can be seen both from how closely points cluster on the line and from the correlation coefficient R. R values near 1 imply very high correlation between the dependent and independent variables, meaning that a change in one characteristic will be accompanied by a change in the other characteristic. Weak correlation means that the variation in the dependent variable is not well explained by the changes in the independent variable. This lack of correlation implies that other variables (including measurement error) may be responsible for the variation in y.

Positive correlation means that as the independent variable increases, so does the dependent variable, and this is shown on the scatter diagram as a line with a positive slope. Negative correlation implies that as the independent variable increases, the dependent variable decreases, and a negative slope is seen on the scatter diagram.

Regression analysis (discussed earlier) provides a prediction model for the relationship between the two variables.

Be careful not to extrapolate beyond the data region because you have no experience on which to draw. Extrapolation should be done with great caution because the relationship between the two variables may change significantly. For example, the size of a balloon will increase as we pump more air into it, but only to a point! Once we pass that point, the outcome will change dramatically.

When we suspect that there are hidden variables, we can stratify our data to

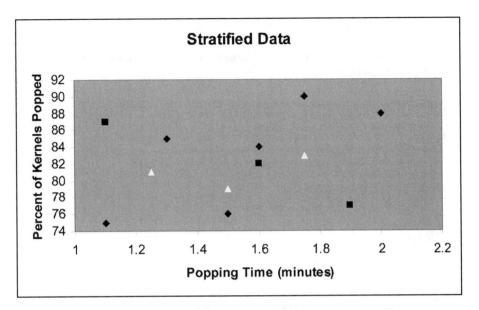

FIGURE F.46 Data that appear to be uncorrelated may be stratified.

see if we can detect the effect of the interactions, as shown in Figure F.46. In this case, there is no clear correlation between the two variables. However, if we recognize that there is a third variable, then we notice three distinctly different patterns. In investigating the effect of cooking time on kernel conversion, suppose that each of the three series, shown in the graph in Figure F.46 as squares, triangles, and diamonds, represents different cooking temperatures. Series one, displayed with diamonds, shows a positive correlation. Series two, in squares, shows a negative correlation. Series three, in triangles, shows less correlation. By looking for these hidden patterns, we may find other key variables that impact our resulting y. We would want to verify these suspicions using additional investigative techniques discussed elsewhere in Part 3, such as multiple regression analysis and design of experiments.

SIPOC

SIPOC, an acronym standing for *s*uppliers, *i*nputs, *p*rocess, *o*utputs, and *c*ustomers, refers to the technique of analyzing a process relative to these parameters to fully understand its impact. In this context, each element of SIPOC is defined as follows:

Suppliers: Those who provide inputs for process

Inputs: The data, knowledge, and resources necessary for the process to generate desired output

Process: The activity that transforms inputs to outputs

Outputs: The result of the process (deliverables)

Customers: The person, persons, or function that receives the outputs

When to Use

Define Stage

- To document the top-level process, its transactions, and its stakeholders

Methodology

We begin a SIPOC analysis by focusing on the process. We map the process using either a flowchart or a process map.

We then define the outputs for the process. These include all the outcomes and results of the process, including the value-added products or services provided as well as documentation, inputs to other processes, and payments. A complete list of outputs will enhance the definitions of customers, inputs, and suppliers, so spend some time making sure that you are complete at this point.

Once the outputs are defined, we can list the customers. A customer is anyone who receives an output from the process and so may include internal as well as external customers.

We then identify the inputs to the process. Consider all the resources necessary for the process. Look particularly at decision points in the process because the information needed to make decisions is a necessary input.

Finally, once we've identified the inputs, we define the source of the input as the supplier.

Table T.18 is a SIPOC example from a publishing company. The process is shown here in text for simplicity, but a process map also could be used. The SIPOC was developed following the guidelines just presented.

TABLE T.18 SIPOC Analysis for a Publisher

Suppliers	Input	Process	Output	Customers
Legal	ISBN	Receive draft	ISBN	Printer
Author	Final draft	Issue ISBN	New cover	Reader
Graphic design	Cover design	Cover	Error list	Marketing
Layout editor	Quark files	Edit layout	Correspondence with editor	
		Proof for errors	PDF files	
		Create PDF for printer		
		Send to marketing		

Interpretation

The results of the SIPOC analysis will assist in proper definition of the project. The process team should have representatives from each of the key customer and supplier groups (collectively, the *stakeholders*). The inputs and outputs to the process provide a check on the process map, and they can assist in project scope definition, as well as general problem solving of sources of variation.

Spaghetti Diagram

A *spaghetti diagram*, as shown in Figure F.47, is a graphic tool used to indicate the movement of material or personnel.

When to Use

Analyze Stage

- To identify unnecessary movement of material or personnel

Methodology

Begin with a floor plan, layout, or map of the physical area used by the process. Write a number 1 at the physical location where the process begins and then a number 2 at the next physical location to which the material or personnel will move. Draw a line from number 1 to number 2. Repeat for all subsequent movements of the material or personnel.

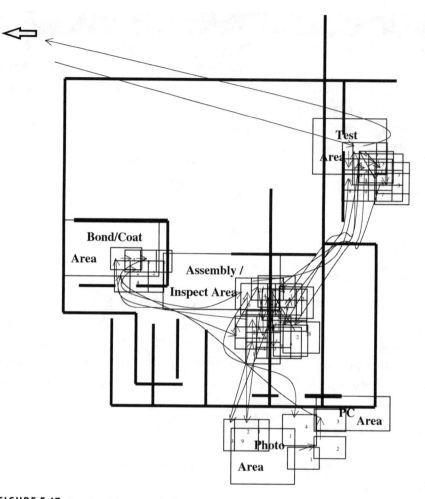

FIGURE F.47 Spaghetti diagram of a floor plan showing poor use of physical space.

An example of a spaghetti diagram is shown in Figure F.47. The floor plan for the process provides the background, complete with walls and doors. The flow of the process is superimposed to show the flow of personnel and material as the process activities are undertaken.

Interpretation

Look for opportunities to move necessary process steps closer to one another. Notice in the example the scrambled mess, resembling the tangles of cooked spaghetti, resulting from excessive movement and poor use of physical space.

Statistical Process Control (SPC) Charts

Walter Shewhart, working for AT&T's Bell Laboratories, developed the concept of *statistical process control* (SPC) in the 1920s. Statistical process control uses data from prior observations of a process to predict how the process will vary in the future. Shewhart offered this definition of *statistical control:* "A phenomenon is said to be in statistical control when, through the use of past experience, we can predict how the phenomenon will vary in the future."

The element of time, which is lacking in enumerative statistical tools (including histograms, confidence intervals, and hypothesis tests), is a critical parameter for investigating process characteristics because processes are, by definition, occurring over the course of time. Enumerative tools pool the data from the past into single estimates of the average and standard deviation—the time element is lost! An enumerative analysis of this nature is valid only when we can assume that all the prior data are from a single distribution.

In contrast, SPC uses the element of time as one of its principal components. Its control charts can be used to verify that a process is stable, implying that the data are from a single distribution.

When to Use

Measure Stage

- To baseline the process by quantifying the common-cause level of variation inherent to the process
- As part of measurement systems analysis to evaluate repeatability and reproducibility

Analyze Stage

- To differentiate between common and special causes of variation

Improve Stage

- To verify the results of process improvement on the process metric

Control Stage

- To monitor the process to ensure the stability of the revised process and the continued benefit of the improvement

A fundamental benefit of control charts is their ability to identify the common-cause operating level of the process. The region between the upper and lower control limits defines the variation that is expected from the process statistic. This is the variation owing to common causes—sources of variation that contribute to all the process observations.

W. Edwards Deming demonstrated the principles behind SPC with his red bead experiment, which he regularly conducted during his seminars. In this experiment, he used a bucket of beads or marbles. Most of the beads were white, but a small percentage (about 10 percent) of red beads were thoroughly mixed with the white beads in the bucket. Students volunteered to be process workers, who would dip a sample paddle into the bucket and produce a day's "production" of 50 beads for the White Bead Company. Other students would volunteer to be inspectors, who counted the number of white beads in each operator's daily production. The white beads represented usable output that could be sold to the White Bead Company's customers, whereas the red beads were scrap. These results then were reported to a manager, who invariably would chastise operators for a high number of red beads. If the operator's production improved on the next sample, he or she was rewarded; if the production of white beads went down, more chastising occurred.

Figure F.48 shows a control chart of the typical white bead output. It's obvious from the control chart that there was variation in the process observations: Each dip into the bucket yielded a different number of white beads. Has the process changed? No! No one has changed the bucket, yet the number of white

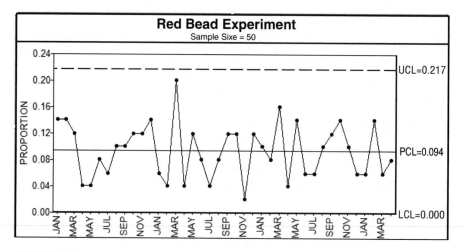

FIGURE F.48 SPC chart.

beads is different every time. The control limits tell us that we should expect anywhere between 0 and 21 percent red beads on a given sample of 50 beads.

When the process is in control, we can use the control limits to predict the future performance of the process. For example, we might use the chart to predict the error levels, which tell us something about the cost to produce the product or deliver the service. If the process variable is the time to deliver the product or service, we can use the chart to plan resources, such as in a doctor's office, or deliver product, such as in a warehouse.

Another fundamental benefit of a control chart is its ability to provide an operational definition of a special cause. Once we accept that every process exhibits some level of variation, we might consider how much variation is natural for the process. If a particular observation seems large, is it unnaturally large, or should an observation of this magnitude be expected? The control limits remove the subjectivity from this decision and define this level of natural process variation.

When a sample subgroup is beyond the control limits, we say that it is a result of a special cause of variation. In other words, something unexpected happened at this point in time (or just prior to this point in time) to influence the process differently from what we've seen before.

Although we may not be able to immediately identify the special cause in process terms (e.g., cycle time increased owing to staff shortages), we have statistical evidence that the process has changed. This process change can occur as a change in process location or a change in process variation.

A change in process location is sometimes simply referred to as a *process shift*. For example, the average cycle time may have changed from 19 to 12 days. Process shifts may result in process improvement (e.g., cycle time reduction) or process degradation (e.g., an increased cycle time). Recognizing this as a process change rather than just random variation of a stable process allows us to learn about the process dynamics, reduce variation, and maintain improvements.

The variation in the process also may increase or decrease. This is evidenced by a change in the width of the control limits. Generally, a reduction in variation is considered a process improvement because the process then is easier to predict and manage.

In the absence of control limits, we assume that an arbitrarily "different" observation is due to a shift in the process. In our zeal to reduce variation, we adjust the process to return it to its prior state. For example, we sample the value highlighted in the leftmost distribution in Figure F.49 from a process that

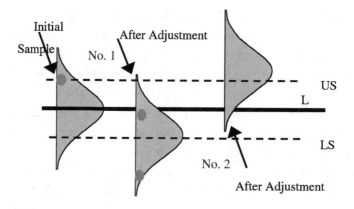

FIGURE F.49 An example of tampering.

(unbeknown to us) is in control. We feel that this value is excessively large, so we assume that the process must have shifted. We adjust the process by the amount of deviation between the observed value and the initial process average. The process is now at the level shown in the center distribution in the figure. We sample from this distribution and observe several values near the initial average, and then we sample a value such as is highlighted in the center distribution. We adjust the process upward by the deviation between the new value and the initial mean, resulting in the rightmost distribution shown in the figure. As we continue this process, we can see that we actually increase the total process variation, which is exactly the opposite of our desired effect.

Responding to these arbitrary observation levels as if they were special causes is known as *tampering*. This is also called *responding to a false alarm* because a false alarm is when we think that the process has shifted when it really hasn't. Deming's funnel experiment demonstrates this principle. In practice, tampering occurs when we attempt to control the process to limits that are within the natural control limits defined by common-cause variation. Some causes of this include

- We try to control the process to specifications or goals. These limits are defined externally to the process rather than being based on the statistics of the process.

- Rather than using the suggested control limits defined at ±3 SDs from the centerline, we use limits that are tighter (or narrower) than these on the faulty notion that this will improve the performance of the chart. Using limits defined at ±2 SDs from the centerline produces narrower control limits than the ±3 SD limits, so it would appear that the ±2σ limits are better at detecting shifts. Assuming normality, the chance of being outside of a ±3 SD control limit is 0.27 percent if the process has not shifted. On average, a false alarm is encountered with these limits once every 370 (1/0.0027) subgroups. Using ±2 SD control limits, the chance of being outside the limits when the process has not shifted is 4.6 percent, corresponding to false alarms every 22 subgroups! If we respond to these false alarms, we tamper and increase variation.

Methodology

In an SPC analysis, we collect samples over a short period of time. Each of these samples is referred to as a *subgroup*. Each subgroup tells us two things about the process—its current location and its current amount of variation.

Once we've collected enough subgroups over a period of time, we can use these short-term estimates to predict where the process will be (its location) and how much the process is expected to vary over a longer time period.

Control charts take many forms depending on the process that is being analyzed and the data available from that process. All control charts have the following properties:

- The *x* axis is sequential, usually a unit denoting the evolution of time.
- The *y* axis is the statistic that is being charted for each point in time. Examples of plotted statistics include an observation, an average of two or more observations, the median of two or more observations, a count of items meeting a criterion of interest, or the percent of items meeting a criterion of interest.
- Limits are defined for the statistic that is being plotted. These control limits are determined statistically by observing process behavior, providing an indication of the bounds of expected behavior for the plotted statistic. They are never determined using customer specifications or goals.

The key to successful control charts is the formation of rational subgroups. Control charts rely on rational subgroups to estimate the short-term variation in the process. This short-term variation then is used to predict the longer-term variation defined by the control limits.

Nelson (1988) describes a *rational subgroup* as simply "a sample in which all of the items are produced under conditions in which only random effects are responsible for the observed variation." Another way of stating this is that the causes of *within*-subgroup variation are equivalent to the causes of *between*-subgroup variation.

A rational subgroup has the following properties:

- The observations comprising the subgroup are independent. Two observations are independent if neither observation influences or results from the other. When observations are dependent on one another, we say the process has *autocorrelation* or *serial correlation*. (These terms mean the same thing.)

- The subgroups are formed from observations taken in a time-ordered sequence. In other words, subgroups cannot be constructed arbitrarily by taking multiple samples, each equal to the subgroup size, from a set of data (or a box of parts). Rather, the data comprising a subgroup must be a "snapshot" of the process over a small window of time, and the order of the subgroups would show how those snapshots vary in time (like a movie). The size of the "small window of time" is determined on an individual process basis to minimize the chance of a special cause occurring in the subgroup (which, if persistent, would provide the situation described immediately below).

- The observations within a subgroup are from a single, stable process. If subgroups contain the elements of multiple process streams, or if other special causes occur frequently within subgroups, then the within-subgroup variation will be large relative to the between-subgroup variation averages. This large within-subgroup variation forces the control limits to be too far apart, resulting in a lack of sensitivity to process shifts.

In Figure F.50, you might suspect that the cause of the tight grouping of

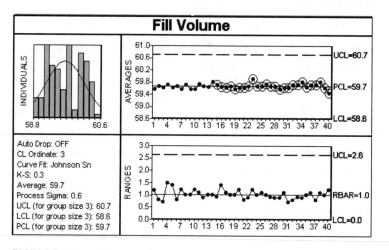

FIGURE F.50 Multiple process streams within each subgroup provide an irrational estimate of process variation.

subgroups about the $\bar{X}$ chart center line is a reduction in process variation. But the range chart fails to confirm this theory.

These data, provided by a major cosmetic manufacturer, represent the fill weight for bottles of nail polish. The filling machine has three filling heads, so subgroups were conveniently formed by taking a sample from each fill head. The problem is that the heads in the filling machine apparently have significantly different average values. This variation between filling heads causes the within-subgroup variation (as plotted on the range chart) to be much larger than the variation in the subgroup averages (represented graphically by the pattern of the plotted points on the $\bar{X}$ chart). The $\bar{X}$ chart control limits, calculated based on the range chart, thus are much wider than the plotted subgroups.

The underlying problem, then, is that the premise of a rational subgroup has been violated: We tried to construct a subgroup out of apples and oranges. But all is not lost (fruit salad isn't so bad) because we've learned something about our process. We've learned that the filler heads are different and that we could reduce overall variation by making them more similar. Note the circles that highlight subgroups 16 through 40 in Figure F.50. The software has indicated a violation of run test 7, which was developed to search for this type of pattern in the data (see "Run-Test Rules").

This type of multistream behavior is not limited to cosmetics filling operations. Consider the potential for irrational subgroups in these processes:

- A bank supervisor is trying to reduce the wait time for key services. She constructs a control chart using subgroups based on a selection of five customers in the bank at a time. Since she wants to include all the areas, she makes sure to include loan applications as well as teller services in the subgroup.
- An operator finish grinds 30 parts at a time in a single fixture. He measures 5 parts from the fixture for his subgroup, always including the two end pieces. His fixture is quite worn, so the pieces on the two ends differ substantially.

Most likely, each of these examples will result in an irrational subgroup owing to multistream processes.

Sampling Considerations

Many times, the process will dictate the size of the rational subgroup. For example, the rational subgroup size for service processes is often equal to 1. A

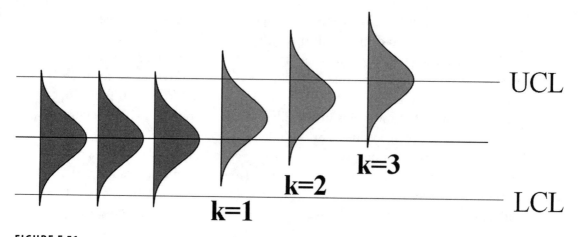

FIGURE F.51 Larger shifts are easier to detect because there is a larger percentage of the process outside the control limits.

larger subgroup taken over a short interval would tend to contain dependent data; taken over a longer interval, the subgroup could contain special causes of variation.

The safest assumption for maintaining a rational subgroup is to use a subgroup size of 1. Since data usually have some cost associated with them, smaller subgroups generally are cheaper to acquire than larger subgroups. Unfortunately, smaller subgroup sizes are less capable of detecting shifts in the process.

As seen in Figure F.51, it is easier to detect larger process shifts than to detect smaller process shifts. The larger shift, shown by the $k = 3\sigma$ shift on the far right, has much more area outside the control limits, so it is easier to detect than the $k = 1\sigma$ shift.

Table T.19 shows the average number of subgroups necessary to detect a shift of size k (in standard deviation units) based on subgroup size n. For example, if we observe the process a large number of times, then, on average, a subgroup of size $n = 3$ will detect a $k = 1\sigma$ shift in 9 subgroups. As you can see from the table, small subgroups will readily detect relatively large shifts of 2σ or 3σ but are less capable of readily detecting smaller shifts. This demonstrates the power of the $\bar{X}$ chart.

| **TABLE T.19** Average Number of Subgroups to Detect Shift | | | | | |
n/k	0.5	1	1.5	2	2.5	3
1	155	43	14	6	3	1
2	90	17	5	2	1	1
3	60	9	2	1	1	1
4	43	6	1	1	1	1
5	33	4	1	1	1	1
6	26	3	1	1	1	1
7	21	2	1	1	1	1
8	17	2	1	1	1	1
9	14	1	1	1	1	1
10	12	1	1	1	1	1

Defining Control Limits

To define the control limits, we need an ample history of the process to define the level of common-cause variation. There are two issues here:

1. Statistically, we need to observe a sufficient number of data observations before we can calculate reliable estimates of the variation and (to a lesser degree) the average. In addition, the statistical "constants" used to define control chart limits (such as d_2) are actually variables and only approach constants when the number of subgroups is "large." For a subgroup size of 5, for instance, the d_2 value approaches a constant at about 25 subgroups (Duncan, 1986). When a limited number of subgroups are available, short-run techniques may be useful.

2. To distinguish between special causes and common causes, you must have enough subgroups to define the common-cause operating level of your process. This implies that all types of common causes must be included in the data. For example, if we observe the process over one shift, using one operator and a single batch of material from one supplier, we are not observing all elements of common-cause variation that are likely to be characteristic of the process. If we define control limits under these limited conditions, then we will likely see special causes arising owing to the natural variation in one or more of these factors.

Control Chart Selection

There are many control charts available for our use. One differentiator between the control charts is the type of data that will be analyzed on the chart:

- *Attributes data* (also known as *count data*). Typically, we will count the number of times we observe some condition (usually something we don't like, such as a defect or an error) in a given sample from the process.

- *Variables data* (also known as *measurement data*). Variables data are continuous in nature and generally capable of being measured to enough resolution to provide at least 10 unique values for the process being analyzed.

Attributes data have less resolution than variables data because we only count if something occurs rather than taking a measurement to see how close we are to a condition. For example, attributes data for a manufacturing process might include the number of items in which the diameter exceeds the specification, whereas variables data for the same process might be the measurement of that part diameter. In a service process, we may measure the time it takes to process an order (variables data) or count the number of times the order processing time exceeds a predefined limit (attributes data).

Attributes data generally provide us with less information than variables data would for the same process. Attributes data generally would not allow us to predict whether the process is trending toward an undesirable state because it is already in this condition. As a result, variables data are considered more useful for defect *prevention*.

There are several attribute control charts, each designed for a slightly different use:

- *np chart:* For monitoring the number of times a condition occurs

- *p chart:* For monitoring the percent of samples having the condition

- *c chart:* For monitoring the number of times a condition occurs, when each sample can have more than one instance of the condition.

- *u chart:* For monitoring the percent of samples having the condition, when each sample can have more than one instance of the condition.

There are also several variables charts available for use. The first selection generally is the subgroup size. The subgroup size is the number of observations, taken in close proximity of time, used to estimate the short-term variation.

Although subgroups of size 1 provide some estimate of the process location, we sometimes choose to collect data in larger subgroups because we obtain a better estimate of both the process location and the short-term variation at that point in time.

Control charts available for variables data include

- *Individual-X charts (also known as* individuals charts, I charts, *and* IMR charts): Used for subgroup size equal to 1.
- $\bar{X}$ *charts*: Used for subgroup size 2 and larger.
- *EWMA (exponentially weighted moving average) charts*: Used for subgroups of size 1 or larger. Suitable for nonnormal data or increased sensitivity to small process shifts.

Figure F.52 shows selection criteria for control charts. Each of these charts is discussed further elsewhere in this part.

Interpretation

When evaluating the results of a control chart, we must realize that reacting to special causes is one of the key reasons for using a control chart. Out-of-control points provide valuable information about the process.

The control charts are designed to detect shifts with a minimal chance of a *false alarm*. That is, there is a negligible chance that the process has not changed

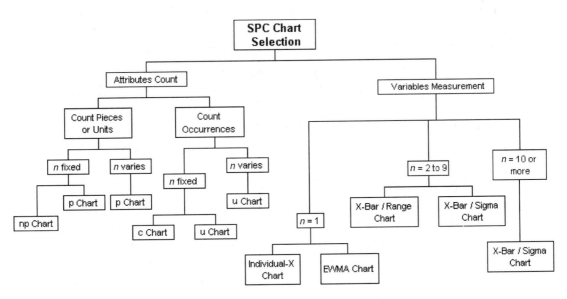

FIGURE F.52 Selection criteria for control charts.

when a special cause has been identified. Conversely, there is overwhelming evidence that the process has changed, and by removing this *special cause*, we will reduce the overall variability of the process. Therefore, whenever a special cause is present, we must not ignore it but learn from it.

When we encounter special causes of variation, we must determine (in process terms) the cause of the process shift. For example, if the control chart indicates that service times are now below the lower control limit, indicating that they were improved, the cause might be that we had *changed the method of customer service by routing clients to more experienced personnel.*

Once we have identified the special cause, we can statistically recalculate the control chart's centerlines and control limits without including the data known to be affected by the special cause. If the process shift is sustained, such as when a new procedure replaces old process procedures, then we simply calculate new control limits for the new, improved process.

As discussed earlier, when the process is in control, subgroups have only an extremely small chance of being outside the control limits. If we incorrectly say that the process has shifted, then we have committed a false alarm. The chance of a false alarm in most control charts is about 1 in 370: For every 370 subgroups plotted, on average, 1 subgroup would be falsely estimated to be out of control. Since we often experience real changes to our process in less time that that, this is considered to be appropriately insignificant.

We start the process of variation reduction by isolating the instances of variation owing to special causes. We can use the time-ordered nature of the control chart to understand what happened (in process terms) at each point in time that represents special causes. When the process does undergo a shift, such as is shown in the three distribution curves on the right of Figure F.51, then we detect the process shift when we happen to sample subgroups from the tail region of the distribution that exceeds the limits. As we can see from the graphic, the larger the process shift, the more tail area is beyond the upper control limit, so the greater chance there is that we will detect a shift.

An important point to remember is that a control chart will not detect all shifts, nor necessarily detect shifts as soon as they occur. Notice in Figure F.51 that even though there was a large tail area outside the upper control limit, the majority of the subgroup samples will be within the control limits. For this reason, we should be suspect of neighboring points, even those within the control limits, once an assignable cause has been detected. Furthermore, we should realize that there are often choices we can make to improve the detection of special causes, including the type of control chart, its options, the use of run test rules, and the method by which we sample from the process.

Once we have differentiated between the variation owing to special causes and the variation owing to common causes, we can separately reduce the variation from each. To reduce the variation owing to common causes, we look to all elements of the system and process for clues to variation. We generally can ignore the point-to-point variation because it represents a combination of factors that is common to all the subgroups. We'll typically use designed experiments and multiple regression analysis to understand these sources of variation.

Transformation

Transformation creates a new variable using one or more original variables, usually to make an analysis more useful.

When to Use

Analyze Stage

- To stabilize variance to meet the assumptions required for ANOVA techniques (a constant level of variance at each response level)
- To calculate parameters based on a measured response or responses (For example, cost may be the preferred response, even though labor time was measured. The effect of the parameter on process variation can also be calculated when there are repeat runs at each operating condition.)

Methodology

Variance Stabilization

Once the condition of nonconstant variance is detected using the F test for equality of variance (discussed earlier), we can plot the log of the standard deviation at each experimental condition with the log of the mean of the experimental condition. The resulting slope of the line will provide an indication of a useful transformation, as shown in Table T.20 (Box, Hunter, and Hunter, 1978). Note that slopes lying between those indicated in Table T.20 should be rounded up or down to the levels provided.

For example, a plot of the log of the averages (of the replicated trials) versus

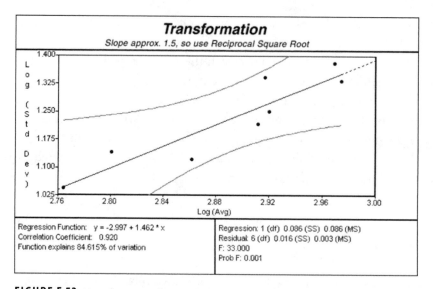

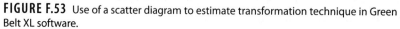

FIGURE F.53 Use of a scatter diagram to estimate transformation technique in Green Belt XL software.

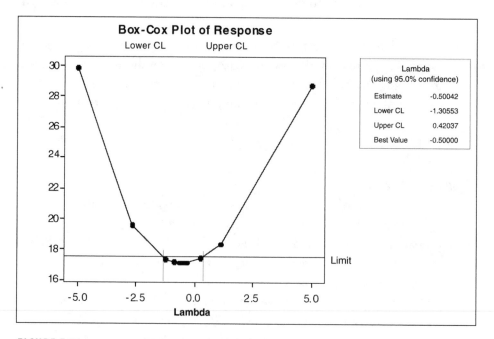

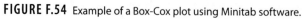

FIGURE F.54 Example of a Box-Cox plot using Minitab software.

the log of the standard deviation (of the replicated trials) indicates a slope of 1.462 in Figure F.53. Since this is close to 1.5, a reciprocal square root transformation will be applied so that the transformed $y_t = 1/\sqrt{y}$.

Box and Cox (1964) developed an iterative approach for determining an optimal λ that minimizes the sum of squares error term. Myers and Montgomery (1995) provide an example of this approach. A sample Minitab output using the preceding example's data is shown in Figure F.54.

In this case, the Box-Cox plot suggests an optimal λ at $-\frac{1}{2}$. This is the same value suggested by the plot of log (SD_i) versus log $(Mean_i)$. From Table T.20, the square root transformation should be applied: Calculate the square root of each raw data value, and use this transformed data in the ANOVA analysis.

Since the confidence interval does not include the value 1 (the λ for no transformation), a transformation would be helpful to stabilize the variance.

TABLE T.20 Suggested Transformations Based on Slope of VAR

Slope	$\lambda = 1 - \alpha$	Transform	Useful for
0	1	None	
½	½	Square root	Poisson data
1	0	Log	Log-normal data
³/₂	−½	Reciprocal square root	
2	−1	Reciprocal	

Transformations: Variance Stabilization

Minitab

Use *Stat\Control Chart\Box-Cox Transformation*. Use the "Options" button to specify column for storage of transformed data.

Excel

Using Green Belt XL Add-On

Data input: Calculate the average and standard deviation of each set of replicated trials using Excel's *AVERAGE* and *STDEV* spreadsheet functions. Calculate the log of each average and each standard deviation.

Menu: *New Chart\ Scatter Diagram*

(Continued)

Data range: Select column of log (averages) as x axis (first column in *Data Range*); select column of log (standard deviations) as y axis (second column in *Data Range*)

Results: Obtain the slope from the plot; round up or down to closest slope in Table T.20

Calculated Parameters

Simple calculated responses occur frequently when a response is measured and then converted to a response with more general interest. For example, the labor required to assemble a piece of furniture may be measured in labor hours and then converted to labor cost because that more directly relates to profitability. Measurement equipment may output a resistance that can be converted to a more meaningful temperature response.

We also can convert multiple responses to a single response. A simple example is the calculation of density based on measured displaced volume and mass. We may similarly calculate utilization based on usage and availability (such as "bed days" in health care).

Finally, we may calculate statistics based on the grouping of repeated runs to better understand how a factor influences the process variation. Taguchi's signal-to-noise ratios are one example of this.

Classical experiments often investigated the effects of a parameter on the mean response. Taguchi popularized investigating parameter effects on the variation of the response using signal-to-noise ratios. Estimating the effects on variation is often useful for designing processes that are robust to parameter variation or in some cases to reduce common-cause variation.

Estimation of the variance requires grouping of responses based on multiple observations at each condition, such as with replication or repeat runs (during the running of the experiment) or after insignificant terms have been discarded. Taguchi's signal-to-noise ratio is a grouped response that considers both the variation of replicated measurements and the proximity of the average response to a specified target value. Taguchi defined over 70 signal-to-noise ratios, 3 of which are most common:

- *Smaller is better*. Used when the target value for the response is zero. The signal-to-noise ratio is calculated as

$$\text{S/N ratio} = -10 \log \left[\Sigma(y_i^2)/n \right]$$

- *Larger is better.* Used when the target value for the response is infinity. The signal-to-noise ratio is calculated as

$$\text{S/N ratio} = -10 \log [\Sigma(1/y_i^2/n)]$$

- *Nominal is better.* Used to minimize the variability of the response. The signal-to-noise ratio is calculated as

$$\text{S/N ratio} = 10 \log [\Sigma(\bar{y}^2)/s^2]$$

Interpretation

Variance Stabilization

The transformed response should be checked for constant variance using the equality-of-variance test. If the transformed response passes the tests for constant variance, then the ANOVA for the transformed response is acceptable for use.

In the preceding example, Bartlett's test for equality of variance is not rejected for the transformed response, so the regression analysis is redone using the transformed response.

Calculated Parameters

Generally, calculated parameters will be analyzed using the same techniques discussed elsewhere in this book.

A simple criticism of signal-to-noise ratios is that they are confusing. A more detailed criticism of the ratios is that they confuse variation of the response with the average response in a single metric, which tends to obscure information. This is particularly dangerous in cases where the variation changes as a function of the average response. A preferred approach is to consider the average and variance of the response as separate metrics (or responses), each to be maximized, minimized, or targeted as necessary (*Note:* Usually a minimized variance is desirable.)

More detailed analysis of signal-to-noise ratios may be found in Box (1988) and Pignatiello and Ramberg (1985).

U Chart

U charts are one of a set of control charts specifically designed for attributes data. The *U* chart monitors the percent of samples having the condition, relative to either a fixed or varying sample size, when each sample can have more than one instance of the condition. For example, we might choose to look at all the transactions in the month (since that would vary month to month) or a set number of samples, whichever we prefer. From this sample, we track the total number of errors in each month.

When to Use

Measure Stage

- To estimate, using attributes data, the process baseline (Generally, we would greatly prefer the use of variable control charts for this purpose.)

Improve Stage

- Since the number of errors tends to be quite small (for even very large samples), the use of attributes charts is limited in the improve stage

Methodology

Samples are collected from the process at specific points each time. Each sample (at each point in time) may have a unique number of units, each of which may have one or more errors.

Plotted statistic: The average count of occurrences per unit of a criterion of interest in a sample of items.

$$u_j = \frac{(\text{count})_j}{n_j}$$

where n_j is the sample size (number of units) of group j.

Centerline:

$$\bar{u} = \frac{\sum_{j=1}^{m}(\text{count})_j}{m}$$

where n_j is the sample size (number of units) of group j, and m is the number of groups included in the analysis.

UCL, LCL (upper and lower control limits):

$$\text{UCL} = \bar{u} + 3\sqrt{\frac{\bar{u}}{n_j}}$$

$$\text{LCL} = \max\left(0, \bar{u} - 3\sqrt{\frac{\bar{u}}{n_j}}\right)$$

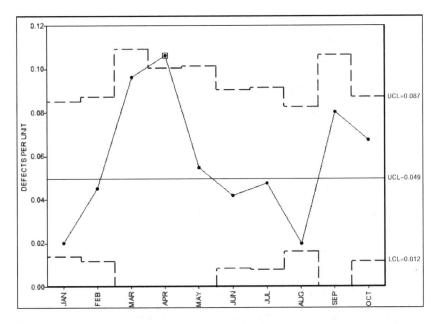

FIGURE F.55 Example of a *U* chart for varying sample size (created using Quality America Green Belt XL software).

where n_j is the sample size (number of units) of group j, and $\bar{u}$ is the average percent.

For example, we observe 500 telemarketing calls each week and record the total number of errors in each call, where each call may have more than one error. Ten months of data are observed, with the following number of errors in each sample: 7 of 350, 14 of 312, 12 of 125, 18 of 170, 9 of 165, 11 of 264, 12 of 254, 8 of 404, 11 of 137, and 21 of 312. The control chart is show in Figure F.55.

U Chart

Minitab

Use *Stat\Control Chart\Attribute Charts\U.* Specify a constant *Subgroup Size* or a column containing variable *Subgroup Sizes* for each group

Options
Use *Options\Display* to specify plotted subgroups.

Use *Scale\Time\Stamp* to set column for *x*-axis labels.

Use *Options\Parameters* for predefined centerline and control limits.

Use *Options\Estimate* to omit subgroups from the calculations.

Use *Options\Stages* to define control regions.

Use *Options\Test* to apply relevant run-test rules.

Excel

Using Green Belt XL Add-On

Use *New Chart\U Chart*. Specify a constant *Subgroup Size* or a column containing variable *Subgroup Sizes* for each group.

Options

Use *Data Range* to specify plotted subgroups.

Use *Options\Title\Label* to set column for *x*-axis labels.

Use *Options\Control Limits* for predefined centerline and control limits, to omit subgroups from calculations, and to define control regions.

Use *Options\Analysis\Auto Drop* checkbox to automatically remove out-of-control groups from the control limit calculations (they are still displayed on the chart).

Use *Options\Run Test* to apply relevant run-test rules.

Interpretation

The upper and lower control limits indicate the bounds of expected process behavior. The fluctuation of the points between the control limits is due to the variation that is intrinsic (built in) to the process. We say that this variation is due to common causes that influence the process. Any points outside the control limits can be attributed to a special cause, implying a shift in the process. When a process is influenced by only common causes, then it is stable and can be predicted.

If there are any out-of-control points, then special causes of variation must be identified and eliminated. Brainstorm and conduct designed experiments to find the process elements that contribute to sporadic changes in process location. To predict the capability of the process after special causes have been eliminated, you should remove the out-of-control points from the analysis, which will remove the statistical bias of the out-of-control points by dropping them from the calculations of the average and control limits. See "Statistical Process Control (SPC) Charts" and "Run-Test Rules" for more detail.

Velocity

Velocity is a lean metric useful for prioritizing cycle time improvement opportunities.

When to Use

Analyze Stage

- To prioritize cycle time improvement opportunities

Methodology

Velocity is calculated by dividing the number of value-added steps by the process lead time:

$$\text{Velocity} = \text{number of value-added steps/process lead time}$$

Little's law is used to calculate the process lead time by dividing the number of items in the process by the completions per hour (George, 2002).

$$\text{Process lead time} = \text{number items in process/completions per hour}$$

For example, if it takes two hours on average to complete each purchase order, then there are 0.5 completions per hour. This is the denominator of the equation for Little's law. If there are 10 purchase orders waiting in queue (the numerator), then Little's law says that we need 10 divided by ½ equals 20 hours of lead time for the process. In other words, we can't process any new orders until the 20-hour lead time has allowed the existing work-in-process to be completed.

If there are five value-added process steps in this process, then the velocity may be calculated as 5 divided by 20 equals 0.25 steps per hour. A process observation log (see Table T.21) is a useful tool for analyzing the velocity of a process. For each step in the process:

- Classify the step as value-added (VA), non-value-added but necessary (NVA type 1), or non-value-added and unnecessary (NVA type 2).

- Calculate the measured distance from the previous process step location to this process step's location.

TABLE T.21 Process Observation Log					
Step Description	**VA/NVA Type**	**Distance from Last Step**	**Average Task Time**	**Average Queue Time**	**Average No. Items in Queue**

- Estimate the average time to complete the process step. This is best determined using a control chart for task time.
- Estimate the average time that the product or customer waits in queue for this process step. This is best determined using a control chart for queue time.
- Estimate the average number of items in queue, as determined through control charting.

After summing the averages, we can use Little's law to calculate the process lead time and the velocity.

Interpretation

The velocity of a process represents the responsiveness or flexibility of the process to customer demand. A long lead time results in slow velocity. Lead time is reduced and velocity increased when work in progress is reduced.

The rationale is simple: New orders from customers cannot be started until work (or items) in process is completed. Thus the activity on new items is stalled. An example from a service process is a doctor's waiting room. The patients are work-in-process. New patients aren't seen by the doctor until those who arrived earlier have been seen.

There are two general methods for increasing velocity, both of which reduce the process lead time: The first method to reduce lead time is to increase the denominator of the equation for Little's law, the *completions per hour*. Completions per hour can be increased by reducing the amount of time necessary for each item to be completed. The second method to reduce lead time is to reduce the numerator of Little's law, the *work-in-process*.

Work Breakdown Structure

A *work breakdown structure* (WBS) is a tree diagram used to break down problems or projects into their components. It reduces "big and complex" issues down to "tiny and manageable" issues that a single project can address.

By breaking the process down into its components, we can recognize that there are really several subprocesses that would each require separate improvement strategies. Limiting our project to one or only a few closely related categories will lead to a better chance of project success. We will need to understand the potentials for each of these subprocesses in financial terms to justify a given project proposal.

When to Use

Define Stage

- To categorize the problems so that the project can focus on one or more key areas (used in conjunction with Pareto analysis)
- To reduce the scope of the project to ensure completion in a reasonable time frame

Analyze Stage

- To break down a problem into its potential components to be addressed in the improve stage.

Methodology

At each level of the tree, brainstorm on categories for each element: How many different ways can this element occur? For example, a project was developed to reduce the cycle time for a purchase order. A work breakdown structure was used to understand the process dynamics. In this case, the process can be broken down into approved and unapproved vendors and then by classification of the purchased items.

Work Breakdown Structure

Excel

Using Green Belt XL Add-On

Open a new file in the MindGenius application.

Enter the problem/project statement as the map title in the initial dialog. Use the "OK" button to start the new branch.

With this main branch selected, simply type each category description into the *Add Branch* dialog, and then select the "OK" button to place the category into the *Map Editor* (drawing surface).

Select a given category, and then type in a subcategory associated with that item.

An example of a work breakdown structure used to isolate potential project issues was shown in Chapter 4.

Interpretation

The output of the WBS will provide input into other tools, generally data-collection tools such as the Pareto diagram. After breaking down the elements of the purchase order process into the different types of products ordered, we then would want to consider which of these types are in most critical need of improvement.

X-Bar Charts

An *X-bar chart*, or $\bar{X}$ *chart*, is a control chart that is useful for variables data. The X-bar chart monitors the process location over time based on the average of a collection of observations called a *subgroup*.

X-bar charts are used with an accompanying chart for monitoring variation between observations in the subgroup over time—either the range chart or the sigma chart.

When to Use

Measure Stage

- To baseline a process by quantifying the common-cause level of variation inherent to the process
- As part of measurement systems analysis to evaluate repeatability and reproducibility

Analyze Stage

- To differentiate between common and special causes of variation

Improve Stage

- To verify the results of process improvement on the process metric

Control Stage

- To monitor the process to ensure the stability of the revised process and the continued benefit of the improvement

X-bar charts are used when you can rationally collect measurements in groups (subgroups) of more than two observations. Each subgroup represents a "snapshot" of the process at a given point in time. The charts' *x* axes are time-based, so the charts show a history of the process. For this reason, you must have data that are time-ordered, that is, entered in the sequence from which they were generated. If this is not the case, then trends or shifts in the process may not be detected but instead attributed to random (common-cause) variation.

For subgroup sizes greater than 10, use sigma charts in place of the range chart for monitoring process variation because the range statistic is a poor estimator of process σ for large subgroups. In fact, the subgroup σ is always a better estimate of subgroup variation than the subgroup range. The popularity of the range chart is due only to its ease of calculation, dating to its use before the advent of computers. For subgroup sizes equal to 1, an individual-X/moving-range or EWMA chart can be used.

Averages are more sensitive to process shift than individual data observations. The distribution of subgroup averages for a given set of data is shown in the top distribution curve in Figure F.56. For the same data, the distribution of observations making up the averages is shown in the bottom distribution curve. We can see that as we drift from the target, the distribution of the average moves from the target value more quickly, increasing our ability to detect the shift.

In fact, as seen by comparing the equations for each distribution (see below), the distribution of the averages is smaller than the distribution of the observations by a factor of 1 over the square root of n, the subgroup size. Thus, for subgroups of size $n = 5$, the distribution of the averages is 45 percent of the width of the distribution of the observations. This is a good reason to *never* show process specifications on an averages chart; the specifications apply to the observations, yet the distribution of the plotted averages will be much tighter even when there are observations outside the specifications. Thus the averages and the specifications are apples and oranges that cannot be compared directly.

$$\sigma_{\bar{x}} = \frac{\bar{R}}{d_2\sqrt{n}}$$

$$\sigma_x = \frac{\bar{R}}{d_2}$$

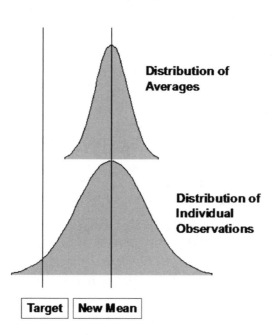

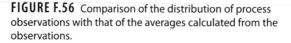

FIGURE F.56 Comparison of the distribution of process observations with that of the averages calculated from the observations.

The sensitivity of X-bar charts to process shifts can be improved with the proper selection of subgroup size. The larger the subgroup, the more sensitive the chart will be to shifts, provided that a rational subgroup can be formed.

Table T.22 shows the average number of subgroups necessary to detect the shift of size k (in standard deviation units) based on the subgroup size n. For example, if we observe the process a large number of times, then on average a subgroup of size $n = 3$ will detect a 1-sigma shift in 9 subgroups. As you can see from the table, small subgroups will readily detect relatively large shifts of 2σ or 3σ but are less capable of readily detecting smaller shifts. For more sensitivity to smaller process shifts, at a given subgroup size, a EWMA chart may be used.

TABLE T.22 Average Number of Subgroups Required to Detect Shift of k Sigma with Subgroup Size of n

n/k	0.5	1	1.5	2	2.5	3
1	155	43	14	6	3	1
2	90	17	5	2	1	1
3	60	9	2	1	1	1
4	43	6	1	1	1	1
5	33	4	1	1	1	1
6	26	3	1	1	1	1
7	21	2	1	1	1	1
8	17	2	1	1	1	1
9	14	1	1	1	1	1
10	12	1	1	1	1	1

Because it attempts to estimate the variation within the subgroup using only two of the observations in the subgroup (the smallest and largest), the range estimate of process variation is not as precise as the sigma statistic. The range chart should not be used for subgroup sizes larger than 10 owing to its poor performance, as shown in Table T.22. Its popularity is largely due to its ease of use in days preceding the advent of computers. As seen in Table T.23, the sigma chart is a more efficient estimator of the standard deviation whenever the subgroup size is greater than 2 (Montgomery, 1991).

TABLE T.23 Efficiency of Range of Statistic Relative to Sigma Statistic	
Subgroup Size (n)	Relative Efficiency
2	1.000
3	0.992
4	0.975
5	0.955
6	0.930
10	0.850

Methodology

After selecting a rational subgroup size and sampling frequency, as discussed under "Statistical Process Control (SPC) Charts," we construct the X-bar and range charts (or X-bar and sigma charts) using the calculations shown below.

X-Bar Chart Calculations

Plotted statistic: Subgroup average

Centerline: Grand average

UCL, LCL (upper and lower control limits):

$$\text{UCL}_{\bar{x}} = \bar{\bar{x}} + 3\left(\frac{\sigma_x}{\sqrt{n}}\right)$$

$$\text{LCL}_{\bar{x}} = \bar{\bar{x}} - 3\left(\frac{\sigma_x}{\sqrt{n}}\right)$$

where $\bar{\bar{x}}$ is the grand average and σ_x is process sigma, which is calculated using the subgroup range or subgroup sigma statistic. *Note:* Some authors prefer to write this as

$$\text{UCL}_{\bar{x}} = \bar{\bar{x}} + A_2\bar{R}$$

$$\text{LCL}_{\bar{x}} = \bar{\bar{x}} - A_2\bar{R}$$

where $\bar{R}$ is the average range or

$$\text{UCL}_{\bar{x}} = \bar{\bar{x}} + A_3\bar{S}$$

$$\text{LCL}_{\bar{x}} = \bar{\bar{x}} - A_3\bar{S}$$

where $\bar{S}$ is the average sigma.

Range Chart Calculations

Plotted statistic:

$$\text{Range}_j = \max(x_1, x_2, \ldots, x_n) - \min(x_1, x_2, \ldots, x_n)$$

where $x_1, x_2, \ldots$ are the n observations in subgroup j

Centerline: Average range.

UCL, LCL (upper and lower control limits):

$$\text{UCL}_R = \bar{R} + 3d_3\sigma_x$$

$$\text{LCL}_R = \max(0, \bar{R} - 3d_3\sigma_x)$$

where $\bar{R}$ is the average range, d_3 is a function of n (tabulated in Appendix 6), and σ_x is process sigma, which is calculated using the average range as $\bar{R}/d_2$. *Note:* Some authors prefer to write this as

$$\text{UCL}_R = \bar{R}\,D_4$$

$$\text{LCL}_R = \bar{R}\,D_3$$

where D_3 and D_4 are a function of n (tabulated in Appendix 6).

Sigma Chart Calculations

Plotted statistic: The subgroup standard deviation:

$$S_j = \sqrt{\frac{\sum_{i=1}^{n}(x_i - \bar{x}_j)^2}{n-1}}$$

where x_i are the observations in subgroup j, $\bar{x}_j$ is the subgroup average for subgroup j, and n is the subgroup size.

Centerline: Average sigma.

UCL, LCL (upper and lower control limits):

$$\text{UCL}_s = \bar{S} + 3\left(\frac{\bar{S}}{c_4}\right)\sqrt{1 - c_4^2}$$

$$\text{LCL}_s = \min\left[0, \bar{S} + 3(\bar{S}/c_4)\sqrt{1 - c_4^2}\right]$$

where $\overline{S}$ is the average sigma, and c_4 is a function of n (tabulated in Appendix 6). *Note:* Some authors prefer to write this as

$$UCL_S = \overline{S} \, B_4$$

$$LCL_S = \overline{S} \, B_3$$

where B_3 and B_4 are a function of n (tabulated in Appendix 6).

X-Bar Chart

Minitab

Use *Stat\Control Chart\Variable Charts for Subgroups\XBar-R*.

Options
Use *Options\Display* to specify plotted subgroups.

Use *Scale\Time\Stamp* to set column for *x*-axis labels.

Use *Options\Parameters* for predefined centerline and control limits.

Use *Options\Estimate* to omit subgroups from calculations.

Use *Options\Stages* to define control regions.

Use *Options\Test* to apply relevant run-test rules.

Excel

Using Green Belt XL Add-On
Use *New Chart\X-Bar* or *Range Chart* or *X-Bar and Sigma Chart*.

Options
Use *Data Range* to specify plotted subgroups.

Use *Options\Title\Label* to set column for *x*-axis labels.

Use *Options\Control Limits* for predefined centerline and control limits, to omit subgroups from calculations, and to define control regions.

Use *Options\Analysis\Auto Drop* checkbox to automatically remove out-of-control groups from the control limit calculations (they are still displayed on the chart).

Use *Options\Run Test* to apply relevant run-test rules;

Interpretation

Always look at the range (or sigma) chart first. The control limits on the X-bar chart are derived from the average range (or average sigma), so if the range (or sigma) chart is out of control, then the control limits on the X-bar chart are meaningless.

Interpreting the Range (or Sigma) Chart

On the range (or sigma) chart, look for out-of-control points. If there are any, then the special causes must be eliminated. Brainstorm and conduct designed experiments to find the process elements that contribute to sporadic changes in variation. To predict the capability of the process after special causes have been eliminated, you should remove the out-of-control points from the analysis, which will remove the statistical bias of the out-of-control points by dropping them from the calculations of the average range (or sigma), the range (or sigma) control limits, and the X-bar control limits.

Also on the range (or sigma) chart, there should be more than five distinct values plotted, and no one value should appear more than 25 percent of the time. If values are repeated too often, then you have inadequate resolution of your measurements, which will adversely affect your control limit calculations. In this case, you'll have to look at how you measure the variable and try to measure it more precisely.

Once you've removed the effect of the out-of-control points from the range (or sigma) chart, the X-bar chart can be analyzed.

Interpreting the X-Bar Chart

After reviewing the range (or sigma) chart, interpret the points on the X-bar chart relative to the control limits and run-test rules. Never consider the points on the X-bar chart relative to specifications because the observations from the process vary much more than the subgroup averages.

If there are any out-of-control points on the X-bar chart, then the special causes must be eliminated. Brainstorm and conduct designed experiments to find the process elements that contribute to sporadic changes in process location. To predict the capability of the process after special causes have been eliminated, you should remove the out-of-control points from the analysis, which will remove the statistical bias of the out-of-control points by dropping them from the calculations of X-doublebar and the X-bar control limits.

Look for obviously nonrandom behavior. Use the run-test rules, which apply statistical themselves for trends to the plotted points.

If the process shows control relative to the statistical limits and run tests for a sufficient period of time (long enough to see all potential special causes), then we can analyze its capability relative to requirements. Capability is only meaningful when the process is stable, because we cannot predict the outcome of an unstable process.

$$S = \sqrt{(1.3s_1)^2 + (1.3s_1)^2 + (1.3s_1)^2 + etc.}$$

$$S = \sqrt{n(1.3s)^2}$$

$$= \sqrt{10(1.3*0.00333")^2}$$

$$S = 0.037"$$

Final Exam

1. **As the Sigma Level for a process increases, its**

    A. error rate and costs of failure increase.

    B. error rate and costs of failure decrease.

    C. error rate decreases as costs of failures increase.

    D. error rate is unaffected and costs of failure increase.

2. **A process operating at a 3σ level of performance**

    A. has a capability of 1.25.

    B. has a field error rate of approximately 7 percent.

    C. can expect to receive customer complaints no more than 3.4 times in a million opportunities.

    D. All the above are true.

3. **Successful Six Sigma deployment is most often achieved**

    A. as a grass-roots effort within an organization.

    B. as an initiative championed by upper management.

    C. through widespread training of most employees in statistical problem-solving techniques.

    D. through teams operating within each department to solve the issues related to their internal processes.

4. **An organization whose key processes are designed at a Six Sigma level of quality will**

    A. spend considerable resources in fixing problems that customers experience.

    B. spend considerable resources in identifying and correcting errors before the customer experiences the error.

    C. spend considerable resources in providing value-added products and services.

    D. All the above are true.

5. **Effective selection of Six Sigma projects to be deployed**

   A. should rest with departmental managers who have authority over their personnel.
   B. should be based on voting within the affected department because department members know best what the issues are.
   C. is a responsibility of more senior management, who have authority over the cross-functional departments affected by the projects and are responsible for achieving the strategic objectives of the organization.
   D. must reside with the black belts and master black belts, who have the technical expertise to know what is achievable.

6. **Effective Six Sigma projects**

   A. are often cross-functional, involving multiple departments across the value stream.
   B. must not cross departmental barriers because that would greatly reduce the chances for longer-term success.
   C. target efficiencies and costs within a given department.
   D. always require advanced statistical techniques, such as multivariate analysis.

7. **Long-term organizational success in Six Sigma**

   A. is achieved one project at a time.
   B. requires a commitment by management to employ data-driven decision-making techniques.
   C. requires a clear understanding of the organization's objectives so that projects can be directed effectively to achieve those objectives.
   D. All the above are true.

8. **The recommended schedule for training in conjunction with a Six Sigma deployment is**

   A. train the process personnel first so that results can be achieved as soon as possible.
   B. train black belts first so that they can be inserted into various departments to correct problems. Once they have achieved some initial results, train the process operators so that they can assist in later projects.
   C. train departmental supervisors and managers first so that they can decide which resources in their department are expendable and can be used for Six Sigma improvement projects.
   D. train management first so that they can develop resources and projects aligned with organizational objectives.

9. **Effective Six Sigma champions**

   A. sponsor Six Sigma projects within their functional authority and cosponsor projects that go beyond their functional authority.
   B. rely on data-driven decision making to achieve their organizational ovjectives.
   C. use data-driven decision making to resolve conflicts.
   D. All the above are true.

10. **A typical 40-hour training course for a Six Sigma green belt**

   A. is designed to develop the green belt as an autonomous Six Sigma project leader.
   B. provides ample understanding of the various problem-solving tools that could be necessary in any Six Sigma project.
   C. exposes the green belt to the DMAIC problem-solving approach and a variety of its tools so that the green belt can retain his or her operational role and actively participate in Six Sigma projects.
   D. All the above are true.

11. **When Six Sigma green belts retain their operational role in an organization,**

   A. their ability to participate effectively in or lead a Six Sigma project team within their functional area is affected by their availability.
   B. the availability of process personnel for working as part of a project team can be improved by building buy-in among the departmental supervisors, such as through awareness training.
   C. the process expertise offered by a trained green belt as part of a project team is enhanced with his or her understanding of the DMAIC approach.
   D. All the above are true.

12. **Project sponsorship by well-positioned members of the management team**

   A. often generates awareness of the importance of the Six Sigma project.
   B. provides the opportunity for the project's objectives to be well aligned with the strategic objectives of the organization.
   C. increases the potential for buy-in among a wider cross section of the organization.
   D. All the above are true.

13. **When selecting projects for deployment, if there are several criteria to be considered and some criteria are more important than other criteria, a useful tool is a**

   A. matrix diagram.
   B. Pareto priority index.
   C. prioritization matrix.
   D. process decision program chart (PDPC).

14. **A project that is scoped properly for a high probability of success will**

   A. involve many stakeholder groups that will each be represented on the project team.
   B. have achievable yet notable objectives within a five- to nine-month project cycle.
   C. address many of the issues affecting the organization.
   D. All the above are true.

15. A particular project has many stakeholder groups. In an attempt to keep the team size at a reasonable level, some of the nonkey stakeholder groups were not included in the team. As a result,

A. the team leader can boost buy-in from these groups by bringing credible group members into the problem solving as ad hoc team members.

B. the team leader should distribute progress reports to both key and nonkey groups to prevent confusion and increase exposure to project data and their interpretation as soon as possible.

C. the sponsor should review each stage of the project reporting to consider its impact on nonkey groups.

D. each of the above considerations, especially used in conjunction with the others, would help to build buy-in among the nonkey groups.

16. To focus a team on a small set of issues when many ideas have been contributed by various sources, the team can use a(n)

A. affinity diagram.

B. flowchart.

C. control chart.

D. brainstorming session.

								0	Cook Training		**Correlation Matrix**	
							3	9	Menu			
						-3	3	0	Plate Prep			
					3	-3	3	0	Pre-Prep			
				-3	-3	-3	9	0	# Cook Staff			
			0	0	0	-1	0	9	# Wait Staff			

Customer Requirements	Import.	**Operational Requirements**							**Competitor Eval.**		
		# Wait Staff	# Cook Staff	Pre-prep	Plate Prep	Menu	Cook Training	Wait Staff Training	House of Italy	Leonardo's	Mama Mia
Service Quality											
Wait Time	3	9	3	3	0	3	3	3	2	5	3
Friendliness of Staff	4	3	0	0	0	0	0	3	1	4	4
Order Accuracy	4	3	1	0	0	3	3	9	5	4	4
Culinary Satisfaction											
Taste	4	0	3	3	3	1	9	3	5	3	2
Temperature	3	3	3	1	9	0	9	3	5	4	3
Pricing											
Some Entrées <$13	3	3	3	3	0	9	0	0	1	4	3
Kids Menu	2	1	1	0	0	9	0	0	1	4	3
Target Value		1:2.5	1:5	30	3	$12	40	60			
Competitor Value		1:2	1:4	30	3	$11.60	40	60			
Importance		71	45	33	39	70	84	78			
Rank		3	5	7	6	4	1	2			

FIGURE F.57 The example QFD matrix.

17. The QFD matrix shown in Figure F.57 indicates that

A. cook training is strongly related to wait time.

B. cook training is strongly related to order accuracy.

C. cook training is strongly related to taste.

D. None of the above are true.

18. **The QFD matrix shown in Figure F.57 indicates that**

    A. the customer places a strong value on the kids' menu.
    B. internal management thinks that friendliness of staff is important.
    C. plate prep is a key process requirement.
    D. wait staff training is a key issue for meeting important customer requirements.

19. **The QFD matrix shown in Figure F.57 indicates that**

    A. preprep is critical to meeting the temperature demands of customers.
    B. the most important operational requirement for culinary satisfaction is the menu offerings.
    C. the most important operational requirement for culinary satisfaction is the cook training.
    D. None of the above are true.

20. **The QFD matrix shown in Figure F.57 indicates that**

    A. the House of Italy provides a good benchmark for culinary satisfaction.
    B. the House of Italy is preferred to Mama Mia's for pricing.
    C. the House of Italy is preferred to Mama Mia's for staff friendliness.
    D. All the above are true.

21. **Comparing the number of cook staff with cook staff training in the QFD matrix shown in Figure F.57 ,**

    A. number of cook staff is more important in meeting customer demands.
    B. cook staff training is more important in meeting customer demands.
    C. number of cook staff is not correlated with any key customers demands.
    D. None of the above are true.

22. **In a SIPOC analysis, inputs include**

    A. data.
    B. output from other processes.
    C. products from suppliers.
    D. all the above.

23. **In a SIPOC analysis, outputs include**

    A. data.
    B. results, value-added products or services, payments, documentation, and input to other processes.
    C. results and value-added products or services.
    D. results, value-added products or services, and resources.

The following data that describe the operations (with cycle times) needed to release a customer order to production are used for questions 24 through 29, which follow the data.

(1) Define bill of materials: 2 days.

(2a) Order and receive materials: 10 days (can be done concurrently with 2b).

(2b1) Schedule job in production: 3 days (can be done concurrently with 2a but must be before 2b2 and 2b3).

(2b2) Define quality plan for product: 1 day (can be done concurrently with 2a but must be after 2b1 and before 2b3).

(2b3) Enter schedule and quality requirements into scheduling software: 1 day (can be done concurrently with 2a but must be after 2b1 and 2b2).

(3) Release to production.

24. **A project to reduce the time it takes to schedule jobs in production (step 2b1) is proposed, with the expectation that it would reduce the time from 3 days to 1 day. In defining the benefits to the company,**

    A. the capacity of the process will be improved, with a potential to handle increased sales.

    B. the cost savings owing to cycle time improvement are difficult to determine, but the project will improve the total delivery time, so it is beneficial.

    C. All the above are true.

    D. None of the above are true.

25. **It is proposed to break step 1 into two steps: verify bill of materials (step 1a) and enter bill of materials into production software (step 2b0). Step 1a replaces step 1 as the initial step of the process, requiring 1 day. Step 2b0, requiring 1 day, must take place before step 2b1 but can be done concurrent with step 2a. The net effect of this change on the total cycle time is**

    A. no change.

    B. reduction of 1 day.

    C. reduction of 2 days.

    D. increase of 1 day.

26. **The total cycle time for the process shown in the example is**

    A. 17 days.

    B. 12 days.

    C. 7 days.

    D. It cannot be determined from the information provided.

27. **To reduce the total cycle time for the process,**

    A. reduce the cycle time for step 1.

    B. reduce the cycle time for step 2a.

    C. reduce the cycle time for step 1 or step 2a.

    D. reduce the cycle time for any of the process steps.

28. **The earliest start time for step 2b2 is**
   A. 5 days.
   B. 6 days.
   C. 12 days.
   D. 15 days.

29. **The latest start time for step 2b2 is**
   A. 5 days.
   B. 6 days.
   C. 10 days.
   D. 11 days.

30. **If we don't define the critical path for a process,**
   A. we can't reduce defect levels effectively.
   B. we may reduce cycle times of noncritical path activities, which won't have as much of an impact on total cycle time.
   C. we may reduce cycle times of noncritical path activities, which will have no impact on total cycle time.
   D. All the above are true.

31. **The advantage of a probabilistic approach to PERT analysis is that**
   A. it properly considers that processes are not deterministic.
   B. it assumes that there is variation in activity times.
   C. it could provide a more realistic estimate of project completion times.
   D. All the above are true.

32. **If the optimistic, pessimistic, and most likely times for step 1 of a process are 2, 9, and 5 days and for step 2 are 4, 13, and 8 days, then the best estimate for the total cycle time for the two steps is**
   A. 13 days.
   B. 13.34 days.
   C. 8 days.
   D. 22 days.

33. **If the optimistic, pessimistic, and most likely times for step 1 of a process are 2, 9, and 5, and for step 2 are 4, 13, and 8 days, then the best estimate for the standard deviation of the total cycle time for the two steps is**
   A. 3.6 days.
   B. 2.67 days.
   C. 1.9 days.
   D. 1.5 days.

34. **Process flowcharts can be used to**

    A. uncover differences in stakeholders' perceptions of the process.
    B. communicate process changes.
    C. discover process complexities that contribute to variation or longer cycle times.
    D. All the above are true.

35. **The prime use of a control chart is to**

    A. detect assignable causes of variation in a process.
    B. detect nonconforming product.
    C. measure the performance of all quality characteristics of a process.
    D. detect the presence of random variation in a process.

36. **Which of the following is the correct control chart for the waiting time for customers in a bank (each individual customer's waiting time will be plotted)?**

    A. U chart
    B. Individual-X/moving range
    C. $\bar{X}$ and s
    D. Np chart

37. **When are control charts for individuals' data necessary?**

    A. The rational subgroup size is 1.
    B. There is only one characteristic to be monitored.
    C. It is always the best choice for control charting.
    D. All the above are true.

38. **A disadvantage of control charts for individuals' data is**

    A. that there are fewer data to collect.
    B. that they are less sensitive to process shifts than larger subgroups.
    C. that they work only for autocorrelated processes.
    D. All the above are true.

39. **An advantage of using control charts for individuals' data is**

    A. that there are fewer data to collect.
    B. that the control limits can be compared directly with the specifications.
    C. that they cost less than larger subgroup sizes.
    D. All the above are true.

40. **When an observation is beyond the 3σ limits on an individual-X chart,**

    A. you should wait to see if more observations go beyond the limits because there is a chance that subgroups will be out of control when the process has not shifted.
    B. you should respond immediately because the chance of an out-of-control point is very small unless the process has shifted.
    C. you should see if the point also fails run-test rules before responding.
    D. you should respond only if the characteristic is critical to the customer.

41. **When the cost of collecting samples is high,**

    A. you shouldn't use control charts because sampling inspection is cheaper.
    B. subgroups of size five are always best, but they increase the time between samples.
    C. a control chart using a subgroup size of one is preferred.
    D. you should ignore the cost because the control chart is always value-added.

42. **When process data occur infrequently, subgroups containing more than one observation**

    A. might include special causes of variation.
    B. generally are not rational subgroups.
    C. are poor indicators of short-term variation.
    D. All the above are true.

43. **Defect detection as a means for process control**

    A. is preferred so long as the detection occurs prior to customer receipt of the product or service.
    B. provides an effective method of improving quality.
    C. is usually not as economical in the long run as a preventive approach.
    D. All the above are true.

44. **When calculating the benefits of training, we should seek to quantify financial benefits of which of the following?**

    A. Improved customer satisfaction
    B. Lower employee turnover
    C. Improved efficiency
    D. All the above

45. **In a process FMEA, process and/or design changes can**

    A. reduce the probability of occurrence.
    B. reduce the severity ranking.
    C. increase the probability of detection.
    D. All the above are true.

46. **With regard to the detection of process errors,**

    A. 100 percent inspection is a preferred approach.
    B. SPC will detect all errors that can occur.
    C. a picture or graphic of the known defects is helpful to guide process operators.
    D. it is not necessary to develop detection plans once you achieve high sigma levels.

47. **We might choose to simulate a process**

    A. when the cost of experimentation is high.
    B. to test a wide variety of conditions.
    C. to generate data useful for training.
    D. All the above are true.

48. **Simulation results**

    A. are usually not useful in preventing errors but often are useful to predict errors.
    B. can be more exact than process data when real distributions are modeled.
    C. should be verified using process data.
    D. All the above are true.

49. **A proper value-stream analysis includes**

    A. all the steps necessary to meet customers' expectations, including transforming raw material to finished good, order placement, service, and delivery.
    B. every process within a given organization.
    C. all process steps within a given department.
    D. all process activities involving customer interaction.

50. **In analyzing the value stream, it is observed that a bottleneck occurs in operation 4, which removes excess material from a part prior to the finishing operation. A response to this should include**

    A. operation 4 needs more personnel.
    B. the operation that produces the excess material prior to operation 4 should be examined.
    C. personnel from downstream processes should be moved as needed to operation 4 to eliminate the bottleneck.
    D. choices a and c in the short term and ultimately choice b to correct the issue.

The remaining questions are intended for those seeking a higher level of technical expertise, such as black belt candidates.

51. **An invoicing process generates 10 to 15 orders per month. In establishing statistical control of the time required for invoicing,**

    A. use a subgroup size of 1 (each plotted group on the individuals chart is a single invoice).
    B. use a subgroup size of 5 based on all orders [each plotted point on the X-bar chart is the average of five successive orders; there will be (on average) two to three subgroups per month].
    C. use a subgroup size of 5 based on a sample of orders each month (each plotted point on the X-bar chart is the average of five random orders each month).
    D. use a subgroup size equal to the maximum order quantity of 15.

52. **To demonstrate compliance with a requirement that the C_{pk} index be at least 1.33 based on a ±3× spread, the quality engineer computed C_{pk} from 50 units selected at random from the production lot before it was delivered to the customer. Which of the following statements describes this approach to capability analysis?**

    A. It is invalid because rational subgrouping was not used.
    B. It is an acceptable method of computing C_{pk}.
    C. It is invalid because the process may be out of control, which would not be detected with this approach.
    D. All the above are true except b.

53. A process shows statistical control using an individual-X chart. Assuming that the implementation cost of a different chart is negligible but the cost of sampling is significant, the most economical method for increasing the sensitivity of the chart to small process shifts is to

    A. increase the subgroup size.
    B. use an EWMA or CuSum chart.
    C. use the $\bar{X}$ range chart.
    D. All the above are true.

54. When a process is extremely nonnormal,

    A. an individual-X chart with control limits defined at plus and minus 3σ from the process mean may predict control limits that don't match the process.
    B. an EWMA or moving-average chart may be useful because the plotted points assume normality.
    C. you should understand why the process is so distributed.
    D. All the above are true.

55. Gauge R&R studies are best done using

    A. calibration standards.
    B. actual samples from the process.
    C. vendor samples.
    D. only the best operators.

56. Gauge R&R studies may be used to

    A. understand and reduce common causes of variation in a process.
    B. ensure that process personnel can take process measurements with minimal error.
    C. compare the performance of new test equipment.
    D. All the above are true.

57. When using a $\bar{X}$ range chart for evaluating gauge repeatability,

    A. the range chart indicates the variation between operators.
    B. the $\bar{X}$ chart should be out of control.
    C. the $\bar{X}$ chart is scaled using the process variation.
    D. All the above are true.

58. A criterion for acceptance of gauge R&R is that

    A. the calculated R&R should be less than 10 percent of process variation.
    B. the calculated R&R should be less than 10 percent of process tolerances.
    C. the calculated discrimination should be more than 8 or 10.
    D. All the above are true.

59. Histograms

    A. give us a graphic view of process location and variation.
    B. provide of quick means of checking process control.
    C. detect subtle trends in the process.
    D. All the above are true.

60. **When using process capability estimates,**
    A. the process must be in control, or the estimate is misleading.
    B. always estimate the process using sample sigma.
    C. we should sort the data prior to analysis.
    D. All the above are true.

61. **A 90% confidence interval for the mean is from 13.8067 to 18.1933. This means that**
    A. there is a 90 percent probability that the true mean lies between 13.8067 and 18.1933.
    B. 90 percent of all values in the population lie between 13.8067 and 18.1933.
    C. 90 percent of all the sample values in the population lie between 13.8067 and 18.1933.
    D. All the above are true.

62. **Assuming normality, the two-sided 95% confidence interval on the mean for a sample of 20 units with an average of 121 and a standard deviation of 15 is**
    A. (112.8, 129.2).
    B. (114.0, 128.0).
    C. (115.2, 126.8).
    D. (114.4, 127.6).

63. **Assuming normality, the one-sided upper 95% confidence interval on the mean for a sample of 20 units with an average of 121 and a standard deviation of 15 is**
    A. 129.2.
    B. 128.0.
    C. 126.8.
    D. 127.6.

64. **For a sample of 20 units with an average of 121 and a standard deviation of 15, a two-sided hypothesis that the mean equals 115 (assuming normality) yields a result of**
    A. reject the null hypothesis that the mean equals 115 because the p value is less than 0.05.
    B. reject the null hypothesis that the mean equals 115 because the p value is greater than 0.05.
    C. assert that the mean equals 115 because the p value is greater than 0.05.
    D. The mean may or may not equal 115; we cannot reject the hypothesis that the mean equals 115 because the p value is greater than 0.05.

65. **For a sample of 20 units with an average of 121 and a standard deviation of 15, for an alternative one-sided hypothesis that the mean is greater than 115 (assuming normality), we should**
    A. reject the null hypothesis that the mean is less than or equal to 115 and assert it is greater than 115 because the p value is less than 0.05.
    B. reject the null hypothesis that the mean is less than or equal to 115 and assert that it is greater than 115 because the p value is greater than 0.05.
    C. reject the null hypothesis that the mean is greater than or equal to 115 and assert that it is less than 115 because the p value is greater than 0.05.
    D. The mean may or may not be greater than 115; we cannot reject the hypothesis that the mean is less than or equal to 115 because the p value is greater than 0.05.

66. For a sample of 20 units with an average of 121 and a standard deviation of 15, a two-sided hypothesis that the standard deviation equals 21 (assuming normality) yields a result of

   A. reject the null hypothesis that the standard deviation equals 21 because the p value is less than 0.05.
   B. reject the null hypothesis that standard deviation equals 21 because the p value is greater than 0.05.
   C. assert that the standard deviation equals 21 because the p value is greater than 0.05.
   D. The standard deviation may or may not equal 21; we cannot reject the hypothesis that the standard deviation equals 21 because the p value is greater than 0.05.

67. For a sample of 20 units with an average of 121 and a standard deviation of 15, for an alternative one-sided hypothesis that the standard deviation is less than 21 (assuming normality), we should

   A. reject the null hypothesis that the standard deviation is greater than or equal to 21 because the p value is less than 0.05.
   B. reject the null hypothesis that standard deviation is greater than or equal to 21 because the p value is greater than 0.05.
   C. assert that the standard deviation is greater than or equal to 21 because the p value is greater than 0.05.
   D. The standard deviation may or may not be greater than or equal to 21; we cannot reject the hypothesis that the standard deviation is greater than or equal to 21 because the p value is greater than 0.05.

68. In a two-sided hypothesis test to compare the equality of two sample variances taken from independent samples, if one sample has a standard deviation of 15 from a sample size of 20, and the other sample has a standard deviation of 21 estimated from a sample of 20, then the test statistic (assuming normality) is

   A. 0.92.
   B. 1.96.
   C. 0.98.
   D. 0.71.

69. In a two-sided hypothesis test to compare the equality of two sample variances taken from independent samples, if one sample has a standard deviation of 15 from a sample size of 20, and the other sample has a standard deviation of 21 estimated from a sample size of 20, then which of the following conclusions (assuming normality) should be made?

   A. Reject the null hypothesis that the variances are equal because the p value is less than 0.05.
   B. Reject the null hypothesis that the variances are equal because the p value is greater than 0.05.
   C. Assert that the variances are not equal because the p value is greater than 0.05.
   D. The variances may or may not be equal; we cannot reject the hypothesis that the variances are equal because the p value is greater than 0.05.

70. **Some useful purposes for model transformations include**

   A. to calculate parameters that are not easily measured directly.
   B. to understand the effect of parameter settings on process variation.
   C. to stabilize the variance to improve parameter estimates.
   D. All the above are true.

71. **When transforming data to stabilize the variance,**

   A. we can plot the log of the standard deviation at each experimental condition against the log of the mean of the experimental condition to determine a suitable transform function.
   B. we should verify that the transformed data have a stabilized variance.
   C. we will use the transformed response in place of the original response when estimating significance of factors or the model.
   D. All the above are true.

72. **Positive correlation implies that**

   A. the dependent variable improves as the independent variable increases.
   B. the dependent variable decreases as the independent variable increases.
   C. the dependent variable increases as the independent variable increases.
   D. the independent variable decreases as the dependent variable increases.

73. **Strong correlation implies that**

   A. the dependent variable improves as the independent variable increases.
   B. there is little error between the predicted response and the actual response as the dependent variable increases.
   C. the dependent variable increases rapidly as the independent variable increases.
   D. All the above are true.

74. **In linear correlation analysis, if the slope of the line is low, then**

   A. the dependent variable is not well predicted by the model.
   B. there is weak correlation between the variables.
   C. as the independent variable changes, there is a small change in the dependent variable.
   D. All the above are true.

75. **If the cycle time of a process is predicted by cycle time = 5.25 × (number of items) + 4.3, with a correlation coefficient R of 0.8, then it is fair to say that**

   A. we can predict cycle time with no error.
   B. only the number of items influences the predicted cycle time.
   C. cycle time is definitely influenced by the number of items.
   D. None of the above are true.

76. **If the correlation coefficient R is 0.9 for a simple linear regression, then**

   A. 90 percent of the variation in y is explained by the regression model.
   B. 81 percent of the variation in y is explained by the regression model.
   C. 90 percent of the variation in y is explained by the variation in x.
   D. approximately 95 percent of the error is explained by the variation in x.

77. **Confidence intervals about the regression line are flared at the ends because**
   A. we can't predict the y values at the extremes with as much certainty.
   B. there are fewer data at the endpoints.
   C. the error in predicting the slope causes greater uncertainty at the extremes.
   D. All the above are true.

78. **If the uncoded expression cycle time (in minutes) = 3 + 1.4 × (number of orders) – 2.1 × (number of clerks) – 0.034 × (process distance),**
   A. the number of clerks is most important.
   B. the process distance is least important.
   C. the cycle time is about 5 minutes when the number of orders equals 5, the number of clerks equals 2, and the process distance equals 14.
   D. All the above are true.

79. **A model of the form $Y = \beta_0 + \beta_1 X_1 + \beta_{11} X_1{}^2 + \beta_2 X_2 + \beta_{12} X_{12}$**
   A. will result in a surface that is nonlinear.
   B. requires experimental trials where X_1 is set to at least three distinct levels.
   C. includes an interaction term.
   D. All the above are true.

80. **To estimate the regression model $Y = \beta_0 + \beta_1 X_1 + \beta_2 X_2 + \beta_{12} X_{12}$,**
   A. using four experimental trials allows for no estimation of error.
   B. it is necessary to use experimental trials where X_1 is set to at least three distinct levels.
   C. we can always use the F statistic to estimate significance of the parameters.
   D. All the above are true.

81. **If an ANOVA does not provide results of the F test, then**
   A. we probably did not run enough trials to estimate error.
   B. the software must be flawed.
   C. we can remove a factor with an effect close to zero to free up trials.
   D. choices a and c are true.

82. **A 3^2 experiment means that we are considering**
   A. two levels of three factors.
   B. two dependent variables and three independent variables.
   C. two go/no-go variables and three continuous variables.
   D. three levels of two factors.

83. **Which of the following purposes are served by replicating an experiment?**
   i. Provide a means for estimating the experimental error.
   ii. Increase the number of treatments included in the experiment.
   iii. Improve the precision of estimates of treatment effects.

   A. Purposes i and ii only
   B. Purposes i and iii only
   C. Purposes ii and iii only
   D. Purposes i, ii, and iii

84. An assembly process is receiving the incorrect pieces for assembly. To ensure that only the correct pieces are sent, the parts tub is redesigned so that only the correct pieces (at their correct number) can fit into the tuB. This is an application of

   A. *kanban.*
   B. *poka yoke.*
   C. visual factory.
   D. 5S.

85. In evaluating an RPN,

   A. a high number indicates high risk.
   B. a high number indicates low risk.
   C. a remote detection ability minimizes the RPN.
   D. a high occurrence minimizes the RPN.

86. Which of the following experimental designs typically has the largest number of replications?

   A. Taguchi
   B. Plackett-Burman
   C. Response surface
   D. EVOP

87. First-order models are often used

   A. to determine optimal conditions for a process.
   B. to narrow down a list of suspected factors influencing a process.
   C. to emphatically prove which factors need to be controlled.
   D. All the above are true.

88. If the fitted model is a good approximation to the data, then

   A. the residuals will have a mean close to zero.
   B. the residuals will have constant variance.
   C. the residuals will be normally distributed.
   D. All the above are true.

89. A good reason to begin with screening designs and a first-order model includes

   A. fewer data are necessary, so time and money are saved.
   B. over limited regions of interest, a first-order model is often a good approximation.
   C. we can often eliminate factors from the experiment.
   D. All the above are true.

90. In a two-level experiment, when factor *A* is run at its high level, factor *B* at its low level, and factor *C* at its high level,

   A. interaction *AB* will be at its low level.
   B. interaction *AC* will be at its low level.
   C. interaction *ABC* will be at its middle level.
   D. all the above are true.

91. **If we alias a factor *F* with the *ABCD* interaction, then**

 A. interaction *BF* is confounded with *ACD*.
 B. we may not be able to distinguish between a measured response owing to *CF* and *ABD*.
 C. we may not be able to distinguish between a measured response owing to *F* and *ABCD*.
 D. all the above are true.

92. **When we fold an entire design,**

 A. we double the total number of experimental runs.
 B. all main factors will be free of confounding with other main factors and two-factor interactions.
 C. we may find that we have extra runs useful for estimating error.
 D. all the above are true.

93. **In a normal probability plot of the effects of a designed experiment,**

 A. points close to the line should be evaluated further for relevance.
 B. points below (but close to) the line are almost significant; those above (and close to) the line are most significant.
 C. points far from the line indicate significance.
 D. both a and b are true.

94. **In a statistical hypothesis test, the reported *p* value provides**

 A. the probability that we don't reject a null hypothesis that is false.
 B. the probability we don't reject a null hypothesis that is true.
 C. the probability of observing samples this extreme if the null hypothesis were true.
 D. the probability that the null hypothesis is true.

95. **In a statistical hypothesis test of the mean, the ability to reject a false hypothesis properly is**

 A. improved when the sample size increases.
 B. improved when the standard deviation of the population increases.
 C. improved when the α value increases.
 D. All the above are true.

96. **Screening designs are often used**

 A. to prove conclusively the factors critical to process control.
 B. to reduce the list of possible factors influencing a process.
 C. to optimize a process.
 D. All the above are true.

97. **We often fold a design**

 A. to produce independent estimation of confounded terms.
 B. when we can't run enough conditions in a given day.
 C. to reduce the number of runs.
 D. All the above are true.

98. Lack-of-fit error may be due to
    A. higher-order effects that are not included in the model.
    B. main factors that are not included in the model.
    C. interactions that are not included in the model.
    D. all the above.

99. If we conduct a screening experiment and conclude that lack-of-fit error is significant,
    A. we need to throw out our data and start over.
    B. we can add center points (if we don't have them) and estimate surface curvature.
    C. we may want to extend the design to add more main factors or interactions.
    D. Both b and c are true.

100. Of the following three types of controls, which is the most desirable, assuming that costs are approximately equal?
    A. Those which prevent the cause or failure mode from occurring or reduce their occurrence
    B. Those which detect the cause and lead to corrective action
    C. Those which detect the failure mode
    D. None of the above strategies are design controls.

Answers to Quizzes and Final Exam

Chapter 1: Deployment Strategy

1. **D.** Cost of quality (see Figure 1.3) and DPMO (see Figure 1.2) decrease as sigma level increases.
2. **D.** Successful Six Sigma deployments are found in many industries, irrespective of company size.
3. **B.** See Figure 1.3.
4. **C.**
5. **D.** Although a DPMO of 20,000 equates to (approximately) a 3.5σ level (Appendix 3), the best answer is choice **D** (all the above) because the reported cost of quality would indicate a much better sigma level (see Figure 1.3). When the cost of quality is underreported, then a "hidden factory" is at work masking those activities.
6. **D.**
7. **A.** Although there may be some resulting improvement in quality owing solely to increased awareness (choice c), the main objective of communicating goals, objectives, and strategy to employees is to build employee buy-in.
8. **C.** Responding to issues only after receiving a large number of customer complaints is usually a sign of poor management because customer retention and revenue are often adversely affected long before the severity of the complaints is recognized. Statistical process control charts rather than confidence intervals would be the appropriate tool for analyzing time-based statistics. A proper evaluation of projects based on their potential to affect the organization in achieving its strategic objectives is an effective use of data in decision making.

9. **B.** Mass training of all employees has been found to be extremely inefficient and ineffective. Training should be conducted just-in-time so that trainees have the opportunity to use their training immediately as part of a project team. Effective teams and the need for building operational buy-in require participation of operational personnel.

10. **D.**

Chapter 2: Developing the Training and Deployment Plan

1. **B.** Leadership is most critically important. Just-in-time training is greatly preferred to broad-based training of employees, most of whom need only minimal training in problem-solving tools.

2. **A.** Executive levels need to understand their role in the deployment more so than the details of analysis methods.

3. **C.** Best results will be achieved when the best minds are tasked with addressing problems of significance to the organization.

4. **D.**

5. **C.** Since green belts are not trained on all the problem-solving methods included in black belt training, and given their operational duties, it is management's responsibility to ensure they have ample time away from their operational duties as well as support from black belts.

6. **A.** Projects involving many stakeholders or those which will consume many resources or take more than 6 months are so are poor candidates for initial waves given the experience level of the individuals and the organization in general.

7. **D.**

8. **B.**

9. **C.** A positive change in behavior, reflective of the materials taught, is the best indicator of training effectiveness.

10. **B.**

Chapter 3: Focusing the Development

1. **C.** Customer expectations are, at times, unknown, so they cannot be assumed to be provided in specifications, even where they do exist. For a bilateral specification (i.e., a requirement dictated by both an upper and lower bound), the midpoint is the preferred process location; as the product or service approaches the bounds, there is less desirability. Process control does not ensure that the process is operating within the specifications unless the process is capable (discussed in more detail in Chapter 5).

2. **A.** Low cost is only preferred when expected quality levels can be assumed. While customer service may be appreciated, problem prevention results in decreased cost for the customer's operations. Customers value predictability, which tends to lower their operational costs.

3. **B.** Specifications tend to obscure real customer expectations, needs, and wants.

4. **D.**

5. **C.**

6. **C.**

7. **B.**

8. **D.** PPI = $(0.75 \times 125{,}000)/(6{,}200 \times 100) = 0.15$.
9. **D.** Labor cost is saved only when it can be reassigned or eliminated.
10. **C.** The prioritization matrix will allow the criteria to be weighted.

Chapter 4: Define Stage

1. **B.** Critical factors are proposed and managed during the analyze stage. Solutions are proposed and evaluated in the improve stage.
2. **C.** A work breakdown structure is used to break down big projects into smaller projects.
3. **D.** A properly defined project charter should include each of these elements, which help to boost buy-in from stakeholders.
4. **C.** The affected department is one of the stakeholders that should have been identified and included in the problem solving, if not the team itself. Involving the sponsor should be a last resort. The team needs to satisfy the department's legitimate concerns and help department members to understand why the proposed solution is the best course (if in fact it is, given the department's concerns).
5. **B.** Replacing team members and asking for intervention from a sponsor would be last resorts after considerable time has been spent on more productive means of resolving the problems. The problems most likely could be best handled by the ideas listed in choice **B.**
6. **C.** This best represents the concept of consensus decision making, which is preferable to voting or mandating decisions. Effective brainstorming will allow greater participation among the team members and yield more ideas of a higher quality than a single person would be capable of generating.
7. **B.** A conflict of ideas is to be expected and is indicative of the various stakeholder groups' varied interests and concerns.
8. **D.**
9. **D.** Since the stated project objectives cannot be realized, the champion must authorize deviations from the previously agreed objectives.
10. **C.**

Chapter 5: Measure Stage

1. **A.** Each stakeholder group may have varied understandings of the process tasks and objectives and has involvement in the current process inputs, tasks, and/or outputs that is useful in documenting the as-is process.
2. **D.**
3. **B.** Defect per unit (DPU) = $300/1{,}000 = 0.3 = 30$ percent. Throughput yield = 1 − DPU = 70 percent.
4. **B.** Defect per unit (DPU) = $300/1{,}000 = 0.3 = 30$ percent. Throughput yield = 1 − DPU = 70 percent.
5. **C.** The process yield calculated with this method does not differentiate between first-pass quality and quality levels after rework. It fails to consider the costs of the hidden factory.
6. **C.** $(0.92)^{1/3} = 0.973$.
7. **B.**

8. **D.**

9. **D.** Special causes of variation, by definition, occur when a subgroup exceeds the statistical limits established in a properly designed statistical process control chart.

10. **A.** Process histograms are inappropriate tools for analyzing variation until the process is shown to be in statistical control. Special causes of variation must be identified and their causes considered relative to the expected project benefits. Confidence intervals are appropriate tools for populations rather than processes and are the incorrect tool for detection of special causes of variation.

Chapter 6: Analyze Stage

1. **D.** Inspection is not value-added because it does not change form, fit, or function. Choice B is incorrect because it confuses a value-added task with the business value-added scenario where the inspection is needed owing to poor process quality. Choice **C** is incorrect in implying that sampling inspection will ensure that customer receives only acceptable product.

2. **B.**

3. **D.**

4. **D.**

5. **D.**

6. **A.** Increasing batch size increases the time required to produce a given unit of production because the given unit must wait for the remainder of the batch to be completed. Setup simplification, rather than adding complexity, will reduce setup time.

7. **D.**

8. **C.**

9. **D.**

10. **C.** Failing to recognize interaction may prevent detection of the interacting factors as being significant.

Chapter 7: Improve Stage

1. **C.** Efforts to reduce cycle time always should be evaluated for their impact on quality

2. **D.**

3. **C.** Useful simulations can be run using rather simple software on a laptop.

4. **C.** In at least some cases, the overall objective in using simulations is to prevent future instances of process errors. While the data generated by a simulation may more precisely model a particular distribution, the actual process data provide the benchmark to which the accuracy of the simulated data can be evaluated. In this regard, the process data, by definition, provide the exact model for the process.

5. **C.**

6. **C.** Evolutionary operations (EVOP) allows the process to continue to generate product.

7. **A.**

8. **D.**

9. **B.**
10. **A.** Prevention of errors is the preferred approach unless its costs cannot be justified.

Chapter 8: Control Stage

1. **B.**
2. **D.**
3. **D.**
4. **D.**
5. **B.**
6. **A.**
7. **A.**
8. **C.**
9. **B.** Behavioral changes are most important, but they may not provide the best measure because they depend on so many other things, such as management systems that encourage the new behavior.
10. **A.** Prevention of errors is the preferred approach unless its costs cannot be justified.

Final Exam

1. **B.**
2. **B,** as shown in Appendix 8.
3. **B.** Success requires commitment of resources, which are controlled by management, as well as linkage with organizational strategy, which is defined by management. Widespread training is often a waste of resources.
4. **C.** Processes designed for Six Sigma (or those which have achieved Six Sigma) will allow process resources to be directed to value-added opportunities. Errors requiring correction are virtually nonexistent.
5. **C.** Project selection is a management responsibility.
6. **A.** Projects deployed only within a specific department often yield less desirable results either because of the lack of broad impact or because the department's resources are optimized at the expense of the system.
7. **D.**
8. **D.** Without management training, training of other resources is often wasted.
9. **D.**
10. **C.** Typical green belt training is designed to expose the green belt to the DMAIC methodology so that he or she can actively lend his or her process expertise as part of a project team. It does not include the technical skills necessary to autonomously lead any project without the support of a qualified black belt or master black belt.
11. **D.**
12. **D.**
13. **C.**
14. **B.** Projects that involve many stakeholder groups decrease the likelihood of success. Any given project is unlikely to solve many of the issues confronting an organization.

15. **D.**
16. **A.**
17. **C.**
18. **D.**
19. **C.**
20. **A.** Choices **B** and **C** are incorrect. A negative interaction implies that as one requirement decreases, the other increases.
21. **B.** Cook staff training has a higher importance than number of cook staff. Choice c is incorrect because number of cook staff has a moderate relationship with taste, which has a customer importance of 4.
22. **D.**
23. **B.**
24. **D.** Step 2b1 is not on the critical path, so any improvement will not improve capacity, nor will it improve the total delivery time.
25. **B.** Step 1a will remain on the critical path. The effect of moving step 2b0 to run concurrent with step 2a is to move it off the critical path, so the cycle time for the critical path is reduced by 1 day.
26. **B.**
27. **C.**
28. **A.**
29. **C.**
30. **C.**
31. **D.**
32. **B.** The average expected time for step 1 is $[2 + (4 \times 5) + 9]/6 = 5.17$, and the average expected time for step 2 is $[4 + (4 \times 8) + 13]/6 = 8.17$. The sum of the two steps then is 13.34 days.
33. **C.** The expected standard deviation of the cycle time for step 1 is $(9 - 2)/6 = 1.17$, and the expected standard deviation of the cycle time for step 2 is $(13 - 4)/6 = 1.5$. The sum of the variances of the two steps then is $(1.17 \times 2) + (1.5 \times 2) = 3.6$. The standard deviation of the two steps is the square root of $3.6 = 1.9$ days.
34. **D.**
35. **A.** Walter Shewhart's main reason for inventing the control chart technique was to detect assignable causes of variation in the process.
36. **B.**
37. **A.**
38. **B.**
39. **D.**
40. **B.**
41. **C.**
42. **D.**
43. **C.**
44. **D.**
45. **A.**
46. **C.**
47. **D.**

48. **C.**
49. **A.**
50. **D.**
51. **A.** Subgroups larger than one would include samples taken over too long a period, increasing the chance of including special causes within the subgroup.
52. **D.**
53. **B.** Although increasing the subgroup size will increase the sensitivity of the chart to small process shifts, it comes at the cost of increased sampling and measurement.
54. **D.**
55. **B.**
56. **D.**
57. **B.**
58. **D.**
59. **A.**
60. **A.**
61. **A.**
62. **B.** In Excel, the 95% two-sided upper and lower confidence limits are calculated as

$$\text{Upper: } =121+\text{TINV}(0.05,20\text{-}1)\text{*}15/\text{SQRT}(20)$$

$$\text{Lower: } =121\text{-}\text{TINV}(0.05,20\text{-}1)\text{*}15/\text{SQRT}(20)$$

63. **C.** In Excel, the 95% one-sided upper confidence limit is calculated as

$$\text{Upper: } =121+\text{TINV}(0.05\text{*}2,20\text{-}1)\text{*}15/\text{SQRT}(20)$$

64. **D.** In Excel, the p value for the two-sided hypothesis that the mean equals 115 is 0.09, calculated as P=TDIST(ABS((121–115)/(15/SQRT(20))),20-1,2). When the p value exceeds 0.05, we fail to reject the null hypothesis. Choice **c** is incorrect because we cannot assert the alternative (because this is the weak conclusion of failing to reject); we can only suggest that there are insufficient data to reject the null hypothesis.
65. **A.** In Excel, the p value for the one-sided hypothesis that the mean is less than or equal to 115 (case 2 in Part 3) is 0.045, calculated (for $t > 0$) as P=TDIST(ABS((121-115)/(15/SQRT(20))),20-1,2). When the p value is less than 0.05, we reject the null hypothesis and can assert the alternative hypothesis (i.e., the strong conclusion).
66. **D.** In Excel, the p value for the two-sided hypothesis that the standard deviation equals 21 is 0.08, calculated (for CHIDIST > 0.5) as P=2*(1-CHIDIST((20-1)*(15^2)/(21^2),20-1)). When the p value exceeds 0.05, we fail to reject the null hypothesis. Choice **c** is incorrect because we cannot assert the alternative (because this is the weak conclusion of failing to reject); we can only suggest that there are insufficient data to reject the null hypothesis.
67. **A.** In Excel, the p value for the one-sided hypothesis that the standard deviation is greater than or equal to 21 (case 1 in Part 3) is 0.040, calculated as P=(1-

CHIDIST$((20-1)*(15^2)/(21^2),20-1))$. When the p value is less than 0.05, we reject the null hypothesis and can assert the alternative hypothesis (i.e., the strong conclusion).

68. **B.** The F statistic for testing equality of variance is calculated (for $s_1^2 > s_2^2$) in Excel as $=(21^2)/(15^2)$.

69. **D.** In Excel, the p value for the two-sided hypothesis that the variances are equal is 0.15, calculated as P$=2*$FDIST$((21^2)/(15^2),20-1,20-1)$. When the p value exceeds 0.05, we fail to reject the null hypothesis. Choice **c** is incorrect because we cannot assert the alternative (because this is the weak conclusion of failing to reject); we can only suggest that there are insufficient data to reject the null hypothesis.

70. **D.**

71. **D.**

72. **C.**

73. **B.**

74. **C.**

75. **D.**

76. **B.**

77. **D.**

78. **C.**

79. **D.** Note the X_1^2 term.

80. **A.** Choice **B** is incorrect because there are no higher-order terms. Choice **C** may not be correct if there are no extra runs (degrees of freedom) to calculate error because only four trials are used.

81. **D.** F tests cannot be performed on the regression when there are insufficient degrees of freedom (unique trials or experimental conditions) to estimate error. Often, factors can be removed from the regression to free up trials for error estimation.

82. **D.** Standard notation for designed experiments where there are n factors all at L levels is Ln.

83. **B.** Increasing the number of observations by replicating an experiment provides the benefits described by i and iii. Note that ii is untrue and that only choice **B** doesn't have ii.

84. **B.**

85. **A.**

86. **D.** Taguchi and Plackett-Burman designs are screening designs that involve a large number of factors with a small number of trials. Response surface designs attempt to fit a nonlinear equation to the response surface. This requires more degrees of freedom than a screening experiment. EVOP is used to make gradual improvements over time. A large number of trials is made; then very small changes are made in the factor levels.

87. **B.**

88. **D.**

89. **D.**

90. **A.** Interaction AB will be at its low level, AC at its high level, and ABC at its low level.

91. **D.**
92. **D.**
93. **C.**
94. **C.**
95. **D.**
96. **B.**
97. **A.**
98. **D.**
99. **D.**
100. **A.**

appendix **1**

Area Under the Standard Normal Curve

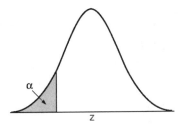

z	0.00	0.01	0.02	0.03	0.04	0.05	0.06	0.07	0.08	0.09
−3.4	0.0003	0.0003	0.0003	0.0003	0.0003	0.0003	0.0003	0.0003	0.0003	0.0002
−3.3	0.0005	0.0005	0.0005	0.0004	0.0004	0.0004	0.0004	0.0004	0.0004	0.0003
−3.2	0.0007	0.0007	0.0006	0.0006	0.0006	0.0006	0.0006	0.0005	0.0005	0.0005
−3.1	0.0010	0.0009	0.0009	0.0009	0.0008	0.0008	0.0008	0.0008	0.0007	0.0007
−3.0	0.0013	0.0013	0.0013	0.0012	0.0012	0.0011	0.0011	0.0011	0.0010	0.0010
−2.9	0.0019	0.0018	0.0018	0.0017	0.0016	0.0016	0.0015	0.0015	0.0014	0.0014
−2.8	0.0026	0.0025	0.0024	0.0023	0.0023	0.0022	0.0021	0.0021	0.0020	0.0019
−2.7	0.0035	0.0034	0.0033	0.0032	0.0031	0.0030	0.0029	0.0028	0.0027	0.0026
−2.6	0.0047	0.0045	0.0044	0.0043	0.0041	0.0040	0.0039	0.0038	0.0037	0.0036
−2.5	0.0062	0.0060	0.0059	0.0057	0.0055	0.0054	0.0052	0.0051	0.0049	0.0048
−2.4	0.0082	0.0080	0.0078	0.0075	0.0073	0.0071	0.0069	0.0068	0.0066	0.0064
−2.3	0.0107	0.0104	0.0102	0.0090	0.0096	0.0094	0.0091	0.0089	0.0087	0.0084

z	0.00	0.01	0.02	0.03	0.04	0.05	0.06	0.07	0.08	0.09
-2.2	0.0139	0.0136	0.0132	0.0129	0.0125	0.0122	0.0119	0.0116	0.0113	0.0110
-2.1	0.0179	0.0174	0.0170	0.0166	0.0162	0.0158	0.0154	0.0150	0.0146	0.0143
-2.0	0.0228	0.0222	0.0217	0.0212	0.0207	0.0202	0.0197	0.0192	0.0188	0.0183
-1.9	0.0287	0.0281	0.0274	0.0268	0.0262	0.0256	0.0250	0.0244	0.0239	0.0233
-1.8	0.0359	0.0351	0.0344	0.0336	0.0329	0.0322	0.0314	0.0307	0.0301	0.0294
-1.7	0.0446	0.0436	0.0427	0.0418	0.0409	0.0401	0.0392	0.0384	0.0375	0.0367
-1.6	0.0548	0.0537	0.0526	0.0516	0.0505	0.0495	0.0485	0.0475	0.0465	0.0455
-1.5	0.0668	0.0655	0.0643	0.0630	0.0618	0.0606	0.0594	0.0582	0.0571	0.0559
-1.4	0.0808	0.0793	0.0778	0.0764	0.0749	0.0735	0.0721	0.0708	0.0694	0.0681
-1.3	0.0968	0.0951	0.0934	0.0918	0.0901	0.0885	0.0869	0.0853	0.0838	0.0823
-1.2	0.1151	0.1131	0.1112	0.1093	0.1075	0.1056	0.1038	0.1020	0.1003	0.0985
-1.1	0.1357	0.1335	0.1314	0.1292	0.1271	0.1251	0.1230	0.1210	0.1190	0.1170
-1.0	0.1587	0.1562	0.1539	0.1515	0.1492	0.1469	0.1446	0.1423	0.1401	0.1379
-0.9	0.1841	0.1814	0.1788	0.1762	0.1736	0.1711	0.1685	0.1660	0.1635	0.1611
-0.8	0.2119	0.2090	0.2061	0.2033	0.2005	0.1977	0.1949	0.1922	0.1894	0.1867
-0.7	0.2420	0.2389	0.2358	0.2327	0.2296	0.2266	0.2236	0.2206	0.2177	0.2148
-0.6	0.2743	0.2709	0.2676	0.2643	0.2611	0.2578	0.2546	0.2514	0.2483	0.2451
-0.5	0.3085	0.3050	0.3015	0.2981	0.2946	0.2912	0.2877	0.2843	0.2810	0.2776
-0.4	0.3446	0.3409	0.3372	0.3336	0.3300	0.3264	0.3228	0.3192	0.3156	0.3121
-0.3	0.3821	0.3783	0.3745	0.3707	0.3669	0.3632	0.3594	0.3557	0.3520	0.3483
-0.2	0.4207	0.4168	0.4129	0.4090	0.4052	0.4013	0.3974	0.3936	0.3897	0.3859
-0.1	0.4602	0.4562	0.4522	0.4483	0.4443	0.4404	0.4364	0.4325	0.4286	0.4247
-0.0	0.5000	0.4960	0.4920	0.4880	0.4840	0.4801	0.4761	0.4721	0.4681	0.4641
-0.0	0.5000	0.5040	0.5080	0.5120	0.5160	0.5199	0.5239	0.5279	0.5319	0.5359
0.1	0.5398	0.5438	0.5478	0.5517	0.5557	0.5596	0.5636	0.5675	0.5714	0.5753
0.2	0.5793	0.5832	0.5871	0.5910	0.5948	0.5987	0.6026	0.6064	0.6103	0.6141
0.3	0.6179	0.6217	0.6255	0.6293	0.6331	0.6368	0.6406	0.6443	0.6480	0.6517
0.4	0.6554	0.6591	0.6628	0.6664	0.6700	0.6736	0.6772	0.6808	0.6844	0.6879
0.5	0.6915	0.6950	0.6985	0.7019	0.7054	0.7088	0.7123	0.7157	0.7190	0.7224
0.6	0.7257	0.7291	0.7324	0.7357	0.7389	0.7422	0.7454	0.7486	0.7517	0.7549
0.7	0.7580	0.7611	0.7642	0.7673	0.7704	0.7734	0.7764	0.7794	0.7823	0.7852
0.8	0.7881	0.7910	0.7939	0.7967	0.7995	0.8023	0.8051	0.8078	0.8106	0.8133
0.9	0.8159	0.8186	0.8212	0.8238	0.8264	0.8289	0.8315	0.8340	0.8365	0.8389
1.0	0.8413	0.8438	0.8461	0.8485	0.8508	0.8531	0.8554	0.8577	0.8599	0.8621
1.1	0.8643	0.8665	0.8686	0.8708	0.8729	0.8749	0.8770	0.8790	0.8810	0.8830
1.2	0.8849	0.8869	0.8888	0.8907	0.8925	0.8944	0.8962	0.8980	0.8997	0.9015
1.3	0.9032	0.9049	0.9066	0.9082	0.9099	0.9115	0.9131	0.9147	0.9162	0.9177

z	0.00	0.01	0.02	0.03	0.04	0.05	0.06	0.07	0.08	0.09
1.4	0.9192	0.9207	0.9222	0.9236	0.9251	0.9265	0.9279	0.9292	0.9306	0.9319
1.5	0.9332	0.9345	0.9357	0.9370	0.9382	0.9394	0.9406	0.9418	0.9429	0.9441
1.6	0.9452	0.9463	0.9474	0.9484	0.9495	0.9505	0.9515	0.9525	0.9535	0.9545
1.7	0.9554	0.9564	0.9573	0.9582	0.9591	0.9599	0.9608	0.9616	0.9625	0.9633
1.8	0.9641	0.9649	0.9656	0.9664	0.9671	0.9678	0.9686	0.9693	0.9699	0.9706
1.9	0.9713	0.9719	0.9726	0.9732	0.9738	0.9744	0.9750	0.9756	0.9761	0.9767
2.0	0.9772	0.9778	0.9783	0.9788	0.9793	0.9798	0.9803	0.9808	0.9812	0.9817
2.1	0.9821	0.9826	0.9830	0.9834	0.9838	0.9842	0.9846	0.9850	0.9854	0.9857
2.2	0.9861	0.9864	0.9868	0.9871	0.9875	0.9878	0.9881	0.9884	0.9887	0.9890
2.3	0.9893	0.9896	0.9898	0.9901	0.9904	0.9906	0.9909	0.9911	0.9913	0.9916
2.4	0.9918	0.9920	0.9922	0.9925	0.9927	0.9929	0.9931	0.9932	0.9934	0.9936
2.5	0.9938	0.9940	0.9941	0.9943	0.9945	0.9946	0.9948	0.9949	0.9951	0.9952
2.6	0.9953	0.9955	0.9956	0.9957	0.9959	0.9960	0.9961	0.9962	0.9963	0.9964
2.7	0.9965	0.9966	0.9967	0.9968	0.9969	0.9970	0.9971	0.9972	0.9973	0.9974
2.8	0.9974	0.9975	0.9976	0.9977	0.9977	0.9978	0.9979	0.9979	0.9980	0.9981
2.9	0.9981	0.9982	0.9982	0.9983	0.9984	0.9984	0.9985	0.9985	0.9986	0.9986
3.0	0.9987	0.9987	0.9987	0.9988	0.9988	0.9989	0.9989	0.9989	0.9990	0.9990
3.1	0.9990	0.9991	0.9991	0.9991	0.9992	0.9992	0.9992	0.9992	0.9993	0.9993
3.2	0.9993	0.9993	0.9994	0.9994	0.9994	0.9994	0.9994	0.9995	0.9995	0.9995
3.3	0.9995	0.9995	0.9995	0.9996	0.9996	0.9996	0.9996	0.9996	0.9996	0.9997
3.4	0.9997	0.9997	0.9997	0.9997	0.9997	0.9997	0.9997	0.9997	0.9997	0.9998

appendix 2

Critical Values
of the t Distribution

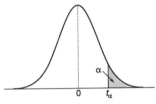

df	0.1	0.05	0.025	0.01	0.005
1	3.078	6.314	12.706	31.821	63.657
2	1.886	2.920	4.303	6.965	9.925
3	1.638	2.353	3.182	4.541	5.841
4	1.533	2.132	2.776	3.747	4.604
5	1.476	2.015	2.571	3.365	4.032
6	1.440	1.943	2.447	3.143	3.707
7	1.415	1.895	2.365	2.998	3.499
8	1.397	1.860	2.306	2.896	3.355
9	1.383	1.833	2.262	2.821	3.250
10	1.372	1.812	2.228	2.764	3.169
11	1.363	1.796	2.201	2.718	3.106

df	0.1	0.05	0.025	0.01	0.005
12	1.356	1.782	2.179	2.681	3.055
13	1.350	1.771	2.160	2.650	3.012
14	1.345	1.761	2.145	2.624	2.977
15	1.341	1.753	2.131	2.602	2.947
16	1.337	1.746	2.120	2.583	2.921
17	1.333	1.740	2.110	2.567	2.898
18	1.330	1.734	2.101	2.552	2.878
19	1.328	1.729	2.093	2.539	2.861
20	1.325	1.725	2.086	2.528	2.845
21	1.323	1.721	2.080	2.518	2.831
22	1.321	1.717	2.074	2.508	2.819
23	1.319	1.714	2.069	2.500	2.807
24	1.318	1.711	2.064	2.492	2.797
25	1.316	1.708	2.060	2.485	2.787
26	1.315	1.706	2.056	2.479	2.779
27	1.314	1.703	2.052	2.473	2.771
28	1.313	1.701	2.048	2.467	2.763
29	1.311	1.699	2.045	2.462	2.756
∞	1.282	1.645	1.960	2.326	2.576

appendix 3

Chi-Square Distribution

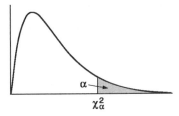

y	0.995	0.99	0.98	0.975	0.95	0.90	0.80	0.75	0.70	0.50
1	0.00004	0.000	0.001	0.001	0.004	0.016	0.064	0.102	0.148	0.455
2	0.0100	0.020	0.040	0.051	0.103	0.211	0.446	0.575	0.713	1.386
3	0.0717	0.115	0.185	0.216	0.352	0.584	1.005	1.213	1.424	2.366
4	0.207	0.297	0.429	0.484	0.711	1.064	1.649	1.923	2.195	3.357
5	0.412	0.554	0.752	0.831	1.145	1.610	2.343	2.675	3.000	4.351
6	0.676	0.872	1.134	1.237	1.635	2.204	3.070	3.455	3.828	5.348
7	0.989	1.239	1.564	1.690	2.167	2.833	3.822	4.255	4.671	6.346
8	1.344	1.646	2.032	2.180	2.733	3.490	4.594	5.071	5.527	7.344
9	1.735	2.088	2.532	2.700	3.325	4.168	5.380	5.899	6.393	8.343
10	2.156	2.558	3.059	3.247	3.940	4.865	6.179	6.737	7.267	9.342
11	2.603	3.053	3.609	3.816	4.575	5.578	6.989	7.584	8.148	10.341
12	3.074	3.571	4.178	4.404	5.226	6.304	7.807	8.438	9.034	11.340

y	0.995	0.99	0.98	0.975	0.95	0.90	0.80	0.75	0.70	0.50
13	3.565	4.107	4.765	5.009	5.892	7.042	8.634	9.299	9.926	12.340
14	4.075	4.660	5.368	5.629	6.571	7.790	9.467	10.165	10.821	13.339
15	4.601	5.229	5.985	6.262	7.261	8.547	10.307	11.037	11.721	14.339
16	5.142	5.812	6.614	6.908	7.962	9.312	11.152	11.912	12.624	15.338
17	5.697	6.408	7.255	7.564	8.672	10.085	12.002	12.792	13.531	16.338
18	6.265	7.015	7.906	8.231	9.390	10.865	12.857	13.675	14.440	17.338
19	6.844	7.633	8.567	8.907	10.117	11.651	13.716	14.562	15.352	18.338
20	7.434	8.260	9.237	9.591	10.851	12.443	14.578	15.452	16.266	19.337
21	8.034	8.897	9.915	10.283	11.591	13.240	15.445	16.344	17.182	20.337
22	8.643	9.542	10.600	10.982	12.338	14.041	16.314	17.240	18.101	20.337
23	9.260	10.196	11.293	11.689	13.091	14.848	17.187	18.137	19.021	22.337
24	9.886	10.856	11.992	12.401	13.848	15.659	18.062	19.037	19.943	23.337
25	10.520	11.524	12.697	13.120	14.611	16.473	18.940	19.939	20.867	24.337
26	11.160	12.198	13.409	13.844	15.379	17.292	19.820	20.843	21.792	25.336
27	11.808	12.879	14.125	14.573	16.151	18.114	20.703	21.749	22.719	26.336
28	12.461	13.565	14.847	15.308	16.928	18.939	21.588	22.657	23.647	27.336
29	13.121	14.256	15.574	16.047	17.708	19.768	22.475	23.567	23.577	28.336
30	13.787	14.953	16.306	16.791	18.493	20.599	23.364	24.478	25.508	29.336

y	0.30	0.25	0.20	0.10	0.05	0.025	0.02	0.01	0.005	0.001
1	1.074	1.323	1.642	2.706	3.841	5.024	5.412	6.635	7.879	10.828
2	2.408	2.773	3.219	4.605	5.991	7.378	7.824	9.210	10.597	13.816
3	3.665	4.108	4.642	6.251	7.815	9.348	9.837	11.345	12.838	16.266
4	4.878	5.385	5.989	7.779	9.488	11.143	11.668	13.277	14.860	18.467
5	6.064	6.626	7.289	9.236	11.070	12.833	13.388	15.086	16.750	20.515
6	7.231	7.841	8.558	10.645	12.592	14.449	15.033	16.812	18.548	22.458
7	8.383	9.037	9.803	12.017	14.067	16.013	16.622	18.475	20.278	24.322
8	9.524	10.219	11.030	13.362	15.507	17.535	18.168	20.090	21.955	26.124
9	10.656	11.389	12.242	14.684	16.919	19.023	19.679	21.666	23.589	27.877
10	11.781	12.549	13.442	15.987	18.307	20.483	21.161	23.209	25.188	29.588
11	12.899	13.701	14.631	17.275	19.675	21.920	22.618	24.725	26.757	31.264
12	14.011	14.845	15.812	18.549	21.026	23.337	24.054	26.217	28.300	32.909
13	15.119	15.984	16.985	19.812	22.362	24.736	25.472	27.688	29.819	34.528
14	16.222	17.117	18.151	21.064	23.685	26.119	26.873	29.141	31.319	36.123
15	17.322	18.245	19.311	22.307	24.996	27.488	28.259	30.578	32.801	37.697
16	18.418	19.369	20.465	23.542	26.296	28.845	29.633	32.000	34.267	39.252
17	19.511	20.489	21.615	24.769	27.587	30.191	30.995	33.409	35.718	40.790

y	0.30	0.25	0.20	0.10	0.05	0.025	0.02	0.01	0.005	0.001
18	20.601	21.605	22.760	25.989	28.869	31.526	32.346	34.805	37.156	42.312
19	21.689	22.718	23.900	27.204	30.144	32.852	33.687	36.191	38.582	43.820
20	22.775	23.828	25.038	28.412	31.410	34.170	35.020	37.566	39.997	45.315
21	23.858	24.935	26.171	29.615	32.671	35.479	36.343	38.932	41.401	46.797
22	24.939	26.039	27.301	30.813	33.924	36.781	37.659	40.289	42.796	48.268
23	26.018	27.141	28.429	32.007	35.172	38.076	38.968	41.638	44.181	49.728
24	27.096	28.241	29.553	33.196	36.415	39.364	40.270	42.980	45.559	51.179
25	28.172	29.339	30.675	34.382	37.652	40.646	41.566	44.314	46.928	52.620
26	29.246	30.435	31.795	35.563	38.885	41.923	42.856	45.642	48.290	54.052
27	30.319	31.528	32.912	36.741	40.113	43.195	44.140	46.963	49.645	55.476
28	31.391	32.620	34.027	37.916	41.337	44.461	45.419	48.278	50.993	56.892
29	32.461	33.711	35.139	39.087	42.557	45.722	46.693	49.588	52.336	58.301
30	33.530	34.800	36.250	40.256	43.773	46.979	47.962	50.892	53.672	59.703

appendix **4**

F *Distribution* (α = 1%)

$$F_{0.99}\,(n_1, n_2)$$
n_1 = degrees of freedom for numerator n_2 = degrees of freedom for denominator

n_2	1	2	3	4	5	6	7	8	9	10
n_1										
1	4052	4999.5	5403	5625	5764	5859	5928	5982	6022	6056
2	98.50	99.00	99.17	99.25	99.30	99.33	99.36	99.37	99.39	99.40
3	34.12	30.82	29.46	28.71	28.24	27.91	27.67	27.49	27.35	27.23
4	21.20	18.00	16.69	15.98	15.52	15.21	14.98	14.80	14.66	14.55
5	16.26	13.27	12.06	11.39	10.97	10.67	10.46	10.29	10.16	10.05
6	13.75	10.92	9.78	9.15	8.75	8.47	8.26	8.10	7.98	7.87
7	12.25	9.55	8.45	7.85	7.46	7.19	6.99	6.84	6.72	6.62
8	11.26	8.65	7.59	7.01	6.63	6.37	6.18	6.03	5.91	5.81
9	10.56	8.02	6.99	6.42	6.06	5.80	5.61	5.47	5.35	5.26
10	10.04	7.56	6.55	5.99	5.64	5.39	5.20	5.06	4.94	4.85
11	9.65	7.21	6.22	5.67	5.32	5.07	4.89	4.74	4.63	4.54
12	9.33	6.93	5.95	5.41	5.06	4.82	4.64	4.50	4.39	4.30
13	9.07	6.70	5.74	5.21	4.86	4.62	4.44	4.30	4.19	4.10
14	8.86	6.51	5.56	5.04	4.69	4.46	4.28	4.14	4.03	3.94
15	8.68	6.36	5.42	4.89	4.56	4.32	4.14	4.00	3.89	3.80
16	8.53	6.23	5.29	4.77	4.44	4.20	4.03	3.89	3.78	3.69

n_2	1	2	3	4	5	6	7	8	9	10
n_1										
17	8.40	6.11	5.18	4.67	4.34	4.10	3.93	3.79	3.68	3.59
18	8.29	6.01	5.09	4.58	4.25	4.01	3.84	3.71	3.60	3.51
19	8.18	5.93	5.01	4.50	4.17	3.94	3.77	3.63	3.52	3.43
20	8.10	5.85	4.94	4.43	4.10	3.87	3.70	3.56	3.46	3.37
21	8.02	5.78	4.87	4.37	4.04	3.81	3.64	3.51	3.40	3.31
22	7.95	5.72	4.82	4.31	3.99	3.76	3.59	3.45	3.35	3.26
23	7.88	5.66	4.76	4.26	3.94	3.71	3.54	3.41	3.30	3.21
24	7.82	5.61	4.72	4.22	3.90	3.67	3.50	3.36	3.26	3.17
25	7.77	5.57	4.68	4.18	3.85	3.63	3.46	3.32	3.22	3.13
26	7.72	5.53	4.64	4.14	3.82	3.59	3.42	3.29	3.18	3.09
27	7.68	5.49	4.60	4.11	3.78	3.56	3.39	3.26	3.15	3.06
28	7.64	5.45	4.57	4.07	3.75	3.53	3.36	3.23	3.12	3.03
29	7.60	5.42	4.54	4.04	3.73	3.50	3.33	3.20	3.09	3.00
30	7.56	5.39	4.51	4.02	3.70	3.47	3.30	3.17	3.07	2.98
40	7.31	5.18	4.31	3.83	3.51	3.29	3.12	2.99	2.89	2.80
60	7.08	4.98	4.13	3.65	3.34	3.12	2.95	2.82	2.72	2.63
120	6.85	4.79	3.95	3.48	3.17	2.96	2.79	2.66	2.56	2.47
∞	6.63	4.61	3.78	3.32	3.02	2.80	2.64	2.51	2.41	2.32

$$F_{0.99}(n_1, n_2)$$

n_1 = degrees of freedom for numerator n_2 = degrees of freedom for denominator

n_2	12	15	20	24	30	40	60	120	∞
n_1									
1	6106	6157	6209	6235	6261	6287	6313	6339	6366
2	99.42	99.43	99.45	99.46	99.47	99.47	99.48	99.49	99.50
3	27.05	26.87	26.69	26.60	26.50	26.41	26.32	26.22	26.13
4	14.37	14.20	14.02	13.93	13.84	13.75	13.65	13.56	13.46
5	9.89	9.72	9.55	9.47	9.38	9.29	9.20	9.11	9.02
6	7.72	7.56	7.40	7.31	7.23	7.14	7.06	6.97	6.88
7	6.47	6.31	6.16	6.07	5.99	5.91	5.82	5.74	5.65
8	5.67	5.52	5.36	5.28	5.20	5.12	5.03	4.95	4.86
9	5.11	4.96	4.81	4.73	4.65	4.57	4.48	4.40	4.31
10	4.71	4.56	4.41	4.33	4.25	4.17	4.08	4.00	3.91
11	4.40	4.25	4.10	4.02	3.94	3.86	3.78	3.69	3.60

n_2	12	15	20	24	30	40	60	120	∞
n_1									
12	4.16	4.01	3.86	3.78	3.70	3.62	3.54	3.45	3.36
13	3.96	3.82	3.66	3.59	3.51	3.43	3.34	3.25	3.17
14	3.80	3.66	3.51	3.43	3.35	3.27	3.18	3.09	3.00
15	3.67	3.52	3.37	3.29	3.21	3.13	3.05	2.96	2.87
16	3.55	3.41	3.26	3.18	3.10	3.02	2.93	2.84	2.75
17	3.46	3.31	3.16	3.08	3.00	2.92	2.83	2.75	2.65
18	3.37	3.23	3.08	3.00	2.92	2.84	2.75	2.66	2.57
19	3.30	3.15	3.00	2.92	2.84	2.76	2.67	2.58	2.49
20	3.23	3.09	2.94	2.86	2.78	2.69	2.61	2.52	2.42
21	3.17	3.03	2.88	2.80	2.72	2.64	2.55	2.46	2.36
22	3.12	2.98	2.83	2.75	2.67	2.58	2.50	2.40	2.31
23	3.07	2.93	2.78	2.70	2.62	2.54	2.45	2.35	2.26
24	3.03	2.89	2.74	2.66	2.58	2.49	2.40	2.31	2.21
25	2.99	2.85	2.70	2.62	2.54	2.45	2.36	2.27	2.17
26	2.96	2.81	2.66	2.58	2.50	2.42	2.33	2.23	2.13
27	2.93	2.78	2.63	2.55	2.47	2.38	2.29	2.20	2.10
28	2.90	2.75	2.60	2.52	2.44	2.35	2.26	2.17	2.06
29	2.87	2.73	2.57	2.49	2.41	2.33	2.23	2.14	2.03
30	2.84	2.70	2.55	2.47	2.39	2.30	2.21	2.11	2.01
40	2.66	2.52	2.37	2.29	2.20	2.11	2.02	1.92	1.80
60	2.50	2.35	2.20	2.12	2.03	1.94	1.84	1.73	1.60
120	2.34	2.19	2.03	1.95	1.86	1.76	1.66	1.53	1.38
∞	2.18	2.04	1.88	1.79	1.70	1.59	1.47	1.32	1.00

F Distribution (α = 5%)

$$F_{0.95}(n_1, n_2)$$

n_1 = degrees of freedom for numerator n_2 = degrees of freedom for denominator

n_2 n_1	1	2	3	4	5	6	7	8	9	10
1	161.4	199.5	215.7	224.6	230.2	234.0	236.8	238.9	240.5	241.9
2	18.51	19.00	19.16	19.25	19.30	19.33	19.35	19.37	19.38	19.40
3	10.13	9.55	9.28	9.12	9.01	8.94	8.89	8.85	8.81	8.79
4	7.71	6.94	6.59	6.39	6.26	6.16	6.09	6.04	6.00	5.96
5	6.61	5.79	5.41	5.19	5.05	4.95	4.88	4.82	4.77	4.74
6	5.99	5.14	4.76	4.53	4.39	4.28	4.21	4.15	4.10	4.06
7	5.59	4.47	4.35	4.12	3.97	3.87	3.79	3.73	3.68	3.64
8	5.32	4.46	4.07	3.84	3.69	3.58	3.50	3.44	3.39	3.35
9	5.12	4.26	3.86	3.63	3.48	3.37	3.29	3.23	3.18	3.14
10	4.96	4.10	3.71	3.48	3.33	3.22	3.14	3.07	3.02	2.98
11	4.84	3.98	3.59	3.36	3.20	3.09	3.01	2.95	2.90	2.85
12	4.75	3.89	3.49	3.26	3.11	3.00	2.91	2.85	2.80	2.75
13	4.67	3.81	3.41	3.18	3.03	2.92	2.83	2.77	2.71	2.67
14	4.60	3.74	3.34	3.11	2.96	2.85	2.76	2.70	2.65	2.60
15	4.54	3.68	3.29	3.06	2.90	2.79	2.71	2.64	2.59	2.54

n_2	1	2	3	4	5	6	7	8	9	10
n_1										
16	4.49	3.63	3.24	3.01	2.85	2.74	2.66	2.59	2.54	2.49
17	4.45	3.59	3.20	2.96	2.81	2.70	2.61	2.55	2.49	2.45
18	4.41	3.55	3.16	2.93	2.77	2.66	2.58	2.51	2.46	2.41
19	4.38	3.52	3.13	2.90	2.74	2.63	2.54	2.48	2.42	2.38
20	4.35	3.49	3.10	2.87	2.71	2.60	2.51	2.45	2.39	2.35
21	4.32	3.47	3.07	2.84	2.68	2.57	2.49	2.42	2.37	2.32
22	4.30	3.44	3.05	2.82	2.66	2.55	2.46	2.40	2.34	2.30
23	4.28	3.42	3.03	2.80	2.64	2.53	2.44	2.37	2.32	2.27
24	4.26	3.40	3.01	2.78	2.62	2.51	2.42	2.36	2.30	2.25
25	4.24	3.39	2.99	2.76	2.60	2.49	2.40	2.34	2.28	2.24
26	4.23	3.37	2.98	2.74	2.59	2.47	2.39	2.32	2.27	2.22
27	4.21	3.35	2.96	2.73	2.57	2.46	2.37	2.31	2.25	2.20
28	4.20	3.34	2.95	2.71	2.56	2.45	2.36	2.29	2.24	2.19
29	4.18	3.33	2.93	2.70	2.55	2.43	2.35	2.28	2.22	2.18
30	4.17	3.32	2.92	2.69	2.53	2.42	2.33	2.27	2.21	2.16
40	4.08	3.23	2.84	2.61	2.45	2.34	2.25	2.18	2.12	2.08
60	4.00	3.15	2.76	2.53	2.37	2.25	2.17	2.10	2.04	1.99
120	3.92	3.07	2.68	2.45	2.29	2.17	2.09	2.02	1.96	1.91
∞	3.84	3.00	2.60	2.37	2.21	2.10	2.01	1.94	1.88	1.83

$$F_{0.95}(n_1, n_2)$$

n_1 = degrees of freedom for numerator n_2 = degrees of freedom for denominator

n_2	12	15	20	24	30	40	60	120	∞
n_1									
1	243.9	245.9	248.0	249.1	250.1	251.1	252.2	253.2	254.3
2	19.41	19.43	19.45	19.45	19.46	19.47	19.48	19.49	19.50
3	8.74	8.70	8.66	8.64	8.62	8.59	8.57	8.55	8.53
4	5.91	5.86	5.80	5.77	5.75	5.72	5.69	5.66	5.63
5	4.68	4.62	4.56	4.53	4.50	4.46	4.43	4.40	4.36
6	4.00	3.94	3.87	3.84	3.81	3.77	3.74	3.70	3.67
7	3.57	3.51	3.44	3.41	3.38	3.34	3.30	3.27	3.23
8	3.28	3.22	3.15	3.12	3.08	3.04	3.01	2.97	2.93
9	3.07	3.01	2.94	2.90	2.86	2.83	2.79	2.75	2.71

n_2	12	15	20	24	30	40	60	120	∞
n_1									
10	2.91	2.85	2.77	2.74	2.70	2.66	2.62	2.58	2.54
11	2.79	2.72	2.65	2.61	2.57	2.53	2.49	2.45	2.40
12	2.69	2.62	2.54	2.51	2.47	2.43	2.38	2.34	2.30
13	2.60	2.53	2.46	2.42	2.38	2.34	2.30	2.25	2.21
14	2.53	2.46	2.39	2.35	2.31	2.27	2.22	2.18	2.13
15	2.48	2.40	2.33	2.29	2.25	2.20	2.16	2.11	2.07
16	2.42	2.35	2.28	2.24	2.19	2.15	2.11	2.06	2.01
17	2.38	2.31	2.23	2.19	2.15	2.10	2.06	2.01	1.96
18	2.34	2.27	2.19	2.15	2.11	2.06	2.02	1.97	1.92
19	2.31	2.23	2.16	2.11	2.07	2.03	1.98	1.93	1.88
20	2.28	2.20	2.12	2.08	2.04	1.99	1.95	1.90	1.84
21	2.25	2.18	2.10	2.05	2.01	1.96	1.92	1.87	1.81
22	2.23	2.15	2.07	2.03	1.98	1.94	1.89	1.84	1.78
23	2.20	2.13	2.05	2.01	1.96	1.91	1.86	1.81	1.76
24	2.18	2.11	2.03	1.98	1.94	1.89	1.84	1.79	1.73
25	2.16	2.09	2.01	1.96	1.92	1.87	1.82	1.77	1.71
26	2.15	2.07	1.99	1.95	1.90	1.85	1.80	1.75	1.69
27	2.13	2.06	1.97	1.93	1.88	1.84	1.79	1.73	1.67
28	2.12	2.04	1.96	1.91	1.87	1.82	1.77	1.71	1.65
29	2.10	2.03	1.94	1.90	1.85	1.81	1.75	1.70	1.64
30	2.09	2.01	1.93	1.89	1.84	1.79	1.74	1.68	1.62
40	2.00	1.92	1.84	1.79	1.74	1.69	1.64	1.58	1.51
60	1.92	1.84	1.75	1.70	1.65	1.59	1.53	1.47	1.39
120	1.83	1.75	1.66	1.61	1.55	1.50	1.43	1.35	1.25
∞	1.75	1.67	1.57	1.52	1.46	1.39	1.32	1.22	1.00

appendix **6**

Control Chart Constants

CHART FOR AVERAGE

CHART FOR STANDARD DEVIATIONS

Observations in Sample, *n*	Factors for Control Limits			Factors for Central Line		Factors for Control Limits			
	A	A₂	A₃	c₄	1/c₄	B₃	B₄	B₅	B₆
2	2.121	1.880	2.659	0.7979	1.2533	0	3.267	0	3.267
0	2.606								
3	1.732	1.023	1.954	0.8862	1.1284	0	2.568	0	2.276
4	1.500	0.729	1.628	0.9213	1.0854	0	2.266	0	2.088
5	1.342	0.577	1.427	0.9400	1.0638	0	2.089	0	1.964
6	1.225	0.483	1.287	0.9515	1.0510	0.030	1.970	0.029	1.874
7	1.134	0.419	1.182	0.9594	1.0423	0.118	1.882	0.113	1.806
8	1.061	0.373	1.099	0.9650	1.0363	0.185	1.815	0.179	1.751
9	1.000	0.337	1.032	0.9693	1.0317	0.239	1.761	0.232	1.707
10	0.949	0.308	0.975	0.9727	1.0281	0.284	1.716	0.276	1.669
11	0.905	0.285	0.927	0.9754	1.0252	0.321	1.679	0.313	1.637
12	0.866	0.266	0.886	0.9776	1.0229	0.354	1.646	0.346	1.610
13	0.832	0.249	0.850	0.9794	1.0210	0.382	1.618	0.374	1.585
14	0.802	0.235	0.817	0.9810	1.0194	0.406	1.594	0.399	1.563
15	0.775	0.223	0.789	0.9823	1.0180	0.428	1.572	0.421	1.544

CHART FOR AVERAGE

CHART FOR STANDARD DEVIATIONS

Observations in Sample, n	Factors for Control Limits			Factors for Central Line		Factors for Control Limits			
	A	A_2	A_3	c_4	$1/c_4$	B_3	B_4	B_5	B_6
16	0.750	0.212	0.763	0.9835	1.0168	0.448	1.552	0.440	1.526
17	0.728	0.203	0.739	0.9845	1.0157	0.466	1.534	0.458	1.511
18	0.707	0.194	0.718	0.9854	1.0148	0.482	1.518	0.475	1.496
19	0.688	0.187	0.698	0.9862	1.0140	0.497	1.503	0.490	1.483
20	0.671	0.180	0.680	0.9869	1.0133	0.510	1.490	0.504	1.470
21	0.655	0.173	0.663	0.9876	1.0126	0.523	1.477	0.516	1.459
22	0.640	0.167	0.647	0.9882	1.0119	0.534	1.466	0.528	1.448
23	0.626	0.162	0.633	0.9887	1.0114	0.545	1.455	0.539	1.438
24	0.612	0.157	0.619	0.9892	1.0109	0.555	1.445	0.549	1.429
25	0.600	0.153	0.606	0.9896	1.0105	0.565	1.435	0.559	1.420

CHART FOR RANGES

X CHARTS

Observations in Sample, n	Factors for Central Line			Factors for Control Limits				
	d_2	$1/d_2$	d_3	D_1	D_2	D_3	D_4	E_2
2	1.128	0.8865	0.853	0	3.686	0	3.267	2.660
3	1.693	0.5907	0.888	0	4.358	0	2.574	1.772
4	2.059	0.4857	0.880	0	4.698	0	2.282	1.457
5	2.326	0.4299	0.864	0	4.918	0	2.114	1.290
6	2.534	0.3946	0.848	0	5.078	0	2.004	1.184
7	2.704	0.3698	0.833	0.204	5.204	0.076	1.924	1.109
8	2.847	0.3512	0.820	0.388	5.306	0.136	1.864	1.054
9	2.970	0.3367	0.808	0.547	5.393	0.184	1.816	1.010
10	3.078	0.3249	0.797	0.687	5.469	0.223	1.777	0.975
11	3.173	0.3152	0.787	0.811	5.535	0.256	1.744	0.945
12	3.258	0.3069	0.778	0.922	5.594	0.283	1.717	0.921
13	3.336	0.2998	0.770	1.025	5.647	0.307	1.693	0.899
14	3.407	0.2935	0.763	1.118	5.696	0.328	1.672	0.881
15	3.472	0.2880	0.756	1.203	5.741	0.347	1.653	0.864
16	3.532	0.2831	0.750	1.282	5.782	0.363	1.637	0.849

CHART FOR RANGES   **X CHARTS**

Observations in Sample, n	Factors for Central Line			Factors for Control Limits				
	d_2	$1/d_2$	d_3	D_1	D_2	D_3	D_4	E_2
17	3.588	0.2787	0.744	1.356	5.820	0.378	1.622	0.836
18	3.640	0.2747	0.739	1.424	5.856	0.391	1.608	0.824
19	3.689	0.2711	0.734	1.487	5.891	0.403	1.597	0.813
20	3.735	0.2677	0.729	1.549	5.921	0.415	1.585	0.803
21	3.778	0.2647	0.724	1.605	5.951	0.425	1.575	0.794
22	3.819	0.2618	0.720	1.659	5.979	0.434	1.566	0.786
23	3.858	0.2592	0.716	1.710	6.006	0.443	1.557	0.778
24	3.895	0.2567	0.712	1.759	6.031	0.451	1.548	0.770
25	3.931	0.2544	0.708	1.806	6.056	0.459	1.541	0.763

appendix **7**

Table of d$^*_2$ *Values*

m = # samples in plotted group

g = # plotted groups

	2	3	4	5	6	7	8	9	10	11	12	13	14	15
1	1.41	1.91	2.24	2.48	2.67	2.83	2.96	3.08	3.18	3.27	3.35	3.42	3.49	3.55
2	1.28	1.81	2.15	2.4	2.6	2.77	2.91	3.02	3.13	3.22	3.30	3.38	3.45	3.51
3	1.23	1.77	2.12	2.38	2.58	2.75	2.89	3.01	3.11	3.21	3.29	3.37	3.43	3.50
4	1.21	1.75	2.11	2.37	2.57	2.74	2.88	3.00	3.10	3.20	3.28	3.36	3.43	3.49
5	1.19	1.74	2.1	2.36	2.56	2.73	2.87	2.99	43.10	3.19	3.28	3.35	3.42	3.49
6	1.18	1.73	2.09	2.35	2.56	2.73	2.87	2.99	3.10	3.19	3.27	3.35	3.42	3.49
7	1.17	1.73	2.09	2.35	2.55	2.72	2.87	2.99	3.10	3.19	3.27	3.35	3.42	3.48
8	1.17	1.72	2.08	2.35	2.55	2.72	2.87	2.98	3.10	3.19	3.27	3.35	3.42	3.48
9	1.16	1.72	2.08	2.34	2.55	2.72	2.86	2.98	3.09	3.18	3.27	3.35	3.42	3.48
10	1.16	1.71	2.08	2.34	2.55	2.72	2.86	2.98	3.09	3.18	3.27	3.34	3.42	3.48
11	1.16	1.71	2.08	2.34	2.55	2.72	2.86	2.98	3.09	3.18	3.27	3.34	3.41	3.48
12	1.15	1.71	2.07	2.34	2.55	2.72	2.85	2.98	3.09	3.18	3.27	3.34	3.41	3.48
13	1.15	1.71	2.07	2.34	2.55	2.71	2.85	2.98	3.09	3.18	3.27	3.34	3.41	3.48
14	1.15	1.71	2.07	2.34	2.54	2.71	2.85	2.98	3.08	3.18	3.27	3.34	3.41	3.48
15	1.15	1.71	2.07	2.34	2.54	2.71	2.85	2.98	3.08	3.18	3.26	3.34	3.41	3.48
>15	1.128	1.693	2.059	2.326	2.534	2.704	2.847	2.970	3.078	3.173	3.258	3.336	3.407	3.472

Capability Index to Sigma Level Conversion

For a given short-term estimate of C_{pk}, the long-term sigma level is provided, assuming normality and a 1.5σ shift.

Short-term Cpk	Long-term Sigma Level	Short-term Cpk	Long-term Sigma Level
0.1	0.3	1.1	3.3
0.2	0.6	1.2	3.6
0.3	0.9	1.3	3.9
0.4	1.2	1.4	4.2
0.5	1.5	1.5	4.5
0.6	1.8	1.6	4.8
0.7	2.1	1.7	5.1
0.8	2.4	1.8	5.4
0.9	2.7	1.9	5.7
1.0	3.0	2.0	6.0

Estimating Sigma Using Long-Term DPMO (from Field Data)

For a given defects per million opportunities (DPMO), the sigma level is provided, assuming normality and a 1.5σ shift. Note that below approximately 3σ, the sigma levels are slightly inaccurate because only one tail of the normal distribution was included for simplicity in the calculation.

DPMO	Sigma	DPMO	Sigma	DPMO	Sigma	DPMO	Sigma
300,000	2.02	6,000	4.01	90	5.25	3	6.03
200,000	2.34	5,000	4.08	80	5.28	2	6.11
100,000	2.78	4,000	4.15	70	5.31	1	6.25
90,000	2.84	3,000	4.25	60	5.35	0.9	6.27
80,000	2.91	2,000	4.38	50	5.39	0.8	6.30
70,000	2.98	1,000	4.59	40	5.44	0.7	6.33
60,000	3.05	900	4.62	30	5.51	0.6	6.36
50,000	3.14	800	4.66	20	5.61	0.5	6.39
40,000	3.25	700	4.69	10	5.77	0.4	6.44
30,000	3.38	600	4.74	9	5.79	0.3	6.49
20,000	3.55	500	4.79	8	5.81	0.2	6.57

DPMO	Sigma	DPMO	Sigma	DPMO	Sigma	DPMO	Sigma
10,000	3.83	400	4.85	7	5.84	0.1	6.70
9,000	3.87	300	4.93	6	5.88	0.09	6.72
8,000	3.91	200	5.04	5	5.92	0.08	6.74
7,000	3.96	100	5.22	4	5.97	0.07	6.77

Durbin-Watson Test Bounds

$$S = \sqrt{(1.3s_1)^2 + (1.3s_1)^2 + (1.3s_1)^2 + etc.}$$

$$S = \sqrt{n(1.3s)^2}$$

$$= \sqrt{10(1.3*0.00333'')^2}$$

$$S = 0.037''$$

	p-1=1		p-1=2		p-1=3		p-1=4		p-1=5	
n	d_L	d_U	d_L	d_U	d_L	d_U	d_L	d_U	d_L	d_U
15	1.08	1.36	0.95	1.54	0.82	1.75	0.69	1.97	0.56	2.21
16	1.10	1.37	0.98	1.54	0.86	1.73	0.74	1.93	0.62	2.15
17	1.13	1.38	1.02	1.54	0.90	1.71	0.78	1.90	0.67	2.10
18	1.16	1.39	1.05	1.53	0.93	1.69	0.82	1.87	0.71	2.06
19	1.18	1.40	1.08	1.53	0.97	1.68	0.86	1.85	0.75	2.02
20	1.20	1.41	1.10	1.54	1.00	1.68	0.90	1.83	0.79	1.99
21	1.22	1.42	1.13	1.54	1.03	1.67	0.93	1.81	0.83	1.96
22	1.24	1.43	1.15	1.54	1.05	1.66	0.96	1.80	0.86	1.94
23	1.26	1.44	1.17	1.54	1.08	1.66	0.99	1.79	0.90	1.92
24	1.27	1.45	1.19	1.55	1.10	1.66	1.01	1.78	0.93	1.90
25	1.29	1.45	1.21	1.55	1.12	1.66	1.04	1.77	0.95	1.89
26	1.30	1.46	1.22	1.55	1.14	1.65	1.06	1.76	0.98	1.88
27	1.32	1.47	1.24	1.56	1.16	1.65	1.08	1.76	1.01	1.86
28	1.33	1.48	1.26	1.56	1.18	1.65	1.10	1.75	1.03	1.85
29	1.34	1.48	1.27	1.56	1.20	1.65	1.12	1.74	1.05	1.84

Level of significance $\alpha = .05$.

n	p-1=1 d_L	p-1=1 d_U	p-1=2 d_L	p-1=2 d_U	p-1=3 d_L	p-1=3 d_U	p-1=4 d_L	p-1=4 d_U	p-1=5 d_L	p-1=5 d_U
30	1.35	1.49	1.28	1.57	1.21	1.65	1.14	1.74	1.07	1.83
31	1.36	1.50	1.30	1.57	1.23	1.65	1.16	1.74	1.09	1.83
32	1.37	1.50	1.31	1.57	1.24	1.65	1.18	1.73	1.11	1.82
33	1.38	1.51	1.32	1.58	1.26	1.65	1.19	1.73	1.13	1.81
34	1.39	1.51	1.33	1.58	1.27	1.65	1.21	1.73	1.15	1.81
35	1.40	1.52	1.34	1.58	1.28	1.65	1.22	1.73	1.16	1.80
36	1.41	1.52	1.35	1.59	1.29	1.65	1.24	1.73	1.18	1.80
37	1.42	1.53	1.36	1.59	1.31	1.66	1.25	1.72	1.19	1.80
38	1.43	1.54	1.37	1.59	1.32	1.66	1.26	1.72	1.21	1.79
39	1.43	1.54	1.38	1.60	1.33	1.66	1.27	1.72	1.22	1.79
40	1.44	1.54	1.39	1.60	1.34	1.66	1.29	1.72	1.23	1.79
45	1.48	1.57	1.43	1.62	1.38	1.67	1.34	1.72	1.29	1.78
50	1.50	1.59	1.46	1.63	1.42	1.67	1.38	1.72	1.34	1.77
55	1.53	1.60	1.49	1.64	1.45	1.68	1.41	1.72	1.38	1.77
60	1.55	1.62	1.51	1.65	1.48	1.69	1.44	1.73	1.41	1.77
65	1.57	1.63	1.54	1.66	1.50	1.70	1.47	1.73	1.44	1.77
70	1.58	1.64	1.55	1.67	1.52	1.70	1.49	1.74	1.46	1.77
75	1.60	1.65	1.57	1.68	1.54	1.71	1.51	1.74	1.49	1.77
80	1.61	1.66	1.59	1.69	1.56	1.72	1.53	1.74	1.51	1.77
85	1.62	1.67	1.60	1.70	1.57	1.72	1.55	1.75	1.52	1.77
90	1.63	1.68	1.61	1.70	1.59	1.73	1.57	1.75	1.54	1.78
95	1.64	1.69	1.62	1.71	1.60	1.73	1.58	1.75	1.56	1.78
100	1.65	1.69	1.63	1.72	1.61	1.74	1.59	1.76	1.57	1.78

Level of significance α = .01.										
15	0.81	1.07	0.70	1.25	0.59	1.46	0.49	1.70	0.39	1.96
16	0.84	1.09	0.74	1.25	0.63	1.44	0.53	1.66	0.44	1.90
17	0.87	1.10	0.77	1.25	0.67	1.43	0.57	1.63	0.48	1.85
18	0.90	1.12	0.80	1.26	0.71	1.42	0.61	1.60	0.52	1.80
19	0.93	1.13	0.83	1.26	0.74	1.41	0.65	1.58	0.56	1.77
20	0.95	1.15	0.86	1.27	0.77	1.41	0.68	1.57	0.60	1.74
21	0.97	1.16	0.89	1.27	0.80	1.41	0.72	1.55	0.63	1.71
22	1.00	1.17	0.91	1.28	0.83	1.40	0.75	1.54	0.66	1.69
23	1.02	1.19	0.94	1.29	0.86	1.40	0.77	1.53	0.70	1.67
24	1.04	1.20	0.96	1.30	0.88	1.41	0.80	1.53	0.72	1.66
25	1.05	1.21	0.98	1.30	0.90	1.41	0.83	1.52	0.75	1.65
26	1.07	1.22	1.00	1.31	0.93	1.41	0.85	1.52	0.78	1.64
27	1.09	1.23	1.02	1.32	0.95	1.41	0.88	1.51	0.81	1.63
28	1.10	1.24	1.04	1.32	0.97	1.41	0.90	1.51	0.83	1.62
29	1.12	1.25	1.05	1.33	0.99	1.42	0.92	1.51	0.85	1.61
30	1.13	1.26	1.07	1.34	1.01	1.42	0.94	1.51	0.88	1.61
31	1.15	1.27	1.08	1.34	1.02	1.42	0.96	1.51	0.90	1.60
32	1.16	1.28	1.10	1.35	1.04	1.43	0.98	1.51	0.92	1.60
33	1.17	1.29	1.11	1.36	1.05	1.43	1.00	1.51	0.94	1.59
34	1.18	1.30	1.13	1.36	1.07	1.43	1.01	1.51	0.95	1.59
35	1.19	1.31	1.14	1.37	1.08	1.44	1.03	1.51	0.97	1.59
36	1.21	1.32	1.15	1.38	1.10	1.44	1.04	1.51	0.99	1.59
37	1.22	1.32	1.16	1.38	1.11	1.45	1.06	1.51	1.00	1.59
38	1.23	1.33	1.18	1.39	1.12	1.45	1.07	1.52	1.02	1.58
39	1.24	1.34	1.19	1.39	1.14	1.45	1.09	1.52	1.03	1.58
40	1.25	1.34	1.20	1.40	1.15	1.46	1.10	1.52	1.05	1.58
45	1.29	1.38	1.24	1.42	1.20	1.48	1.16	1.53	1.11	1.58
50	1.32	1.40	1.28	1.45	1.24	1.49	1.20	1.54	1.16	1.59
55	1.36	1.43	1.32	1.47	1.28	1.51	1.25	1.55	1.21	1.59
60	1.38	1.45	1.35	1.48	1.32	1.52	1.28	1.56	1.25	1.60
65	1.41	1.47	1.38	1.50	1.35	1.53	1.31	1.57	1.28	1.61
70	1.43	1.49	1.40	1.52	1.37	1.55	1.34	1.58	1.31	1.61
75	1.45	1.50	1.42	1.53	1.39	1.56	1.37	1.59	1.34	1.62
80	1.47	1.52	1.44	1.54	1.42	1.57	1.39	1.60	1.36	1.62
85	1.48	1.53	1.46	1.55	1.43	1.58	1.41	1.60	1.39	1.63
90	1.50	1.54	1.47	1.56	1.45	1.59	1.43	1.61	1.41	1.64
95	1.51	1.55	1.49	1.57	1.47	1.60	1.45	1.62	1.42	1.64
100	1.52	1.56	1.50	1.58	1.48	1.60	1.46	1.63	1.44	1.65

n	$p-1=1$		$p-1=2$		$p-1=3$		$p-1=4$		$p-1=5$	
	d_L	d_U	d_L	d_U	d_L	d_U	d_L	d_U	d_L	d_U
65	1.41	1.47	1.38	1.50	1.35	1.53	1.31	1.57	1.28	1.61
70	1.43	1.49	1.40	1.52	1.37	1.55	1.34	1.58	1.31	1.61
75	1.45	1.50	1.42	1.53	1.39	1.56	1.37	1.59	1.34	1.62
80	1.47	1.52	1.44	1.54	1.42	1.57	1.39	1.60	1.36	1.62
85	1.48	1.53	1.46	1.55	1.43	1.58	1.41	1.60	1.39	1.63
90	1.50	1.54	1.47	1.56	1.45	1.59	1.43	1.61	1.41	1.64
95	1.51	1.55	1.49	1.57	1.47	1.60	1.45	1.62	1.42	1.64
100	1.52	1.56	1.50	1.58	1.48	1.60	1.46	1.63	1.44	1.65

Glossary

Alias   Factors or interactions are aliased or confounded when an independent estimate cannot be made for a parameter that is the alias of another parameter. See also "Factorial Designs" in Part 3.

Attributes Data   Attributes data are also known as *count data*. Typically, we will count the number of times we observe some condition (usually something we don't like, such as an error) in a given sample from the process. This is different from measurement data in its resolution. Attributes data have less resolution because we only count if something occurs rather than taking a measurement to see how close we are to the condition. For example, attributes data for a health care process might include the number of patients with a fever, whereas variables data for the same process might be measurement of the patients' temperature.

Attributes data generally provide us with less information than measurement (variables) data would for the same process. Using attributes data, we generally will not be able to predict whether the process is trending toward an undesirable state because it is already in this condition.

Average   The average, sometimes called *X-bar*, is calculated for a set of n data values as

$$\overline{X} = \frac{1}{n}\sum_{i=1}^{n} x_i$$

Simply, the sum of each observation x_i is divided by the number of observations n. An example of its use is as the plotted statistic in an X-bar chart. Here, the n is the subgroup size, and $\bar{x}$ indicates the average of the observations in the subgroup.

When dealing with subgrouped data, you also can calculate the overall average of the subgroups. It is the average of the subgroups' averages, so it is sometimes called X-doublebar.

$$\bar{\bar{X}} = \frac{1}{m \times n} \sum_{j=1}^{m} \sum_{i=1}^{n} x_i$$

where n is the subgroup size and m is the total number of subgroups included in the analysis.

When the subgroup size is 1, this equation simplifies to

$$\bar{\bar{X}} = \frac{1}{m} \sum_{j=1}^{m} x_j$$

Average Range   The average of the subgroup ranges (R-bar).

$$\bar{R} = \frac{1}{m} \sum_{j=1}^{m} R_j$$

where R_j is the subgroup range of subgroup j, and m is the total number of subgroups included in the analysis.

Average Sigma   The average of the subgroup sigma (S-bar).

$$\bar{S} = \frac{1}{m} \sum_{j=1}^{m} S_j$$

where S_j is the subgroup sigma of subgroup j, and m is the total number of subgroups included in the analysis.

Backward Elimination   Regression by backward elimination involves an interactive series of regressions starting with the initial model (the interaction array). At each step, the significance of the t statistic for each remaining parameter is compared with the specified probability criterion. The lowest (poorest comparison) parameter is discarded, and the regression is run again until all remaining parameters meet the criterion. See "Regression Analysis" in Part 3.

Balance   Balance in a designed experiment is used in two contexts. First, the levels in a design may be balanced; second, the data may be distributed in a balanced way. When a design is balanced, each column of the design array has the same number of levels of that parameter. When the data are balanced, the data points are distributed over the experimental region so that they have an equal contribution to the parameter estimates. Although many designs satisfy both criteria, some, such as central composite designs, forgo design balance in favor of data balance. Balance of both kinds is often forfeited in favor of adding points to better estimate the experimental error. At times, it may be preferable to void the balance by removing runs to make a smaller design that can meet a time or resource constraint.

Bias   Also known as *accuracy*, bias is an estimate of the error in a measurement system. Bias is estimated by taking repeat samples of a part or standard using the measurement system and comparing the average of these measurements with a measurement taken of the same piece using equipment with higher accuracy.

$$\text{Bias} = \text{average of measurements} - \text{reference value}$$

$$\%\text{Bias} = (\text{bias/process variation}) \times 100\%$$

Process variation may be estimated as six times the process sigma value calculated from a control chart.

Blocking Factor   When all runs cannot be completed under the same environment (homogeneous conditions), exclusive of the factors themselves, blocking may be necessary. The maximum block size may be limited by such constraints as the number of runs that can be done in one day or shift. Blocking factors may not interact with main factors. Blocking factors are evaluated as random factors in an ANOVA.

Box-Behnken Design   A Box-Behnken design (named for the authors who originally proposed it) uses a selection of corner, face, and central points to span an experimental space with fewer points than a complete factorial design (see Figure F.58). It is similar in intent to a central composite design, but it differs in that no corner or extreme points are used. It has no extended axial points, so it uses only three-level factors. They usually require fewer runs than a three-level fractional factorial design, and they are useful to avoid the extreme factor level combinations that central composite designs might require.

In the example shown in Figure F.59, notice that instead of corner points, factors are run at midpoints and the center on the cube.

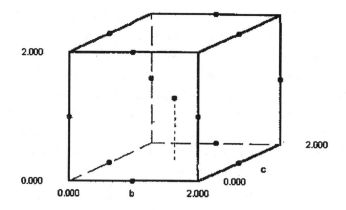

FIGURE F.58 Example of a Box-Behnken design.

Casual Factor   Also known as *random variable* or *covariate*. Occasionally, an experimental factor will be present that is not controllable for an experimental run. Such a factor cannot be included in a design but can be recorded and included in the experimental data, for example, outside air temperature, run sequence, and day of the week. A poor fit of the data to the model is sometimes an indicator of the presence of a significant casual factor.

Central Composite Design   A central composite design (CCD) spans a set of quantitative factors with fewer points than a standard fractional factorial multilevel design without a large loss in efficiency. Central composite designs consist of central points, corner points (as in the fractional factorial design), and either face-centered points or extended axial points. Central composite designs with face points require three levels. With extended axial points, five levels are required.

These three-level designs are often used for response surface analysis to map out the shapes of the quadratic surfaces. The center and axial points allow estimates of quadratic terms. (Recall that two-level designs only can be used to estimate linear surfaces.) Repeat center points provide an estimate of pure error.

An example of a face-centered central composite design is shown in Figure F.59. Note the points on the face of the cube. In this case, a standard 2^3 fractional factorial design is supplemented with the six face-centered points and two centerpoints.

Figure F.60 is an example of a central composite design with axial points. In this case, a standard 2^3 fractional factorial design is supplemented with the six axial points and two centerpoints.

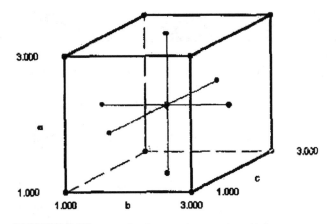

FIGURE F.59 Example of a central composite with face-centered points.

The location of the axial points (or more precisely, the levels of the factors) is often determined to achieve a *rotatable* design. A design is rotatable if the variance of the predicted response is constant at all points equidistant from the center of the design. Most design-generation software will define the axial points to achieve rotatable designs. For example, with $k = 2$ factors, design points are equally spaced at plus and minus 1.414, as shown in Table T.24.

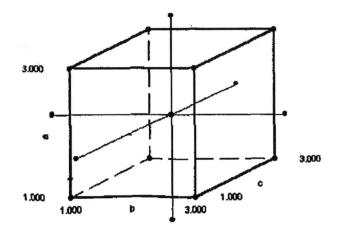

FIGURE F.60 Example of a central composite design with axial points.

TABLE T.24				
K	2	3	4	5
α	1.414	1.682	2.00	2.378

For central composite designs, it is not uncommon for the data to be collected in blocks owing to the size of the experiment. For example, we may begin with a screening fractional factorial and then add center and axial points.

Recall that *orthogonal* designs are designs that allow all parameters to be estimated independently. Orthogonal blocking implies that the block effects do not affect the ability to estimate parameters independently. In a blocked central composite design, the choice of the axial point locations and the number of centerpoint replicates affect orthogonal blocking.

The recommendations suggested for central composite designs with blocking are shown in Table T.25. The last column refers to a half-fractional design for five factors.

TABLE T.25					
Number Factors		**2**	**3**	**4**	**5(1/2)**
Blocks within cube	Points in cube	4	8	16	16
	Blocks in cube	1	2	2	1
Center point replicates in each block		3	2	2	6
Axial block	Axial points	4	6	8	10
Center point replicates		3	2	2	1
Total observations (N)		14	20	30	33
α		1.414	1.633	2.0	2.0

Coefficient   The multiplicative term preceding each parameter in a regression equation. For example, in the regression equation response = 3.5(factor A) + 4.2(factor B) + 1.6(factor AB) + 25.64, 3.5 is the coefficient of factor A and 25.64 is the coefficient of the mean term (i.e., in simple linear regression, the y intercept).

Coefficient of Determination R Squared   The coefficient of determination (COD) indicates how much of the total variation in the dependent variable can be accounted for by the regression function. For example, a COD of 0.70

implies that 70 percent of the variation in y is accounted for by the regression equation. Most statisticians consider a COD of 0.7 or higher for a reasonable model.

$$COD = R^2$$

where R is the correlation coefficient.

Coefficient of Determination, Adjusted   The coefficient of determination, corrected for the number of terms in the regression equation. It is typically lower and more stable than R^2 when there is more than one independent variable.

$$R_a^2 = 1 - c(1 - R^2)$$

where $c = (n - 1)/(n - p - 1)$

    n = number of runs

    p = number of parameters estimated by regression

Complete Factorial Design   A complete factorial design (CFD) consists of all combinations of all factor levels. A CFD is capable of estimating all factors and their interactions. For example, a complete factorial design of three factors, each at two levels, would consist of $2^3 = 8$ runs. See "Factorial Designs" in Part 3.

Confounding   Confounding exists in a multiple regression when two or more factors cannot be estimated independently of one another. Usually this means that there are not enough of the proper runs to form the required estimates for each factor. Confounding may result when runs are removed from a designed experiment without changing the parameter requirements.

An extended design may be generated to add runs to eliminate the confounding. See "Factorial Designs" in Part 3.

Correlation Coefficient R   A measure of how much linear relationship exists between the values for the two variables. The correlation coefficient can range between +1 and −1. Positive values indicate a relationship between X and Y variables so that as X increases, so does Y. Negative values imply that the relationship between X and Y is such that as values for X increase, values for Y decrease. A value near zero means that there is a random, nonlinear relationship between the two variables.

$$R = \frac{S_{xy}}{S_{xx} \times S_{yy}}$$

$$S_{yy} = \sigma_y^2(N-1)$$

$$S_{xx} = \sigma_x^2(N-1)$$

$$S_{xy} = \sum_{j=1}^{N}(x_j - \bar{\bar{x}})(y_j - \bar{\bar{y}})$$

where N is the total number of observations, $\bar{\bar{x}}$ and $\bar{\bar{y}}$ are the averages of x and y, respectively, and σ_x and σ_y are the sample sigma of the x and y values, respectively.

Critical Path   Those tasks which, if not completed in the minimum amount of time, will cause subsequent tasks to be delayed and upset the entire project (or process) completion schedule. See "Gantt Chart" in Part 3.

Degrees of Freedom   A measure of how many runs are used to form an estimate of a parameter. Each parameter estimate absorbs one degree of freedom from the total number of degrees of freedom available. Before any estimates are made, the number of degrees of freedom available equals the number of independent data values.

F Statistic   Provides an indication of the lack of fit of the data to the estimated values of a regression.

$$F = \frac{MS_{reg}}{MS_E}$$

where the mean square regression is $MS_{reg} = SS_{reg} = \beta_1 S_{xy}$. *Note:* The degrees of freedom for the regression = 1, and the mean square error (residual) is

$$MS_E = \frac{SS_E}{df_E} = \frac{S_{yy} - \beta_1 S_{xy}}{N-2}$$

$$S_{yy} = \sigma_y^2(N-1)$$

$$S_{xy} = \sum_{j=1}^{N}(x_j - \bar{\bar{x}})(y_j - \bar{\bar{y}})$$

where N is the total number of observations, $\bar{\bar{x}}$ and $\bar{\bar{y}}$ are the averages of x and y, respectively, and σ_y is the sample sigma of the y values.

Several examples of F tests are presented in Part 3.

Fixed Effects   Fixed effects are factors chosen at specific levels of interest, spanning a region of interest, for which a systematic effect on model response is expected. In a separate context, factors are said to be fixed when held at a constant level during an experiment. The alternative to a fixed effect is a *random effect*.

Fractional Factorial Design   A fractional factorial design is a design that is a regular fraction ($\frac{1}{2}$, $\frac{1}{4}$, $\frac{1}{8}$, . . . , $\frac{1}{3}$, $\frac{1}{9}$, $\frac{1}{27}$, . . . , $\frac{1}{5}$, $\frac{1}{25}$, . . .), a $\frac{3}{4}$ fraction, or an irregular unbalanced fraction of a complete factorial design. See "Factorial Designs" in Part 3.

Gauge   An instrument or scale used to measure a process parameter.

Interactions   When the influence of one parameter on a response depends on the setting of another parameter, this suggests that the interaction of the two parameters may be significant.

In practice, it is often found that only two-factor interactions have a significant effect. The effect of quadratic terms (A^2, B^2, etc.) depends on the process. Some processes are inherently nonlinear with respect to the factor values used in the model. If the data can be fitted only by using many higher-order terms or are not well fitted even with all possible linear and quadratic terms, it may indicate that the process is oscillating over the range of one or more factors. It also may mean that the factor levels or the response should be transformed. Quadratic terms for qualitative factors are often very difficult to interpret and generally should be avoided.

The decision to include or exclude interactions between main factors is extremely important. A screening experiment, which allows for no interactions, may be useful when there is little understanding of the process and no interactions are believed to exist. During the analysis of a screening experiment, it may be found that some main factors are unimportant. If this is the case, the effect of some unplanned interactions may be estimated. There is, however, no assurance that important interactions will not remain confounded with main factors. A better choice is to use a resolution IV design instead of the screening (resolution III) design. The R-IV design will ensure no confounding between main effects and two-factor interactions, although the two-factor interactions cannot be estimated.

During the analysis of an experiment planned with interactions, it is often possible to eliminate one or more main factors and to add unplanned interactions to the analysis. See "Factorial Designs" in Part 3.

John's ¾ Designs   John's ¾ designs are ¾ fractions of regular fractional factorial designs. For example, designs can be constructed of 12 runs (¾ of 16 runs) and 24 runs (¾ of 32 runs). Conditions are chosen to maximize the number of interactions independently estimated. In this way, the designs are constrained by the interactions.

Usually, for the same number of runs, the John's ¾ designs can accommodate more interactions than a Placket-Burman or fractional factorial design. See "Factorial Designs" in Part 3.

K-S Statistic   The Kolmogorov-Smirnov (K-S) statistic can be used as a relative indicator of curve fit. See "Goodness-of-Fit Tests" in Part 3.

Kurtosis   A measure of the flatness or peakedness of a distribution. Kurtosis is 0 for a normal distribution. Values greater than 0 imply that the distribution has more of a peak than a normal distribution. Values less than 0 imply that the distribution is flatter than a normal distribution.

$$\text{Kurtosis} = \left[\frac{N(N+1)}{(N-1)(N-2)(N-3)} \sum_{j=1}^{N} \frac{(x_j - \bar{\bar{x}})^4}{\sigma_x^4} \right] - \frac{3(N+1)^2}{(N-2)(N-3)}$$

where x_j is observation j, N is the total number of observations, $\bar{x}$ is the average, and σ_x is the sample sigma.

Lack of Fit   The difference between the total sum of squares of the residuals and the pure error sum of squares, that is, a measure of lack of fit between the data and the fitted response. An F test is used to express the significance of the lack of fit, which is expected to be nonsignificant for a well-fitted model. See "Response Surface Analysis" in Part 3.

Median   The 50th percentile. The median of a sample of data is found by rank-ordering the data from smallest to largest value and then selecting the data value that is in the middle of the sample. It will have an equal number of data values greater than it and less than it. When there are an even number of data values, use the average of the two central values.

For normal distributions, the median value occurs at the average of the distribution. This is also where the mode, or high point (most frequently occurring value), of the distribution occurs.

For distributions skewed left, both the median and mode occur to the left of (are smaller than) the distribution's average.

For distributions skewed right, both the median and mode occur to the right of (are larger than) the distribution's average.

Minimum Detectable Effect   A design's minimum detectable effect (MDE) refers to the minimum main effect that can be detected at a specified α significance and β confidence. The MDE is measured in units of standard deviation. An MDE of 2.6 or less is recommended.

Mixed-Level Designs   Mixed-level designs have factors in which at least one factor has a different number of levels than another factor. For example, a two-factor design in which one factor has two levels and another has three levels is a mixed-level design; so is a design consisting of a 2-level factor, a 3-level factor, and a 12-level factor. Mixed-level designs are generated using pseudofactors.

To determine the number of runs required to estimate each possible factor and interaction in a mixed-level design, multiply the number of runs calculated separately for each fixed-level case. For example, a design with five two-level factors and one three-level factor would require $2^5 \times 3^1 = 32 \times 3 = 96$ runs. See "Factorial Designs" in Part 3.

Mixture Design   Formulations, blends, combinations, compounds, amalgams, and recipes are designs in which the factor levels in each run either all sum to a fixed quantity (volume, charge, load) or are restricted to a range of quantities.

Mixture designs differ from ordinary fractional factorials because the levels for the factors in a run cannot be chosen independently of one another. Each factor level must be measurable in some common unit of measure; the common measure need not be the experimental factors' units of measure. The common unit may be cubic feet, with factor measures in gallons, pounds, and cubic inches. A factor level may have a minimum or maximum; in addition, the sum of all the factor levels in a run may be specified to not fall below some minimum quantity or exceed some maximum quantity. Standardized designs are based on a nondimensional unit, which may have upper and lower bounds on the sum of all factor levels in a run or which may have upper or lower bounds on the levels for each factor.

Mixture designs are usually special forms of response surface designs, except for screening designs, which have no center or other interior points. Mixture designs usually are constructed to estimate linear interactions only; that is, they estimate interactions such as AB or ABC but cannot estimate AB^2, A^2B^2, or higher interaction forms.

Noise Factors   See *Subsidiary Factor*.

Normalization   Normalizing is one of several useful transformation techniques. The effect is to transform the values of the variable to a −1 to +1 range when the experimental array is balanced so that the parameters (factors or response) are in a common range. This allows the effects (the relative importance of any factor or interaction) to be identified more clearly. It improves the numerical accuracy of the regression and the computation of significance. Often, the parameters to be retained or discarded thus are identified more easily. Usually either all or none of the quantitative factors to be used in a particular regression run are normalized. Normalizing has no useful purpose for qualitative factors.

Where the experimental situation is nonlinear, the linear model will not fit well, and normalizing is of limited value, except as a first step in screening out factors or interactions that have minimal effect on the response. After an initial determination of significant parameters, a regression may be done on transformed experimental values. Often it's convenient to do a final analysis with the experimental values so that the results in plotting are displayed in conventional units.

$$\text{Normalized value} = (\text{value} - \text{mean of value})/(0.5 \times \text{range of values})$$

Orthogonality   Orthogonality refers to the property of a design that ensures that all specified parameters may be estimated independent of any other.

The degree of orthogonality is measured by the normalized value of the determinant of the information matrix. An orthogonal design matrix having one row to estimate each parameter (mean, factors, and interactions) has a measure of 1. It's easy to check for orthogonality: If the sum of the factors' columns in standard format equals 0, then the design is orthogonal.

Some writers lump orthogonality with balance, which is different. *Balance* implies that the data are distributed properly over the design space. It implies a uniform physical distribution of the data and an equal number of levels of each factor.

Designs do not necessarily need balance to be good designs. Rather, some designs (such as central composite designs) sacrifice balance to achieve better distribution of the variance or predicted error. Balance also may be sacrificed by avoiding extreme combinations of factors, such as in the Box-Behnken design.

For example, a complete factorial design is both orthogonal and balanced if in fact the model that includes all possible interactions is correct. Such a design, although both balanced and orthogonal, would not be a recommended experimental design because it cannot provide an estimate of experimental error. When an additional point (row) is added (which for a complete factorial design must be a repeated run), the design is still orthogonal but unbalanced. If the complete interaction model were not correct, then the design is balanced, but the distribution of data is not balanced for the parameters to be estimated.

Fractional factorial and Plackett-Burman designs are normally constructed to have both orthogonality and balance; however, they may have more rows than are required for estimating parameters and error. In such cases, appropriate rows may be trimmed so that orthogonality is preserved but balance is lost. Central composite designs are orthogonal in that all the parameters for the central composite model may be estimated, but the design itself is unbalanced. A greater or lesser number of centerpoints is used to achieve an estimating criterion and an error estimate.

PCL   The PCL, or process centerline, is the average when a normal distribution is assumed for the control chart statistic, or it is typically the median of the distribution for nonnormal distributions.

Plackett-Burman Designs   Plackett-Burman (PB) designs are quite useful as screening designs. Plackett-Burman designs are generated in steps of four runs, from 4 to 100 runs. The number of runs n must be at least $k + 1$, where k is the number of parameters. For example, a design can be constructed in 12 runs to estimate 11 parameters.

When the number of runs is a power of 2 (i.e., 2^x, such as 8-, 16-, or 32-run experiments), the design is the same as a standard fractional factorial. When the number of runs equals a factor of 4 (such as 12-, 20-, or 24-run experiments), the design can be more efficient than the fractional factorial.

Usually, for the same number of runs, the John's ¾ designs can accommodate more interactions.

Process Sigma   An estimate of the standard deviation of a controlled process. Based on the moving-range chart (when subgroup size $n = 1$),

$$\sigma_x = \frac{\overline{MR}}{d_2}$$

where $\overline{MR}$ is the average moving range, and d_2 (available in Appendix 6) is based on $n = 2$.

Based on the range chart (when subgroup size $n > 1$) *Note:* This is the standard deviation of the observations, *not* the standard deviation of the subgroup averages, which may be calculated by dividing this estimate by the square root of n.

$$\sigma_x = \frac{\overline{R}}{d_2}$$

where $\overline{R}$ is the average range and d_2 (available in Appendix 6) is a function of n.

Based on the sigma chart (when subgroup size $n > 1$) *Note:* This is the standard deviation of the observations, *not* the standard deviation of the subgroup averages, which may be calculated by dividing this estimate by the square root of n.

$$\sigma_x = \frac{\overline{S}}{c_4}$$

where $\overline{S}$ is the average sigma and c_4 (available in Appendix 6) is a function of n.

Population Sigma   The standard deviation of the population from which the sample was drawn.

$$\sigma_x = \sqrt{\frac{\sum_{j=1}^{N}(x_j - \overline{\overline{x}})^2}{N}}$$

where N is the total number of observations, x_j is the observation at time j, and $\overline{\overline{x}}$ is the average.

Pure Error   Experimental error, the differences between repeated runs of the same condition. The total error includes both pure error and lack-of-fit error.

We can estimate pure error as the variation between the repeat runs using the sum of squares deviations between each observation and the average at that design condition. To estimate pure error, we need to repeat at least one of the run conditions.

In some cases, we may even have a full design replicate, such as when we remove a factor from the analysis if it is not statistically significant. For example, if we ran a two-level complete factorial design for three factors (2^3) and determined that the *ABC* interaction was insignificant, we would have a replicated 2^{3-1} design.

We also can extend designs to estimate error. See "Factorial Designs" in Part 3.

Qualitative Factors Qualitative factors are those which are not assigned measurable levels, such as on/off or blue/green/red. The levels of a qualitative factor are nominal; they do not have a natural order or a measure of separation between them. Qualitative factors often exist in a few discrete categories only. When numerical calculations are made using qualitative data, a numerical value must be assigned to each factor category for regression analysis.

Quantitative Factors Quantitative factors have a natural order that may be quantified, such as weight or distance. Often they are referred to as continuous variables or variable data. Quantitative factors may be measured as an interval between levels or with respect to some common origin. In some cases, qualitative information may be expressed quantitatively for the purpose of analysis, such as setting slow = 0, medium = 7, and fast = 10. Such quantification need not be related to any recognized scale, but it should be spaced realistically. Quantitative factors can describe a specific response curve or surface, whereas the shape of the response to qualitative factors depends on an arbitrary factor ordering.

Random Effects Random effects result from factors having levels that are representative of a larger set of levels. An assumption is made that the random levels included in the design are representative because they are chosen randomly from a population having normally distributed effects. They are included in a design as a nonsystematic source of variation. Blocking factors are used as random effect factors. Random factors are often nuisance parameters; they may be a source of variation, but they are generally not useful for control. They are often included in a design with the hope, if not the expectation, that they will be found to be nonsignificant.

Rational Subgroups Most control charts, including the X-bar and individual-X charts, rely on rational subgroups to estimate the short-term variation in the process. This short-term variation is then used to predict the longer-term variation defined by the control limits. But what is a rational subgroup?

A rational subgroup is simply "a sample in which all of the items are produced under conditions in which only random effects are responsible for the observed variation" (Nelson, 1988). As such, it has the following properties:

1. The observations comprising the subgroup are independent. Two observations are independent if neither observation influences or results from the other. When observations are dependent on one another, we say the process has autocorrelation or serial correlation (these terms mean the same thing). Many processes are subject to autocorrelation. Examples include

   - *Chemical processes.* When dealing with liquids, particularly in large baths, samples taken close together in time are influenced by one another. The liquid retains the effect of the first observation, such as temperature, which carries over into subsequent temperature observations for a period of time. Subgroups formed over a small time frame from these types of processes are sometimes called *homogeneous subgroups* because the observations within the subgroups are often nearly identical (except for the effect of measurement variation).

   - *Service processes.* Consider the wait time at a bank. The wait time of any person in the line is influenced by the wait time of the person in front of him or her.

   - *Discrete part manufacturing.* Although this is the "classic" case of independent subgroups, when feedback control is used to change a process based on past observations, the observations become inherently dependent.

   When observations within a subgroup are autocorrelated, the within-subgroup variation is often quite small and not a reflection of the between-subgroup process variation. The small within-subgroup variation forces the control limits to be too narrow, resulting in frequent out-of-control conditions. This leads to tampering.

2. The observations within a subgroup are from a single, stable process. If subgroups contain the elements of multiple process streams, or if other special causes occur frequently within subgroups, then the within-subgroup variation will be large relative to the variation between subgroup averages. This large within-subgroup variation forces the control limits to be too far apart, resulting in a lack of sensitivity to process shifts. Run-test 7 (15 successive points within 1σ of centerline) is helpful in detecting this condition.

3. The subgroups are formed from observations taken in a time-ordered sequence. In other words, subgroups cannot be randomly formed from a set of data (or a box of parts); instead, the data comprising a subgroup must be a "snapshot" of the process over a small window of time, and the order of the subgroups would show how those snapshots vary in time (like a movie). The size of the "small window of time" is determined on an individual process basis to minimize the chance of a special cause occurring in the subgroup.

Replicated Designs   Replicated designs are designs in which all or almost all of the main factor design is repeated a few or several times. Replication allows an estimate of variance for each run of the main factor design, thereby allowing for an analysis of variation over the full range of the experiment.

Regression Function   The equation of the least squares fit line through the data, used to estimate values of the dependent variable (the y axis) for given values of the independent variable (the x axis) or variables (X_1, X_2, etc.).

Residuals   A residual is the difference between the observed response and the value calculated from the regression model (the fitted response) for that combination of factor levels. The residual includes the effect of both experimental error (pure error) and the lack of fit between the assumed model and the true model.

Resolution   Resolution provides an indication of the interaction types that can be estimated independently with the design. Recall that when factors and interactions are confounded, they cannot be estimated independently.

Resolution, as a way of describing performance of a design, is most useful when complete sets of interactions are required.

- *Resolution III.* At least one main factor may be confounded with an interaction. These are typically useful only as a preliminary screening design.
- *Resolution IV.* Main factors are not confounded with two-factor interactions but may be confounded with higher-order interactions. Two-factor interactions may be confounded with each other and with higher-order interactions.
- *Resolution V.* Main-factor and two-factor interactions are not confounded with one another but may be confounded with higher-order interactions. Three-factor and higher-order interactions may be confounded.

- *Resolution VI.* Main-factor and two-factor, interactions are not confounded with each other or with three-factor interactions. Three-factor and higher-order interactions may be confounded with one another.

- *Resolution VII.* Main-factor, two-factor, and three-factor interactions are not confounded with one another but may be confounded with higher-order interactions. Four-factor and higher-order interactions may be confounded.

Resolution V or VI designs provide the most detail needed for first-order models.

As the resolution increases, the number of trials also increases quite dramatically with the number of factors.

Mixed-resolution designs are also possible. That is, we may not need estimates of all the three-factor interactions or even all the two-factor interactions. This often happens with mixture experiments (where the levels of the individual factors contribute to the whole of the factors) as well as for response surfaces (where quadratic effects may exist for only some factors).

Reducing designs, by eliminating extraneous runs, can produce mixed-resolution designs.

Sample Sigma   The standard deviation of the samples drawn from the population.

$$\sigma_x = \sqrt{\frac{\sum_{j=1}^{N}(x_j - \bar{\bar{x}})^2}{N-1}}$$

where x_j is the observation at time j, N is the total number of observations, and $\bar{\bar{x}}$ is the average.

Screening Designs   Screening designs are initial designs with a minimum number of runs (design conditions, trials) used to eliminate factors from subsequent designs. Screening designs often do not estimate interactions. Regular and irregular Plackett-Burman designs may be used for screening. Screening designs may satisfy resolution III or IV. See "Factorial Designs" in Part 3.

Skewness   A measure of the symmetry of a distribution around its mean. Positive values indicate a shift or tail to the right; negative values indicate a shift or tail to the left. Skewness is 0 for a normal distribution.

$$\text{Skewness} = \frac{[(N-1)(N-2)]}{N}\sum_{j=1}^{N}\frac{(x_j - \bar{\bar{x}})^3}{\sigma_x^3}$$

where x_j is the observation j, N is the total number of observations, $\bar{\bar{x}}$ is the average, and σ_x is the sample sigma.

Slack Time   The amount of time that a particular task may be delayed without delaying completion of the entire project. The latest start time minus the earliest start time on the time schedule is equal to the slack time. See "Gantt Chart" in Part 3.

Standard Error of Mean   Used as an indication of the reliability of the average as an estimate of the mean of the population. Smaller numbers mean that the estimate of the population average has less variability.

$$\text{Standard error} = \frac{\sigma_x}{\sqrt{N}}$$

where x_j is the observation j, N is the total number of observations, and σ_x is the sample sigma.

Standardized Short-Run c Statistic   The c statistic can be standardized for use in short-run processes as follows. Once standardized, the data can be plotted on a c chart.

$$z_i = \frac{c_i - \bar{c}_r}{\sqrt{\bar{c}_r}}$$

where n is the sample size, and $\bar{c}_r$ is a constant based on prior data or a desired value.

When based on prior data, $\bar{c}_r$ may be calculated as

$$\bar{c}_r = \frac{\sum_{j=1}^{r}(\text{count})_j}{r}$$

Standardized Short-Run np Statistic   The np statistic can be standardized for use in short-run processes as follows. Once standardized, the data can be plotted on a np chart.

$$z_i = \frac{np_i - n\bar{p}_r}{\sqrt{n\bar{p}_r(1 - \bar{p}_r)}}$$

where n is the sample size, and $n\bar{p}_r$ is a constant based on prior data or a desired value.

When based on prior data, $\overline{np}_r$ may be calculated as

$$\overline{np}_r = \frac{\sum_{j=1}^{r}(\text{count})_j}{r}$$

Standardized Short-Run Observations   Observations can be standardized for use in short-run processes as follows. Once standardized, the data can be plotted on any variables control chart.

For use as nominal control charts,

$$z_i = x_i - \text{nominal}$$

where x_i is the observation, and nominal is a constant based on prior data or a desired value.

For use as stabilized control charts,

$$z_i = \frac{x_i - \text{nominal}}{\sigma}$$

where x_i is the observation, σ is the standard deviation of the observations, and nominal is a constant based on prior data or a desired value.

Standardized Short-Run p Statistic   The p statistic can be standardized for use in short-run processes as follows: Once standardized, the data can be plotted on a p chart.

$$z_i = \frac{p_i - \overline{p}_r}{\sqrt{\frac{1}{n}[\overline{p}_r(1 - \overline{p}_r)]}}$$

where n is the sample size, and $\overline{p}_r$ is a constant based on prior data or a desired value.

When based on prior data, $\overline{p}_r$ may be calculated as

$$\overline{p}_r = \frac{\sum_{j=1}^{r}(\text{count})_j}{\sum_{j=1}^{r} n_j}$$

Standardized Short-Run u Statistic   The u statistic can be standardized for use in short-run processes as follows. Once standardized, the data can be plotted on a u chart.

$$z_i = \frac{u_i - \bar{u}_r}{\sqrt{(\bar{u}_r)(1 / n)}}$$

where n is the sample size, and $\bar{u}_r$ is a constant based on prior data or a desired value.

When based on prior data, $\bar{u}_r$ may be calculated as

$$\bar{u}_r = \frac{\sum_{j=1}^{r}(\text{count})_j}{r}$$

Stationary Point   The point (if it exists) on a response surface that may be located at a maximum, minimum, or saddle point. The stationary point may be outside the experimental range. When the stationary point is far from the data region, it should be used only to indicate a general direction, requiring additional data for validation. See "Response Surface Analysis" in Part 3.

Studentized Residual   See "Residuals Analysis" in Part 3.

Subsidiary Factor   Subsidiary factors are factors that may be contributors to the response but are not controlled in normal operations; however, they must be controlled for the experiment. When not included in the design, they contribute to error. If the effect of a subsidiary factor is suspected of being strong, it should be included as a main factor so that its interaction effects can be estimated properly.

Taguchi uses the labels inner array for main factors and outer array for subsidiary factors. Taguchi's noise factors refer to factors that usually cannot be controlled in practice. In classical design literature, these factors are often referred to as subsidiary factors. Many times we fail to recognize these process variables, and their effect contributes to experimental error.

Taguchi defined three types of noise:

- *External*—such as temperature, dust, or vibration
- *Internal*—such as material wear or aging
- *Unit-to-unit*—such as time of day for order arrival or material composition

Attempts to control these process variables are often costly. Instead, it is often preferred to determine optimal regions for the process or product that minimize the impact of these uncontrollable factors. Designing processes and products in this way is known as a robust design.

The effect of interaction between a subsidiary factor and a main factor cannot be estimated. When subsidiary factors are incorporated in a design, they are usually considered as random effects during the analysis or as noise factors.

When subsidiary (or noise) factors are included in an experiment, we can construct a subsidiary design (Taguchi's outer array). We can specify interaction among the subsidiary factors, but the subsidiary factors cannot interact with any of the main factors (or their interactions). The final design repeats each run of the main design for each subsidiary design trial. For example, a 16-run main design coupled with a 4-run subsidiary design created for two noise factors results in a final design of $16 \times 4 = 64$ trials.

If the analysis indicates significance of a noise factor, then it is possible that main and noise factors interact. If interaction is suspected, it is best to run additional experimental trials treating the significant noise factors as main factors to look for interaction between the noise and (original) main factors. For this reason, it is always better to try to incorporate a subsidiary factor as a main factor in the initial design.

Taguchi Designs   Taguchi designs are fractional factorial designs with the order of the factors or rows revised from the standard order. In this way, Taguchi did not develop any new designs. Some practitioners feel that his design construction is more complicated than others, obscuring the interactions or factor effects.

Instead, Taguchi's contributions to design were in his recommendations for screening designs to include the effect of variance. Taguchi emphasized the use of replicates, including subsidiary (or noise) factors, to estimate variance.

Tampering   Tampering with a process occurs when we respond to variation in the process (such as by adjusting the process) when the process has not shifted. In other words, it is when we treat variation owing to common causes as variation owing to special causes. This is also called *responding to a false alarm* because a false alarm is when we think that the process has shifted when it really hasn't.

In practice, tampering generally occurs when we attempt to control the process to limits that are within the natural control limits defined by common-cause variation. Some causes of this include:

- We try to control the process to specifications or goals. These limits are defined externally to the process rather than being based on the statistics of the process.

- Rather than using the suggested control limits defined at ±3 standard deviations from the centerline, we instead choose to use limits that are tighter (or narrower) than these (sometimes called *warning limits*). We might do this based on the faulty notion that this will improve the performance of the chart because it is more likely that subgroups will plot outside these limits. For example, using limits defined at ±2 standard deviations from the centerline would produce narrower control limits than the ±3 standard deviation limits. However, you can use probability theory to show that the chance of being outside of a ±3 standard deviation control limit for a normally distributed statistic is 0.27 percent if the process has not shifted. On average, you would see a false alarm associated with these limits once every 370 subgroups (1/0.0027). With ±2 standard deviation control limits, the chance of being outside the limits when the process has not shifted is 4.6 percent, corresponding to false alarms every 22 subgroups!

Deming showed how tampering actually increases variation. It easily can be seen that when we react to these false alarms, we take action on the process by shifting its location. Over time, this results in process output that varies much more than if the process had just been left alone. See "Statistical Process Control (SPC) Charts" in Part 3.

Taguchi Ratios   See "Transformation" in Part 3.

Variance Analysis Ratio   A plot of the variance analysis ratio may be used to select a transform of the response. Transforms are sometimes used to stabilize the variance over the range of the data. See "Transformation" in Part 3.

References

AIAG (1995). *Potential Failure Modes and Effects Analysis Reference Guide.* Automotive Industry Action Group.

———— (1995). *MSA Reference Manual.* Automotive Industry Action Group.

Box, G. E. P. (1988). "Signal-to-Noise Ratios, Performance Criteria and Transformations." *Technometrics* 30, 1–40.

———— and Cox, D. R. (1964). "An Analysis of Transformations." *Journal of the Royal Statistical Society, Series B* 26, 211–246.

———— and Draper, N. R. (1969). *Evolutionary Operation: A Statistical Method for Process Improvement.* New York: Wiley.

———— and Jenkins, G. M. (1970). *Time Series Analysis, Forecasting and Control.* San Francisco: Holden-Day.

————, Hunter, W. G., and Hunter, J. S. (1978). *Statistics for Experimenters.* New York: Wiley.

Carlzon, J. (1989). *Moments of Truth.* New York: HarperCollins.

Deming, W. E. (1986). *Out of the Crisis.* Cambridge, MA: MIT Press.

Derringer, G., and Suich, R. (1980). "Simultaneous Optimization of Several Response Variables." *Journal of Quality Technology* 12, 214–219.

Duncan, A. J. (1986) *Quality Control and Industrial Statistics*, 5th ed. Homewood, IL: Richard D. Irwin.

Forum Corporation (1996). Annual Report. Available at www.forum.com/publications/esub_archive/sales.html.

General Electric (1997–2000). Annual Reports to Shareholders.

George, M. L. (2002). *Lean Six Sigma*. New York: McGraw-Hill.

Harry, M., and Schroeder, R. (2000). *Six Sigma*. New York: Doubleday.

Johnson, N. L., and Kotz, S. eds. (1983). *Encyclopedia of Statistical Sciences*, pp. 303–314. New York: Wiley.

Juran, J. M., and Gryna, F. M. (1988). *Juran's Quality Control Handbook*, 4th ed. New York: McGraw-Hill.

Keller, Paul (1993). "Demystifying SPC: III. EWMA Makes It Easy." *PI Quality*, September–October, 50–52.

Keller, Paul (2001). *Six Sigma Deployment*. Tucson, AZ: QA Publishing.

Montgomery, D. C. (1991). *Introduction to Statistical Quality Control*. New York: Wiley.

Myers, R. H., and Montgomery, D. C. (1995). *Response Surface Methodology*. New York: Wiley.

Nelson, Lloyd S. (1984). "The Shewhart Control Chart: Tests for Special Causes." *Journal of Quality Technology* 16(4), 237–239.

——— (1988). "Control Charts: Rational Subgroups and Effective Applications." *Journal of Quality Technology* 20(1), 73–75.

Pignatiello, J. J., Jr., and Ramberg, J. S. (1985). "Discussion of Off-Line Quality Control, Parameter Design and the Taguchi Method by R. N. Kackar." *Journal of Quality Technology* 17, 98–206.

Pyzdek, T. and Keller, P (2009). *Six Sigma Handbook*, 3rd Ed. New York: McGraw-Hill.

Revelle, J. (2000). *What Your Quality Guru Never Told You*. Tucson, AZ: QA Publishing.

Slater, R. (1999). *Jack Welch and the GE Way*. New York: McGraw-Hill.

——— (2000). *The GE Way Fieldbook*. New York: McGraw-Hill.

Snee, R. D. (2002). "The Project Selection Process." *Quality Progress*, September, 78–80.

Taguchi, G. (1986). *Introduction to Quality Engineering*. Tokyo: Asian Productivity Organization.

Western Electric Company (1958). *Statistical Quality Control Handbook*, 2nd ed. New York: Western Electric Company.

Womack, J. P., and Jones, D. T. (1996). *Lean Thinking*. New York: Simon & Schuster.

Index

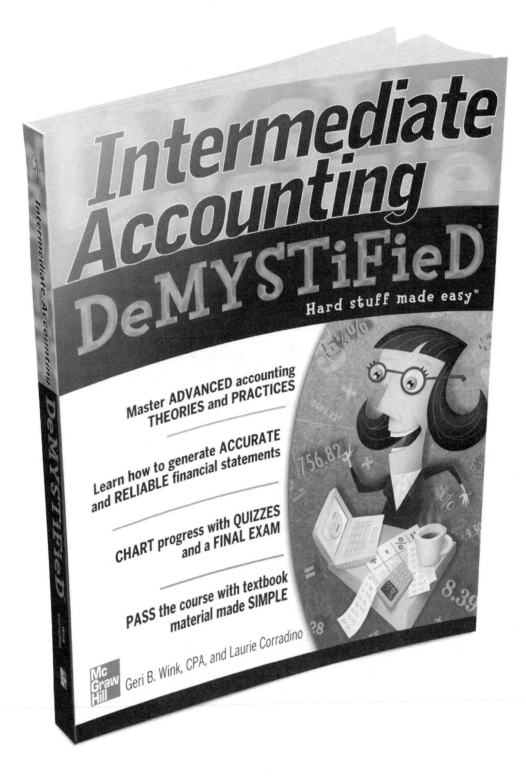

Intermediate Accounting

DeMYSTiFieD®

Hard stuff made easy™

Master ADVANCED accounting THEORIES and PRACTICES

Learn how to generate ACCURATE and RELIABLE financial statements

CHART progress with QUIZZES and a FINAL EXAM

PASS the course with textbook material made SIMPLE

McGraw Hill

Geri B. Wink, CPA, and Laurie Corradino

Making complex accounting principles as easy as 1-2-3!

Contents

DeMYSTiFieD®

Hard stuff made easy

The DeMYSTiFieD series helps students master complex and difficult subjects. Each book is filled with chapter quizzes, final exams, and user friendly content. Whether you want to master Spanish or get an A in Chemistry, DeMYSTiFieD will untangle confusing subjects, and make the hard stuff understandable.

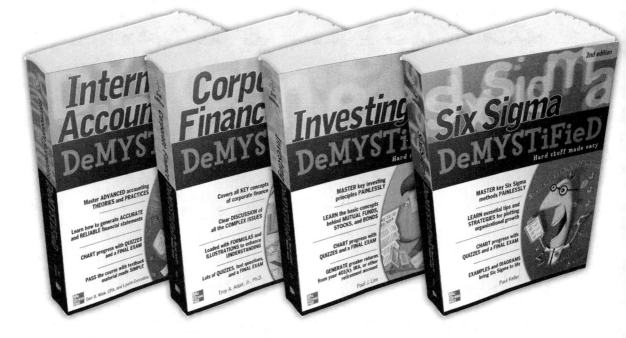